For the Life of the World

For the Life of the World

Jesus Christ and the Church in the Theologies of Dietrich Bonhoeffer and Stanley Hauerwas

ROBERT J. DEAN

☙PICKWICK *Publications* · Eugene, Oregon

FOR THE LIFE OF THE WORLD
Jesus Christ and the Church in the Theologies of Dietrich Bonhoeffer and Stanley Hauerwas

Copyright © 2016 Robert J. Dean. All rights reserved. Except for brief quotations in critical publications or reviews, no part of this book may be reproduced in any manner without prior written permission from the publisher. Write: Permissions, Wipf and Stock Publishers, 199 W. 8th Ave., Suite 3, Eugene, OR 97401.

Pickwick Publications
An Imprint of Wipf and Stock Publishers
199 W. 8th Ave., Suite 3
Eugene, OR 97401

www.wipfandstock.com

PAPERBACK ISBN 13: 978-1-4982-3319-4
HARDCOVER ISBN 13: 978-1-4982-3321-7
EBOOK ISBN: 978-1-4982-3320-0

Cataloguing-in-Publication data:

Dean, Robert J.

Title: For the life of the world : Jesus Christ and the church in the theologies of Dietrich Bonhoeffer and Stanley Hauerwas / Robert J. Dean.

Description: Eugene, OR: Pickwick Publications, 2016 | Includes bibliographical references and index(es).

Identifiers: ISBN 978-1-4982-3319-4 (paperback) | ISBN 978-1-4982-3321-7 (hardcover) | ISBN 978-1-4982-3320-0 (ebook)

Subjects: LCSH: Jesus Christ—Person and offices. | Bonhoeffer, Dietrich, 1906–1945. | Hauerwas, Stanley, 1940–. | Title.

Classification: LCC: BR53 D43 2016

Manufactured in the U.S.A.   05/11/16

Unless otherwise stated, all Scripture quotations are taken from the New Revised Standard Version Bible, copyright 1989, Division of Christian Education of the National Council of the Churches of Christ in the United States of America. Used by permission. All rights reserved.

For Melissa

Contents

Acknowledgments | ix
Abbreviations | xi

1 **Introduction** | 1
   Why Bonhoeffer and Hauerwas? | 1
   The Importance of Karl Barth for Bonhoeffer and Hauerwas | 6
   Bonhoeffer and Hauerwas: Christ, Church, and World | 12

2 **"This Man is God!": The Person of Jesus Christ** | 16
   Part 1: The Christology of Dietrich Bonhoeffer | 17
   Part 2: The Christology of Stanley Hauerwas | 41
   Part 3: Christological Conclusions | 64

3 **A Peculiar People: The Church of Jesus Christ** | 72
   Part 1: The Ecclesiology of Dietrich Bonhoeffer | 73
   Part 2: The Ecclesiology of Stanley Hauerwas | 101
   Part 3: Ecclesiological Conclusions | 130

4 **For the Life of the World: Church and World** | 153
   Part 1: Church and World in the Theology Dietrich Bonhoeffer | 154
   Part 2: Church and World in the Theology of Stanley Hauerwas | 188
   Part 3: Concluding Thoughts on Church and World | 214

5 **Conclusion** | 230
   Summary | 230
   For Further Consideration | 233

APPENDIX: The Ethics of Tyrannicide | 241

Bibliography | 253
Index | 279

Acknowledgments

In working on a project such as this, one becomes acutely aware that they are standing on the shoulders of giants. This is perhaps most evident when considering the two theological titans who are the focus of the book. However, it is equally true when one stops to think of the many scholars who have devoted their lives to preserving and passing on the Bonhoeffer legacy and also, more generally, when one recognizes that one's work stands within a tradition of theological inquiry made possible by the faithfulness of men and women, both known and unknown, which stretches back over two millennia. While it would be impossible to fully acknowledge all of my debts, I will attempt to give thanks for some of the "concretions of divine grace" I have experienced within the church catholic while working on this project.

    This book originated as a dissertation submitted to Wycliffe College at the University of Toronto. I have benefited greatly from the collegiality of the Wycliffe community and particularly from the careful supervision of my thesis director, Joseph Mangina. In his willingness to read an earlier draft of my dissertation, Stanley Hauerwas demonstrated the graciousness for which he is rightfully renowned. David Schuchardt, Paul Johansen, Craig Shugart, Lisa Barber, and Robyn Elliott, faithful servants of the church of Jesus Christ, read and responded to drafts of various sections as the project unfolded. They represent the type of readership that both Bonhoeffer and Hauerwas have imagined for their work. I am fortunate to be able to count them as friends. It was a privilege to have my dissertation read by an examination committee representative of both excellence in scholarship and an abiding ecumenicity. I learned greatly from the incisive comments and probing questions of Professors John Berkman, Reid Locklin, Ephraim Radner, and Philip Ziegler. The current book is stronger to the extent that I have been able to address and incorporate their comments and concerns. Of course, none of the people mentioned above are to be held responsible for any mistakes or shortcomings that remain in the current book—they are entirely my own.

I am grateful for the many expressions of the body of Christ that have blessed me along the way. The congregation of Good Shepherd Community Church has served throughout as a living exhibition of the fragile gift of grace bestowed in the church. Muskoka Woods Sports Resort generously provided office space for me during the summer months. Tyndale Seminary entrusted me with the privilege of teaching theology students and gave me the opportunity to teach courses in which the writings of both Bonhoeffer and Hauerwas featured prominently. Knox Presbyterian Church in Toronto, Ontario, and Byron United Church in London, Ontario provided opportunities for me to share about the life and work of Dietrich Bonhoeffer in congregational settings.

Finally, my father and mother, Tom and Ruth Dean, have continued to eagerly follow my progress, offering their encouragement and grammatical advice from afar. Anastasia, who was born near the beginning of the project, and Nathanael, who arrived just in time for the submission of the dissertation and its defense, have been a source of continuing joy and have helped to keep my work in proper perspective. Finally, it is impossible to express in words my gratitude to Melissa, without whom this work would not have been possible. In addition to being an excellent proofreader, she has been an unfailing support and source of encouragement. Whether the correlate to "Hauerwas's rule"—"You always marry the right person!"—is generally valid, I can't say, but it has certainly been true in my case.

Abbreviations

WORKS BY DIETRICH BONHOEFFER

DBWE	Dietrich Bonhoeffer Works
SC (DBWE 1)	Sanctorum Communio
AB (DBWE 2)	Act and Being
CF (DBWE 3)	Creation and Fall
D (DBWE 4)	Discipleship
LT (DBWE 5)	Life Together
E (DBWE 6)	Ethics
LPP (DBWE 8)	Letters and Paper from Prison
DBWE 10	Barcelona, Berlin, New York: 1928–1931
DBWE 11	Ecumenical, Academic and Pastoral Work: 1931–1932
DBWE 12	Berlin: 1933
DBWE 13	London: 1933–1935
DBWE 14	Theological Education at Finkenwalde: 1935–1937
DBWE 15	Theological Education Underground: 1937–1940
DBWE 16	Conspiracy and Imprisonment: 1940–1945
CC	Christ the Center
WF	The Way to Freedom: Letters, Lectures and Notes, 1935–1939
WP	Worldly Preaching: Lectures on Homiletics

WORKS BY STANLEY HAUERWAS

AC	*After Christendom: How the Church is to Behave if Freedom, Justice, and a Christian Nation are Bad Ideas*
AN	*Against the Nations: War and Survival in a Liberal Society*
ATE	*Approaching the End: Eschatological Reflections on Church, Politics, and Life*
BH	*A Better Hope: Resources for a Church Confronting Capitalism, Democracy, and Postmodernity*
CCL	*Character and the Christian Life: A Study in Theological Ethics*
CET	*Christian Existence Today: Essays on Church, World, and Living in Between*
ComC	*A Community of Character: Toward a Constructive Christian Social Ethic*
CSC	*Cross-Shattered Christ: Meditations on the Seven Last Words*
CSChu	*A Cross-Shattered Church: Reclaiming the Theological Heart of Preaching*
DFF	*Dispatches from the Front: Theological Engagements with the Secular*
DT	*Disrupting Time: Sermons, Prayers, and Sundries*
HC	*Hannah's Child: A Theologian's Memoir*
HR	*The Hauerwas Reader*
IGC	*In Good Company: The Church as Polis*
Mt	*Matthew*
PK	*The Peaceable Kingdom: A Primer in Christian Ethics*
PTF	*Performing the Faith: Bonhoeffer and the Practice of Nonviolence*
SP	*Suffering Presence: Theological Reflections on Medicine, the Mentally Handicapped, and the Church*
STT	*Sanctify Them in the Truth: Holiness Exemplified*
SU	*The State of the University: Academic Knowledges and the Knowledge of God*
TT	*Truthfulness and Tragedy: Further Investigations into Christian Ethics*
US	*Unleashing the Scripture: Freeing the Bible from Captivity to America*
VV	*Vision and Virtue: Essays in Christian Ethical Reflection*
WA	*Without Apology: Sermons for Christ's Church*

WAD	*War and the American Difference: Theological Reflections on Violence and National Identity*
WGU	*With the Grain of the Universe: The Church's Witness and Natural Theology*
WW	*Wilderness Wanderings: Probing Twentieth-Century Theology and Philosophy*
WWW	*Working with Words: On Learning to Speak Christian*

WORKS JOINTLY WRITTEN OR EDITED BY HAUERWAS

BCCE	*The Blackwell Companion to Christian Ethics*
CAV	*Christians among the Virtues: Theological Conversations with Ancient and Modern Ethics*
CDRO	*Christianity, Democracy, and the Radical Ordinary: Conversations between a Radical Democrat and a Christian*
DFH	*Dissent from the Homeland: Essays after September 11*
LGVW	*Living Gently in a Violent World: The Prophetic Witness of Weakness*
RA	*Resident Aliens: Life in the Christian Colony*
TAG	*The Truth about God: The Ten Commandments in Christian Life*
WRAL	*Where Residents Aliens Live: Exercises for Christian Practice*

WORKS BY KARL BARTH

CD	*Church Dogmatics*

1

Introduction

WHY BONHOEFFER AND HAUERWAS?

"Why Dietrich Bonhoeffer and Stanley Hauerwas?" The deceptively simple question of the examiner pierced the silence of the board room where I was defending my dissertation. Of course, this was not the first time that I had considered this question, but sometimes the most obvious questions are the most difficult to answer. It was a question that had accompanied me throughout my years of research and writing as a doctoral student, sometimes prominently impressing itself and other times retreating to the background, yet always present. At times it was a question I asked myself in exasperation, like whenever a new trail opened up down the rabbit-hole of Bonhoeffer secondary literature or when yet another volume from the prolific pen of Hauerwas arrived on my desk.

Moving from the existential to the substantial, there are many different ways that one could attempt to answer the question, Why Bonhoeffer and Hauerwas? It would not be a stretch to argue that Bonhoeffer and Hauerwas are two of the most influential figures in contemporary theology.[1] At the

---

1. For a survey of the wide-ranging reception and vastly different interpretations of Bonhoeffer, see Haynes, *Bonhoeffer Phenomenon*. However, it should be noted that during his own lifetime Bonhoeffer was not widely known or recognized and could even be considered to have been a marginal figure in the German Church Struggle and resistance movements. Barnett, "Bonhoeffer Legacy," 96–97. The prominent Princeton professor of religion and occasional Hauerwas sparring partner, Jeffrey Stout, asserts that "Stanley Hauerwas is surely the most prolific and influential theologian

beginning of the twenty-first century the influence of their theological legacies does not appear to be abating. Each one's work transcends the boundaries drawn by theological departments in modern universities in striking ways. Their published writings include systematic theology (although it is worth noting that neither have presented a comprehensive systematic account of their theology), ethics, philosophical theology, biblical commentary, pastoral theology, sermons, prayers, and other works of "popular theology." The inter-disciplinary, or even eclectic, character of their work contributes to the appeal of their theology.[2] Yet in spite of their massive influence, Bonhoeffer's legacy remains susceptible to misappropriation and Hauerwas is still too quickly dismissed as a sectarian.[3]

The case for a study bringing together the theologies of Bonhoeffer and Hauerwas is further strengthened by the compelling character of their life stories.[4] On the one hand, there is Bonhoeffer, the theological prodigy born with a silver-spoon in his mouth, who through his costly discipleship learned "to see the great events of world history from below" and eventually met his end on Nazi gallows.[5] On the other hand, there is Hauerwas, the brash, famously foul-mouthed son of a Texan bricklayer, whose hard work eventually led to him being acclaimed "America's best theologian" by *Time* magazine—a somewhat ironic designation in light of his enduring criticisms of the American project.[6] While from a sociological perspective their lives

---

now working in the United States" (*Democracy and Tradition*, 140). Nation, writing at the turn of the millennium, has plausibly suggested that "probably no one has more substantially changed the field of Christian ethics within the last twenty-five years than Stanley Hauerwas" ("Stanley Hauerwas," 19).

2. Cavanaugh describes Hauerwas's work as the exemplification of the unique genre of "not-boring theology" ("Stan the Man," 30–31). The broad appeal of Bonhoeffer's work suggests that it also belongs in this category.

3. Green and Carter maintain that "one could argue that he [Bonhoeffer] is simultaneously the most quoted and most misinterpreted Christian theologian of the twentieth century" (*Interpreting Bonhoeffer*, xi). Perhaps the most influential charge of "sectarianism" against Hauerwas was raised by Gustafson in "The Sectarian Temptation."

4. Bonhoeffer biographies continue to be written, but the definitive biographical source remains Bethge, *Dietrich Bonhoeffer*. Of the recent additions to the field, worthy of honorable mention is Schlingensiepen, *Dietrich Bonhoeffer*, and Marsh, *Strange Glory*. The most concentrated source of biographical information about Hauerwas is found in his memoir *Hannah's Child*. An informative and entertaining short biographical piece on Hauerwas is Cavanaugh's essay, "Stan the Man."

5. Bonhoeffer's thoughts on "the view from below" are found in an essay he wrote for his co-conspirators in 1942. *LPP* (*DBWE* 8), 52. In 1998, a likeness of Dietrich Bonhoeffer was unveiled alongside of Mother Elizabeth of Russia, Martin Luther King, and Oscar Romero, among others, in the gallery of modern martyrs at Westminster Abbey.

6. Elshtain, "Christian Contrarian."

may have taken differing trajectories, there are some striking similarities between their ecclesial locations at the twilight of Christendom. Bonhoeffer lived and served amongst a church divested of its position of social privilege and responsibility that proved incapable of resisting the allure of the Nazi promise of Germanic glory. Hauerwas remains haunted by the German church of Bonhoeffer's day and the fear that the church in America has so confused the Gospel and the American Dream that it would fare no better if it found itself thrust into a similar situation.[7] Bonhoeffer's life and witness shines brightly against the stark backdrop of the horrors of Nazi Germany. Hauerwas's full and productive life lacks the concentrated drama of Bonhoeffer's relatively short life, but there is a similar prophetic character to his work.[8] Neither Bonhoeffer nor Hauerwas shied away from controversy, which at times made them unpopular figures amongst their ecclesial and academic colleagues, but this also contributes to the fascinating character of their lives.[9] Although this present work is not intended to be a study of "biography as theology," it is important at the outset to note that Bonhoeffer and Hauerwas are figures who are interesting in their own right.[10]

Additional impetus for a book-length study of these two theologians has been provided by Hauerwas himself, who has drawn upon the work of Bonhoeffer in several works published since the turn of the millennium.[11] However, this appropriation of Bonhoeffer's work by Hauerwas has proven to be controversial in some quarters. There are some who question whether Hauerwas has really allowed Bonhoeffer to speak in his own distinct voice or whether he has simply assimilated Bonhoeffer to his own "high-church Mennonite" vision.[12] The question arises whether Bonhoeffer, in Hauerwas's

---

7. For one manifestation of this haunting in Hauerwas's work, see *RA*, 24–25, 43–48.

8. Kelly and Nelson observe that "Hauerwas's critique of militarism and of the churches' failure to emphasize the teachings of Jesus Christ in assessing moral issues is uncannily reminiscent of Bonhoeffer's own unpopular, lonely struggle for a restoration of gospel values in the Hitler era" (*Cost of Moral Leadership*, 127).

9. Ericksen has sounded an important caveat about the danger of becoming too comfortable with Bonhoeffer and failing to note that even the Confessing Church of Bonhoeffer's day was not entirely comfortable with him. "Dietrich Bonhoeffer in History," 127. Some of the controversies surrounding both figures will come to the fore in various parts of the current work.

10. For a seminal account of doing theology biographically, see McClendon, *Biography as Theology*. McClendon extends this project into his three volume *Systematic Theology*, which includes a treatment of Bonhoeffer in *Ethics*, 193–212.

11. *PTF*, 13–72; Hauerwas, "Bonhoeffer and Yoder"; *WWW*, 270–85. Bonhoeffer also appears as one of Hauerwas's favorite interlocutors in his biblical commentary *Matthew*.

12. Hauerwas's description of his ecclesial aspiration to be a "high-church Mennonite" is found in *ComC*, 6. For criticisms of Hauerwas's appropriation of Bonhoeffer

hands, simply becomes John Howard Yoder redux? Conversely, it could be asked whether Hauerwas has picked up on an important strand in Bonhoeffer's thought that resonates with his own? This study is very much interested in such questions, but its purview is much broader.

While an increasing number of essays and books have drawn upon the work of both Bonhoeffer and Hauerwas in supporting their own constructive arguments, there are relatively few essays and no manuscripts that I am aware of that focus on reading Bonhoeffer and Hauerwas on their own terms and bringing them into direct dialogue with one another.[13] When Bonhoeffer's and Hauerwas's theologies are brought into dialogue in scholarly literature, it tends to be within the context of a discussion of an area of specific interest and specialization to the author and hence, while often interesting and insightful, they are not able to engage at a more comprehensive level with the major themes and claims of each theologians' work.[14] The rationale, "because no one has ever done it," certainly carries some weight for a young theologian hoping to make a scholarly contribution through writing a dissertation, but it does not present an entirely satisfying rationale for either the one who is called to undertake such a project or for the reader who is entertaining the option of reading the finished work.

While all of the ground traversed in the previous few paragraphs contributes in some way to answering the question, Why Bonhoeffer and Hauerwas? the answer remains incomplete without addressing some of the substantive material convictions which underlie the project. To put those convictions in the most simple and straightforward manner, I believe Bonhoeffer and Hauerwas have something important to say about the church—something that the contemporary North American church with its recurring patterns of cultural accommodation needs to hear if it is to faithfully bear witness to Christ in the midst of navigating its increasingly diasporic existence amidst the ruins of Christendom. Furthermore, it is my contention that both Bonhoeffer and Hauerwas have something interesting and important to say about the church and its mission in the world, because

---

ranging from the comprehensive to the particular, see DeJonge, "How to Read Bonhoeffer's Peace Statements"; Heuser, "Cost of Citizenship," 54–56; and Brock, "Bonhoeffer and the Bible," 28.

13. For examples of works that draw upon the writings of both Bonhoeffer and Hauerwas in advancing their own constructive theological proposals, see Lawson, "Theological Formation"; Nessan, "What if the Church"; Nation, "First Word Christians Have to Say"; Badcock, *House Where God Lives*; Harper and Metzger, *Exploring Ecclesiology*; and Jones, *Embodying Forgiveness*.

14. E.g., Marsh, "In Defense of a Self"; Richardson, "*Sanctorum Communio*"; Nullens, "Dietrich Bonhoeffer"; Heuser, "Cost of Citizenship" and Brock, "Bonhoeffer and the Bible."

of who they understand Jesus to be. For both, Jesus makes all the difference. Hence, in some respects, this book could be considered to be a study of "the difference Christ makes," both in their theologies and for the church negotiating the complexities of its relationship to the modern world.[15]

If Christ-church-world forms the *cantus firmus*—to borrow terminology from Bonhoeffer's prison letters—of the current work, its clear sounding also allows for the development of some interesting contrapuntal themes.[16] While the careful reader will undoubtedly recognize many such themes, some of which are perhaps not even perceptible to the author, there are three which warrant particular attention at this point. All three pertain to the conviction that Christ makes all the difference. First, the current work will present a reading of Bonhoeffer that argues for the fundamental continuity of his thought based upon the perduring christological center of his thought. While the writings emerging from Bonhoeffer's desk and cell during the Second World War undoubtedly mark a development of Bonhoeffer's thought they should not be read as marking a decisive break with or abandonment of what has gone before. Second, this work seeks to make a contribution to the understanding of Hauerwas's work through highlighting the often overlooked christological center of his thought. A recognition that the person of Jesus Christ stands as the true animating center of Hauerwas's work serves to both counter some of the objections raised to his work and reframe some of the questions of his interlocutors.[17] Third, the christological concentration of both thinkers reflects the profound influence that Karl Barth and his break with theological liberalism has had upon them. Both Hauerwas and Bonhoeffer could be considered to be "mildly rebellious Barthians," who have come through the other-side of the Barthian revolt while still managing to retain some of the classic interests of the liberal theological

---

15. "The Difference Christ Makes" is the title of an essay delivered by Samuel Wells at a celebration held to commemorate Hauerwas's recent retirement from Duke Divinity School. The title is shared with the book which contains the rest of the essays from the occasion, Collier, *Difference Christ Makes*.

16. For Bonhoeffer's development of the theme of the *cantus firmus*, see *LPP* (*DBWE* 8), 393–95. See also the discussion of "the polyphony of life" in chapter 4 of the present work.

17. One of the most significant set of objections that has been recently raised is found in Healy's *Hauerwas: A (Very) Critical Introduction*. Unfortunately, Healy's work was only published after I had finished writing the dissertation which formed the basis of the current book. I have attempted to incorporate some engagement with Healy's book in both the footnotes and the body of the text, but extensive engagement with Healy would have required writing a rather different book. In some ways, the christological reading of Hauerwas I present in this book is itself a response to some of Healy's charges.

tradition, but now transposed into a new key.[18] In order to set the stage for the chapters which follow, we will need to briefly examine the significance of Barth's theological breakthrough and its appropriation by both Bonhoeffer and Hauerwas.

THE IMPORTANCE OF KARL BARTH FOR BONHOEFFER AND HAUERWAS

The Swiss theologian Karl Barth sought to recover the evangelical character of theology by directing theology back to its true subject matter—the God who has acted for us and revealed Himself to us in Jesus Christ. Stemming from his renewed engagement with the Bible, and especially the apostle Paul, Barth came to recognize the shortcomings of liberal theology which was at times in its speech about God nothing more than humankind speaking about itself in a loud voice. Theological liberalism, in its false confidence, had blurred the infinite qualitative distinction between God and humanity, and in its misplaced optimism, had failed to recognize the continuing impact of sin upon humanity. Such theology, as Barth initially discovered during the First World War, leaves the church especially susceptible to co-option by other powers and ideologies. It was therefore essential for both the practice of theology and the life of the church (and as it would also turn out, the world) to recover the evangelical character of theology by affirming as the Confessing Church did at Barmen through the pen of Karl Barth that "Jesus Christ, as he is attested to us in Holy Scripture, is the one Word of God whom we have to hear, and whom we have to trust and obey in life and in death."[19] The freedom of the theologian, like the freedom of the Christian, is found in obedience to Jesus Christ who is theology's proper object, but who also always remains the true subject of theology. As a result, Barth understood that the practice of theology must always be located within and in the service of the church.[20]

Bonhoeffer first encountered Barth's theology in the winter of 1924–1925 when he came across *Das Wort Gottes und die Theologie*. Bonhoeffer

---

18. Of course, the presence of these classic liberal theological interests might lead some to conclude that Bonhoeffer and Hauerwas are not simply "mildly rebellious Barthians," but are, in fact, "heretical Barthians." It seems like an incredibly un-Barthian thing to say, but perhaps Barthianism is in the eye of the beholder!

19. "The Theological Declaration of Barmen," in Matheson, *Church and the Third Reich*, 46.

20. This conviction is reflected in the title Barth ascribed to his magnum opus: *Kirchliche Dogmatik* (*Church Dogmatics*).

immediately appointed himself the "propagandist for this book."[21] He would continue to advocate for Barth within the theological faculty for the duration of his time at the University of Berlin. Bonhoeffer's own perception of his indebtedness to Barth is displayed in a letter of September 19, 1936 addressed to the Swiss theologian after Bonhoeffer had been left off the list of contributors to the *Festschrift* for Barth's fiftieth birthday. In the letter Bonhoeffer expresses his disappointment at not being "counted among the theologians associated with you," which, he goes on to say, they both know "is not true."[22] Hauerwas first encountered the theology of Karl Barth while a student at Yale Divinity School. He was immediately impressed by how Barth's "recovery of the Christological center of the Christian faith" allowed him to "rightly recognize the Nazis for who they were" while many of the liberal theologians of his day failed to do so.[23] Years later, Barth would become the hero of Hauerwas's Gifford Lectures.[24] In an autobiographical essay, Hauerwas would make his understanding of his own appropriation of Barth more explicit by stating that his "Barthianism" is "just another way of saying my Christology."[25]

It lies beyond the scope of this chapter to trace Bonhoeffer's and Hauerwas's appropriation of the theology of Karl Barth throughout the breadth of their respective corpuses. For our purposes, it will be sufficient to examine one representative essay from each thinker—Bonhoeffer's seminar paper "The Theology of Crisis and Its Attitude toward Philosophy and Science" and Hauerwas's essay "On Doctrine and Ethics"—to display how the two have incorporated Barth's christological overturning of liberal theology.

Bonhoeffer: "The Theology of Crisis . . ."

Bonhoeffer presented the paper "The Theology of Crisis and its Attitude toward Philosophy and Science" in the second semester of a year-long seminar with John Baillie on the philosophy of religion during his first visit to the United States in 1930–1931.[26] Although Bonhoeffer had raised some critical questions of Barth's early theology in his *Habilitationsschrift*, during his time at Union Seminary he set those questions aside in order to act as a travelling evangelist for the great Swiss theologian in the midst of

21. Bethge, *Bonhoeffer: Man of Vision*, 51, quoted in Pangritz, *Karl Barth*, 15.
22. *WF*, 116, quoted in Pangritz, *Karl Barth*, 56.
23. *HC*, 51.
24. *WGU*, 141–204.
25. *DT*, 237.
26. Green, editor's introduction to *DBWE* 10:44.

this new frontier.[27] Near the beginning of the paper, Bonhoeffer audaciously suggests to the students that the only way that they will be able to come into real contact with Barth's thought is if they forget "at least for this one hour everything you have learned before concerning this problem."[28] In the context of the lecture, these remarks appear as a radical indictment of the course. In light of Bonhoeffer's reflections elsewhere on the theological education of the students at Union, however, it is not outside of the realm of possibility that Bonhoeffer may have been encouraging the students to forget everything they had learned in their studies up to that point![29] In contrast to the philosophers that had been discussed in the class—Kant, Bergson, and Dewey are named—Bonhoeffer maintains that Barth is a Christian theologian "in the tradition of Paul, Luther, Kierkegaard, in the tradition of genuine christian thinking."[30] Barth is to be found within the line of genuine Christian thinking because he holds to "the proper presupposition of christian theology," namely, "that God entered history in Jesus Christ, [and] made himself known to the world in this revelation."[31] The revelation of God in Jesus Christ is not the revelation of an idea or general truth congenial to humankind's deepest essence, but rather is revelation in the concealment of the concrete, historical event of the scandalous suffering and death of Christ.[32] Bonhoeffer commends Barth for his theological reading of the Scriptures, which places God at the center as the primary subject: "This precisely is the logic of the Bible, God's coming which destroys all human attempts to come, which condemns all morality and religion, by means of which man tries to make superfluous God's revelation."[33] To the fallen human being entrapped within the circle of sin, the liberating and justifying word of God must always come "straight from above, from *outside* of man" and therefore can only ever be the presupposition and never the deduction of a theological argument.[34] Having introduced the theo-logic of Karl Barth, Bonhoeffer now turns to the problem of philosophy and attempts to trace

27. According to Baillie's recollections, Bonhoeffer was "the most convinced disciple of Dr. Barth that had appeared among us up to that time, and withal as stout an opponent of liberalism as had ever come my way" ("Some Reflections," 8, quoted in Bethge, *Dietrich Bonhoeffer*, 158).

28. *DBWE* 10:462. It should be noted that this seminar paper is the one of the few surviving theological works by Dietrich Bonhoeffer that was written in English.

29. See *DBWE* 10:305–20.

30. *DBWE* 10:463.

31. Ibid., 464.

32. Ibid., 464–65.

33. Ibid., 466.

34. Ibid., 467.

out the implications of Barth's thought for the discipline of philosophy. In the process, as Bethge has observed, Bonhoeffer frequently mingles together Barth's propositions with his own.[35] In a manner reminiscent of the argument forwarded in *Act and Being*, Bonhoeffer suggests that all philosophical systems are attempts by the autonomous ego with its omnivorous appetite to pull all of reality into itself.[36] Bonhoeffer maintains that Barth recognizes that humankind is stuck in the spiral of its own egocentricity from which there is no escape. From the human perspective it is a hopeless situation:

> Man must die in his sin in spite of philosophy, must remain alone in his overpowered and misinterpreted world. But now, the christian message comes: entirely from outside of the world of sin God himself came in Jesus Christ, he breaks as the holy Ghost into the circle of man, not as a new idea, a new value by virtue of which man could save himself, but in concreteness as judgment and forgiveness of sin, as the promise of eschatological salvation. God makes himself known to man who is sinner in his whole existence. The whole existence of man in his egocentric world has to be shaken (erschütert) before man can see God as really outside of himself.[37]

As a result there can be for Bonhoeffer no such thing as Christian philosophy, only critical philosophy which recognizes its limitations in the face of the radical irruption of judgment and grace in the revelation of Jesus Christ.[38] Bonhoeffer's concluding remarks provide a concise representation of the theological convictions he has acquired from Barth which will contribute to the shaping of his unfolding theological project: "Here at the end we stand again where we stood in the beginning; and that cannot be otherwise; for *everything* is included in God's revelation in Christ, in the justification of the sinner by faith and grace alone. And must not the solution of *everything* be there, where *God himself* is?"[39]

Hauerwas: "On Doctrine and Ethics"

Karl Barth receives pride of place in Stanley Hauerwas's essay, "On Doctrine and Ethics." Hauerwas describes the purpose of the essay as an attempt "to

---

35. Bethge, *Dietrich Bonhoeffer*, 159.
36. DBWE 10:473.
37. Ibid., 473.
38. Ibid., 474.
39. Ibid., 476.

provide a narrative which explains how the disjunction between doctrine and ethics arose and why, as Barth claims, such a division cannot be justified theologically."[40] Hauerwas maintains that Christian ethics is a peculiarly modern endeavor, going so far as to claim that "at one time Christian ethics did not exist."[41] In stating this, Hauerwas does not mean that "Christians did not think about how best to live their lives as Christians,"[42] but rather that they did not make the hard and fast distinction between their belief and their behavior that is so characteristic of modern individuals. Hauerwas provides a genealogical sketch in support of his contention, demonstrating how the theological and ethical formed an inseparable unity through the patristic and medieval periods.[43] This unity began to be threatened following the Protestant Reformation, as ethics came to be associated with "works," which stood opposed to "faith," as sinful humanity's attempt to secure its own righteousness before God. Not only did the Protestant Reformation contribute to a new way of understanding ethics for Christians, it also led to a profound shift in the ways that Christians related to their world. Hauerwas explains:

> In earlier centuries, the Christian understanding of life could be articulated in the language of natural law, but it was assumed that natural law was only intelligible as part of divine law as mediated by the church. What was lost after the Reformation was exactly this understanding of the church as the indispensable context in which order might be given to the Christian life. For example, with the loss of the rite of penance in Protestantism, casuistry as an activity of moral theologians was lost. Such a loss did not seem to be a problem as long as it was assumed that everyone 'knew' what it meant to be Christian. However, as it became less and less clear among Protestants what it 'means' to be Christian there have increasingly been attempts to 'do' ethics. The difficulty is that no consensus about what ethics is or how it should be done exists. As a result, theologians have often turned to philosophy for resources in their search for an ethic—resources that ironically helped create the problem of how to relate theology and ethics, because now it is assumed that 'ethics' is an autonomous discipline that is no longer dependent on religious conviction.[44]

40. Stanley Hauerwas, "On Doctrine and Ethics," 22.
41. Ibid., 24.
42. Ibid., 24.
43. Ibid., 24–28.
44. Ibid., 29.

Hauerwas continues his genealogy by turning to the work of Immanuel Kant. In response to the breakdown of the Christian world, Kant attempted to exorcise the ghosts of relativism and secure a foundation for ethical activity through his formulation of the "categorical imperative." By grounding ethics in reason alone, Kant thought that he had freed the subject from the grasp of religious and cultural provincialism and in the process preserved space for faith. In this way, Hauerwas maintains, "Kant becomes the greatest representative of Protestant liberalism; that is, Protestant liberal theology after Kant is but a series of footnotes to his work."[45] Following Kant, "Protestant theologians no longer sure of the metaphysical status of Christian claims, have sought to secure the ongoing meaningfulness of Christian convictions by anchoring them in anthropological generalizations and/or turning them into ethics."[46] The apex of this trajectory is found, according to Hauerwas, in the thoroughly apologetic theology of Friedrich Schleiermacher. Even more significant than "Schleiermacher's explicit views about ethics was his conception of the dogmatic task as a civilisational and thus ethical task."[47] The driving force of this enterprise was, for Schleiermacher, the university; hence, the necessary inclusion of a faculty of theology for the training of clergy who are understood to be servants of the state. The modern disciplinary divisions and structuring of theological curriculum, which arose under Schleiermacher's influence, serves to reinforce the notion that theology and ethics are discrete entities.[48]

Enter Karl Barth, for whom, Hauerwas observes:

> there can be no ethics that is not from beginning to end theological. Indeed, ethics is theological through and through because for Barth theology is more than simply one discipline among others. Theology rather is the exposition of how God's word as found in Jesus Christ provides not only its own ground but the ground for all that we know and do. Barth, therefore rejects Schleiermacher's attempt to make theology part of a "larger essential context, of a larger scientific problem-context," by returning theology to its proper role as servant of the church's proclamation of Jesus Christ. For Barth dogmatics cannot have access to a higher or better source of knowledge than that which is found in the church's proclamation that the God Christians worship is triune.[49]

45. Ibid., 30.
46. Ibid., 30.
47. Ibid., 31.
48. Ibid., 32.
49. Ibid., 32–33.

Hauerwas proceeds to approvingly cite John Webster, who argues that Barth's *Church Dogmatics* is a moral ontology which is "a depiction of the world of human action as it is enclosed and governed by the creative, redemptive, and sanctifying work of God in Christ, present in the power of the Holy Spirit."[50] The ethical task of post-Enlightenment liberal theology is thus thrown on its head. Theology must be understood as an ecclesial discipline, in service of the church which lives in service of the Triune God and not as a tool for underwriting universal values essential for the upholding of the state. The ambiguous categories of Enlightenment ethics, "such as 'the good' or the 'categorical imperative' are far too abstract to give the guidance that can only come from the concreteness of God's command as found in Jesus Christ."[51] Those who wish to do theology and ethics after Barth must be "Christian speakers for whom doctrine is speech that does work."[52] Only then, when Christians relearn to take seriously the particularity of their convictions, will the church once again have something truly interesting to say to the world.

BONHOEFFER AND HAUERWAS: CHRIST, CHURCH, AND WORLD

Both Bonhoeffer and Hauerwas have come away from their engagement with Barth firmly convinced that God's self-revelation in Jesus Christ is the presupposition of all Christian thought and action. In their appropriation of Barth's christological overturning of liberal theology, Bonhoeffer and Hauerwas discover that the church's mission in the world is cast in a different light than in the regnant paradigms of cultural Christianity. In light of the event of God's self-revelation and reconciliation of the world in Jesus Christ, the task of the church is not to change the world, but to witness to the fact that the world has already been definitively changed in the life, death, and resurrection of Jesus Christ. Flowing from Barth's christological recovery, and reflected in the work of both Bonhoeffer and Hauerwas, are the reclamation of theology as an ecclesial discipline and the restoration of the connection between theology and ethics that had been severed in modernity. Under Barth's influence, Bonhoeffer and Hauerwas recognize that any attempt to address the church-world problematic must begin with the person of Jesus Christ.

---

50. John Webster, *Barth's Ethics of Reconciliation*, 1–2, quoted in ibid., 33.
51. Hauerwas, "On Doctrine and Ethics," 33.
52. Ibid., 35.

In light of this, I will begin in the next chapter with an exploration of the Christologies which lie at the heart of each thinker's theological vision. Although both Bonhoeffer and Hauerwas are deeply indebted to Barth's formal recovery of the christological center of the Christian faith, each of them is also influenced in the material development of their Christologies by other figures whose influence allows them to retain Barth's apocalyptic stance while at the same time opening the door to a more catholic conception of the church. The chapter will, accordingly, be governed by a consideration of the following research questions applied to the work of both figures: Who is Jesus Christ? What has he accomplished? What is the relationship between his person and work? Through consideration of these questions, I hope to demonstrate how the person of Jesus Christ, fully divine and fully human, stands at the center of each theologian's work resulting in distinctly evangelical theologies whose Christology is both apocalyptic and participatory in character.

In the third chapter, we will begin to see how both Bonhoeffer's and Hauerwas's judicious appropriation of Barth's legacy leads to the emergence of important distinctions from their theological mentor in the area of ecclesiology. Whereas Barth could famously assert that "the world would not necessarily be lost if there were no Church," both Bonhoeffer and Hauerwas are insistent that *extra ecclesiam nulla salus*.[53] Against the gnosticizing forces of modernity which seek to privatize, spiritualize, and individualize the Christian faith, Bonhoeffer and Hauerwas both insist that salvation is inseparably intertwined with the concrete life of the Christian community.[54] The chapter will seek to be informed by the following questions: How do Bonhoeffer and Hauerwas understand the identity and mission of the church? What is the nature of the church's relationship to Jesus Christ? What is the place of the church within the economy of salvation? Through engaging with these questions I trust that it will become apparent that, for both Bonhoeffer and Hauerwas, a catholic ecclesiology is a necessary implicate of an evangelical Christology. As a result, both thinkers understand concern for the church's identity to be of supreme missional significance.

The fourth chapter will in many ways simply be the outworking of the christological and ecclesiological commitments held by the two thinkers which were articulated in the previous chapters. It will consider how both

---

53. *CD* 4/3.2:826.

54. Reno has observed that "for much of modern thought, and for nearly all of what passes as ethical reflection in modern Protestant theology, a Gnostic sensibility prevails" ("Stanley Hauerwas," 305). For more extensive explorations of the gnostic character of modern North American Christianity, see Hart, *In the Aftermath*, 43–62; Lee, *Protestant Gnostics*; Bloom, *American Religion*.

Bonhoeffer and Hauerwas conceive of the unique ministry of the church as a distinct evangelical and catholic community in the world. Stemming from their christological commitments, both men have a profound interest in the world and could be considered to be advocates of a certain type of Christian humanism or worldliness. However, the form of this worldliness cannot be dictated by the terms of the world, but must be received from the saving activity of the Triune God made manifest in Jesus Christ. Central questions shaping the agenda of this chapter include: How does the church inhabit and serve the world? How did Bonhoeffer and Hauerwas understand the particular worlds they inhabited? As we explore these questions, we will see that the radical christological concentration of both men and their corresponding recovery of the importance of the identity of the church allows for a different orientation to the church-world problematic than the predominant approaches to the problem in modernity.

Each of these three chapters will consist of three major sections. The first section of each chapter will be devoted to the attempt to understand Bonhoeffer's thought on its own terms and will be followed in the second section by an attempt to come to grips with Hauerwas's understanding of the topic under consideration. Although particularly pertinent issues emerging in the secondary literature will be engaged in the text, most of the engagement with secondary sources will be restricted to the footnotes.[55] The primary focus of these sections will be upon concrete engagement with each figure's thought through the close reading of relevant primary texts. Each chapter will conclude with a summary section that will provide the opportunity to bring the theologies of Bonhoeffer and Hauerwas into dialogue with one another. In addition to presenting a synthesis of the major points of agreement shared between the two theologians, these summary sections will also present potential areas of disagreement where one theologian may be able to offer correction to the other on the basis of their own shared and stated christological convictions. The book will draw to a close with a concluding chapter that will briefly restate the major findings of the project, give voice to unanswered questions, and propose areas for further research.

While this concludes the argument proper of the book, a work which brings together the theologies of Dietrich Bonhoeffer—a famous anti-Nazi

---

55. Undoubtedly, some will question the choice of interlocutors and wonder why this voice and not another was represented in the discussion. This is the reader's right and from the reader I can only ask for patience and charity. However, in light of the vast swaths of Bonhoeffer literature which now appear in print and the rapidly proliferating secondary sources pertaining to Hauerwas's work a degree of selectivity had to be exercised if the material was going to be presented in a manageable format that did not over-burden the reader.

conspirator—and Stanley Hauerwas—perhaps the most prominent contemporary advocate of a theologically-informed pacifism—would remain incomplete for many readers if it did not address the theological and ethical questions surrounding Bonhoeffer's alleged involvement in the conspiracy. Therefore, an appendix on the "The Ethics of Tyrannicide" has been included following the conclusion.

2

"This Man is God!"
The Person of Jesus Christ

In this chapter I will argue that the person of Jesus stands at the center of the theological projects of both Dietrich Bonhoeffer and Stanley Hauerwas and that both cling to the conviction that the concrete reality of the church and its distinct mission in the world springs forth from the irreducible particularity of the person of Jesus Christ. This chapter will examine the Christologies of Bonhoeffer and Hauerwas and seek to uncover the central place that Jesus Christ occupies within their work.

Bonhoeffer's Christology will be examined through an exploration of the Christology lectures he delivered in 1933 at the University of Berlin. The reading of these lectures provides a point of entry into Bonhoeffer's Christology, as they incorporate many of the key concepts from Bonhoeffer's earlier academic writings and anticipate many of the later christological developments in his thought.

The second major part of the chapter will consider Hauerwas's Christology. While Hauerwas's theology is most frequently considered from an ecclesiological, ethical, or philosophical perspective, there has been little attention given to the radical christological thrust of his work.[1] Analysis of an early essay, entitled "The Humanity of the Divine," will disclose that this

---

1. A notable exception is Samuel Wells's recent essay, "The Difference Christ Makes," which originated as an address delivered as part of a celebration of Hauerwas's career upon the occasion of his retirement from Duke Divinity School. The writing of this chapter preceded the publication of Wells's essay, but there are a striking number of similarities between our analyses. Some of the similarities will be documented in the footnotes.

christological concentration was present at a very early point in Hauerwas's academic career. The development of Hauerwas's Christology will then be traced through an examination of two definitive essays from the early 1980s when his distinctive project was coming into focus: "Jesus: The Story of the Kingdom" and "Jesus: The Presence of the Peaceable Kingdom." This will be followed by a consideration of two of Hauerwas's more recent writings, which serve to materially supplement his Christology: *Cross-shattered Christ* and his biblical commentary, *Matthew*.

PART 1: THE CHRISTOLOGY OF DIETRICH BONHOEFFER

The Centrality of Jesus Christ in Bonhoeffer's Thought

The correspondence between Bonhoeffer and his close friend Eberhard Bethge during the former's incarceration in Tegel military prison reveals that throughout this period Bonhoeffer was haunted by the piercing question: "who is Christ actually for us today?"[2] This was certainly not the first time that the christological question had occupied Bonhoeffer's thoughts. Bethge, who was the recipient of much of the prison correspondence, maintains that Bonhoeffer's "one question, with certain variations, was always, 'Who is he, Christ?'"[3] Although commentators are in widespread agreement about the central place of Christology in Bonhoeffer's thought,[4] Bonhoeffer himself did not publish any text exclusively dedicated to this topic. Bonhoeffer did, however, deliver a series of lectures on Christology during the summer semester of 1933 while teaching as a member of the faculty at the University of Berlin. These lectures have survived in the form of notes taken by several of the students who participated in the class.[5]

Although we do not have access to Bonhoeffer's original manuscripts, the student notes that have been preserved underscore the importance of

   2. *LPP* (*DBWE* 8), 362.
   3. Wright, "Aftermath of Flossenburg," 657.
   4. E.g., Pangritz, "Who is Jesus Christ," 134; Green, *Theology of Sociality*, 1; Robertson, translator's preface to *CC*, 10; Phillips, *Christ For Us*, 27; Ott, *Reality and Faith*, 368; Feil, *Theology of Dietrich Bonhoeffer*, 86, 95; Godsey, "Bonhoeffer and Christian Spirituality," 81; Dumas, *Dietrich Bonhoeffer*, 167; Tietz, "Bonhoeffer's Strong Christology," 188.
   5. A composite reconstruction of the lectures attempted by Eberhard Bethge based upon the notes of several of the students was published in English in 1966 under the title *Christ the Center* in America and *Christology* in England. A new English translation of this composite reconstruction was prepared by Edwin H. Robertson and published in 1978. A different version of the lectures, based substantially upon the notes of a single student, Gerhard Reimer, has been published in *DBWE* 12:299–360.

the Christology lectures for Bonhoeffer's own theological development. Eberhard Bethge has described these lectures as "the high point of Bonhoeffer's academic career,"[6] for in preparing them Bonhoeffer had to "bring together all of his thoughts, statements, and experiments and test their validity and foundation."[7] In the immediate context of Bonhoeffer's life, it appears that these lectures provided the christological grounding for his subsequent reflections on Christian discipleship famously published under the title *Nachfolge* (*Discipleship*), whose key themes Bonhoeffer was already wrestling with as early as 1932.[8] Matthews appears to be quite correct in suggesting that in Bonhoeffer's Christology lectures we are granted "a glimpse of the theological foundation that would ground him until his dying day."[9] In the section that follows, we will engage in a close reading of Bonhoeffer's Christology lectures, pausing at various points along the way to consider how he has integrated key themes from his previous work and how these lectures anticipate later developments in his thought.

Background to the Christology Lectures

"The years 1932–33 in Germany," Rasmussen notes, "can still leave the observer baffled—as it did some living at the time—by the spectacle of a civilized society disintegrating into barbarism."[10] The aftershocks of these tumultuous years would continue to rattle Germany for years to come and would profoundly influence the shape of Bonhoeffer's life. The beginning of 1933 saw Hitler, riding a wave of popular support, appointed on January 30 to the position of Reich Chancellor by President Hindenburg. Two days later, Bonhoeffer was found behind a microphone giving a radio address entitled, "The Younger Generation's Altered View of the Concept of the Führer."[11] In this address, Bonhoeffer called into question "the messianically tinged expectations of the Führer held among the younger generation itself."[12]

Young people were not the only ones whose imaginations were enraptured by Hitler and the burgeoning National Socialist party. For a German

---

6. Bethge, *Dietrich Bonhoeffer*, 219.

7. Ibid., 219.

8. Kelly and Godsey, editors' introduction to *D* (*DBWE* 4), 4–5; Kuske and Tödt, editor's afterword to *D* (*DBWE* 4), 292–93; Plant, *Bonhoeffer*, 94.

9. Matthews, *Anxious Souls*, 49. For similar assessments of the importance of the Christology lectures to Bonhoeffer's theological development, see Rasmussen, editor's introduction to *DBWE* 12:37; Plant, *Bonhoeffer*, 146; Green, *Theology of Sociality*, 234.

10. Rasmussen, editor's introduction to *DBWE* 12:3.

11. *DBWE* 12:266–68.

12. Scharffenorth, editor's afterword to *DBWE* 12:503.

people devastated by the rabid inflation which accompanied the Great Depression and disgraced by what they considered to be a humiliating treaty enacted at the conclusion of the First World War at Versailles, the Nazi rhetoric which spoke of a return to Germanic glory proved to be particularly appealing.[13] The churches, which had seen their place of influence diminish during the time of the Weimar Republic, were also swept up in this wave of enthusiasm for Hitler, enamored with his promises to restore Christianity as "the basis of our whole morality" and to place Christianity under his "firm protection."[14] Within a year, the following prose passage, which reflects the frightening messianic projections of the period, was being taught in schools:

> As Jesus set men free from sin and hell, so Hitler rescued the German people from destruction. Both Jesus and Hitler were persecuted; but, while Jesus was crucified, Hitler was exalted to Chancellor. While the disciples of Jesus betrayed their master and left him in his distress, the sixteen friends of Hitler stood by him. The apostles completed the work of their Lord. We hope that Hitler will lead his work to completion. Jesus built for heaven; Hitler, for the German soil.[15]

On the night of February 27, 1933 the *Reichstag* building, where the German parliament assembled, was set ablaze. This act of terror was all that Hitler needed to begin quickly consolidating power. The next day President Hindenburg, at Hitler's request, announced an Emergency Decree which suspended many of the civil liberties protected by the Weimar constitution. In the weeks that followed, a series of laws was passed which increasingly consolidated power under Hitler and deprived citizens of constitutional rights under the guise of freedom, including the Law for the Reconstitution of the Civil Service with its infamous "Aryan paragraph," which banned from the civil service those of non-Aryan descent and others who were considered to be politically subversive, such as communists and socialists. In parallel with these governmental developments, the Reich Conference of German Christians was held on April 3 and 4, which advocated: "*Gleichschaltung* (the alignment of all sectors with Nazi goals), the *Führer* principle, the Reich church, and racial conformity."[16]

Bonhoeffer began his Christology lectures on Wednesday, May 3—a week before students and professors joined with Nazi stormtroopers to burn

---

13. Bonhoeffer himself during his first visit to America spoke of the negative impact of Versailles upon the German people. *DBWE* 10:411–18.

14. Hitler's proclamation to the German people published in *Völkischer Beobachter* (Feb. 1, 1933), quoted in Bethge, *Dietrich Bonhoeffer*, 261–62.

15. Robertson, *Christians against Hitler*, 18, quoted in Robertson, *Persistent Voice of Dietrich Bonhoeffer*, 79.

16. Bethge, *Dietrich Bonhoeffer*, 270.

hundreds of volumes of books in a bonfire beneath the Humboldt monument[17]—and lectured Wednesdays and Saturdays from 8:00 am to 9:00 am until July 22, 1933.[18] By the end of the year, over ninety percent of the theology students had joined the National Socialist Party and a swastika banner had been draped over the front entrance of the building where the faculty of theology was housed.[19] Amidst the surrounding political turbulence, Bonhoeffer focused upon these lectures, the preparations for which he considered to be the most challenging of his academic career up to that point.[20] Close to two hundred students attended the young professor's lectures—a quite astounding fact considering the demanding nature of the material and the early morning start time![21] Otto Dudzus, one of Bonhoeffer's students, recalls:

> He looked like a student himself when he mounted the platform. But then what he had to say gripped us all so greatly that we no longer came because of this very young man but because of what he had to say—even though it was dreadfully early in the morning. I have never heard a lecture that impressed me nearly so much as this one.[22]

Bonhoeffer's Prolegomena to the Christology Lectures

One can only imagine the anxious hush that must have fallen over the lecture hall as the young, broad-shouldered, blond-haired, bespectacled professor stepped behind the lectern. Bonhoeffer's "high and slightly tremulous" voice pierced the silence:[23]

> Teaching about Christ begins in silence. "Be still, for that is the absolute," writes Kierkegaard. That has nothing to do with the silence of the mystics, who in their dumbness chatter away secretly in their soul by themselves. The silence of the Church

---

17. Rasmussen, editor's introduction to *DBWE* 12:4.

18. *DBWE* 12:299 n. 1. Bonhoeffer cancelled his final lecture, so that he and his students could dedicate themselves to the preparations of the Young Reformation Movement for the upcoming church elections. Bethge, *Dietrich Bonhoeffer*, 295.

19. Marsh, *Strange Glory*, 165.

20. Bethge, *Dietrich Bonhoeffer*, 219.

21. The lecture schedule must have been demanding for Bonhoeffer himself, who was known to be somewhat of a night-owl.

22. Bethge, *Dietrich Bonhoeffer*, 219.

23. Marsh, *Strange Glory*, 151.

is silence before the Word. In so far as the Church proclaims the Word, it falls down in silence before the inexpressible: "In silence I worship the unutterable" (Cyril of Alexandria). The spoken Word is the inexpressible; this unutterable is the Word. "It must become spoken, it is the great battle cry" (Luther). Although it is cried out by the Church in the world, it remains the inexpressible. To speak of Christ means to keep silent; to keep silent about Christ means to speak. When the Church speaks rightly out of a proper silence, then Christ is proclaimed.[24]

This dramatic opening salvo indicated to attentive listeners that this would be no ordinary course of lectures. What was being embarked upon was no mere academic undertaking conducted by a detached observer operating within the realm of supposed scholarly neutrality. On the contrary, those gathered to study Christology found themselves called to participate in an ecclesial discipline rooted in the worshipping life of the church and nourished by the life-giving springs of prayer.[25] This does not mean that Christology is some sort of marginal discipline. Since it deals with the incarnation of the Logos of God, it is, in fact, "the invisible, unrecognized, hidden center of scholarship, of the *universitas litterarum*."[26] This claim can only be affirmed within the Christian church, for the transcendence of the object of Christology can only be acknowledged in faith and never proven on other grounds.

In describing the condition of fallen humanity, Bonhoeffer, as he previously did in his *Habilitationsschrift* employs the traditional Lutheran terminology of the *cor curvum in se* (the heart turned in upon itself).[27] The concept of the *cor curvum in se*, which first rose to prominence in Luther's lectures of 1515–1516 on the epistle to the Romans,[28] may have been mediated to Bonhoeffer through his teacher Karl Holl.[29] For Bonhoeffer, the *cor curvum in se* of fallen humanity is like a black hole which attempts to pull everything into itself. Through the operation of its classifying logos, the *cor curvum in se* attempts to assimilate everything into its own ordering, thus removing any potential threats posed to its own being by the question of transcendence. The classifying logos is extraordinarily resilient, as

---

24. *CC*, 27.

25. "To pray is to keep silent and at the same time cry out, before God in both cases, in the light of God's Word" (*DBWE* 12:301).

26. Ibid., 301.

27. *AB* (*DBWE* 2), 137.

28. Lohse, *Martin Luther's Theology*, 71.

29. Rumscheidt, "Formation of Bonhoeffer's Theology," 57.

demonstrated by Hegel's sophisticated dialectic in which the human logos assimilated the divine counter Logos into itself:

> But what happens if the counter Logos suddenly presents its demand in a wholly new form, so that it is no longer an idea or a word that is turned against the autonomy of the [human] logos, but rather the counter Logos appears, somewhere and at some time in history, as a human being, and as a human being sets itself up as judge over the human logos and says, "I am the truth," I am the death of the human logos, I am the life of God's Logos, I am the Alpha and the Omega? Human beings are those who must die and must fall, with their logos, into my hands. Here it is no longer possible to fit the Word made flesh into the logos classification system. Here all that remains is the question: Who are you?[30]

Who? is the proper christological question. It is the question of transcendence, which expresses the "otherness of the other," as opposed to How?, which is the question of immanence.[31] According to Bonhoeffer, the question How? (i.e., How are you possible?) is the "godless question" upon which the early Church foundered.[32] (On the other hand, modern theology has shipwrecked itself on the "that" question of the truth of revelation.)[33] Who are you? remains the central and only appropriate question of Christology. However, the fallen human logos is not capable of asking the question, Who? As fallen human beings we remain "chained to our own authority" and hence whatever language we use, our intention remains, How?[34] Echoing his insistence in *Act and Being* that human beings cannot place themselves into the truth, Bonhoeffer insists that the Who? question can only be asked where the other has already revealed himself, namely in the church.[35] It is here, as one is encountered by the Risen One, that the question Who? is truly elicited and subsequently turned around so that the questioner herself becomes the questioned. In the face of such an encounter, there are only two possibilities: "the human being must either die or kill Jesus."[36] There are many different ways that we attempt to be finished with Christ, ranging from outright rejection to death by flattery. No

---

30. *DBWE* 12:302.
31. Ibid., 303.
32. Ibid.
33. Ibid., 304.
34. Ibid., 303.
35. *AB* (*DBWE* 2), 58, 81, 90.
36. *DBWE* 12, 307.

one is immune from participating in this conspiracy—not even, or perhaps especially, the theologians![37] The christological question "can be asked only within the context of faith, and there it will receive its answer."[38] Within the act of faith the true identity of Jesus Christ is disclosed, as is also the identity of the believer, for as Bonhoeffer asserts in a manner reminiscent of the opening lines of Calvin's *Institutes of the Christian Religion*, "it is only from God that man knows who he is."[39]

Bonhoeffer concludes his prolegomena by emphasizing that "Christology is not soteriology."[40] At this point Bonhoeffer summons Luther to testify against the Lutheran tradition that has developed under the influence of Melanchthon's famous dictum, "to know Christ is to know his benefits."[41] In referring "the christological question back to the soteriological question," Melanchthon initiated an epochal shift which paved the way for the rise of modern liberal theology and its absorption of Christology into soteriology, ultimately rendering any specific Christology superfluous.[42] Although it is commonplace to speak of the soteriological concentration of Luther's thought and the indissoluble connection between Christology and soteriology in Luther's theology, Luther recognized that the two could not be conflated.[43] For Luther, "soteriology has its basis in Christology" and what was of the utmost importance was the identity of the person who was performing the work.[44] Following Luther, in contradistinction to Melanchthon, Bonhoeffer insists that only when the identity of the one who does the work

---

37. Ibid., 307. It is interesting to observe Bonhoeffer's summoning of Kierkegaard in the opening paragraph of the lectures. As Kelly has observed, both Bonhoeffer and Kierkegaard were united in their disdain for "the grandiosity of theological blather that so cavalierly bestows honorific titles on Jesus while ignoring the real meaning of Jesus for Christian living" ("Kierkegaard as 'Antidote,'" 157). A further similarity has been identified by Ziegler, who has drawn attention to Bonhoeffer's development of the promeity of Christ in the Christology lectures and its resonances with Kierkegaard's Christology. "Christ for Us Today," 29–35, 39–41. For a full manuscript-length treatment of the relationship between Kierkegaard and Bonhoeffer, see Kirkpatrick, *Attacks on Christendom*.

38. *DBWE* 12:307.

39. *CC*, 31. John T. McNeill observes that the French version of the 1560 edition of Calvin's *Institutes* begins with the sentence, "In knowing God, each of us also knows himself" (*Institutes*, 36 n. 3).

40. *DBWE* 12:308.

41. *CC*, 37.

42. Ibid., 37. For a similar assessment of the dangers of a soteriological approach to Christology, see Pannenberg, *Jesus*, 47–49.

43. E.g., Slenczka, "Christus," 382; Lohse, *Martin Luther's Theology*, 34, 223; Lienhard, *Luther*, 41.

44. Lohse, *Martin Luther's Theology*, 224; see also Slenczka, "Christus," 382–83.

is known, can what it is he does be recognized. Bethge succinctly captures the essence of Bonhoeffer's argument:

> Contrary to the view of Melanchthon, Bonhoeffer was of the opinion that "Christology is not soteriology" (CC 37); that the work does not interpret the person, but, as Luther says, the person the works; that the *extra nos* must not be dissolved into the *pro nobis* and that the *pro nobis* rests on the *extra nos*; that the Who-question preserves the priority of the christological question over the soteriological.[45]

This does not mean that the person and the work can be separated, for the "complete Christ is the historical Jesus, who can never in any way be separated from his work."[46] It is only for the purpose of establishing a theological method that Christology is given theological priority over soteriology. Having established the proper theological relationship between the person and work of Christ, Bonhoeffer concludes his introduction by stating the true subject matter of Christology which he will pursue in the following parts of the lectures: "To put it in the abstract: The personal ontological structure [*personale Seinstruktur*] of the whole, historical Christ is the subject matter of Christology."[47]

The Present Christ

John Webster has intriguingly suggested that "one illuminating way of writing the history of modernity would be to envisage it as the story of the steady eclipse of belief in Jesus' presence—as the gradual erosion of confidence in the basic Christian conviction that, *sub specie resurrectionis*, everything looks different."[48] In his opening remarks to the first major part of his Christology lectures, Bonhoeffer further signals his break with the trajectory of this modern narrative:

> As the Crucified and Risen One, Jesus is at the same time the Christ who is present now. This is the first statement: that Christ is the Christ who is present in history. He is to be understood as present in time and space. *Nunc et hic*, the two flow together in the concept of the church. Christ in his person is indeed present in the church as person. Thus the presence of Christ is there in

---

45. Bethge, "Bonhoeffer's Christology," 73.
46. *CC*, 39.
47. *DBWE* 12:310.
48. Webster, *Word and Church*, 2.

the church. Only because Christ is the Christ who is present are we still able to inquire of him. Only because proclamation and the sacraments are carried out in the church can we inquire about Christ.[49]

Standing behind the lectern at the university whose chair of theology was first occupied by Friedrich Schleiermacher, the young professor boldly pronounced that his liberal theological forbearers had gotten it wrong. According to Bonhoeffer's judgement, in neglecting the reality of the resurrection, Schleiermacher, Ritschl, and Herrmann had each in their own way reduced Christ from a present person to a mere influence, value, or power. Drawing upon the doctrine of the ascension, another neglected doctrine in modernity, Bonhoeffer is able to assert with Luther that it is only on account of "sitting at God's right hand, Christ is able to be present to us."[50] It is the presence of the risen Christ in the church that makes possible an understanding of his person. Just how exactly Jesus Christ is present with us we cannot say. It is enough to know that "the presence of Jesus Christ in the Church, at a particular time and place, is because of the fact that there is one whole person of the God-Man."[51] To attempt to establish how the human Jesus can be present with us or how the eternal God could be present within time is to tear asunder what has been joined together in the hypostatic union by asking the godless question, How? Only the personal question Who? is appropriate. For this reason, "the starting point for Christology has to be the God-human."[52] The influence of Luther is very much apparent in Bonhoeffer's insistence on focusing upon the concrete person of the God-man and his avoidance of abstract speculation concerning the natures. According to Luther's line of thought, "the one agent of salvation is the person; if Christ's works could be assigned to one or the other nature, this, in Luther's view, would mean that he was not in fact one person at all and that there was no incarnation."[53] It is this emphasis upon the hypostasis of the complete God-human that provides the foundation for Bonhoeffer's recovery of the life and teachings of Jesus later in the lectures, which he then develops further in *Discipleship* and returns to again while in prison.

Reflecting the soteriological thrust of Luther's Christology, Bonhoeffer insists "I can never think of Jesus Christ in his being-in-himself, but only

---

49. *DBWE* 12:310.
50. Ibid., 312.
51. *CC*, 45.
52. *DBWE* 12:313.
53. Jenson, "Luther's Contemporary Theological Significance," 277.

in his relatedness to me."⁵⁴ The existential implications of this assertion for Christology arise not from the reflective human subject, but stem from the *pro-me* personal ontological structure of Jesus Christ himself. To attempt to think of Christ-in-himself is a godless abstraction, for Christ in his very being is for me. As Bonhoeffer asserts, "This *pro-me* is not to be understood as an effect that issues from Christ or as a form that he assumes incidentally, but is to be understood as the very being of his person."⁵⁵ In employing the *pro-me* in this way, Bonhoeffer is able to sail between the Scylla of scholasticism which makes the person of Christ into an object for study apart from his existential impact upon us and the Charybdis of theological liberalism which neglects the person of Christ to focus solely on the effect of his works upon us. Bonhoeffer's christological employment of the *pro-me* is of central significance to his theological project as it allows him to hold together the person and work of Christ.⁵⁶ It also, reflecting the concerns of his *Habilitationsschrift*, allows him to transcend the competing claims of ontological and actualistic understandings of revelation, as respectively informed by the phenomenological and transcendental philosophical traditions.⁵⁷ It is the *pro-me* structure that holds together the being and act of Christ; for in the *pro-me* structure "being-there-for-*you* comes together with being-*there*-for-you."⁵⁸ Along with Karl Barth, Bonhoeffer recognized that being-conceptions of revelation run the risk of reducing revelation to a human possession.⁵⁹ However, the actualistic theology of the early Barth and the dialectical theological movement, in Bonhoeffer's judgment, threatened the continuity of God's relationship to humanity and therefore had difficulties accounting for the continuity of the Christian life.⁶⁰ According to Bonhoeffer, the theologies based upon an actualistic understanding of revelation had misconstrued the freedom of God.⁶¹ It is worth quoting Bonhoeffer here at some length:

> In revelation it is not so much a question of the freedom of God—eternally remaining within the divine self, aseity—on the other side of revelation, as it is of God's coming out of God's own

---

54. *DBWE* 12:314.

55. Ibid., 314.

56. As also does his concept of Christ as *Stellvertreter*, which will be explored momentarily. Green, *Theology of Sociality*, 61.

57. DeJonge, *Bonhoeffer's Theological Formation*, 93.

58. *DBWE* 12:315.

59. Marsh, *Reclaiming Dietrich Bonhoeffer*, 127.

60. DeJonge, *Bonhoeffer's Theological Formation*, 56–58.

61. Green, *Theology of Sociality*, 85.

self in revelation. It is a matter of God's *given* Word, the covenant in which God is bound by God's own action. It is a question of the freedom of God, which finds its strongest evidence precisely in that God freely chose to be bound to historical human beings and to be placed at the disposal of human beings. God is free not from human beings, but for them. Christ is the word of God's freedom. God *is* present, that is, not in eternal nonobjectivity but—to put it quite provisionally for now—"haveable," graspable in the Word within the church. Here the formal understanding of God's freedom is countered by a substantial one. If the latter can be understood to be a true understanding of God's freedom, then we are guided toward concepts of being by the understanding of revelation as pure act.[62]

In this quite remarkable passage, the twenty-four-year-old postdoctoral student offers an important correction to the work of his theological mentor, in terms congruent with Barth's theological project, by redefining the freedom of God from a christological perspective.[63] Echoing "the magnificent theme of *Act and Being*," Bonhoeffer reaffirms in the Christology lectures that Jesus Christ "is the one who has really bound himself in the freedom of his existence to me. And he is the one who has preserved his contingency freely in being there for me."[64] It is this understanding of Jesus Christ in his *pro-me* personal structure which allows for "the coordination or unity of contingent acts and historically continuous being."[65] This development of the understanding of Christ as person present in the church has fittingly been described by Michael DeJonge as a type of "post-Barthian, Lutheran theology."[66] Drawing upon similar descriptive nomenclature, Jens Zimmerman describes Bonhoeffer as a "deeply Lutheran theologian with a Barthian twist" because of his ability to "combine a genuine appreciation of the historical, of faith as existing concretely in time and culture, with an equal stress on God's transcendence."[67]

---

62. *AB* (*DBWE* 2), 90–91.

63. On the basis of the texts available to him at the time of writing his *Habilitationsschrift* in 1930, Bonhoeffer's criticisms of Barth's early theology and the dialectical theology movement in general appear to be warranted. Barth's later writings do not appear to be as vulnerable to the same criticisms. See especially *CD* 4/1–3 and Barth, *Humanity of God*.

64. *CC*, 48. Marsh describes God's binding of Godself to humanity in freedom as "the magnificent theme of *Act and Being*" (*Reclaiming Dietrich Bonhoeffer*, 133). Ziegler similarly interprets the promeity of the Christology lectures in connection with the understanding of divine freedom advanced in *Act and Being*. "Christ for Us Today," 31.

65. DeJonge, *Bonhoeffer's Theological Formation*, 93.

66. DeJonge, "Presence of Christ," 114.

67. Zimmerman, "Suffering with the World," 23.

Bonhoeffer's understanding of the freedom of God as freedom for humanity lies at the heart of his conception of the *pro-me* structure of Christ, which allows him to maintain the connection between the person and work of Christ. This organic unity of the person and work of Christ is perhaps most clearly displayed within the lectures in Bonhoeffer's explication of the implications of the *pro-me* structure for the relation of Christ to the new humanity.[68] According to Bonhoeffer there are three key implications of the *pro-me* structure; namely, that Jesus Christ is the inaugurator of the new humanity, that he stands in the place of the new humanity before God, and that Christ is in the new humanity and it is in him.[69] In speaking of the "new humanity," Bonhoeffer utilizes a term he first introduced in his doctoral dissertation *Sanctorum Communio*, which he appears to have appropriated from the work of his dissertation advisor, Reinhold Seeberg.[70] In *Sanctorum Communio*, the new humanity is closely linked with Bonhoeffer's concept of the "collective person."[71] Each human community, whether it is as small as a family or as large as a nation, can be considered as a collective person with its own objective *Geist*.[72] At the most universal level, the fallen human race has its being in Adam, which is a being-in-sin or "being-for-self," characterized by fragmentation and isolation.[73] In Adam's attempt to be like God all of humanity has fallen, and in this old humanity, "the whole of humanity falls anew, so to speak, with every person who sins."[74] Human beings are unable to escape the gravitational pull of the *cor curvum in se*; hence fallen humanity remains in a state of fragmentation, unable to unify itself by restoring itself to communion with God or others.[75] Salvation must therefore come from the outside—*extra nos*. Bonhoeffer elaborates:

> While the old humanity consists of countless isolated units—each one an Adam—that are perceived as a comprehensive

---

68. *DBWE* 12:315; *CC*, 48.

69. *DBWE* 12:315; *CC*, 48. Zimmerman links Bonhoeffer's understanding of the new humanity with that of the Fathers, describing both as *"participatory ontology"* ("Being Human," 33).

70. Rumscheidt, "Formation of Bonhoeffer's Theology," 58.

71. *"We maintain that community can be interpreted as a collective person with the same structure as the individual person"* (SC (*DBWE* 1), 77; italics original).

72. For a more detailed exposition of "Person" as a corporate concept in *Sanctorum Communio*, see Green, *Theology of Sociality*, 36–48.

73. *SC* (*DBWE* 1), 121. The description of Bonhoeffer's understanding of sin as "being-for-self" is introduced in Green, *Theology of Sociality*, 49.

74. Ibid., 146.

75. Krötke highlights Bonhoeffer's affinity with Luther in emphasizing the ubiquity and inescapability of sin. "Bonhoeffer and Luther," 70.

unity only through each individual, the new humanity is entirely concentrated in the one single historical point, Jesus Christ, and only in Christ is it perceived as a whole. For in Christ, as the foundation and the body of the building called Christ's church-community, the work of God takes place and is completed. In this work Christ has a function that sheds the clearest light on the fundamental difference between Adam and Christ, namely the *function of vicarious representative* [*Stellvertreter*].[76]

As the *Stellvertreter*, Jesus both stands in the place of sinners and is himself the presence of the eschatologically reconstituted humanity. Green helpfully elaborates: "By his becoming human, Christ vicariously dies the death of every sinful human being and of sinful humanity corporately, and liberates people to the new life of resurrection and grace; the new humanity has its concrete social form in the church, and there people are incorporated into Christ and reunited with each other, having been freed from the egocentricity, domination and isolation of their own power."[77] As a result Bonhoeffer can speak of *Stellvertretung* as being the "life-principle of the new humanity,"[78] which is characterized by "*being-with-each*-other" and "*being-for-each*-other."[79] This understanding of Christ as *Stellvertreter* and the accompanying concept of *Stellvertretung* run like a red thread through Bonhoeffer's writings.[80] Furthermore, it is not difficult to discern the line that runs from Bonhoeffer's christological concept of the *Stellvertreter* through the *pro-me* personal structure to his famous prison presentation of Jesus as "the human being for others."[81]

Bischoff has drawn attention to the uniqueness of Bonhoeffer's understanding of Christ's redemptive work as *Stellvertreter* by introducing the analogy of a cross with its horizontal and vertical beams. The horizontal beam represents the anthropological dimension of salvation, whereas the vertical beam represents the theological dimension. Bischoff observes that contemporary "liberal-evangelical polarization has split/reduced

---

76. *SC* (*DBWE* 1), 146.

77. Green, *Theology of Sociality*, 182.

78. *SC* (*DBWE* 1), 147.

79. Ibid., 182.

80. E.g., in *Discipleship* Christ is described as the one who "suffers as vicarious representative for the world," whose sufferings bring salvation (*D* (*DBWE* 4), 90). In the *Ethics* manuscript, "History and Good [1]," Bonhoeffer explicitly connects Christian ethical conduct with Christ's *Stellvertretung*: "All human responsibility is rooted in the real vicarious representative action of Jesus Christ on behalf of all human beings. Responsible action is vicarious representative action" (*E* (*DBWE* 6), 232).

81. *LPP* (*DBWE* 8), 382.

redemption into the horizontal beam in the former and the vertical beam in the latter."[82] Bonhoeffer's understanding of the saving work of Christ, however, holds together the vertical and horizontal beams of the cross where other modern attempts fail.[83] Generally speaking the introduction of this analogy is a helpful addition to the ongoing discussion. However, one must keep in mind that like all analogies, Bischoff's analogy of the cross with its vertical and horizontal beams does have its limitations. For instance, if pushed too far, the analogy seems to suggest that one can in fact have one of the beams in place without the other. Bonhoeffer would not be content to suggest that modern liberals need only to add to their abstract concepts of social justice an individualistic, metaphysical account of redemption as found in some popular forms of evangelicalism in order to complete their portrait of salvation, or vice versa. Rather for Bonhoeffer, theology and anthropology are indivisible on account of the incarnation.

Phillips has correctly noted the centrality of the *pro me* to Bonhoeffer's argument, observing:

> The heart of Bonhoeffer's lectures is his argument that the total orientation of the personal structure of Christ is *pro me*: Christ's being-for-me is not some "power" which he possesses but rather the definition of his being. His determination *pro me* is the centre of his personal structure. Two questions are thus proper to Christology: *In what form* is Christ present *pro me*, and *where* is Christ present *pro me*?[84]

In answer to the first question, Bonhoeffer maintains that "the God-human Jesus Christ is the one who, in his *pro-me* structure, is present in his person to the church as Word, sacrament and church-community."[85] The connection between Christ's ascension and his presence to his church is made explicit in an Ascension Day sermon Bonhoeffer delivered at the Kaiser Wilhelm Memorial Church on May 25, 1933. Bonhoeffer expounds the significance of the ascension, proclaiming:

> He is close to us in his church, in his Word, in his sacrament, in love among the brethren. Here he comforts us who are abandoned; here he soothes our homesickness ever anew; here he takes us who are estranged from God, who are in barren empty places, who don't know the way, who are alone, and makes us

---

82. Bischoff, "Ecclesiology of the Cross," 60.

83. Ibid., 60. Bischoff's unfortunate choice of the term "re-incarnation" as a way of describing the relation between Christ and the church is not as helpful.

84. Phillips, *Form of Christ*, 80.

85. *DBWE* 12:315.

joyful in his Christly presence. Joy in the sermon, joy in the sacrament, joy in brothers and sisters—that is the joy of the believing church in its unseen, heavenly Lord.[86]

"That Christ is the Word means that he is the truth."[87] Christ does not merely have the Word, but is the Word, who encounters humanity not in the form of idea, but in the form of address, which renders the hearer response-able and responsible. As address, the Word is not a timeless truth, but an event of encounter which occurs again and again within history. Christ is not merely *in* the Word of the Church, but rather is present *as* the Word of the Church, having freely bound himself to the human words of the Church's proclamation. The famous marginal note to the Second Helvetic Confession (1566), which states that "The preaching of the Word of God *is* the Word of God," resonates with Bonhoeffer's theology of preaching.[88] As Bonhoeffer would later frame the matter, "The proclaimed word is not a medium of expression for something else, something that lies behind it, but rather it is the Christ himself walking through his congregation as the Word."[89] Yet the person of the God-human who has bound Himself to the proclaimed word, remains hidden under the veil of the flesh in the human word of preaching, revealed only when and where God chooses. In this way, "Christ as Word expresses both the contingent character of his revelation and his commitment [Bindung] to humankind."[90]

If preaching is "the form in which the Logos reaches the human logos,"[91] then the sacrament must be understood as "the form in which the Logos reaches man in his nature."[92] The sacrament must not be thought of as a representation of the Word, "for only that which is not present can be represented."[93] The corporeality of the sacrament counters gnosticizing tendencies which attempt to reduce Jesus to an idea, abstracted from an existence in history and nature.[94] Against all accounts of the sacraments

---

86. Ibid., 469.
87. Ibid., 315.
88. Second Helvetic Confession, 1.4, quoted in Wainwright, *For Our Salvation*, 27.
89. *WP*, 101.
90. *DBWE* 12:317.
91. *CC*, 53.
92. Ibid., 53.
93. *DBWE* 12:318.
94. Hall has drawn attention to the way the early church fathers drew upon the Eucharist to counter the gnostic threat in the early centuries of the church in *Worshipping with the Church Fathers*, 51–80. Lee suggests that the recovery of the significance and regular celebration of the Eucharist is essential if the Protestant church in North America is to overcome its latent gnosticism in *Against the Protestant Gnostics*, 272.

which attempt to place the locus of activity within the individual's subjectivity, Bonhoeffer insists that the sacraments, "do not *mean* something—they *are* something."[95] The question How is Christ present in the sacrament? is inadmissible according to Bonhoeffer and results in the dead end of the *extra Calvinisticum* of Reformed theology and the corresponding Lutheran response of the doctrines of ubiquity and ubiviolipresence.[96] The inadequacy of Luther's doctrines of ubiquity and ubiviolipresence is that "both fail to understand Christ's presence as Christ's way of being."[97] They are the result of the attempt to answer on Lutheran grounds the speculative question How? originally introduced by Reformed theology. Instead, the Lutheran tradition must be restored to its best insights by focusing on the only question that is admissible, "*Who* is present in the sacrament?"[98] In the sacrament Jesus Christ is completely present in the fullness of his humanity and divinity. The hidden presence of the God-human in bread and wine is his continuing humiliation in the present. Yet as a result of his presence, the bread and wine participate in the new creation. Whereas in the world the continuity between creation and nature has been lost as a result of the fall, in the sacrament, the bread and wine are liberated from their bondage to decay so that they may communicate the reality of God—existing no longer in and for themselves but for others.[99] "This being-for-the-person," Bonhoeffer asserts, "is their being newly created."[100]

The third form that Bonhoeffer emphasizes is Christ's presence *in* and *as* the church. Here Bonhoeffer returns to a theme that has been central to his theology since his doctoral dissertation where he first introduced the phrase, "Christ existing as church-community."[101] For Bonhoeffer, the

---

95. *DBWE* 12:319.

96. The *extra Calvinisticum* was the pejorative title given by Lutheran theologians to the Reformed understanding that with respect to the incarnation the second Person of the Trinity is not constrained in activity or presence to the flesh of Jesus. Luther's doctrine of ubiquity arises from his commitment to the communication of attributes between the divine and human natures in the person of the God-man and allows for the assertion that Christ is present everywhere in his humanity. Bonhoeffer describes ubivolipresence as the doctrine that "Christ is only there when he wants to be there for you" (*DBWE* 12:321).

97. *DBWE* 12:322.

98. *CC*, 57.

99. Bonhoeffer reflects upon the discontinuity between creation and nature following the fall in *Creation and Fall*, where he writes, "The trees and animals, which once immediately represented God's word as the Creator, now in often grotesque ways point instead as though to the incomprehensibility and arbitrariness of a despot who is hidden in darkness" (*CF* (*DBWE* 3), 134).

100. *DBWE* 12:322.

101. *SC* (*DBWE* 1), 140–41. The phrase "Christ existing as church-community" is a

Church is not only "the receiver of the Word of revelation, but is itself revelation and Word of God."[102] Using language paralleling the sacramental realism reflected in his discussion of Christ as sacrament, Bonhoeffer maintains, "The Church *is* the body of Christ, it does not *signify* the body of Christ."[103] A paragraph later, he adds, "Christ is not only the head of the Church, but also the Church itself (see 1 Corinthians 12 and Ephesians)."[104] Harvey has observed that "Bonhoeffer's basic axiom that *die Kirche ist Christus als Gemeinde existierend*, the church is Christ existing as community, represents in significant ways a recovery and restatement of Augustine's contention that in the church we encounter the whole Christ, *totus Christus*, consisting of both head and body."[105] Augustine, of course, is drawing upon the widespread use of language referring to the church as "the body of Christ" in the writings of the apostle Paul.[106] It is clear then, as Dumas argues, that "from the very beginning Bonhoeffer's interest in the church grows out of christological realism far more than out of an attempt to make a 'case for the church,' or out of fears about the failures and shortcomings of existing empirical churches."[107] The church is of extreme importance for Bonhoeffer because it *is* the bodily presence of the risen Christ in the time between his ascension and *parousia*. At this point the question can be raised as to whether Bonhoeffer conflates Christ and the church; "whether Bonhoeffer leaves adequate room for the freedom of the person of Christ relative to the church."[108] Although there are hints within the lectures that it is possible for Christ to stand over and against the church, as evidenced in the Counter Logos narrative at the beginning of the lectures and the concluding comments of the lectures which speak of Christ being an offense or stumbling block to the church, on the basis of the lectures as a whole this is a legitimate question to ask. However, in the subsequently published *Discipleship*, Bonhoeffer insists upon the necessity of affirming both the unity of and distinction between Christ and his church. In *Discipleship*, Bonhoeffer appears to have

---

christological adaptation of Hegel's "God existing as community," which may have been mediated to Bonhoeffer through his teacher Reinhold Seeberg (198 n. 218). McBride maintains that "'Christ existing as community' is a—if not the—definitive concept in Bonhoeffer's corpus" ("Christ Existing as Concrete Community Today," 92).

102. *CC*, 58.

103. Ibid., 59.

104. Ibid., 59.

105. Harvey, "Augustine and Aquinas," 12.

106. Rom 12:3–8; 1 Cor 12:12–31; Eph 4:1–16. The theme is most pronounced in Augustine's sermons and pastoral writings. Mallard, "*Totus Christus*."

107. Dumas, *Dietrich Bonhoeffer*, 84.

108. Holmes, "Wholly Human," 218.

moved beyond his casual dismissal in the Christology lecture of the distinction between head and members in Ephesians as being "not originally Pauline," so that he is now able to insist that "the unity between Christ and his body, the church, demands that we at the same time recognize Christ's lordship over his body."[109]

Green has offered a helpful clarification with regards to Bonhoeffer's presentation of Christ as church, stressing that "it is imperative to recognize that when Bonhoeffer speaks of the church-community as the third aspect of the Gestalt or Personstruktur of Christ, he is stressing the *social nature of Christ's presence in Word and sacrament*; he is not speaking of a third form autonomous from Word and Sacrament."[110] Bonhoeffer's unfolding of the *pro me* structure of the person of Christ serves to concretize the concept of transcendence by rooting the personal transcendence of Christ within the concrete life of the community. As Green has observed elsewhere in commenting upon Bonhoeffer's Christology lectures:

> God's transcendence is not remote otherness or absence; God's otherness is embodied precisely in the other person who is real and present, encountering me in the heart of my existence with the judgement and grace of the gospel. In this way Christ is present *pro me*, for me. Bonhoeffer's Christology is simultaneously incarnational and communal.[111]

In response to the question Where is Christ present *pro me*? Bonhoeffer answers that Christ is present as the center of human existence, as the center of history, and as the center of nature.[112] As the true and renewed center [*Mitte*] of all things, Christ also stands as the boundary or limit [*Grenze*] to fallen human existence, history, and creation. As the one who stands in the center [*Mitte*], Christ can properly be spoken of as the mediator [*Mittler*].[113] While clearly related to Bonhoeffer's conception of Christ as *Stellvertreter*, Green has observed that the introduction of this new terminology "enables Bonhoeffer to relate his Christology more concretely to history, politics, and nature, and in doing so he makes Christ a more active, present agent."[114]

The centrality of Christ to human existence cannot be empirically verified, as it is an ontological or theological statement, not a psychological

---

109. D (*DBWE* 4), 220.

110. Green, *Theology of Sociality*, 219.

111. Green, "Human Sociality," 124.

112. "It is the nature of Christ's person to be in the center" (*DBWE* 12:324).

113. The integral connection between the center [*Mitte*] and the mediator [*Mittler*] in German is somewhat obscured in English translation.

114. Green, *Theology of Sociology*, 236.

one. Similarly, there can be no question of proving that Christ occupies the center of history. Instead, Christ stands as the hidden center of history, as "the destroyer and fulfiller of all the messianic expectations of history."[115] In this way the presence of Christ in the church calls into question the messianic assumptions of all of the world's ideologies and political programs—a particularly poignant observation in light of the events that had already transpired in Germany by mid-1933. Just as Christ is the center and boundary of human existence, the church as the presence of Christ is both the hidden center of history and the boundary of the state; "Christ as the center of history is the mediator between the state and God in the form of the church."[116] Bonhoeffer strikes a further blow at the heart of the Nazi program by insisting that Israel must be understood as the hidden center of history where the Messianic promise of history is fulfilled. Bonhoeffer's use of the Jewish title Messiah in this section, in place of the more commonly used Hellenized title of Christ, further emphasizes the "interrelation between Jesus the Jew and his primary context: the people of Israel."[117] This understanding of the Jewish Messiah Jesus as the hidden center of history mitigates against both ahistorical accounts of salvation and progressivist understandings of history. Bonhoeffer's awareness of the Jewishness of Jesus and his inseparable connection with the people Israel would only increase over the duration of his life, as evidenced by: his publication of *Creation and Fall*, a theological commentary on Genesis 1–3 in the fall of 1933, at a time when it was academically and politically unfashionable to engage with the Old Testament;[118] his dire warning to Western civilization in his *Ethics* manuscript that "driving out the Jew(s) from the West must result in driving out Christ with them, for Jesus Christ was a Jew";[119] his renewed interest in the Old Testament while in prison,[120] which contributed to what has been described as a "primordially Jewish" way of thinking about "religionless Christianity."[121] This recovery of Jesus's place within the context of the unfolding history between God and Israel contributes to the distinct earthiness and worldly character of salvation in Bonhoeffer's prison writings.[122]

115. *CC*, 62.
116. *DBWE* 12:327.
117. Pangritz, "Who is Jesus Christ?," 144.
118. Tödt, *Authentic Faith*, 89.
119. *E* (*DBWE* 6), 105.
120. *LPP* (*DBWE* 8), 213–14, 367, 373, 394, 491–93.
121. This description was offered by the Jewish theologian Pinchas Lapide in *Internationales Bonhoeffer Forum*, 2:122, quoted in Rütter and Tödt, editor's afterword to *CF* (*DBWE* 3), 173.
122. In an intriguing passage in a letter dated April 30, 1944 Bonhoeffer brings

Christ is the center not only of human existence and history, but also of nature. The natural world was created to proclaim the glory of God, but now lies silent, subject to servitude under the curse. Nature finds its redemption in Christ, the new creation who is its center. In the sacraments the elements of the old creation "are set free from their dumbness and proclaim directly to the believer the new creative Word of God."[123] Although brief and largely undeveloped, Bonhoeffer's sketch of Christ as the center of nature is suggestive with regards to pointing a way forward for developing a christologically grounded eco-theology.[124] Bonhoeffer himself would only begin to explore the fuller implications of Christ as the mediator between God and nature in his *Ethics* manuscripts.[125]

The categories of human existence, history, and nature are actually abstractions as "human existence is also and always history, always and also nature."[126] These abstractions, however, are helpful in indicating that "the mediator as fulfiller of the law and liberator of creation is all this for the whole of human existence."[127] This understanding of Christ as the comprehensive center of all things is reflected in the later christological developments of *Ethics* where Bonhoeffer speaks of Jesus as "the Real One" who is "the origin, essence, and goal of all reality."[128] Its influence is also apparent in *Letters and Papers from Prison* where Bonhoeffer seeks to understand Christ at the center of life and not simply at the boundaries where human understanding fails.[129]

---

together the themes of transcendence, the center, reading the Old Testament, and religionless Christianity: "God is beyond in the midst of our lives. The church stands not at the point where human powers fail, at the boundaries, but in the center of the village. That's the way it is in the Old Testament, and in this sense we don't read the New Testament nearly enough in light of the Old. I am thinking a great deal about what this religionless Christianity looks like, what form it takes, and I'll be writing you more about it soon" (*LPP* (*DBWE* 8), 367).

123. *CC*, 65.

124. Rasmussen has drawn upon Bonhoeffer's writings as a resource for developing an "earth faith" and "earth ethic." See *Earth Community, Earth Ethics*, 295–316. Rasmussen also returns to Bonhoeffer in his recent work *Earth-Honoring Faith*, 305–31.

125. In particular, see "Natural Life" in *E* (*DBWE* 6), 171–218.

126. *CC*, 65.

127. Ibid., 65.

128. *E* (*DBWE* 6), 263.

129. *LPP* (*DBWE* 8), 367, 406–7.

The Historical Christ

Bonhoeffer begins the second part of his lecture series, "The Historical Christ," with the affirmation that, "The present Christ of whom we have spoken so far is the historical Christ."[130] There can be no question of separating a "Jesus of history" from a "Christ of faith." Attempts to secure an approach to the absolute through historical research are ultimately futile and serve as a poor substitute for a personal encounter with the Risen One. It is the "Jesus of history" who bears witness to himself by the miracle of his presence in the church, rendering attempts at historical confirmation irrelevant. This is not license for empty emotionalism or vacuous sentimentality in the life of the church, "because the witness of Jesus Christ to himself is none other than that which the Scriptures deliver to us and which comes to us by no other way than by the Word of Scriptures."[131] These Scriptures must be read with all of the human resources available to us without lazily settling into a doctrine of verbal inspiration, which itself is a "poor surrogate for the resurrection."[132]

Critical or negative Christology serves, according to Bonhoeffer, to safeguard the mystery of the incarnation. Christological heresies are the result of attempts to get behind the fact of the incarnation through the attempt to answer the question, How? In the process, the full humanity and/or the full divinity of Christ are inevitably diminished. The high-point of critical Christology is found in the Chalcedonian Definition, which effectively rules the How? question out of bounds and directs attention to the question of identity. In contrast to the heretical alternatives which had approached Christology though objectified notions of humanity and deity:

> The Chalcedonian Definition had also given an answer to the question, "How?"; but in its answer, the question, "How?," was already superseded. It had, in fact, superseded the doctrine of the two natures by its firm adherence to the negative in contradictory opposites. In reality, it says that the matter of Jesus Christ is not to be settled with the concept of "natures," neither is it possible to bring a demonstrable unity that way. This critical sense of the Chalcedonian Definition can take us further. This can only happen when the idea of deity and humanity as something which can be discovered is superseded, and discussion no longer starts from isolated natures. The starting point is given: the man Jesus *is* the Christ, *is* God. This "*is*" may no longer be

---

130. *CC*, 69.
131. Ibid., 73.
132. *DBWE* 12:331.

derived. It is the presupposition of all the thinking and must not be constructed as a conclusion. Since Chalcedon, it is no longer possible to ask how the natures can be thought of as different while the person remains one, but quite clearly *who* is this man, of whom it is declared, "He is God"?[133]

As a result, any theology which strays from the concrete figure of the God-human who is testified to in the Scriptures into abstract speculation concerning the natures, whether that be an abstract separation of the natures as in the case of the Reformed doctrine of the *logos asarkos* or an abstract unity as in the case of the Lutheran *genus majestaticum*, is guilty of trespassing upon territory that Chalcedon has already ruled out of bounds.[134]

Of particular interest in this section on critical Christology is Bonhoeffer's discussion of docetism. Docetism, on Bonhoeffer's reading, is rooted in the Hellenistic antithesis between idea and appearance, alongside a way of thinking about redemption which understands human beings as standing in need of redemption from "their captivity to individuality."[135] Thus a docetic way of thinking presupposes that "the appearance is that which is incidental, and the idea is the substance. Jesus as a human being is incidental, as opposed to the substance that is God."[136] As a result, liberal theology which has attempted to understand Jesus as the carrier or embodiment of certain preconceived values or religious ideals, must be understood as docetic:

> Liberal theology only wanted to see, in Jesus, the embodiment of a certain doctrine. Thus the humanity of Jesus is basically not taken seriously, even though liberal theology has so much to say about Jesus as a human being. The idea of Jesus' humanity bypasses here the reality of Jesus as a human being, confuses the ideal of his humanity with its reality, in short, makes his humanity into a symbol.[137]

We have previously observed how Bonhoeffer fought to preserve the integral connection between Jesus and the people of Israel. In this section

---

133. *CC*, 98.

134. *DBWE* 12:345–46. The *genus majestaticum* speaks of the communication of divine properties to the humanity of Christ by virtue of the hypostatic union. On the other hand, the Reformed tradition in its desire to avoid the confusion of the natures has allowed a place for speaking of the *logos asarkos*—the continuing existence of the second person of the Trinity apart from the flesh of Jesus.

135. *DBWE* 12:333.

136. Ibid., 335.

137. Ibid., 337.

it is important to note how Bonhoeffer combats the prevailing docetism of his time through a subtle terminological shift. It was customary in the German theological tradition to employ the word *Inkarnation* and the accompanying term *Fleischgewordene* (literally, 'becoming flesh') to speak of the incarnation.[138] Bonhoeffer, however, consistently utilizes the term *Menschgewordene* (literally, 'becoming human') to emphasize God's complete identification with humanity and, I would suggest, the particular human life lived by the God-man Jesus Christ.[139]

Only after critical Christology has done its work in ruling the question How? out of bounds and directing our attention to the concrete person of the God-human, who is present in his indissoluble unity, is one in a position to begin to formulate a positive Christology. As a result, positive Christology focuses its attention upon the figure of Jesus Christ, affirming that "Jesus the human being is God, and that he is so as the human being, not in spite of his humanity or beyond his humanity."[140] In attending to the figure of Jesus Christ as his identity is rendered in the Scriptures, it becomes apparent that at the heart of positive Christology lies the consideration of the humiliation and exaltation of the Incarnate One.

Although impossible to distinguish from a temporal perspective, the doctrines of the incarnation and the humiliation must be carefully distinguished at the conceptual level. Bonhoeffer insists, "To be humiliated does not mean to be *more* human and *less* God, and to be exalted does not mean to be *more* God and *less* human. Both in being humiliated and in being exalted Jesus remains wholly human and wholly God."[141] The humiliation is found in Christ's taking on of sinful flesh, which results in the veiling of the God-man. As a result, Jesus Christ "goes incognito, as a beggar among beggars, as an outcast among outcasts, as despairing among the despairing, as dying among the dying."[142] The presence of the God-man hidden in "the likeness of sinful flesh" is the "stumbling block" which is "the central problem of Christology."[143] "The doctrine that Jesus was without sin is not

---

138. Ibid., 334 n. 94; Rasmussen, editor's introduction to *DBWE* 12:45.

139. In his discussion of docetism, Bonhoeffer raises a curious objection to the doctrine of the *enhypostasis*. Bonhoeffer suggests that the *enhypostasis* poses a threat to the full humanity of Jesus, for in affirming that the Word assumed human nature it seems to deny the particularity of Jesus's human existence. In the doctrine of the *enhypostasis*, Bonhoeffer sees a re-inscription of the docetic presupposition of the opposition of idea and appearance. *DBWE* 12:335–36.

140. Ibid., 354.

141. Ibid., 355.

142. *CC*, 107.

143. Ibid., 46.

just one word [logos], one doctrine [among others]," Bonhoeffer asserts, "but rather the central point that decides everything."[144] Jesus Christ truly bears our sinful flesh, but because he is *the One* who bears it, he bears it without sin. Reflecting the influence of Luther, Bonhoeffer states that Jesus is at one and the same time the "*peccator pessimus*" and "the Holy One, the Eternal, the Lord, the Son of the Father" and because of this we are saved.[145] Bonhoeffer elaborates upon the soteriological significance of the Son's assumption of sinful flesh in the final chapter of *Discipleship*, where he argues that "God must conform to the human image, since we are no longer able to conform to the image of God."[146] The connection between the humiliation of the God-man and its soteriological significance is further taken up in the *theologia crucis* of the prison letters, perhaps most clearly in Bonhoeffer's famous words of reflection: "God consents to be pushed out of the world and onto the cross; God is weak and powerless in the world and in precisely this way, only so, is at our side and helps us."[147]

Since the actions of Jesus take place in the likeness of sinful flesh, they are shrouded in historical ambiguity. The sinlessness of Jesus cannot be read off the pages of history, but can only be confessed in faith. It is Christ's presence in the form of the humiliated one, which is the form of Christ *pro nobis*; for, "if Christ had proved himself by miracles, we would have believed the visible *theophany* of deity, but that would not have been faith in Christ *pro me*. It would not have been inner conversion, but simply acknowledgement."[148] It is only through the resurrection and exaltation that we come to know that it is the God-man who is hidden in this incognito. However, even in the resurrection, Christ does not discard his incognito, as the resurrection itself does not escape the realm of historical ambiguity. The incognito has only been lifted for those who have received the news in faith. Those who respond in faith will find that "the Church must go its own way of humiliation" with the humiliated one.[149] There can be no question of the church seeking visible confirmation of its way, either boasting in its success or finding self-satisfaction in its humiliation, rather it must confess its

---

144. *DBWE* 12:356.

145. Ibid., 357. Krötke highlights the inseparability of the *peccator pessimus* from Luther's understanding of Christ as our vicarious representative in bearing our sin. The presence of both themes, and the prominence of the latter, in Bonhoeffer's work point to the profound influence of Luther upon his Christology. "Bonhoeffer and Luther," 60–64.

146. *D* (*DBWE* 4), 282.

147. *LPP* (*DBWE* 8), 479.

148. *CC*, 110.

149. Ibid., 113.

sins, allow itself to be forgiven, and continually look to its Lord, the hidden center of all things.

Eternal Christ

After devoting time to the consideration of the Present Christ and the Historical Christ, Bonhoeffer intended to complete his course of lectures on Christology with a final section devoted to exploration of the theme of the Eternal Christ. Unfortunately, much like the riveting seminal thoughts from prison which Bonhoeffer was never able to fully develop, the Christology lectures remain tantalizingly unfinished.[150] Since no manuscript evidence exists for this section, it is uncertain as to whether Bonhoeffer himself ever got around to writing it.[151] Although it is tempting to speculate what conclusions Bonhoeffer might have come to in this final section, by this point it should be apparent that the lectures that were presented and the notes that have been preserved are a valuable treasure which provide us with crucial insight into the center of Bonhoeffer's thought.

PART 2: THE CHRISTOLOGY OF STANLEY HAUERWAS

Early Influences

Christology is not the first thing that comes to mind for most people when they hear the name Stanley Hauerwas.[152] Hauerwas himself has even admitted that he is "not even sure what a 'full-blown Christology' would look like,"[153] nor does he believe "in anyone having a well worked-out Christology."[154] These statements, however, must not be read as a repudiation of the centrality of Jesus Christ to his theological project, but rather as a rejection of speculative approaches to Christology which attempt to explain the mystery of the incarnation. They are also a reflection of Hauerwas's en-

---

150. Student records indicate that Bonhoeffer ran out of time in his course and never delivered his lectures on the Eternal Christ.

151. Robertson, translator's preface to *CC*, 15.

152. Although that perception may now be changing. E.g., Hays remarked on the occasion of Hauerwas's retirement that "the deepest theme of Stanley's work, the consistent thread running through all his thought, is his emphasis on the centrality of Jesus Christ" (foreword to *Difference Christ Makes*, 5). See also Wells's essay in the same volume, "Difference Christ Makes."

153. *Mt*, 20.

154. *HC*, 59.

during conviction that the work of theology remains perpetually unfinished due to its very subject matter—the God of Israel who has revealed himself in Jesus Christ—and its character as a communal enterprise. Hauerwas's christological reflection operates within the realm of what Bonhoeffer referred to as "positive Christology"—that is, reflection upon the identity of Jesus Christ as rendered in the Scriptures governed by the conviction that "this man is God."

It appears that Hauerwas's central christological convictions began to take shape during his time as a seminary student at Yale Divinity School. Not only was Yale the site of Hauerwas's introduction to the thought of Karl Barth, it was also at Yale that Hauerwas, as a result of participating in Hans Frei's course on Christology, came to an appreciation of the liberal lives of Jesus.[155] Reflecting upon this stage in his own theological development, Hauerwas writes, "I saw that the liberal emphases on the life of Jesus could be interpreted as the rightful refusal to let go of the life of Jesus. Both more 'orthodox' Christologies and the Protestant emphasis on justification seemed to give in to the temptation to leave Jesus behind."[156]

It was Hauerwas's immersion in the theology of Karl Barth and his reflections upon the importance of attending to the life of Jesus which paved the way for his encounter with the work of John Howard Yoder. In the summer of 1970, Hauerwas received from Yoder a mimeograph of a book that would be published two years later under the title *The Politics of Jesus*.[157] In *The Politics of Jesus* and in Yoder's work more generally, Hauerwas discovered a "high Christology" which took the life and teachings of Jesus seriously.[158] In fact, it is because Jesus Christ is fully God and fully human that his life and teachings cannot be ignored. Yoder cuts to the heart of the issue with a series of incisive rhetorical questions: "What becomes of the meaning of the incarnation if Jesus is not normatively human? If he is human but not normative, is this not the ancient ebionitic heresy? If he be somehow authoritative but not in his humanness, is this not a new gnosticism?"[159] In this way, Yoder's recovery of the social and political significance of Jesus Christ by attending to his life and ministry proves to be "more radically Nicene and Chalcedonian than other views."[160] The politics of Jesus, for Yo-

---

155. *HC*, 62. Interestingly, this was the only course that Hauerwas took with either Frei or George Lindbeck.

156. Ibid., 62.

157. Ibid., 117.

158. *DT*, 238.

159. Yoder, *Politics of Jesus*, 10.

160. Ibid., 102.

der, is the politics of the cross. The cross is the culmination of Jesus's refusal to entertain the options of either quietist withdrawal or armed insurrection in the face of the powers dominating the Jewish people.[161] The cross is the definitive embodiment of God's refusal to redeem coercively. From Yoder, Hauerwas came to understand not only that "the politics of Jesus was a public affair with cosmic consequences,"[162] but that nonviolence is indissolubly linked with Christology. Furthermore, *The Politics of Jesus* reinforced for Hauerwas the fact that "Christology cannot be abstracted from accounts of discipleship," a realization he first came to while reading Bonhoeffer's *Discipleship* in seminary.[163]

It is the combination of these influences and fundamental christological convictions that contribute to the development of Hauerwas's unique theological voice and give his writings their distinctive character. This conclusion is affirmed by Hauerwas's own reflections upon his writing career and the reception of his work:

> What many people find hard to understand, or at least what strikes them as unusual, is how I combine what I hope is a profound commitment to fundamental Christian convictions with a socially radical ethic. At bottom, the convictions involve the claim that Jesus is both fully God and fully human. If he is not fully both, then we Christians are clearly idolaters. A socially radical ethic follows from this theological conviction because our worship of Jesus is itself a politics through which a world is created that would not exist if Jesus were not raised from the dead. Basic to such politics is the refusal of a violence that many assume is a "given" for any responsible account of the world.[164]

In what follows I will trace the development of Hauerwas's christological thought: showing how many of his core christological convictions were already evident in one of his earliest essays, investigating how these christological convictions were incorporated into and amplified within the context of his developing theological project particularly in conjunction with his "narrative turn," and finally examining the explicit christological character of two of his more recent works.

---

161. Ibid., 36
162. *HC*, 160.
163. *PTF*, 35.
164. *HC*, 136.

"The Humanity of the Divine"

In 1972 a brief essay, which could perhaps be best described as a theological meditation, appeared in *The Cresset*, a publication of Valparaiso University Press, under the title "The Humanity of the Divine."[165] Many of Hauerwas's core christological commitments are already on display in this early essay. Hauerwas prefaces his reflections with an affirmation possessing a distinctly creedal character:

> *Christ*, the *Lord* of creation,
> *Reconciler* of the world to the Father,
> *Redeemer* of sinful humanity,
> *Victor* over death through his crucifixion and resurrection,
> *Foretaste* and *Herald* of the Kingdom of God,
> *Incarnation* of God, very God and very man.[166]

One could hardly ask for a higher Christology than that expressed in this short stanza. Unlike much of modern preaching, which Hauerwas understands to be hopelessly preoccupied with the self, Hauerwas, in a prototypically Barthian move, unabashedly begins with the person of Jesus Christ. "In the light of God's action in Christ," Hauerwas insists, "this preoccupation with self is insignificant; in theological terms, it is but an attempt to have the atonement without the incarnation and crucifixion."[167]

Turning from our preoccupation with our own subjectivities to the reality of Christ, however, is not without its difficulties. For the very phrase "very God and very man" is enough to trigger within us "metaphysical flights of fancy" which attempt to imagine how God-substance and human-substance are held together or to cause us to embark upon bouts of "psychological speculation" which aspire to attribute different faculties and functions of Jesus to either his humanity or divinity.[168] At this point Hauerwas draws upon Kierkegaard's fairy tale of the young prince in order to illustrate a further popular misconception surrounding the incarnation.[169] In Kierkegaard's tale, the prince, who has fallen in love with a lovely maiden, disguises himself in order to win the hand of his beloved on the basis of his own personal merits and not his wealth and social status. The lure of the

---

165. Hauerwas, "Humanity of the Divine."
166. Ibid., para. 1.
167. Ibid., para. 7.
168. Ibid., para. 8.
169. Although Kierkegaard references are relatively rare in the Hauerwas corpus, one must not underestimate the influence of the great Danish philosopher and theologian, who in Hauerwas own terms continues to "haunt" him. *HC*, 53.

story is not whether the prince will get the maiden, for we know that he will, but rather it is found in wondering when the prince will reveal his identity to the maiden by ripping through his peasant's disguise to reveal the royal purple. In this regard, the difficulty with the Gospel is that "at no time does Jesus ever rip back the veil of flesh and reveal the purple of deity."[170] The one who is the long-awaited Messiah, the fulfillment of Israel's hopes, suffers the ignominy of being mocked, beaten, and hung upon the cross.

This is a scandal to us because we approach Jesus with the preconception that he "is a man who is doing divine things."[171] Against this Hauerwas affirms, "The gospel's good news and mystery of the incarnation is not that this is the human doing the divine, but that the very action of Jesus is divine action; it is what God does about the salvation of the world."[172] The true mystery of the incarnation then is not how God-substance and human-substance coexist in one person, but rather how God has freely bound himself to humanity, undergoing suffering and even death, "so that man can be capable of being in love with God."[173] Hauerwas presents a more nuanced understanding of the work of Christ in the writings which we will subsequently examine. At this point, however, it is important to note the presence of the influence of Aquinas and his interpretation of charity as friendship with God.[174] Becoming a friend of God involves learning to walk in the way of the man of sorrows, which leads to the cross. In this way Christology and discipleship are interwoven, for "the ambiguity of the figure of Jesus is the necessary christological requirement to draw us into the very commitment that is necessary in order to recognize that this was surely the Christ."[175] It turns out then, that the real difficulty with the doctrine of the incarnation in modernity is not intellectual, but rather it is a moral-ethical problem rooted in our refusal to be drawn out of ourselves and into the life of the crucified Christ.

"Jesus: The Story of the Kingdom"

We turn now to two important essays from the early 1980s which demonstrate the centrality of the person of Jesus Christ to Hauerwas's unfolding project and also the reciprocal influence of his developing approach to

---

170. Hauerwas, "Humanity of the Divine," para. 12.
171. Ibid., para.16.
172. Ibid., para. 17.
173. Ibid., para. 19.
174. See especially Aquinas, *Summa Theologica* 2.2.23.
175. Hauerwas, "Humanity of the Divine," 20.

Christian ethics upon his christological thought.[176] The first of the essays, "Jesus: The Story of the Kingdom," is motivated by the observation that although Jesus is confessed as central to the Christian faith, Christians in modernity have frequently left Jesus behind when engaging with questions pertaining to social ethics.[177] The fact that nothing strikes us as unusual about the question, What is the relation between Christology and social ethics? is in itself revealing. In the face of these developments, Hauerwas forwards the radical counter-proposal that "a christology which is not a social ethic is deficient."[178] Christologies that are unconcerned with "the social form of Jesus' work or the sociological situation of the church" fail to understand the kind of Messiah Jesus is.[179] Jesus's work as Messiah necessarily implies the existence of a Messianic people, which means that Christology must "direct our attention to how we are required to make the story of Jesus' life our own."[180] So-called "orthodox" theologies built upon the christological dogma of Chalcedon can give the impression that "one can know who Jesus is or 'what' he was in terms of essences, substances, and natures, without the necessity of in some way knowing Jesus himself—without, that is, being his disciple."[181] Furthermore, Chalcedon's exclusive concern with the inner constitution of Jesus Christ, in the words of Walter Kasper cited approvingly by Hauerwas, obscures "the total eschatological perspective of biblical theology."[182] Without corresponding attention to the specifics of Jesus's life, the christological affirmations of the creeds run the risk of promoting the very docetic impulse which they sought to defend against.[183]

Much like Bonhoeffer, Hauerwas is interested in avoiding the dangers associated with separating Christology from soteriology and subordinating Christology to soteriology. When soteriological concerns take precedence over Christology, Jesus becomes the answer or solution to the universal human predicament—a predicament which is understood apart from

---

176. Wells suggests that the two books within which these essays are found—*A Community of Character* and *The Peaceable Kingdom*—along with *With the Grain of the Universe*, are "the Christological center of Stanley's work and hence his most abiding achievement" ("Difference Christ Makes," 16).

177. *ComC*, 36–37.

178. Ibid., 37.

179. Ibid., 233 n. 4.

180. Ibid., 37.

181. Ibid., 41.

182. Kasper, *Jesus the Christ*, 238, quoted in *ComC*, 41.

183. *ComC*, 40. Hauerwas has no interest in rejecting the classical christological formulas. Rather he is warning of the dangers of abstracting the Creed from the life of the community gathered around the Scriptures.

Jesus himself, expressed in the metaphysical terms of neo-orthodoxy or the moralities of liberal Protestantism. However, Jesus is not a universally significant figure because he is the embodiment of a universal principle or ethic. Rather, Jesus is universally significant because, through the witness of the community that lives according to his particular story, all are invited to become his disciples. Hauerwas is insistent that "Jesus' person cannot be separated from his work, the incarnation from the atonement."[184] Showing his indebtedness to his teacher, Hans Frei, Hauerwas asserts that "there is no moral point or message that is separate from the story of Jesus as we find it in the Gospels."[185] Jesus is not the embodiment of a saviour figure, rather the Saviour is Jesus and therefore "Jesus' identity is prior to the 'meaning' of the story."[186] In other words, if one wants to know what salvation is all about, one must look to the story of Jesus. As Hauerwas argues, "the narrative character of the Gospels is integral to the affirmation of Jesus' redemptive significance."[187]

Jesus's story, according to Hauerwas, is most simply, "the story of a man who had the authority to preach that the Kingdom of God is present."[188] The concept of the Kingdom of God has been particularly attractive to Christian ethicists on account of the fact that a kingdom is by necessity a social and political reality of some sort. Hauerwas avoids the pitfalls of liberal theology, which has tended to equate the Kingdom with abstract ideals,[189] through his retrieval of Origen's understanding of Jesus as the *autobasileia*, the personal presence of the Kingdom.[190] If Jesus is Himself the personal presence of the Kingdom, then it follows that "there is no way to know the Kingdom except by learning of the story of this man Jesus."[191] The story of Jesus calls into question all of our preconceptions about the political, for, as Hauerwas puts it, "to know the Kingdom through the story of Jesus requires us to believe that the polity into which we are called can only be based on that power that

---

184. Ibid., 43.

185. Ibid., 42; cf. Frei, *Identity of Jesus Christ*, 101–22.

186. ComC, 43.

187. Ibid., 44.

188. Ibid., 37.

189. The paradigmatic example of this development for Hauerwas is found in the work of the great proponent of the Social Gospel, Walter Rauschenbusch, who transformed "the theocratic image of the Kingdom of God into the democratic ideal of the brotherhood of man" (AN, 111).

190. The influence of Karl Barth is also evident at this point, as Hauerwas's reference to Origen is preceded by the quotation, "Jesus is Himself the established Kingdom of God" (CD 2/2:177, quoted in ComC, 45).

191. ComC, 45.

comes from trusting in the truth."[192] Such a polity is an aberration amongst the kingdoms of this world built upon domination and fueled by fear. That is why the truth of the Kingdom, which is the story of Jesus, can only be discovered by those whose lives are transformed in the process of following Him. Discipleship, for Hauerwas, is an epistemological prerequisite for truly knowing Christ.

Christian discipleship creates a cruciform polity. The summons to discipleship calls into existence a people who live by the truth of Jesus amidst a world ruled by the very powers that sent him to the cross. It is at the cross where the social character of Jesus's mission is on clearest display, for the arrival of the Kingdom is nothing less than the eschatological irruption of a new world made possible through the person and work of Christ.[193] Unlike the passing world, this new world is not ruled by the threat of death, but rather by the Lord who rules by the paradoxical powerlessness which is the power of truth. In trusting in the power of truth which is Jesus, disciples are liberated from the necessity to secure their own future as they learn to be forgiven and to receive their lives as gifts. As the church—"the organized form of Jesus' story"[194]—learns to name and resist the competing powers which seek to claim our lives, it will necessarily appear as a type of "contrast model" to the surrounding world. It is at this point that Hauerwas introduces a formulation that will later, in a refined form, become one of his signature turns of phrase: "the church first serves the world by helping the world to know what it means to be the world."[195] This service of the world can only occur as the church allows itself to be formed by the story of Jesus. The Gospels play a central role in this formation, for they are "the constitutions of this new polity" called the church, the training manuals of the new community which seeks to make the story of Jesus its own.[196] The call to make the story of Jesus one's own is incumbent upon all Christians, for Hauerwas insists that "we, no less than the first Christians, are the continuation of the truth made possible by God's rule."[197]

192. Ibid., 46.

193. Ibid., 48–49. Wells observes, "The uniqueness of Jesus lies fundamentally in his acceptance of the cross as the way of disarming the powers that oppress us, and in the vindication of his nonviolent witness in the resurrection. Christ is at the centre of Hauerwas' theology, in so far as Christ inaugurates and makes possible the peaceable kingdom—the nonviolent witness of the Christian community" (*Transforming Fate*, 128).

194. *ComC*, 50.

195. Ibid., 50.

196. Ibid., 49. Hauerwas asserts that the fact that there are four Gospels reminds the Church that "Jesus' story is a many-sided tale," which means that there are various ways in which disciples may learn to make the story of Jesus their own (52).

197. Ibid., 52.

The significance of this landmark essay, "Jesus: The Story of the Kingdom," to Hauerwas's developing project and to the field of Christian ethics as a whole must not be underestimated. In it, Hauerwas found a way to integrate the christological impulse he inherited from Barth and Yoder into the center of his ethical thought amongst the constellations of character, virtue, narrative, and community by speaking of Jesus as the story which forms the church. In doing so, he made an important contribution to recovering the theological character of Christian ethics. There are also many specific christological insights within the essay that are to be commended, including: the refusal to separate the person and work of Christ, the emphasis upon the particularity of Jesus and the importance of his whole life, and the organic connection between Christology and discipleship. The essay does, however, open the door to at least one line of christological questioning. The question revolves around to what degree narrative or story is an adequate conceptual tool to speak of the person of Jesus Christ and his relationship to the church. Although to speak of Jesus as story makes great sense within Hauerwas's developing project, the repeated referrals to Jesus as story ring strangely in the ears of those attuned to the historic affirmations of the Christian tradition, which has preferred to speak of Christ as person.[198] Now admittedly, we come to know a person only as we come to know their story and by drawing upon the category of story Hauerwas is able to combat docetic Christologies which fail to attend to the life of the first-century Jewish rabbi Jesus of Nazareth.[199] However, in repeatedly referring to Jesus as story, it does appear that Hauerwas runs the risk of instrumentalizing Jesus. This raises an important question: does Hauerwas in this essay, against his own stated intentions, inadvertently separate the person and work of Christ, so that the work of Christ is understood as providing a truthful story according to which we may live our lives? Toward the end of the essay, Hauerwas approvingly cites Nils Dahl who maintains that "there is a close relationship between the church and Jesus, but within this relationship Jesus retains priority and sovereignty."[200] However, it is not at all clear, at this point, how Jesus retains this priority and sovereignty over the church. Does Jesus retain his priority and sovereignty in the sense that his story is the governing story which the church must continually test its life and practices against? If this is

198. E.g., "I cannot hope to provide the scriptural basis to defend the view that Jesus is best understood as the story that authorizes the preaching of the Kingdom" (ibid., 46–47).

199. One of the key insights of the Protestant Reformer Martin Luther was his retrieval of the narrative shape of the Gospel. See Luther, *Basic Theological Writings*, 104–11.

200. Dahl, *Jesus in the Memory*, 171, quoted in *ComC*, 51.

the case, in what sense can it be said that Jesus continues to be present in the ongoing life of his church?[201] Is Jesus present to the church simply through the continuing influence of his story, and if so, is this not a rather underwhelming reading of Christ's promise to be with his church until the end of the age?[202] Hauerwas's next foray into the realm of explicit christological reflection, "Jesus: The Presence of the Peaceable Kingdom," both expands upon the fruitful insights of "Jesus: The Story of the Kingdom" and begins to address some of these deficiencies.

"Jesus: The Presence of the Peaceable Kingdom"

"Everything I have done in this book has been preparation for this chapter."[203] So reads the first sentence of the chapter entitled "Jesus: The Presence of the Peaceable Kingdom" found within Hauerwas's self-described "primer in Christian ethics," *The Peaceable Kingdom*. Since *The Peaceable Kingdom* is perhaps the closest thing to an attempt to "pull it all together" that Hauerwas has published, his opening admission should alert us to the central significance of this essay not only to *The Peaceable Kingdom*, but to his corpus as a whole.[204]

The reader who turns to "Jesus: The Presence of the Peaceable Kingdom" having already encountered "Jesus: The Story of the Kingdom" will find much that is familiar. The discussion of the ethical significance of Jesus, the eschatological character of Jesus's ministry in proclaiming and inaugurating the Kingdom, the emphasis upon discipleship and the close connection between Christ and His church all echo themes touched upon in the previous essay. The careful reader, however, will also find much that is new. The shift in terminology between the two titles, "Jesus: The Story of the Kingdom" and "Jesus: The Presence of the Peaceable Kingdom," is revealing in this regard. Although the importance of the story of Jesus is still

201. This concern is also raised by Fergusson, "Another Way of Reading," 245–46.
202. Matt 28:20.
203. *PK*, 72.
204. In the introduction to *The Peaceable Kingdom* Hauerwas acknowledges the pressure he has been under to "pull it all together" in one book, but denies that he has done that for "theology's inherently practical character, its unmistakable status as a pastoral discipline, simply defies strong systematization." That being said, Hauerwas does acknowledge that in this book "I try to make more explicit than I have in the past the conceptual foundation underlying the suggestions I have made about how theology, and in particular Christian ethics, should be done" (ibid., xvi). Cartwright and Thomson have both drawn attention to the centrality and significance of *The Peaceable Kingdom* within Hauerwas's corpus. Cartwright, afterword to *HR*, 627; Thomson, *Ecclesiology of Stanley Hauerwas*, 3.

stressed, Jesus is no longer spoken of as a story. Rather, Jesus is "the presence of the peaceable kingdom." This phrase links together two of the major developments which distinguish this essay from its predecessor; namely, a concentrated emphasis upon non-violence and a more developed treatment of the resurrection. The final significant innovation of the essay is Hauerwas's setting of the Jesus's story within the context of the story of Israel's life with God. In the section that follows, we will explore the new developments represented in "Jesus: The Presence of the Peaceable Kingdom."

The Kingdom of God continues to occupy a central place in Hauerwas's exposition of the person and work of Christ. However, it is the concentrated emphasis upon the peaceable character of this Kingdom which distinguishes Hauerwas's treatment of this theme from the previous essay. The arrival of Jesus on the scene and his proclamation of the Kingdom is an eschatological irruption of God's reign of peace, bringing an end to any notions that the way things are in the world is the way they have to be. Jesus's welcoming of the stranger, his proclaiming of the radical ethic of the Kingdom in the Sermon on the Mount, his casting out of demons, his meals with outsiders, and his calling of the disciples to leave everything behind, all point to the presence of the new age. As in the previous essay, Hauerwas once again insists that the cross is the kingdom come. The cross is the demonstration of Jesus's unwillingness to ensure the success of his ministry through violently seizing the levers of power, which is but the flip side of his trust in God. In going to his death, Jesus entrusts the future to God and out of obedience wholly abandons Himself into the hands of His Father. The cross then becomes the site of "Jesus' ultimate dispossession through which God has conquered the powers of this world."[205] Jesus's death is not a mistake, but rather what is to be expected when the violence of the world is confronted and unmasked by the peace of God. The cross is the shape of God's way with the world.[206] It is the very love of God that is displayed at the cross; "a love that would overcome the powers of this world not through coercion and force but through the power of this one man's death."[207]

---

205. *PK*, 87.

206. Stout maintains that Hauerwas's theology lacks "a persuasive account of the full range of biblical passages that have a bearing on his pacifist interpretation of scripture" ("Spirit of Democracy," 13). While there is something to this criticism, in that Hauerwas has not put forward a biblical theology of peace and violence that systematically considers the scriptural witness, it fails to recognize the christological concentration of Hauerwas's thought and the centrality of the cross to Hauerwas's reading and telling of the story of God.

207. *PK*, 76.

Of course, none of this would be known, were it not for the resurrection. The resurrection vindicates Jesus's life and ministry as the personal presence of the Kingdom and testifies to the character of the God who raised him from the dead. The resurrection is "God's decisive eschatological act" which stands as "the absolute center of history."[208] It is because the resurrection testifies to the present reality of God's peace made possible through the forgiveness of sins that we can remember our sin without it destroying us—that is, because of the resurrection we can claim our stories as our own.[209] Hauerwas elaborates upon the significance of the resurrection:

> Only if our Lord is a risen Lord, therefore, can we have the confidence and the power to be a community of forgiveness. For on the basis of the resurrection we have the presumption to believe that God has made us agents in the history of the kingdom. The resurrection is not a symbol or myth through which we can interpret our individual and collective dyings and risings. Rather the resurrection of Jesus is the ultimate sign that our salvation comes only when we cease trying to interpret Jesus' story in the light of our history, and instead we interpret ourselves in the light of his. For this is no dead Lord we follow but the living God, who having dwelt among us as an individual, is now eternally present to us making possible our living as forgiven agents of God's new creation.[210]

There is much that is noteworthy in this paragraph including the connection drawn between the resurrection and the community of forgiveness, the affirmation that the kingdom has a history, the emphasis upon the irreducible particularity of Jesus and the corresponding rejection of correlational approaches to theology, but what is perhaps most significant is that by the end of the paragraph Hauerwas has shifted from speaking about the significance of the resurrection for us to affirming that the resurrection is significant for Jesus. The resurrection not only confirms that the story of Jesus is a truthful story that is worth making our own, it furthermore means that Jesus is alive and personally present and active in the life of his people. Although one might wish that Hauerwas had said more at this point about how Christ is personally present and active in the midst of the congregation, it is important that he has at the very least made this affirmation, for it indicates that the continuing influence of Christ upon his community extends beyond that of simply being a moral exemplar.

208. Ibid., 88, 90.
209. Ibid., 89.
210. Ibid., 90.

That being said, it can hardly be denied that there is a distinct emphasis upon *imitatio Christi* in "Jesus: The Presence of the Peaceable Kingdom." Hauerwas draws upon the story of Israel to fill in his conception of *imitatio Christi* and to demonstrate that in learning to imitate Jesus, disciples are learning to imitate God. In emphasizing the unintelligibility of the Gospels apart from the story of God's dealings with Israel, Hauerwas is simply affirming what the Church has in theory affirmed since its early conflict with Marcion, but what it has in practice all too often neglected. Reflecting back upon his work, some thirty years after the publication of his first collection of essays, Hauerwas acknowledges that one of his major concerns has been the "re-Judaization of Christianity," which involves showing "that Christianity is unintelligible without the Jews."[211] In "Jesus: The Presence of the Peaceable Kingdom," Hauerwas seeks to recover the connection between the story of Jesus and the story of the people of Israel. Israel's experience with God had trained the Jews to see the world eschatologically, that is "in terms of a story, with a beginning, a continuing drama, and an end."[212] Without Israel's identification of the God who had created all things, elected them as a people, and promised to bring all things to their fitting conclusion, the story of Jesus is ripe for idealistic distortion. The docetic tendencies of modernity which seek to make the Christian faith into a matter of rational assent to a set of propositions, on the one hand, or private inner illumination, on the other, are confounded by the fleshly reality of the Jews. For Israel, the life of faith takes the form of the concrete history of their journey with the Lord. Hauerwas goes on to assert that "the task for Israel, indeed the very thing that makes Israel Israel, is to walk in the way of the Lord, that is, to imitate God through the means of the prophet (Torah), the king (Sonship), and the priest (Knowledge)."[213] The holders of the offices of prophet, priest and king were commissioned to embody "in their lives and work the vocation of Israel to 'walk' in the 'way' of the Lord" and in doing so to provide visible exemplars for the people to imitate.[214] At points within Israel's story and self-understanding the three offices coalesce in one figure, as in Moses or the figure of the Servant in Isaiah. This is significant for christological reflection, as Hauerwas explains:

> It is against this background that the early Christians came to understand and believe in Jesus' life, death, and resurrection. They had found a continuation of Israel's vocation to imitate

---

211. *DT*, 191.
212. *PK*, 82.
213. Ibid., 77. Hauerwas at this point is drawing upon Tinsley, *Imitation of God*, 35.
214. *PK*, 78.

God and thus in a decisive way to depict God's kingdom for the world. Jesus' life was seen as the recapitulation of the life of Israel and thus presented the very life of God in the world. By learning to imitate Jesus, to follow in his way, the early Christians believed they were learning to imitate God, who would have them be heirs of the kingdom.[215]

Hauerwas's appropriation of the doctrine of recapitulation within the context of Israel's vocation to imitate God allows him to move beyond individualistic understandings of *imitatio Christi*, towards an ecclesially-centered vision of the imitation of Christ. In addition, by drawing upon the story of Israel's journey with the Lord, Hauerwas is able to situate the concerns he first raised in his doctoral dissertation about the continuity and growth of the subject and about sanctification within the context of a more biblically-shaped vision.[216] The influence of the insights that Hauerwas has gleaned from his engagement with the story of Israel is apparent in the concluding section of the essay in which he addresses faith and justification. Against those who spuriously understand justification by faith to be the cancellation of the ethical, faith, according to Hauerwas, "is our appropriate response to salvation, and it is fundamentally a moral response and transformation."[217] Faith is the integrated response of the entire human being to the peaceable Kingdom which is present in Christ. To be "in Christ" is to be "part of that community pledged to be faithful to this life as the initiator of the kingdom of peace."[218] When the terms justification and sanctification are separated from the unsubstitutable life and death of Jesus, they cannot help but be abstractions which distort the Christian life.[219] Hauerwas reminds us that "'Sanctification' is but a way of reminding us of the kind of journey we must undertake if we are to make the story of Jesus our story. 'Justification' is but a reminder of the character of that story—namely, what God has done by providing us a path to follow."[220]

"Jesus: The Presence of the Peaceable Kingdom" marks a decisive step forward along the path laid out in "Jesus: The Story of the Kingdom." Hauerwas's establishment of the centrality of non-violence, the Israel-context

---

215. Ibid., 78.

216. *CCL*, 179–228.

217. *PK*, 93.

218. Ibid., 93.

219. Cartwright has drawn attention to Hauerwas's concerns about how secondary forms of theological discourse (e.g., nature, grace, creation, redemption) have come to preempt the story of Jesus in modern ethics and theology. Afterword to *HR*, 648.

220. *PK*, 94.

of the Jesus story, and the significance of the resurrection are crucial christological developments in his maturing theological project. However, there are gaps which still remain in Hauerwas's Christology. One of the most significant lacunae comes to light in Hauerwas's treatment of Israel. Hauerwas's presentation of the offices of prophet, priest and king in terms of providing "suitable models for the people to imitate" seems to be a rather reductionistic understanding of the offices.[221] Although recovering the exemplaristic dimension of the offices may be a helpful contribution to Christian ethics, it seems to be somewhat of a stretch to consider the primary purpose of the offices of prophet, priest, and king to be the provision of an example. To state the obvious, the names of the offices themselves point to their predominant function in the life of Israel. For example, the priest is one who has been anointed to represent the people before God and God to the people within the context of the cultus. By limiting his discussion primarily to exemplarist terms, Hauerwas provides a skewered presentation of the offices of prophet, priest and king, which by implication leads to a relatively thin conception of the *munus triplex* of Christ. A similar tendency also appears to be evident in Hauerwas's assertion that "the very thing that makes Israel Israel, is to walk in the way of the Lord."[222] Certainly Hauerwas is correct to emphasize the ethical character of Israel's calling. However, in phrasing it in such a way, he risks obscuring the prior theological reality that Israel's calling is just that, a calling rooted in the gracious election of God.

These observations tie in with criticisms raised by Colin Gunton and David Fergusson. Due to the material connection of these criticisms with what has just been discussed, along with the fact that they were voiced prior to the writings which we will be examining next, it seems appropriate to consider them at this point. Gunton, in considering Hauerwas's contribution to the recovery of the importance of virtue to the Christian life, stresses that due to the fallen nature of humanity an ethic of virtue is insufficient and potentially dangerous if it is not rooted in a theology of redemption. He then ponders aloud, placing on the table the question of whether Hauerwas is "in danger of an exemplarism of the cross, an implicit Pelagianism which lays upon human agents a burden too great for them to bear?"[223] Fergusson expresses similar concerns in evaluating Hauerwas's attempt to demonstrate the ethical significance of Jesus's mission, particularly with regard

---

221. Ibid., 78.

222. Ibid., 77.

223. Gunton, "The Church as a School of Virtue?," 220. Healy, in his recent volume, gives voice to a similar set of concerns. *Hauerwas*, 122–26.

to "Jesus: The Presence of the Peaceable Kingdom" and "Jesus: The Story of the Kingdom":

> Yet the outcome of this concern is that Jesus is generally characterised as the prototype of Christian existence, the founder of the church, and the one in whom God reveals how we are to live. The christological language tends to be that of revelation rather than redemption. The latter seems confined to quality of life realised only in the church . . . In particular, it is not clear in what sense the work of Christ can be described as completed in his resurrection and ascension, or in what sense Christ is active in the church by the power of the Spirit.[224]

We have previously seen how Hauerwas's treatment of Jesus in "Jesus: The Story of the Kingdom" raised questions concerning the resurrection and the nature of Jesus's continuing presence in the church. Although Hauerwas's treatment of the resurrection in "Jesus: The Presence of the Peaceable Kingdom" points the way towards possible solutions to these problems, from a material perspective, they remain largely unaddressed. Hauerwas, on account of what he has failed to say in his christological explorations up to this point, has left himself open to the line of criticism raised by Gunton and Fergusson.[225] Ultimately, I do not believe that the charges are applicable and in what follows I will attempt to demonstrate why this is the case. Hauerwas himself in a brief response to Gunton's essay suggests that the difference between the two may be the result of what Hauerwas has learned from the Anabaptists, namely that discipleship is the epistemological prerequisite of knowing who Christ is.[226] This may be a contributing factor, but it seems that both Gunton's and Fergusson's criticisms also arise out of a failure to understand the nature of Hauerwas's project and his understanding of the work of theology. Theology, for Hauerwas, is always a communal enterprise. It is work that is conducted within and for the church, which in a sense is the ongoing argument about the way the Scriptures should be interpreted and lived. As a result, the theologian is never alone; she discovers what she believes as she enters into dialogue with her friends and even her enemies. The theologian is always "standing on the shoulders of giants." Taken together with the ultimate telos of theology in the life of God, this means that

---

224. Fergusson, "Another Way of Reading," 245.

225. Even a highly sympathetic reader of Hauerwas, like Kallenberg, feels inclined while reviewing *With the Grain of the Universe* to ask why Hauerwas is content, unlike the book's heroes—Yoder and John Paul II—to "spend so little time writing about Jesus" ("Strange New World," 211).

226. Hauerwas, "Where Would I Be," 321–22.

theology is always embedded within a conversation that remains necessarily incomplete. With this in mind, I would suggest that Hauerwas enters into the christological conversation of the church, not with the intention of saying the last or definitive word, but rather with the intention of recovering a particularly important part of the tradition that has been obscured or lost. He has, after all, up to this point, been writing explicitly within the field of Christian ethics.[227] When the context and purpose of these writings is taken into consideration, Hauerwas's emphasis upon the normative humanity of Jesus should not be seen as a denial of his redemptive significance or the finished character of his work, but rather as a helpful corrective or recovery of a more complete christological vision. If we take Hauerwas at his word, when he expresses his hope that he is "a thoroughly orthodox Christian" who wants "to believe everything the church believes,"[228] then we must not conflate his failure to thoroughly engage with specific dimensions of Christ's work, for example, by not providing a full-orbed investigation of the *munus triplex*, with their denial. Rather it is more in keeping with Hauerwas's understanding of the work of theology to presume that up to this point he has not felt the need to develop these aspects of Christology because they either lie outside the scope of his particular project or he has recognized that they have already been addressed by others with a degree of clarity and elegance that would be hard for him to match.[229]

For these reasons, I believe Hauerwas evades the charges forwarded by Gunton and Fergusson. However, his later writings seem to indicate that the charges have not been without impact and that he is interested in addressing what has been perceived to be his sins of omission. In these later writings we observe Hauerwas unashamedly and regularly employing Trinitarian language and engaging a broader scope of dogmatic themes. In his memoirs Hauerwas observes that as he entered into his seventh decade he began to notice a difference in his work. Reflecting upon this, Hauerwas writes, "I do not know if the difference was enough to say that I was 'changing,' but I noticed I was able to write and speak with less hesitancy about God."[230] This

---

227. Consider the the subtitles of the two books in which the two essays we have just considered appear: "Toward a Constructive Christian Social Ethic" and "A Primer in Christian Ethics."

228. *DT*, 191.

229. For example, my suspicion is that Hauerwas felt no need to provide a full theological explication of the *munus triplex* because he recognized that Karl Barth in volume 4 of his *Church Dogmatics* had already brilliantly done so. This suspicion is supported in Hauerwas's memoir where he refers to his "Barthianism" as a synonym for his Christology. *HC*, 237.

230. Ibid., 277.

shift was first noticeable to Hauerwas when he wrote a series of meditations on the seven last words of Christ and continues to be evident in his commentary on the Gospel of Matthew. One cannot help but wonder whether the distinct ecclesial context in some way contributed to both the change in tone and the fuller dogmatic resourcement evident in these works, to which we now turn.

The Christology of *Cross-Shattered Christ* and *Matthew*

The first decade of the new millennium witnessed the publication of two works which cannot be ignored by anyone interested in studying the Christology of Stanley Hauerwas. Both works are the result of particular commissions. The first, *Cross-Shattered Christ*, emerged from a series of meditations on the seven last words of Christ that Hauerwas was asked to give as part of a Good Friday service at Saint Thomas Church Fifth Avenue in New York in 2003. The second came into being as a result of the invitation to contribute a commentary on the Gospel of Matthew for the Brazos Theological Commentary on the Bible—a commentary series committed to recovering the practice of theological exegesis according to the rule of faith embodied in the Nicene tradition, rooted in the conviction that when it comes to biblical interpretation, "dogma clarifies rather than obscures."[231]

As Hauerwas is forced to engage with the Scriptures, for and with the church, what emerges is a more robust, multi-orbed Christology than we have seen from him up to this point[232]—a Christology which is explicitly

---

231. Reno, series preface to the Brazos Theological Commentary on the Bible in *Mt*, 12. Long before Hauerwas's biblical commentary on Matthew, Wells had remarked upon the centrality of the synoptic gospels to Hauerwas's scriptural understanding. *Transforming Fate*, 64. In light of this observation, it is interesting to ponder what type of commentary would have emerged and how Hauerwas's own theological work would have been affected if instead of Matthew he were assigned a different book, such as the Gospel of John or the Epistle to the Hebrews.

232. Both those highly critical of and those more favorably inclined towards Hauerwas's commentary on Matthew have raised questions concerning the extent of Hauerwas's engagement with the particular words of the text. Along this spectrum see Johnson, "Matthew or Stanley?," 29–34; Bockmuehl, "Ruminative Overlay," 20–28; and Mangina, "Hidden From the Wise," 13–19. An evaluation of Hauerwas's exegetical practice lies beyond the scope of the current study, however it does seem that more sustained concentration upon the exegetical task would have been beneficial to Hauerwas's volume. Some of the further criticisms seem to arise from a lack of clarity surrounding the larger Brazos project and just what exactly constitutes a "theological commentary." Hauerwas, for his part, suggests that his commentary is best understood, in the words of Ephraim Radner, as a "ruminative overlay" of the Gospel of Matthew. *Mt*, 18.

rooted in the doctrine of the Trinity.[233] This christological development should not be construed as a radical break or a charting of a new course by Hauerwas, for in the preface of *Cross-Shattered Christ* he himself expresses the hope that "readers will find here the animating center that I hope has informed the way I have tried to do theology."[234] Rather, in this new context, freed from the polemical concerns which have frequently dominated his occasional essays and the need of his earlier work to demonstrate the significance of Jesus for social ethics, Hauerwas is able to enter into a deeper, more sustained theological reflection on the person of Christ, the second person of the Trinity.[235] This does not mean that some favorite themes do not reappear in these works. Readers familiar with his earlier works will recognize such distinctive Hauerwasian emphases as: Jesus as the *autobasileia* and the one who inaugurates the new age,[236] the crucifixion as the kingdom come,[237] the significance of the Jews,[238] Jesus as the recapitulation of Israel's life,[239] the christological basis of nonviolence,[240] disciple-making as the purpose of the Gospels and the inseparability of Christology and discipleship,[241] an emphasis upon the whole life of Jesus informing the whole life of the Church,[242] and even an allusion to the purple of Kierkegaard's story.[243] In his introduction to *Matthew*, Hauerwas acknowledges the recurrence of some previously developed themes, before ultimately defining the true subject matter of the Gospel of Matthew:

> I do stress the politics of Matthew as well as the role of nonviolence in Jesus' ministry, but I hope I have avoided making the political character of Matthew "what Matthew is all about." Jesus the Son of God is what Matthew is all about. That means the subject of Matthew's gospel is inexhaustible and, therefore, defies any attempt to make the story that Matthew tells conform to an overarching theme.[244]

---

233. Mangina has also noted an importance ascribed to the Trinity in *Matthew* that may have been lacking in Hauerwas's early work. "Hidden from the Wise," 18.

234. *CSC*, 11.

235. Not all agree with this assessment; cf. Healy, *Hauerwas*, 69–71.

236. *CSC*, 44; *Mt*, 96, 115, 166, 202.

237. *CSC*, 85.

238. Ibid., 53, 73; *Mt*, 106, 187.

239. *CSC*, 86; *Mt*, 27.

240. *CSC*, 54–55; *Mt*, 72, 224.

241. *Mt*, 19, 91, 247.

242. Ibid., 30.

243. Ibid., 56.

244. Ibid., 20.

Reminiscent of Luther who boldly proclaimed that one "must delight in assertions, or he will be no Christian,"[245] Hauerwas in writing his commentary on Matthew "discovered that writing a commentary is an invitation to indulge in assertions."[246] Many of these assertions cluster around the subject of Matthew's Gospel, Jesus the Son of God who is described as: the new Joshua,[247] the new Moses,[248] the new David,[249] the Father's prayer for us,[250] the Law,[251] *the* human being,[252] the parable of the Father,[253] God's glory,[254] the Passover Lamb for the world,[255] God's covenant,[256] and God's psalm for the world.[257] Jesus's flesh is described as the booth of God's presence.[258] Jesus is the great high priest and the temple,[259] and, perhaps most offensively to New Testament scholars, Jesus's crucifixion is the "desolating sacrilege."[260] These affirmations which are distributed liberally throughout the commentary are both evocative and provocative and frequently beg for further elucidation. Woven together, however, they represent a rich christological tapestry shrouded in the mystery of YHWH the Triune God.[261]

Hauerwas's treatment of Jesus's cry of dereliction from the cross, which is treated in both volumes, provides an illustrative point of entry into the character of the christological reflection of this period. The cry "My God, my God, why have you forsaken me?" poses a stark challenge to the biblical

245. Luther, "Bondage of the Will," 105.
246. *Mt*, 20.
247. Ibid., 36.
248. Ibid., 40–41.
249. Ibid., 56.
250. Ibid., 76.
251. Ibid., 93.
252. Ibid., 99.
253. Ibid., 127, 135.
254. Ibid., 156.
255. Ibid., 214.
256. Ibid., 218.
257. *CSC*, 43, 101; *Mt*, 237.
258. *Mt*, 157.
259. Ibid., 205.
260. Ibid., 205, 226.
261. The phrase "YHWH the Triune God" is the title of an essay by R. Kendall Soulen exploring the lack of connection between the recent revivals in trinitarian theology and the church's reevaluation of its teaching regarding the Jewish people. In a recent sermon Hauerwas expresses the following conviction which clearly resonates with Soulen's phrase, "That is why the heart of our confession that God is Triune is the church's insistence that the God we worship, the Father, Son, and Holy Spirit, is Israel's God" (*CSChu*, 57).

interpreter. Some interpreters attempt to meet this challenge with the flight into speculation about Jesus's subjectivity, but Hauerwas has no interest in such attempts to get behind the text.[262] Rather, in these enigmatic words from the cross we are confronted by "the sheer, unimaginable *different-ness*—of God."[263] In the face of this mystery, Hauerwas gives voice to the questions that rise up within:

> What are we to make of such a cry if this is the Son of God? We cannot suppress the thought: "If you are the Son of God, should you be saying this? If you are God, if you are the Second Person of the Trinity, how can you be abandoned?" This is clearly a God with a problem.[264]

In order to save ourselves from the embarrassment of these questions and to rescue Jesus from the absurdity of being abandoned, Christians feel that they must offer some type of explanation as to why Jesus had to die, often called atonement theories. Atonement theories are problematic for Hauerwas on several different levels. First, atonement theories have a tendency of subordinating Christology to soteriology, with the result that Jesus's cross becomes all about us; i.e., "Jesus had to die because we needed and need to be forgiven."[265] Atonement theories, then, are simply another form of the liberal theological project and hence draw the corresponding condemnation from Hauerwas. "Ironically," Hauerwas writes, "by trying to understand what it means for us to need forgiveness, too often our attention becomes focused on something called the 'human condition' rather than the cross and the God who hangs there."[266] Second, atonement theories are also problematic because they "risk isolating Jesus' crucifixion from his life."[267] Here the conservative side of theological spectrum, perhaps best exemplified in Mel Gibson's film *The Passion of the Christ*, comes in for criticism.[268] Although satisfaction, exemplarist, and *Christus Victor* accounts of the atonement all have some scriptural warrant, they fail to recognize that "Matthew's gospel, Matthew's story of Jesus's mission to Israel, Matthew's understanding of discipleship, Matthew's description of the beginning of

---

262. *Mt*, 20, 44.
263. Williams, *Christ on Trial*, 37, quoted in *CSC*, 64; *Mt*, 240.
264. *CSC*, 26–27; cf. *Mt*, 240.
265. *CSC*, 28.
266. Ibid., 28.
267. *Mt*, 238.
268. Hauerwas identifies this as a problem with Mel Gibson's *The Passion of the Christ* in Sheahen, "'Why Have You Forsaken Me?,'" para. 8.

the church—all climax in the death of Jesus."[269] Earlier in his commentary, Hauerwas drew upon Barth's appropriation of the *anhypostatos* and *enhypostatos*, to emphasize the significance and unsubstitutability of the particular life of Jesus.[270] We must attend to the entire life of Jesus because it is the human life of the Second Person of the Trinity, or, to put it quite simply, "the gospel is this man."[271] Finally, atonement theories are dangerous because they can suggest a god other than the Triune God of the Gospel. Here Hauerwas has in mind accounts of the atonement that suggest that Jesus must be sacrificed in order to satisfy some abstract theory of justice. Against this view, Hauerwas vigorously maintains that:

> The Father's sacrifice of the Son and the Son's willing sacrifice is God's justice. Just as there is no God who is not the Father, Son, and Holy Spirit, so there is no god who must be satisfied that we might be spared. We are spared because God refuses to have us lost.[272]

From this quotation it is clear that although Hauerwas has strong reservations about atonement theories, he does have a stake in affirming that atonement or reconciliation has occurred. However, it is the Gospels themselves which stand in the place of a theory of atonement in Hauerwas's thought. Hauerwas approvingly cites Robert Jenson: "There is no other story behind or beyond it [the story of the Crucifixion presented in the Gospels] that is the real story of what God does to reconcile us, no story of mythic battles or of a deal between God and his Son or of our being moved to live reconciled lives."[273] Instead, the cry of dereliction must be heard within the context of Israel's story for "only a people like Israel, a God-possessed people, can know what it might mean to be abandoned by God."[274] In a manner reminiscent of Luther's *theologia crucis*, Hauerwas insists that God is most clearly revealed in the hidden form of the man upon the cross. Hauerwas writes, "These words from the cross, and the cross itself, mean that the Father is to be found when all traces of power, at least as we understand power, are absent; that the Spirit's authoritative witness is most clearly revealed when all forms of human authority are lost; and that God's power and authority

---

269. *Mt*, 238.
270. Ibid., 100.
271. Ibid., 103.
272. *CSC*, 66.
273. Jenson, *Systematic Theology*, 1:189, quoted in *Mt*, 238.
274. *CSC*, 61.

is to be found exemplified in this captive under the sentence of death."[275] Hauerwas insists that we must not equate this death, particularly the cry of dereliction with human suffering in general, rather "My God, my God why have you forsaken me?" is "the cry of the long-expected Messiah, sacrificed in our stead and thus becoming the end of sacrifice."[276] Christ's death is the sacrifice which frees us from the sacrificial systems which dominate our lives, particularly the sacrificial language and logic of the nation-state which calls us to sacrifice our unwillingness to kill.[277] In a particularly poetic paragraph, Hauerwas takes up the motif of the "happy exchange" to describe Christ's work on the cross:

> In the cross of Christ God refuses to let our sin, the sin of his tormentors, determine our relation to him. God's love for us means that he can only hate that which alienates his creatures from the love manifest in our creation. Cyril of Jerusalem observes that by calling on his Father as "my God," Christ does so on our behalf and in our place. Hear these words, "My God, my God, why have you forsaken me?" and know that the Son of God has taken our place, become for us the abandonment that our sin produces, so that we may live confident that the world has been redeemed by this cross.[278]

"Through the cross of Christ" Hauerwas insists, "we are drawn into the mystery of the Trinity."[279] This means that although it is proper to speak of Christ's work on the cross as being complete or finished, at the same time there is a place within the economy of salvation to speak of Christ's continuing work in the church through the Holy Spirit. This truth is elegantly captured in a paragraph from Hauerwas's reflection upon the sixth word from the cross, "It is finished":

> God has finished what only God could finish. Christ's sacrifice is a gift that exceeds every debt. Our sins have been consumed, making possible lives that glow with the beauty of God's Spirit. What wonderful news: "'It is finished.' But it is not over." It is not over because God made us, the church, the "not over." We are made witnesses so the world—a world with no time for a

---

275. Ibid., 64; see also *Mt*, 240.
276. *CSC*, 61.
277. *Mt*, 28.
278. Ibid., 241; see also *CSC*, 65.
279. *CSC*, 31.

crucified God—may know that we have all the time of God's kingdom to live in peace with one another.[280]

PART 3: CHRISTOLOGICAL CONCLUSIONS

In the preceding pages, we have explored the animating christological center of two of the twentieth century's most important theological voices. In their own unique ways, the theologies of both Dietrich Bonhoeffer and Stanley Hauerwas can be fruitfully understood as explications of the earliest Christian confession, "Jesus is Lord!"[281] The confession "Jesus is Lord!" provides a helpful rubric for presenting a summary of the major christological themes and emphases shared between these two theologians and for bringing their theology into dialogue around potential areas of divergence.

Jesus Is Lord!

Following the conviction of the New Testament authors and the earliest Christian communities, Bonhoeffer and Hauerwas both affirm that the Gospel entails the recognition that a particular first-century Palestinian Jew who proclaimed and enacted the advent of the Kingdom of God, ran afoul of the political and religious authorities of his time, and suffered execution on a Roman cross outside of Jerusalem during a Passover weekend, has been exalted to the right hand of God and enthroned as Lord of all. The proper name Jesus identifies this particular individual and stands as shorthand for his unique, personal history—a history which is narrated in the Scriptures. The Risen One bears witness to Himself through the testimony of Scripture, rendering moot any attempt to get behind the text in order to separate the Jesus of history from the Christ of faith.[282] For both Bonhoeffer and Hauerwas, the Jesus of history *is* the Christ of faith.

This shared emphasis upon the unique, unsubstitutable identity of Jesus Christ rubs against the grain of the docetic temptation to leave Jesus behind. Liberal theology, which on the surface has been so interested in the humanity of Jesus, often ends up making Jesus the manifestation of some

---

280. Ibid., 90. The internal quotation—"'It is finished.' But it is not over."—is a recurring refrain in Neuhaus's reflections on the seven last words, *Death on a Friday Afternoon*, 190, 191, 205, 216.

281. See for example Rom 10:9, 1 Cor 12:3, Phil 2:11.

282. That being said, Bonhoeffer does not speak with same animus against the historical-critical method as Hauerwas sometimes does. For what is perhaps Hauerwas's most polemical engagement with the historical-critical method, see *US*, 1–44.

universal ideal which can be known on other grounds. Hans Frei introduced the term "epistemological monophysitism" to describe that way that modern theology has acknowledged the humanity of Jesus in theory, but failed to attend to the details of Jesus's life-story to such an extent that Christ's true humanity is compromised.[283] In the place of the particular, unsubstitutable identity that is rendered by the Gospels, liberal theology imports a general anthropology, which is sometimes even justified by the use of the adjective incarnational. Those of a more conservative perspective are not immune from this docetic tendency, often succumbing to the temptation of replacing the living Christ with "orthodox" religious ideas and principles. Bonhoeffer's famous diatribe against "cheap grace" in the opening chapter of *Discipleship* is directed against those who have made justification by faith into such a principle.[284] Hauerwas, for his part, sees something similar going on in the "ethical realism" of Reinhold Niebuhr, in which, "justification by faith is loosed from its Christological context and made a truth to underwrite a generalized virtue of humility in order to make Christians trusted players in the liberal game of tolerance."[285] The theologies of Bonhoeffer and Hauerwas transcend the contemporary divisions between left and right, liberal and conservative, by calling all Christians to renewed attention to the concrete figure of Jesus Christ whose unique identity is rendered in the Scriptures.

This shared emphasis upon the particularity of the person of Jesus Christ places the event of revelation firmly within time and therefore opens the door to an understanding of the Christian life that takes seriously the historicity of human existence. This implication will be explored further in the coming chapters. At this point it is worth pausing to consider whether both Bonhoeffer's and Hauerwas's accounts would be further strengthened through focusing even greater attention upon the timeful character of Jesus's life and ministry. Although both theologians go to great lengths to affirm the truly human character of Jesus's existence, the question could be raised as to whether their christological portrayals are capable of affirming that "Jesus grew in wisdom and stature, and in favor with God and men."[286] At times the fallen humanity assumed by the Son seems to function merely as a cloak or disguise, as in Bonhoeffer's "incognito" and Hauerwas's employment of Kierkegaard's parable of the purple, rather than also as the object of

283. Higton, *Christ, Providence and History*, 68. For further discussion of "epistemological monophysitism," see Sonderegger, "Epistemological Monophysitism," 255–62.

284. "Cheap grace is grace without discipleship, grace without the cross, grace without the living, incarnate Jesus Christ" (*D* (*DBWE* 4), 44).

285. *WGU*, 136.

286. Luke 2:52.

the sanctifying work of the Triune God.[287] An appropriation of an account of the sanctification of fallen human flesh in the incarnation of the Son which understands the history of reconciliation as being played out over the course of the entirety of the life of Christ would appear to strengthen the Christologies of both Bonhoeffer and Hauerwas, without seeming to in any way mitigate their interest in the full humanity of Jesus and the historicity of human existence.[288]

A further implication of the assertion "*Jesus* is Lord" is that our understanding of lordship must now be shaped and re-defined by the particular life of Jesus. Against popular conceptions of lordship which are nothing more than idolatrous projections of our own will-to-power, both Bonhoeffer and Hauerwas make recourse to a *theologia crucis*. However, the cruciform shape of Lordship cannot be separated from the Crucified One who is the Lord. Both Bonhoeffer's conception of Jesus as "the man for others" and Hauerwas's emphasis upon nonviolence must remain subject to christological control or else they run the risk of becoming empty, and possibly even idolatrous, abstractions.[289]

Jesus Is *Lord*!

The emphasis upon the sole lordship of Jesus Christ within the theologies of Bonhoeffer and Hauerwas is perhaps the predominant factor contributing to the uniquely prophetic character of their work. Put quite simply, if Jesus is Lord, then Hitler is not. Nor is the modern nation-state, Western liberal democracy, Mammon, or any of the other persons, objects, or ideologies competing for the allegiance of Christians. The New Testament scholar Larry Hurtado has observed that there are three different contexts in which Jesus is referred to as *Kyrios* in Paul's letters: liturgical contexts, eschatological contexts, and ethical contexts.[290] As in the letters of the apostle, the boundaries between these usages remain rather fluid within the Christologies of Bonhoeffer and Hauerwas. However, this threefold division can serve as a helpful heuristic device.

---

287. *DBWE* 12:355–60; Hauerwas, "Humanity of the Divine," para. 9–12; *Mt*, 56.

288. One such account is provided in Torrance, *Incarnation*, 63–65; 114–16; 206. Another is offered in McIntosh, *Divine Teaching*, 105–10.

289. Dumas warns of the danger of extracting the phrase "man for others" from Bonhoeffer's rich Christology. *Dietrich Bonhoeffer*, 228. Hauerwas criticizes such a use of the phrase "man for others," but it does not appear that he has Bonhoeffer specifically in view. *US*, 54.

290. Hurtado, *Lord Jesus Christ*, 115–18.

Within the context of early Christian worship the confession "Jesus is Lord!" can be understood as an affirmation that Jesus shares in the divine identity of YHWH, the God of Israel.[291] There are several important implications of this affirmation that are prominent in the thought of both Bonhoeffer and Hauerwas.

First, if Jesus is one with the God of Israel, the Creator of heaven and earth, then Jesus must be understood as the ultimate truth of human existence, and beyond that, of the entire created order. For Bonhoeffer, Jesus Christ is the center of history, nature, and human existence and any attempt "to understand reality without the Real One means living in an abstraction."[292] Hauerwas similarly affirms that "the kingdom present in Jesus Christ is the ultimate realism."[293] As a result, Hauerwas can affirm that "those who bear crosses are working with the grain of the universe."[294] Although the two may at times differ in how this is materially worked out within their projects, they do appear united in the theological conviction that "the reality of Christ determines all that is."[295]

Second, a correlation of the just-discussed conviction is a commitment by both thinkers to what could be considered a type of non-foundationalism. The shared reasoning which commits both thinkers to a type of non-foundationalism can be simply stated as follows: "Christology deals with that which grounds all things and therefore cannot itself be grounded."[296] The Word of God revealed in Jesus Christ is always the prerequisite for theology; as such it creates its own foundation for Christian thought and existence.[297] This means that faith is necessary for true theological knowledge and correspondingly that discipleship and the church are epistemological prerequisites for the true knowledge of God.[298]

---

291. For full monographs elucidating this point see Bauckham, *God Crucified* and Hurtado, *Lord Jesus Christ*.

292. *E* (*DBWE* 6), 262.

293. *HR*, 389.

294. *WGU*, 17, quoting Yoder, "Armaments and Eschatology," 58.

295. *PTF*, 45.

296. Webster, *Word and Church*, 117. Hauerwas frames the matter in the following way: "If one needs a standard of truth to insure that Jesus is the Messiah, then one ought to worship that standard of truth, not Jesus" (*Mt*, 185).

297. *DBWE* 12:315; Hauerwas, "On Doctrine and Ethics," 32.

298. E.g., "Knowledge cannot be separated from the existence in which it was acquired" (*D* (*DBWE* 4), 51). "The truth that is Jesus is a truth that requires discipleship, for it is only by being transformed by what he has taught and by what he has done that we can come to know the way the world is" (*Mt*, 247).

Third, inseparable from these implications is the understanding shared by both Bonhoeffer and Hauerwas that the confession "Jesus is Lord!" requires a commitment to the exclusivity of the revelation of God in Jesus Christ. If one wishes to know who God is and what He is like, one has no recourse but to attend to the person of Jesus Christ. For both Bonhoeffer and Hauerwas there is no question of turning to secondary sources apart from God's revelation in Christ to supplement our knowledge of God. Their rejection of so-called "natural theology" is as vehement as the "Nein!" pronounced by their theological mentor Karl Barth. However, their commitment to understanding all of reality in the light of Christ will not allow them to abandon the natural world, but rather presses them forward towards developing a truly natural theology emerging from God's revelation in Christ.[299]

Finally, the confession that Jesus shares in the identity of YHWH the God of Israel, highlights the importance of the Old Testament and the people of Israel for Christology. Both Bonhoeffer and Hauerwas share a common interest in restoring Jesus to his primary context within the people of Israel. They each recognize that attending to the people of Israel cuts against the gnosticizing currents of modernity which seek to spiritualize and de-politicize Christ's saving work. While offering tantalizing clues to a way forward, the material content of the significance of the people of Israel within their respective Christologies, however, remains largely underdeveloped and has been left for their students and colleagues to work through.[300]

The confession "Jesus is Lord!" is rich with eschatological overtones. The eschatological dimension of this confession contributes greatly to the palette of the christological portraits painted by both Bonhoeffer and Hauerwas. For both theologians, Jesus is the human being eschatologically re-constituted in the image of God. Just as Bonhoeffer and Hauerwas are insistent that if one wishes to know who God is they must look to Jesus Christ,

---

299. See Bonhoeffer's attempt to rehabilitate the category of 'the natural' within Protestant ethics in his manuscript "Natural Life" in *E* (*DBWE* 6), 171–218. See also Hauerwas's provocative presentation of Karl Barth as the "natural theologian" *par excellence* in his Gifford Lectures. *WGU*, 173–204. Wells asserts that "the claim that Stanley should be famous for" is the assertion that "Jesus is the shape of natural theology" ("Difference Christ Makes," 27).

300. Bonhoeffer's friend and literary executor Eberhard Bethge became particularly interested in matters pertaining to Jewish-Christian relations, an interest which informed some further christological reflection. For an overview of this involvement see De Gruchy, *Daring, Trusting Spirit*, 181–94. For an example of a work written by a former student of Hauerwas that is largely congenial to his work, but which seeks to offer a helpful corrective in this area, see Bader-Saye, *Church and Israel after Christendom*.

in a similar way if one wishes to know what it means to be truly human one must look to Jesus.[301]

The new humanity of Christ is both vicarious and participatory in the thought of both Bonhoeffer and Hauerwas. For Bonhoeffer, Jesus Christ is the eschatological irruption of God's salvific power and presence which comes to us *extra nos*. As the *Stellvertreter*, Jesus Christ stands in the place of sinful humanity before God, reconciling human beings to God and one another. In place of the old humanity infinitely fragmented along the faultlines of each individual's sinful egocentricity, the new humanity, characterized by its being with and for others, has been realized in Jesus Christ and is taking form in the world within the church-community, which is Christ's body. For Hauerwas, Jesus Christ is the apocalyptic presence of God's peaceable kingdom. On the cross Jesus unmasked the principalities and powers which seek to rule our world through violence and falsehood and through his resurrection he has broken the power of the last enemy, Death. Freed from the fear of death, those called to be church can venture to live "out of control" lives that are dependent solely upon the gracious gifts of God. Through the forgiveness of sins made available through Jesus Christ, human beings can now face the truth about themselves and speak truthfully to one another without it being the cause of their destruction. This eschatological dimension of both of their Christologies, alongside of the epistemological convictions previously discussed, contributes a distinctly apocalyptic flavor to their writings.[302]

It is interesting to observe that although the work of the eschatological Spirit is implicitly central to both of their ecclesiological proposals, as will be shown in the next chapter, neither to the best of my knowledge devotes more than passing remarks to the significance of the Holy Spirit for the life and ministry of Jesus.[303] If anything, further attention to the pneumatological dimension of Christology would only serve to further strengthen

---

301. E.g., "Jesus is not a human being but *the* human being" (*E* (*DBWE* 6), 85). "But Jesus is not the exemplification of humanity. He is this man and no other. Indeed, he is the only true human being" (*Mt*, 99–100).

302. Philip Ziegler has explored the apocalyptic character of Bonhoeffer's *Ethics* in "Dietrich Bonhoeffer—An Ethics of God's Apocalypse?" Douglas Harink has presented a case for the apocalyptic character of Hauerwas's thought in *Paul among the Postliberals*, 67–103.

303. Although Kelly and Nelson insist that an important aspect of Bonhoeffer's pneumatology is that "every referent is always to Jesus in his human ministry as a man in whom the Spirit of God dwells in its fullness" (*Cost of Moral Leadership*, 66). It appears that Hauerwas may be developing his pneumatological thinking along these very lines. See the recently appearing online article, "How to be Caught by the Holy Spirit."

not only their Christologies, but also the significant relationship between Christology and ecclesiology that exists in both of their work.

The confession "Jesus is Lord!" entails that he alone demands exclusive allegiance. In this early Christian confession the theological and the ethical exist in organic unity. Like the early church, Bonhoeffer and Hauerwas are united in the conviction that Christianity is not a set of beliefs about Jesus, but rather a way of life lived in the commanding and empowering presence of the risen Lord. Both Bonhoeffer and Hauerwas are convinced that as a result of the incarnation of the Word and the ascension of Jesus to the right hand of the Father that the world has been reconfigured and the rule of the Lord Jesus Christ extends over the entirety of life. In the words of an old aphorism, Jesus must be truly Lord of all, or else he is not Lord at all. Both Bonhoeffer and Hauerwas would affirm this statement as long as it is not understood to be merely a statement about making Jesus one's "personal Lord," as in pietism, but rather as an affirmation of Christ's rule over the entire cosmos. Life cannot be compartmentalized or divided up among different spheres, for as Bonhoeffer puts it, there is "only *the one realm of the Christ-reality*" and within that realm Jesus "demands undivided obedience."[304] A similar christological sentiment lies behind one of Hauerwas's favorite refrains, "Any God who won't tell you what to do with your pots and pans and genitals isn't worth worshipping."[305]

Jesus *Is* Lord!

The two-letter verb *is* binds together the first-century Palestinian Jew who is identified by the proper name Jesus with the Creator of the Universe. In this grammatical context, the *is* functions as a channel opening up a realm of commerce between the human and the divine, in this way anticipating the great christological formulations of Nicaea and Chalcedon. As we have seen, both Bonhoeffer and Hauerwas are interested in affirming the full divinity and full humanity of Christ as confessed in these classic creedal statements. However, they are both equally insistent that the Creeds are not static formulas that serve as the basis for abstract operations of metaphysical calculus. Rather, they are safeguards which preserve the mystery of the incarnation and ultimately direct our attention back to the concrete figure of the crucified and risen Jesus Christ.

It is at this point that the little verb *is* takes flight, demonstrating that it is more than an inert equal sign. In Bonhoeffer's and Hauerwas's theologies

---

304. *E* (*DBWE* 6), 58; *D* (*DBWE* 4), 135.
305. *TAG*, 20; cf. *HR*, 531.

the *is* pulsates with the vitality of the Risen One. There is dynamism to their thought stemming from the conviction that the risen Lord Jesus Christ is present to and in his church and is even now making all things new through the power of the Holy Spirit. As a result, both Bonhoeffer and Hauerwas are able to speak as if God matters and as if God makes a difference here and now, because the "as if" has been rolled away with the stone and the Risen One is at loose in the world.

The confession "Jesus is Lord!" presupposes the mission of the Triune God. The existence of the human being Jesus is the sole result of the Father's sending of the Son in the power of the Holy Spirit. To assert otherwise is to fall into the related complex of adoptionistic christological heresies such as Ebionism and Nestorianism. An implication of rooting the human existence of Jesus of Nazareth within the Trinitarian mission is that Jesus's entire life must be understood as mission. While neither consistently utilizes this language of the *missio Dei*, it naturally flows from their shared steadfast conviction that the person and work of Christ are inseparable. Both recognize that subordinating Christology to soteriology inevitably leads to the effacement of the unsubstitutable identity of Christ. As opposed to theological streams which separate soteriology from the person of Christ, the theologies of Bonhoeffer and Hauerwas reflect the conviction that Jesus *is* salvation. As we will see in the next chapter, this refusal to separate the person of Christ from his work will have significant implications for their understanding of the identity and mission of Christ's body, the church.

In this chapter I have attempted to make plain the animating center of the theologies of Dietrich Bonhoeffer and Stanley Hauerwas. The animating center, shared by both theologians, is nothing other than the person of Jesus Christ in the irreducible uniqueness of his personal presence. It is their central concern for the person of Jesus Christ that allows their theologies to transcend contemporary divisions amongst theological camps and resist easy classification. It is the christological concentration of their thought that leads to the compelling, even prophetic, character of their writings.

3

A Peculiar People
The Church of Jesus Christ

Based upon the christological commitments explored in the previous chapter, both Dietrich Bonhoeffer and Stanley Hauerwas have something of profound importance to say about the church. Their works of "popular ecclesiology" written about the church, for a broader reading constituency within the church, will serve as the gateway into their respective ecclesiological imaginations. In these works, we see both Bonhoeffer and Hauerwas attempting to diagnose what ails the church through providing genealogies which endeavor to account for the condition of the church in their day. Both Bonhoeffer and Hauerwas are convinced that in their respective contexts the church must recover its public presence as an identifiable community of disciples. Furthermore, both complement their conception of the church as a community of radical discipleship with what could be considered to be a more catholic ecclesiology that understands the existence of the concrete church-community to be internal to the Gospel. Both theologians perceive that this development brings them into conflict with Karl Barth, whose theology has otherwise had such a profound influence upon them. However, their emphases upon practicing the presence of Christ suggest a constructive way beyond their critical impasses with Barth. The trajectory just outlined will provide the road map for the exploration, in turn, of each theologian's ecclesiological vision. This analysis will be followed by a summary section shaped around the traditional creedal notes of the church. This will present the opportunity for observing how the work of the two theologians provides the impetus for a revitalized deployment of the creedal notes of the church, while at the same time providing an occasion to bring their ecclesiological insights into constructive dialogue with one another.

PART 1: THE ECCLESIOLOGY OF DIETRICH BONHOEFFER

Background to the Finkenwalde Writings

A fascination with the concept of the church marked Dietrich Bonhoeffer's theological career from the outset. His doctoral dissertation, *Sanctorum Communio: A Theological Study of the Sociology of the Church*, completed in 1927 at the tender age of 21, attempted to employ contemporary sociology and social philosophy within the overarching dogmatic framework of a theology of revelation.[1] It was followed less than three years later by a daring *Habilitationsschrift* in which Bonhoeffer would appeal to the concept of the church as a means of overcoming the divide between actualistic and ontological accounts of revelation.[2] As central as the church was in Bonhoeffer's academic dissertations, it was not until the events of 1933 and the immediately following years, as Bonhoeffer was thrust into the crucible of the Church Struggle and Germany fell increasingly under the spell of Nazism, that his ecclesiological writings truly came into their own. The two published works emerging from the period during which Bonhoeffer directed the illegal preachers' seminary at Finkenwalde—*Discipleship* and *Life Together*—demonstrate a remarkable combination of pastoral depth and theological insight. Absent from these writings are the cumbersome academic apparatuses and labyrinthine turns of phrase of the dissertations. Instead we encounter works whose existential urgency is aptly communicated through the clarity and eloquence of their simple and straightforward prose.[3]

In 1935, as the Church Struggle intensified, Bonhoeffer was recalled from his pastorate in London, England to direct the preachers' seminary planted by the Confessing Church in Zingst on the Baltic Sea. The seminary, like all those established by the mandate of the Dahlem synod, was

---

1. Karl Barth considered it a "theological miracle" that such a dissertation could emerge from within the theological faculty of the University of Berlin. Marsh, *Strange Glory*, 57. Bethge presents the reflections of Bonhoeffer's cousin Hans-Christoph von Hase, who wrote to Bonhoeffer about the dissertation remarking, "There will not be many who really understand it, the Barthians won't because of the sociology, and the sociologists won't because of Barth" (*Dietrich Bonhoeffer*, 83).

2. *AB* (*DBWE* 2).

3. Webster maintains that this development is a result of Bonhoeffer becoming "in effect, a practical, biblical theologian" (*Word and Church*, 99).

deemed to be illegal by the governing authorities before it even opened. In a letter to his brother Karl-Friedrich, written several months before his return to Germany, Bonhoeffer speculated that "the restoration of the church must surely depend on a new kind of monasticism, which has nothing in common with the old but a life of uncompromising discipleship, following Christ according to the Sermon on the Mount."[4] The preachers' seminary, which within two months of opening was moved to Finkenwalde, provided the very opportunity for such a venture. The result was a unique experiment in community living and theological training, the likes of which had not been seen in Germany before. It gave rise to rumors throughout the Evangelical Church "about the terrible heresies in Finkenwalde—Catholic practices, enthusiastic pacifist activities, and radical fanaticism."[5] *Discipleship* emerged from the lectures which were the animating center of Bonhoeffer's theological curriculum at Finkenwalde.[6] *Life Together* was Bonhoeffer's attempt to provide a theologically-informed description of the community life at Finkenwalde after the seminary was closed and sealed by the Gestapo in September 1937.[7] The two works belong together, for not only do they emerge from the same period, but *Discipleship* and *Life Together* point to the same reality; for "to be together as a group of people in that place [Finkenwalde] thus presupposed a willingness to stake one's life on faith in and obedience to the God revealed in Jesus Christ, to reject the Nazi gods of blood and soil, and to repudiate the Nazification of German Protestantism in the *Reichskirche*."[8]

How the Church Became Worldly through the Peddling of Cheap Grace

"Cheap grace is the mortal enemy of our church. Our struggle today is for costly grace."[9] This dramatic opening salvo sets the tone for Bonhoeffer's evaluation of the ecclesial environment of his time. The opening pages,

---

4. *DBWE* 13:285.

5. Bethge, *Dietrich Bonhoeffer*, 433.

6. Three years after its publication, Bonhoeffer would be surprised to find the monks at the Benedictine monastery of Ettal, where Bonhoeffer at that time was working on his *Ethics*, reading aloud passages of *Discipleship* during dinner—a testament to the wide influence of the book during Bonhoeffer's lifetime. Bethge, *Dietrich Bonhoeffer*, 453.

7. Bethge reports that *Life Together* was the most widely read of Bonhoeffer's books during Bonhoeffer's lifetime. Ibid., 469.

8. Badcock, *House Where God Lives*, 180–81.

9. *D* (*DBWE* 4), 43.

which read like a litany, first lamenting the distortion of cheap grace and then extolling the truth and beauty of costly grace, are among the most well-known of all of Bonhoeffer's writings. "Cheap grace," Bonhoeffer asserts, "means grace as bargain basement goods, cut-rate forgiveness, cut-rate sacrament; grace as the church's inexhaustible pantry, from which it is doled out by careless hands without hesitation or limit."[10] It is "grace as a doctrine, as principle, as system" and "justification of sin but not of the sinner."[11] Bonhoeffer brings his lament to a close with the summation: "Cheap grace is preaching forgiveness without repentance; it is baptism without the discipline of community; it is the Lord's Supper without confession of sin; it is absolution without personal confession. Cheap grace is grace without discipleship, grace without the cross, grace without the living, incarnate Jesus Christ."[12] "Costly grace," on the other hand, "is the hidden treasure in the field, for the sake of which people go and sell with joy everything they have."[13] "It is costly," Bonhoeffer explains, "because it calls to discipleship; it is grace, because it calls us to follow *Jesus Christ.*"[14] In the life of the Christian, "grace and discipleship belong inseparably together."[15]

However, within the German Protestant Church of the 1930s, the vital nerve connecting grace to discipleship had been severed. A supposedly Christian nation had been swept up into the nationalistic and militaristic fervor surrounding Adolf Hitler and the Nazi Party.[16] Even the church, in its eagerness to ensure its institutional survival and retain its clerical privileges, was stumbling over itself in its eagerness to display its loyalty to the government.[17] In Bonhoeffer's estimation it was not the Nazis who were responsible for wielding the scalpel which severed the nerve joining grace to discipleship, rather the nerve atrophied and died over the course of the church's long history. Painting in broad brushstrokes, Bonhoeffer asserts that "the expansion of Christianity and the increasing secularization of the church caused the awareness of costly grace to be gradually lost. The world

10. Ibid.
11. Ibid.
12. Ibid., 44.
13. Ibid.
14. Ibid., 45.
15. Ibid., 46.
16. Within this context, Ziegler proposes that the first chapter of *Discipleship* on "costly grace" can be read as "a passionate case for acknowledgement of the claims of Barmen II regarding the evangelical use of the law" ("Not to Abolish," 284).
17. Perhaps the most embarrassing incident involved the introduction in 1938 by the consistory of the Evangelical Church of an oath of loyalty to the *Führer* which was required of all pastors. See Bethge, *Dietrich Bonhoeffer*, 599–603.

was Christianized; grace became common property of a Christian world. It could be had cheaply."[18] In protest against the secularization of the church and the cheapening of grace, people fled to monasteries, which preserved the memory of costly grace and the necessity for discipleship. However, the protest of the monastic movement was relativized by the church which tolerated its existence and, in doing so, justified its own secular life and relegated the demands of discipleship to the small extraordinary minority found in the holy orders. A two-tiered mode of Christian existence arose in which the call to discipleship was understood to be for the elite few who entered into monastic life, while for the majority the claim of Christ was limited to the realm of religious rites and observances. Costly grace was lost when those in the monastic orders began to believe this narrative and to look upon their own life as one of special merit. According to Bonhoeffer, "the gospel of pure, costly grace" was reawakened during the Reformation when God called Martin Luther out of the monastery, back into the world, after showing him "through scripture that discipleship is not the meritorious achievement of individuals, but a divine commandment to all Christians."[19] In leaving the monastery, Luther engaged in "a frontal assault" upon the world; "following Jesus now had to be lived out in the midst of the world."[20] It is a perverse misconstrual of Luther to think that the pure grace of the gospel which he proclaimed releases Christians from obedience to Jesus Christ. If that were the case then "the Reformation's main discovery would then be the sanctification and justification of the world by grace's forgiving power."[21] This, however, is exactly the way of thinking that has emerged victorious following the Reformation. What for Luther was a divine conclusion, has become for his descendants a principled presupposition.[22] The results have been disastrous. Although the propagation of cheap grace has led to the Christianization of the world in name, in reality "Christianity has become the world under this grace as never before."[23]

Bonhoeffer perceived that justification by faith becomes the article by which the church falls, if the article becomes an abstract principle divorced from the living person of Jesus Christ. Bonhoeffer observed that in Lutheran Germany, "the pure doctrine of grace became its own God, grace itself."[24] However, from Bonhoeffer's perspective one is not justified by holding a

18. D (DBWE 4), 46.
19. Ibid., 47.
20. Ibid., 48.
21. Ibid., 49.
22. Ibid., 50.
23. Ibid.
24. Ibid., 53.

correct understanding of the doctrine of justification, rather one is justified as they are called and claimed by the Just One, Jesus Christ.

In the long run cheap grace had proven to be terribly costly to the church. Bonhoeffer attributes the hardening of individuals in disobedience and the collapse of the organized churches to the peddling of cheap grace. The proliferation of cheap grace in Germany had resulted in a comfortable, cultural Christianity. In surrendering the demands of discipleship in exchange for continuing influence and privilege in society, the church in Germany discovered that it lacked the resources to resist the false gods of *Volk, Blut und Boden*. Within this context, Bonhoeffer perceived the central challenge facing the church to be the need "to understand grace and discipleship again in correct relationship to each other."[25]

The Church as a Visible Community of Disciples

In order to address this challenge Bonhoeffer turns to the Synoptic Gospels. There he finds not an abstract ideal of grace, but rather the person of the living Lord Jesus Christ who summons disciples to faith and obedience, never one without the other. This call to discipleship is not "anything preprogrammed, idealistic, or legalistic," for it has "no other content besides Jesus."[26] Jesus Christ, the Son of God in human flesh, is the mediator between God and humanity. Since the Son of God became a human being, that human being must be followed. The call of the mediator "creates existence anew."[27] Each person stands alone as a responsible individual in the presence of the call of Christ. No longer can they hide amongst the anonymity of the crowd, or abdicate responsibility for the call by clinging to the apparent "God-given" orders of family, race, or nation, for Jesus Christ has stepped into the center ending all immediacy with the world. Those who attempt to live in immediate relationships are living in a dream world. Bonhoeffer elaborates, "There is no genuine tie to the given realities of the created world; there are no genuine responsibilities in the world without recognition of the break, which already separates us from the world. There is no genuine love for the world except the love with which God has loved the world in Jesus Christ."[28]

---

25. Ibid., 55. Ford observes that Bonhoeffer "united under the heading of discipleship what Reformed theologians treated under 'Faith,' 'Justification' and 'Sanctification'" (*Self and Salvation*, 246).

26. *D (DBWE* 4), 59.

27. Ibid., 62.

28. Ibid., 96.

The new life of the disciple takes the form of simple obedience to the call and command of Christ. Bonhoeffer is insistent that the desire to recover the place of simple obedience in the life of the disciple is not "enthusiasm."[29] On the contrary, those who attempt to dismiss simple obedience to Jesus as "enthusiasm" have actually replaced the true hermeneutical key to Scripture, the living Lord Jesus Christ, with an abstract principle of grace.[30] In the opening chapters of *Discipleship*, Bonhoeffer is hard at work to ensure that faith is not confused with mere credulity. Faith, for Bonhoeffer, is the existential orientation of the entire human being towards Jesus Christ in response to His call. Hence, Bonhoeffer's famous aphorism, "*only the believers obey,* and *only the obedient believe.*"[31] Lurking in the background is Bonhoeffer's distinction in *Act and Being* between *actus directus* and *actus reflexus*.[32] The immediate act of faith (*actus directus*) sees only Christ, while the consciousness of reflection (*actus reflectus*) is one step removed from the act of faith itself.[33] In a phrase within *Act and Being* which anticipates the later developments of *Discipleship*, Bonhoeffer writes, "Faith looks not on itself, but on Christ alone."[34] When the distinction between *actus directus* and *actus reflexus* is understood, it becomes apparent that for Bonhoeffer, as Charles Marsh has observed, "knowing Christ *is* following Christ—it *is* obedience."[35]

The call of Jesus Christ invites the disciple into community with the Crucified One. In the words of Reginald Fuller's original English translation of *Discipleship*: "When Christ calls a man, he bids him come and die."[36] Bonhoeffer insists that the cross must not be interpreted "as one's daily misfortune, as the predicament and anxiety of our natural life."[37] Such an understanding could only arise within a Christianity which had left the adventurous seas of discipleship behind, in order to take up mooring in the shallow waters of cheap grace. Instead, the cross must be understood as "that suffering which comes from our allegiance to Jesus Christ alone."[38]

29. Ibid., 77.
30. Ibid., 81–82.
31. Ibid., 63.
32. *AB* (*DBWE* 2), 28.
33. Ibid., 158.
34. Ibid., 133.
35. Marsh, *Reclaiming Dietrich Bonhoeffer*, 107.
36. *D* (*DBWE* 4), 87 n. 11. The new translation lacks the poetic and existential punch of Fuller's rendering of the sentence, but more closely reflects the German text; "Whenever Christ calls us, his call leads to death" (87).
37. Ibid., 87.
38. Ibid., 86.

The call of Jesus Christ creates a visible community of the cross. This theme comes most clearly to the fore in Bonhoeffer's extensive treatment of the Sermon on the Mount, which takes up approximately a third of the pages of *Discipleship*. Bonhoeffer's interest in the Sermon on the Mount seems to have been sparked by the French theologian and pastor Jean Lasserre, who befriended Bonhoeffer during his time at Union Seminary in 1930–31. Lasserre was the first Christian of pacifist convictions that Bonhoeffer had personally encountered, but in Lasserre Bonhoeffer found a kindred spirit who shared "his longing for the concretion of divine grace."[39] Lasserre introduced Bonhoeffer to a way of reading the Sermon on the Mount which liberated the Sermon from its marginalization in Lutheran theology.[40] Bonhoeffer's literal reading of the Sermon on the Mount in *Discipleship* is simple, but it is not simplistic. Bonhoeffer presents a christological interpretation of the Sermon, which understands it to be the outworking of Jesus's calling of the disciples into communion with his passion.[41] This call creates a visible community of the cross, which has been appointed by Christ as the salt and light of the world. Bonhoeffer draws attention to the fact that Christ's pronouncements regarding salt and light are given in the indicative, not the imperative. The disciples are not encouraged to be salt or light; rather the call of Christ has made them both. Nor should the disciples confuse the message of Jesus by thinking that what he is really saying is "you have the salt." Bonhoeffer insists:

> It would diminish the meaning to equate the disciples' message with salt, as the reformers did. What is meant is their whole existence, to the extent that it is newly grounded in Christ's call to discipleship, that existence of which the Beatitudes speak. All those who follow Jesus' call to discipleship are made by that call to be the salt of the earth in their whole existence.[42]

What distinguishes Christians from nonbelievers can be summarized by a single word which appears in Matthew 5:47: "what is Christian is what is '*peculiar*,' περισσόν, the extraordinary, irregular, not self-evident."[43] Bon-

---

39. Bethge, *Dietrich Bonhoeffer*, 154.

40. As a young pastor in Barcelona, Bonhoeffer had dismissed a literal interpretation of the Sermon by classifying it as law that had been abolished by Christ. See *DBWE* 10:359–78.

41. Ziegler draws attention to the christological character of the interpretations of the Sermon on the Mount offered by Bonhoeffer and his Reformed contemporary Eduard Thurneysen in "Not to Abolish."

42. *D* (*DBWE* 4), 111–12.

43. Ibid., 144.

hoeffer elaborates, "What is Christian depends on the 'extraordinary.' That is why Christians cannot conform to the world, because their concern is the περισσόν."[44] The περισσόν is "the way of self-denial, perfect love, perfect purity, perfect truthfulness, perfect nonviolence."[45] In short, "it is the love of Jesus Christ himself, who goes to the cross in suffering and obedience."[46] Like the cross of Christ, "which became outrageously visible in the complete darkness," so the extraordinary must become visible in the life of the community of disciples.[47]

Like the cross itself, which to the world seems to be the site of shame and debasement, but which the eyes of faith recognize as the coronation of the King of Glory, there is a dialectical quality to visibility of the community of the Crucified. The extraordinary character of the life of the disciple is hidden from the disciple herself, who acting in obedience to the call of her Lord, sees only Jesus. The true disciple of Jesus does not commit himself to the extraordinary for the sake of the extraordinary. If that were the case, the disciple would be no different from the enthusiast who acts for the sake of becoming visible and separating himself from others. "It is not the faith community which separates itself from others," Bonhoeffer warns those prone to enthusiastic tendencies. Lest he be misunderstood as advocating an accomodationist form of cultural Christianity, he goes on to insist that "this separation necessarily takes place in the call by the Word."[48] The call of Christ separates a small community of disciples from the world. This set apart community of disciples should "never invest their trust in numbers," for "the disciples are few and will always be only a few."[49] As they keep company with Jesus, the disciples discover that they have not been called to a position of private privilege. Rather, they have been appointed "coworkers and helpmates" of Christ, and as such are sent to the great mass of people upon whom Christ looks with compassion.[50] The disciples are sent out by Christ into the midst of an apocalyptic struggle, "participating in his power over the unclean spirits and the devil, who has taken hold of humanity."[51] It is Christ himself who is present in their midst, at work in and through them.

44. Ibid.
45. Ibid.
46. Ibid.
47. Ibid., 114.
48. Ibid., 175.
49. Ibid., 175–76. Richardson has observed that Bonhoeffer's notion of the church as minority has natural resonances with Hauerwas's ecclesiology. "*Sanctorum Communio*," 111.
50. D (*DBWE* 4), 198.
51. Ibid., 186.

Bonhoeffer elaborates upon the connection between the work of Christ and the work to which the disciples have been commissioned:

> The message and the effectiveness of the messengers are exactly the same as Jesus Christ's own message and work. They participate in his power. Jesus commands that they proclaim the coming of the kingdom of heaven, and he commands the signs which authenticate the message. Jesus commands them to heal the sick, cleanse the lepers, raise the dead, and cast out demons! Proclamation becomes an event, and the event gives witness to the proclamation. The kingdom of God, Jesus Christ, the forgiveness of sins, justification of the sinner by faith: all this is nothing other than the destruction of demonic power, healing, and raising the dead. As the word of the almighty God, it is deed, event, miracle. The *one* Jesus Christ goes out through the country in his twelve messengers and does his work. The royal grace with which the disciples are equipped is the creative and redemptive word of God.[52]

Lest those sent out in the power of Jesus Christ suffer from triumphalistic delusions, Bonhoeffer is quick to remind the reader that there are limits to the mission given to the disciples. The disciples are subject to the same constraints as the Word, whose "power is veiled in weakness."[53] The disciples cannot be strong where the Word is weak. Any attempt to force the Word upon the world results in the replacement of the living Word with a conquering idea and is ultimately nothing more than peddling cheap grace. Against such a Christendom mentality, Bonhoeffer reminds us, "For the Word, there are such things as hardened hearts and locked doors."[54] The disciples must not cast their pearls before swine, but rather must be willing, if necessary, to shake the dust from their feet and bear rejection with the Word.

Objections to Bonhoeffer's Construal of Discipleship

Bonhoeffer's attempt to recover an understanding of the church as a community of radical discipleship has not been without its share of controversy. Lingering over his impassioned reflections on discipleship and the monastic-like discipline of the Finkenwalde community itself is the question of whether Bonhoeffer had established a law of holiness or what has been

52. Ibid., 189.
53. Ibid., 173.
54. Ibid.

described as a "law of works."⁵⁵ When Karl Barth received Bonhoeffer's letter of September 19, 1936, informing him that the young seminary director was engaged in a work which took up the great questions of justification and sanctification, the towering Swiss theologian was not without his own concerns. Barth was particularly worried that Bonhoeffer's quest for concretion in this area could easily lead to a "return to the fleshpots of Egypt" and renewed captivity to the anthropological orientation of theological liberalism.⁵⁶ Barth discerned a common thread running amongst those who had criticized him on this score in the past, namely, "resignation over against the original christological and eschatological approach in favor of (in fact, increasingly abstract!) actualizations in a specifically human sphere."⁵⁷ Bonhoeffer shared Barth's concern about a misplaced longing for visibility, but he also realized that a Christianity which is not realized in the human sphere is a denial of the incarnation and that same christological-eschatological beginning which both men so deeply valued.⁵⁸ Later, Bonhoeffer himself, while incarcerated in Tegel prison, came to recognize the dangers lying latent within *Discipleship*. In a letter written to Bethge on the day following the failed coup attempt, Bonhoeffer reflects upon his own spiritual pilgrimage. Remembering a conversation he once had with the French pacifist pastor, Jean Lasserre, Bonhoeffer writes:

> We had simply asked ourselves what we really wanted to do with our lives. And he said, I want to become a saint (—and I think it's possible that he did become one). This impressed me very much at the time. Nevertheless, I disagreed with him, saying something like: I want to learn to have faith. For a long time I did not understand the depth of this antithesis. I thought I

---

55. Ott, *Reality and Faith*, 251. Gerhard Krause, a former Finkenwalde student, wrote to Bonhoeffer in February of 1939 to inform him of his decision to pursue legalized status in the Reich Church. He included in the letter the following theological appraisal of *Discipleship*, in particular, and of Bonhoeffer's theological position more generally: "I simply sense errors in the doctrine of justification [Rechtfertigungslehre] and even more errors in the doctrine of the church (esp. in the 'questions,' *Ev. Theol.* 36:10) that I otherwise know of only in Catholic theology" ("Letter of February 18, 1939," in *DBWE* 15:149). The "questions" Krause speaks of were Bonhoeffer's response to the controversy swirling around his paper "On the Question of Church Communion" in *DBWE* 14:689–97.

56. Barth, "Letter of October 14, 1936," in *DBWE* 14:267.

57. Ibid., 267.

58. Years later, in his own discussion of the doctrine of sanctification Barth would commend *Discipleship* as "easily the best that has been written on this subject." However, Barth would qualify his commendation by noting that he was not referring to all parts of *Discipleship*, but rather only to the opening sections: "The Call to Discipleship," "Simple Obedience," and "Discipleship and the Individual." *CD* 4/2:533.

myself could learn to have faith by trying to live something like a saintly life. I suppose I wrote *Discipleship* at the end of this path. Today I clearly see the dangers of that book, though I still stand by it.[59]

In the sentences which follow this quotation, Bonhoeffer expresses the concern that when read in a certain way, *Discipleship* could give the impression that the life of faith, which is discipleship, is about making something of oneself.[60] Bonhoeffer recognized that there is the danger his reflections upon discipleship could lead to the petrification of the living call of the risen Christ into an all-too-human ethical system or pietistic program. What is frequently overlooked in the above quotation, however, is Bonhoeffer's continuing affirmation of *Discipleship*.[61] In spite of these dangers, Bonhoeffer insists that he still stands by what he had written there. *Discipleship*, in Bonhoeffer's judgement, was a necessary protest against the comfortable cultural Christianity of the day that had transformed grace into an ideal. This cheap grace had become an unmerciful law unto itself with devastating consequences for the life and witness of the Protestant church in Germany. In this context, *Discipleship*, for all its dangers, was a risk that had to be taken. Even within the pages of *Discipleship* itself, Bonhoeffer seems aware of the danger of misconstruing the call to discipleship as a law of holiness. He constantly stresses that discipleship is not a self-chosen program for making something of oneself, but rather it is a *passio passiva*, in which disciples must be who they already are in Christ.[62] The disciples do not set out to separate or distinguish themselves from others; rather this occurs only through the call of Jesus Christ himself.[63] Bonhoeffer's treatment of the topic of the righteousness of the disciples makes clear that what he has in mind is no law of holiness:

> Disciples live completely out of the bond connecting them with Jesus Christ. Their righteousness depends only on that bond and never apart from it. Therefore, it can never become a standard

---

59. *LPP* (*DBWE* 8), 485–86.

60. Ibid., 486.

61. For a recent example of a reading of the letter which overlooks the significance of Bonhoeffer's continuing affirmation of *Discipleship*, see Marsh, *Strange Glory*, 375. Moberly suggests, rightly I believe, that Bonhoeffer's comment may be read as a caveat, but certainly not as a retraction of *Discipleship*. *Virtue of Bonhoeffer's Ethics*, Loc. 3778. Nation et al., similarly propose that these comments are best understood as a "correction" and not a "repudiation" of the argument of Discipleship. *Bonhoeffer the Assassin?*, 177.

62. *D* (*DBWE* 4), 89, 113.

63. Ibid., 175.

which the disciples would own and might use in any way they please. What makes them disciples is not a new standard for their lives, but Jesus Christ alone, the mediator and Son of God himself. The disciples' own righteousness is thus hidden from them in their communion with Jesus. They can no longer see, observe, and judge themselves; they only see Jesus and are seen, judged, and justified by grace by Jesus alone.[64]

Spiritual disciplines, like the ones advocated in *Life Together*, are always vulnerable to being construed in legalistic terms. However, when they are located within a dynamic understanding of the life of discipleship rooted in the gracious command of the living Lord Jesus Christ, they are properly understood as a means of grace. Bonhoeffer explains, "Because consideration of the Scriptures, prayer, and intercession involve a service that is our duty, and because the grace of God can be found in this service, we should train ourselves to set a regular time during the day for them, just as we do for every other service we perform. That is not 'legalism,' but discipline and faithfulness."[65] A disciplined approach to meditating upon the Scriptures, prayer and intercession, is not a human attempt to get God in hand, but rather is part of the all-encompassing response of those who have heard the call to discipleship and take God at his word.

The Church in the Economy of Salvation

Whereas Bonhoeffer's treatment of the theme of discipleship in the Synoptic Gospels, which occupies the first part of *Discipleship*, has generated great interest and excitement in many quarters over the years, his discussion of "The Church of Jesus Christ and Discipleship" in Part Two has been largely overlooked. On occasion, it has even been met with open disdain. Hanfried Müller failed to understand the connection between the two parts of the book. In his opinion, *Discipleship* fell apart into two pieces.[66] Others, according to the characterization of Ernst Feil, have considered the second part of *Discipleship* to be "a distortion, caused by inadmissible sacramentalizing" and/or "a withdrawing of the statement made in the first part."[67] What both the objectors and over-lookers fail to recognize is that the catholic ecclesiology of the second part of *Discipleship* is the necessary

---

64. Ibid., 170.
65. *LT* (*DBWE* 5), 91.
66. Kuske and Tödt, editors' afterword to *D* (*DBWE* 4), 311, referring to Müller, *Von der Kirche zur Welt*, 230–44.
67. Feil, *Theology of Dietrich Bonhoeffer*, 81.

correlate to the theology of discipleship presented in the first part. Without the ecclesiology of the second part, discipleship must either be dismissed as historically irrelevant (after all, Jesus is not physically walking the streets of Galilee today calling people to follow him), or reduced to a matter of casting oneself in the role of a particular biblical character who is encountered by Christ and attempting to imitate them (but the question then arises whether one should see oneself, for example, as Levi whom Jesus called to leave everything or the paralytic to whom he extended forgiveness). Within the writings of the apostle Paul and his testimony to the presence of the risen Christ in the church, Bonhoeffer finds the resources to address these questions. If one wishes to hear Jesus's call to discipleship, one must look for Christ where he has promised to be present, namely in the preaching and sacraments of the church.[68] The first disciples had to leave everything in order to be in the company of Jesus, but now, following the resurrection and ascension, "through word and sacrament, the body of Christ is no longer confined to a single geographical location."[69] Bonhoeffer's bringing together of the Christ of Paul with the Jesus of the Synoptic Gospels is necessary, on the one hand, for displaying the continuing relevance of the theme of discipleship, and on the other, for combating a pseudo-Lutheran reading of Paul prevalent in Bonhoeffer's day which dismissed discipleship as a type of works-righteousness standing in opposition to the central article of justification by faith. Bonhoeffer makes the connection by insisting that "what the Synoptics describe as hearing and following the call to discipleship, Paul expresses with the concept of *baptism*."[70] Baptism marks an apocalyptic break in which "Christ invades the realm of Satan and lays hold of those who belong to him, thereby creating his church-community [Gemeinde]."[71] This break with the world is accomplished through "the grace-filled death of baptism," through which the sinner is put to death in community with the death of Christ upon the cross.[72] This means that "the death of baptism means *justification away from sin*" and not merely justification in sin.[73] The gift of death received in baptism, is equivalent in content to Jesus's calling of his disciples in the Synoptic Gospels into the community of his cross.[74]

---

68. D (*DBWE* 4), 202.
69. Ibid., 238.
70. Ibid., 207.
71. Ibid.
72. Ibid., 208.
73. Ibid., 209.
74. Ibid.

Having established this connection between the Synoptic Gospels and the writings of Paul, Bonhoeffer is now free to employ the writings of the apostle in presenting his ecclesiological portrait. The ecclesiology which emerges from the pages of the second part of *Discipleship* proves to be heavily reliant upon the insights of Bonhoeffer's academic dissertations, but shorn of their cumbersome, and at times problematic, philosophical vocabulary. Salvation for Bonhoeffer is found in bodily community with Christ.[75] In his body, Jesus Christ has borne the sinful flesh of all humanity and therefore his body has become the site of humanity's acceptance by God. As the one who bears all of humanity into death and also into resurrection, Jesus Christ is "both an individual self and the new humanity."[76] Bonhoeffer explains:

> The body of Jesus Christ is identical with the new humanity which he has assumed. The body of Christ is his church-community [Gemeinde]. Jesus Christ at the same time is himself and his church-community (1 Cor. 12:12). Since Pentecost Jesus Christ lives here on earth in the form of his body, the church-community. Here is his body crucified and risen, here is the humanity he assumed. To be baptized therefore means to become a member of the church-community, a member of the body of Christ (Gal. 3:28; 1 Cor. 12:13). To be in Christ means to be in the church-community. But if we are in the church-community, then we are also truly and bodily in Jesus Christ. This insight reveals the full richness of meaning contained in the concept of the body of Christ.[77]

In the preceding paragraph, many of the themes from Bonhoeffer's earlier ecclesiological writings are represented in condensed form. There is an allusion to the concept of Christ as collective person first articulated in *Sanctorum Communio* and the accompanying axiom "Christ existing as church-community."[78] The identification of the church as the presence of Christ's body on earth between the time of Pentecost and the *parousia* indicates that the church must itself be understood as a form of revelation.[79] This has epistemological implications, for if the church is a reality of revelation,

---

75. Ibid., 214.
76. Ibid., 215.
77. Ibid., 217–18.
78. E.g., *SC* (*DBWE* 1), 121, 140, 192, 214, 260.
79. Ibid., 141. This understanding of the church as revelation is prevalent throughout Bonhoeffer's academic dissertations and is expressed with particular clarity and forcefulness in the following quotation from *Act and Being*: "The community of faith is God's final revelation as 'Christ existing as community [Gemeinde],' ordained for the end time of the world until the return of Christ" (*AB* (*DBWE* 2), 112).

then it is a reality that can only be grasped in faith.[80] The reality of the church is not deducible from empirical observation, for God's revelation in the church remains concealed under the veil of historical ambiguity, just as during his earthly ministry the Son of God remained incognito under the veil of sinful flesh. It is only as one is taken up in Christ into the existence of the new humanity of the church-community that the true reality of the church becomes apparent. Being in the church is the presupposition for faith and the being of the church is known only in faith.[81] It is for this reason that Bonhoeffer can assert as he does above that "to be in Christ means to be in the church-community."[82]

By insisting that "there is no community with Jesus Christ other than the community with his body," Bonhoeffer sounds a strong note against the gnostic and docetic tendencies which seem to continually lap at the church.[83] It is through the sacraments that we come to participate in the community of the body of Christ. "The sacraments," Bonhoeffer writes, "have their origin and goal in the body of Christ. Sacraments exist only because there is a body of Christ."[84] The sacrament of baptism "makes us members of the body of Christ," while the Lord's Supper "keeps us in this community (κοινωνία) with Christ's body."[85] This emphasis upon bodily community with Christ also counters the rampant individualism which frequently accompanies a gnostic outlook, for it allows Bonhoeffer to assert that "the new human being is not the single individual who has been justified and sanctified; rather, the new human being is the church-community, the body of Christ, or Christ himself."[86]

Outside of the church-community, which is the new human being, there is only the old Adam—the internally divided, infinitely fragmented human being, who exists in a state of perpetual turning inward upon himself (*cor curvum in se*).[87] In Adam, "human beings live without truly being human," no longer able to conform to the image of God.[88] However, in Jesus Christ, God has conformed to the human image, creating anew the

---

80. SC (*DBWE* 1), 127.

81. AB (*DBWE* 2), 117–18.

82. D (*DBWE* 4), 218. This resonates with his earlier assertion in *Sanctorum Communio* that "*there is no relation to Christ in which the relation to the church is not necessarily established as well*" (SC (*DBWE* 1), 127; italics original).

83. D (*DBWE* 4), 216.

84. Ibid.

85. Ibid.

86. Ibid., 219.

87. Ibid., 218; AB (*DBWE* 2), 137.

88. D (*DBWE* 4), 282.

divine image upon the face of the earth. From now on, to be truly human means to be conformed to the One who became human.[89] This happens in the church, not as individuals strive to realize some type of ideal, but as the living Christ forms his people into his own image as "the *incarnate, crucified*, and the *transfigured one*."[90] This interest in the concept of conformation continues into *Ethics*, where Bonhoeffer writes, "*The church is the place where Jesus Christ's taking form is proclaimed and where it happens.*"[91] This implies that the church is not merely an instrument or accessory necessary for announcing the good news, but is in fact intrinsic to the Gospel itself. The church is the site where Christ takes form in the world.[92] As Bonhoeffer stresses repeatedly throughout *Sanctorum Communio*, "the *church is both a means to an end and at the same time an end in itself.*"[93] The church is a means to an end in that the entirety of its corporate life is "oriented toward effectively proclaiming Christ to all the world";[94] however, as it participates in the new humanity of Christ's being-for-others, "the goal of the divine mandate of proclamation and the beginning of its fulfillment has already been reached."[95] Just as the person and work of Christ are inseparable for Bonhoeffer, so too are the identity and mission of the church.

As the body of Christ, the church takes up visible space on earth. The visibility of the church is a consequence of the incarnation of Christ and is the result of the work of the Holy Spirit. Bonhoeffer's intense christological concentration sometimes leads readers to overlook the important place of the Holy Spirit in his theology.[96] Although Bonhoeffer's pneumatology remains materially underdeveloped, it is important to recognize that for Bonhoeffer the church arises at the nexus of Christology *and* pneumatology.[97] Since his doctoral dissertation, Bonhoeffer was of the view that the Holy Spirit actualizes in time within the church-community the reconcili-

---

89. *E* (*DBWE* 6), 94.

90. *D* (*DBWE* 4), 285.

91. *E* (*DBWE* 6), 102.

92. Contra Phillips' bizarre claim that Bonhoeffer utilizes the terminology of "formation" and "conformation" to free his Christology from his ecclesiology. *Christ for Us*, 137.

93. *SC* (*DBWE* 1), 261. See also 141, 176, 190.

94. *E* (*DBWE* 6), 404.

95. Ibid., 404.

96. For an investigation of the place of the Holy Spirit in Bonhoeffer's theology of discipleship, see Kelly and Nelson, *Cost of Moral Leadership*, 51–82.

97. Among those who have remarked upon the implicit pneumatology which is operative at the center of Bonhoeffer's theology are Ford, "Bonhoeffer, Holiness, and Ethics," 368; and Badcock, *House Where God Lives*, 183.

ation between God and humanity and between human beings themselves that Jesus Christ has realized for all eternity in his body on the cross.[98] The intersection of Christology and pneumatology in ecclesiology is most apparent in Bonhoeffer's discussion of "The Visible Church-Community" in *Discipleship* and his Finkenwalde lecture on the "Visible Church in the New Testament."[99] Just as Christ in becoming human took up space among us, it must be understood that "the body of the exalted Lord is likewise a visible body, taking the form of the church-community."[100] Wherever the attempt is made to separate the essence of the church from the appearance of the church, there "one surrenders faith in Christ, the one who became flesh."[101] Bonhoeffer also sounds the corresponding pneumatological warning, writing, "Wherever the church withdraws into invisibility, it is in fact scorning the reality of the Spirit."[102] The church, as the body of Christ, is the special visibility of the Holy Spirit. The coming of the Holy Spirit marks the dawning of the new creation. Bonhoeffer draws a helpful parallel between God's original creation of the world and the new creation of the church: "As little as the first creation was a 'religious' matter, being rather the reality of God, so also the second creation of God through Christ in the Holy Spirit."[103] In light of this, baptism must not be thought of as a quaint religious rite which grants one access to Sunday morning religious observances, but rather as the passing through the primeval waters of the new creation through which a new people is brought into being—a people whose life together is entirely reconfigured around the living reality of God-for-us in Jesus Christ.

The visibility of the church-community cannot be limited to its liturgical gatherings. Living bodies require order and differentiation. Bonhoeffer observes, "A body lacking in differentiation is in the process of decomposition."[104] In this, the body of Christ is no different; it is an ordered and differentiated community which receives both offices and gifts for those offices from the Holy Spirit.[105] In addition to the ordering of the church-community, the body of Christ also becomes visible in the life of its

---

98. *SC* (*DBWE* 1), 139, 157–61. See also *DBWE* 14:455–56.
99. *D* (*DBWE* 4), 225–52; *DBWE* 14:434–76.
100. *D* (*DBWE* 4), 226.
101. *DBWE* 14:463; *D* (*DBWE* 4), 229–30.
102. *DBWE* 14:439.
103. *DBWE* 14:442–43.
104. *D* (*DBWE* 4), 229.
105. Reflecting his own experience of the Nazi state's attempt to interfere in church politics and practices, Bonhoeffer emphatically insists that "any tampering with the church's order from the outside is an infringement on the visible form of Christ's body itself" (ibid., 231).

members in the world. Because the Son of God wholly and truly became a human being, Christ's claim upon the human being embraces the entirety of life.[106] Christians live out their daily lives in the world as members of the body of Christ. Disciples will encounter definite limits as they attempt to live out their secular vocation; some professions are simply "incompatible with being a member of the Christian community."[107] In addition, there will be occasions when the concrete situation in the workforce requires Christians to make a public confession of faith in Christ, which may result in dismissal from their jobs. For the sake of the body of Christ—the incarnate Christ and his church-community—Christians are to remain in the world "in order to engage the world in a frontal assault."[108] The church is the visible contradiction of the world from within the world for the sake of the world, so that the world may know that it is loved and reconciled by God.[109] As it engages the world in this way, "the visible church-community will always more closely assume the form of its suffering Lord."[110]

This interest in distinguishing the visible church-community from the world is a reflection of Bonhoeffer's interest in retrieving the theological categories of sanctification and holiness for church life. In the mainstream Protestantism of Bonhoeffer's day sanctification had been largely eclipsed by the doctrine of justification. Meanwhile, in the pietistic tradition, where some memory of sanctification lived on, holiness had been relegated to the realm of personal interiority. Sanctification, for Bonhoeffer, is a public reality whose foundation is located in God's desire to have a peculiar people unto Himself. "Sanctification," Bonhoeffer writes, "is the fulfillment of the will of God, who says: 'You shall be holy, for I am holy,' and 'I, the Lord, I who sanctify you, am holy.'"[111] Bonhoeffer notes that Christians in the New Testament are referred to as "the saints" and never as "the just," for the latter "is not equally capable of describing the full content of the gift received."[112] Christians are not only justified freely through Christ, they also receive from him the gift of sanctification. The two gifts are distinguishable, but inseparable. Bonhoeffer elaborates, "Whereas, in justification, believers are being included in the community with Jesus Christ through Christ's death that took place once for all, sanctification, on the other hand preserves

---

106. *DBWE* 14:471.
107. *D* (*DBWE* 4), 246.
108. Ibid., 244.
109. *E* (*DBWE* 6), 63.
110. *D* (*DBWE* 4), 248.
111. Ibid., 260. The internal biblical references are to Lev 19:2 and 21:8.
112. *D* (*DBWE* 4), 259.

them in the sphere into which they have been placed."¹¹³ This preservation is accomplished through the seal of the Holy Spirit. The church will always find this seal under attack from without and within. In its struggle with the world without, the church must resist the world's desire to be the church. This resistance is necessarily political in form, not in the sense of the church becoming another lobby-group within the political apparatus of the nation-state, but rather in the realization of the political character of the embodied life of the church-community itself. Bonhoeffer elaborates:

> Since the church-community is the city on the hill, the "polis" (Matt. 5:14), established on this earth by God and marked with a seal as God's own, its "political" character is an inseparable aspect of its sanctification. The "political ethics" of the church-community is grounded solely in its sanctification, the goal of which is that world be world and community be community, and that, nevertheless God's word goes out from the church-community to all the world, as the proclamation that the earth and all it contains is the Lord's. That is the "political" character of the church-community.¹¹⁴

Church politics will also necessarily entail the struggle for personal sanctification out of the recognition that "in the midst of the church-community there still lives a piece of the world within this sacred realm."¹¹⁵ In its struggle with the world within, the church must resist its own desire to become the world. As the saints of God, Christians have been liberated from the power of sin and live from the memory that they have been crucified with Christ; "through dying daily under this cross, their thinking, speaking, and their bodies are being sanctified."¹¹⁶ If it is to preserve the seal of its sanctification and avoid becoming a peddler of cheap grace, the church must relearn the importance of exercising the power of the keys through naming and retaining specific sins. The flesh must be put to death through the practice of private confession to another Christian and unrepentant sinners must be held accountable through the practice of church discipline. In fact, as Bonhoeffer maintains, "the whole life of the church-community

---

113. Ibid., 259.

114. Ibid., 261–62. Bonhoeffer also refers to the church as a *polis* in a letter to Erwin Sutz during the Finkenwalde period. In the letter, Bonhoeffer warns that if the Confessing Church were to go the way of the Oxford Movement then "the price we pay is that we are no longer a church, that is, [that] *we are no longer a polis*, and that means we can no longer preach the gospel of the polis" (*DBWE* 14:272).

115. *D* (*DBWE* 4), 262.

116. Ibid., 269.

is permeated by discipline."[117] The disciplined life of the community in its struggle with the world and the flesh is "directed toward being able to stand firm on the day of Jesus Christ."[118] On that day the Lord will bring to completion the good work he has begun in his church-community and the sanctification which, to this point, has been hidden from the eyes of the disciples will become plain.

Bonhoeffer's Ecclesiological Criticism of Barth

Bonhoeffer's understanding of the place of the church in the economy of salvation signifies his divergence from his theological mentor, Karl Barth. Within his doctrine of reconciliation, Barth ventures the following three statements: "1. the world would be lost without Jesus Christ and His Word and work; 2. the world would not necessarily be lost if there were no Church; and 3. the Church would be lost if it had no counterpart in the world."[119] Bonhoeffer would stand in strong solidarity with Barth with respect to the first and third statements, but as we have seen from our exploration of Bonhoeffer's understanding of the church in the economy of salvation, he would surely be uneasy with Barth's second statement. For Bonhoeffer, Cyprian's dictum *extra ecclesiam nulla salus* rings true.[120] This was most explicitly expressed in the context of the Church Struggle when Bonhoeffer published his controversial remark: "Whoever knowingly separates himself from the Confessing Church in Germany separates himself from salvation."[121] In the statement, "the world would not necessarily be lost if there were no Church," Bonhoeffer would likely have understood Barth to be returning to a formalistic understanding of the freedom of God similar to the one that characterized Barth's earlier dialectical period, which Bonhoeffer had criticized in *Act and Being*.[122] As was discussed in the previous chapter, Bonhoeffer insisted that the aseity of God must be understood in terms of the promeity of God in Jesus Christ. God's freedom is not a formal abstrac-

---

117. Ibid., 271.
118. Ibid., 276.
119. *CD* 4/3.2:826.

120. *DBWE* 11:310. Bender has drawn attention to the fact that Barth does at earlier places speak positively of *extra ecclesiam nulla salus* (*CD* 4/2:620–622; cf. *CD* 4/1:725–39; also *CD* 1/2:211, 215, 217, 220), noting, however, that all these references should be considered in light of Barth's assertion that "the intention behind this dictum is better expressed by saying '*Extra Christum nulla salus*' (*CD* IV.1, 688)" (*Karl Barth's Christological Ecclesiology*, 245 n. 32).

121. *DBWE* 14:675.
122. *AB* (*DBWE* 2), 90–91.

tion, but rather is the concrete reality of his freedom for us in the person of Jesus Christ present in the church-community. With this in mind, Bonhoeffer could only look upon the statement "the world would not necessarily be lost if there were no Church" as a dangerous flight into speculative fancy which moves beyond the concrete reality given in the economy of salvation and threatens to obscure, in docetic fashion, the truth of the incarnation. Of course, Karl Barth was no docetist, as Bonhoeffer himself acknowledged, but he did recognize the potential for Barth's theology to be misinterpreted in an idealistic-docetic direction.[123]

These concerns may also have something to do with the enigmatic charge of "positivism of revelation" that Bonhoeffer famously raised against Barth within the context of his prison correspondence with Eberhard Bethge.[124] In the present context, I cannot hope to provide an exhaustive examination of the charge "positivism of revelation."[125] Instead, I will attempt to make some connections that are of particular relevance to the ecclesiological discussion at hand. As several scholars have noted, the charge of "positivism of revelation" frequently occurs in close connection with Bonhoeffer's own references to recovering the "arcane discipline" [*Arkandisziplin*].[126] Unfortunately, there is almost as little scholarly consensus surrounding Bonhoeffer's understanding of the "arcane discipline" in the prison letters as there is around "positivism of revelation." Bonhoeffer's interest in the *Arcanum* appears to go back to at least 1932, where in his lectures on "The Nature of the Church" he insisted that the Christian confession of faith belongs to the mysteries that are shared by the gathered congregation and must not be confused with propaganda which can be used

---

123. *DBWE* 14:435–36. This observation occurs in the context of Bonhoeffer's discussion of the twin dangers facing the church within the context of the church's conflict with the state—an idealistic-docetic ecclesiology and a materialistic-secular or magical-sacramental ecclesiology. Bonhoeffer goes on to wryly note, "The first derives from a misunderstanding of Barthian theology, the second from correctly understanding Dibelius's theology."

124. *LPP* (*DBWE* 8), 364, 373, 429.

125. It should be noted that the charge of "positivism" appears to have been one of Bonhoeffer's favorites, which he threw around with playful, and perhaps reckless, abandon. See Wolf-Dieter Zimmerman's account of his time with Bonhoeffer in London in *I Knew Dietrich Bonhoeffer*, 78. Unfortunately, as Pangritz has observed, many who have latched on over the years to Bonhoeffer's assessment of "positivism of revelation" have been "motivated by anti-Barthian prejudice rather than by a thorough reading of Bonhoeffer's writings" (*Karl Barth*, 245). The result being that rather than thinking with Bonhoeffer beyond Barth, they have returned to sailing within the channels of liberal theology which both Barth and Bonhoeffer had left behind.

126. Ott, *Reality and Faith*, 122; Pangritz, *Karl Barth*, 5. Some older translations of Bonhoeffer's work referred to *Arkandisziplin* as the "discipline of the secret."

as a weapon against the godless.[127] The "arcane discipline" continued to fascinate Bonhoeffer throughout his time as leader of the Confessing Church seminary at Finkenwalde. In his homiletics lectures from that period, Bonhoeffer attributes the origins of the "arcane discipline" to the time of Origen, when congregations began to dismiss the catechumens and unbelievers before receiving the sacraments, reciting the confession of faith, and praying the Lord's Prayer in their own private gathering. "This closed meeting," Bonhoeffer writes, "was begun to provide protection for the church against the mockery of the world."[128] This theme recurs in *Discipleship* where the "arcane discipline" is alluded to in contrast with the "cheap grace" of cultural Protestantism, which is metaphorically described as throwing bread to the dogs and casting pearls before swine.[129] In light of the events which Bonhoeffer had witnessed in the early to mid-1930s—including the rise of the German Christians and the ensuing Church Struggle, the adoption of the Aryan paragraph, and the Brown Synod—it is not surprising that Bonhoeffer would be concerned with protecting the mysteries of the church against profanation.[130] However, in the context of the prison letters his primary concern in referring to the "arcane discipline" does not seem to be protecting against profanation, but rather to preserve the existential character of the Christian life. Bonhoeffer seemed to fear that a "positivism of revelation" that treated revelation as axiomatic for the derivation of a theological system risked betraying the ever-deepening immersion in the mystery of God which properly characterizes Christian existence. This "positivism of revelation" which seems to be overly determined by its negative reaction to liberal theology, not only leaves the world to its own devices by refusing to engage with its questions, it also threatens to become an oppressive "law of faith."[131] The "arcane discipline" stands against this tendency as a reminder that in the life of faith and personal theological understanding there are "degrees of cognition and degrees of significance."[132] Adding fuel to the fire was Bonhoeffer's perception that Barth's "positivism of revelation" had morphed into a form of conservative restoration within the Confessing

127. *DBWE* 11:315 n. 331.

128. *WP*, 99.

129. *D* (*DBWE* 4), 45, 172.

130. Pugh rightly observes that "these boundaries were not to be protected because of a desire for personal piety, or the religious path of withdrawal from the world, rather the mysteries of the church were to be guarded and protected lest they become reduced to something that does not bear the power of God in the world" (*Religionless Christianity*, 146).

131. *LPP* (*DBWE* 8), 373.

132. Ibid., 373.

Church which could be characterized as possessing "an 'objective' interest in Christianity," but including "little personal faith in Christ."[133] For Bonhoeffer, the "arcane discipline" prevents the Christian faith from becoming a conquering ideology, by standing as concrete evidence that the Christian faith is not a system of beliefs to be mastered, but a life to be lived in the presence of Jesus Christ.[134] This life takes the form of a pilgrimage leading ever further into the mystery of the Triune God.[135] As David Ford has observed, this mystery or secret "cannot simply be known as a fact, a positivist datum. Being conformed to it (language Bonhoeffer uses in the *Ethics*) is intrinsic to knowing it truly."[136]

Kathryn Tanner has drawn attention to how "the category of revelation becomes the overarching rubric for all that Christ does" in the early volumes of Barth's *Church Dogmatics*.[137] This trend, which has characterized modern theology, tends to push an understanding of Christ's work in a subjectivist direction. In order to de-emphasize the importance of the human reception of revelation and preserve the aseity of God, Barth makes a secondary move in which "Jesus has to do with the objective pole of revelation; the Holy Spirit with the subjective pole of human apprehension."[138] In making such a move, Barth "short-circuits" the work of the Holy Spirit in the divine economy, by reducing the Spirit's work to the noetic dimension of enlightening individuals to the reality of revelation in Jesus Christ.[139] Bonhoeffer, as we have seen, has a more robust conception of the work of the Holy Spirit, which includes the recognition from his doctoral dissertation onwards that the work of the Holy Spirit is a distinct sociology known as church. Furthermore, Bonhoeffer and Barth seem to have different con-

---

133. Ibid., 500.

134. Hence Ford's contention that Bonhoeffer views Barth as failing to do justice to the priority of the vocative in the life of the worshipping self. *Self and Salvation*, 257 n. 41.

135. Floyd offers the intriguing suggestion that "Bonhoeffer's writing can best be encountered as the 'spirituality' of the 'pastor' as much as the 'theology' of the 'professor.' That is to say, he is as concerned to articulate a 'pastoral' theology of vocation as to state any systematic 'answers' to the mysteries of faith. He is best understood as himself a perpetual pilgrim—for whom being a Christian was a *task* rather than an *accomplishment*—who as a theologian longed to provide that grammar of faith capable of putting into play all the grand voices of the theological greats before him—and more importantly, capable of giving voice to the transformative capacity of the gospel to remake life anew" ("Dietrich Bonhoeffer," 56).

136. Ford, *Self and Salvation*, 263.

137. Tanner, "Jesus Christ," 264.

138. Ibid., 267.

139. Mangina, "Bearing the Marks," 270.

ceptions of the knowing self and its knowledge of God. John Godsey, who wrote a dissertation on Bonhoeffer under the direction of Barth, attempts to elucidate the difference in the following quotation:

> Knowledge of God for Bonhoeffer, because of its foundation in Christ, could not be gained apart from immersion in the joys and sufferings of everyday existence, which is where one meets Christ in the other. Knowledge of God for Barth involves cognitive acknowledgment of a *fait accompli*, namely, the predetermination of human destiny in the works and ways of the same Christ.[140]

There is a sense in which Barth's knowing subject seems to reflect a much more modern Kantian understanding of the self, than does the knowing subject of Bonhoeffer's writings. Bonhoeffer's epistemology seems to more closely resemble that of the desert fathers, the Church fathers, and the people of Old Testament Israel, all of whom equated knowledge of God in some way with the transformation of the self, stemming from participation in the reality of God.[141] In a representative quotation from *Act and Being*, Bonhoeffer asserts, "It is in being known by God that human beings know God. But to be known by God means to become a new person."[142] To summarize, for Bonhoeffer, to know Christ is to be taken up into the messianic event so that one finds oneself in Christ, that is within the community that, through the work of the Holy Spirit, is being conformed to the form of the incarnate, crucified, and risen Jesus Christ.

Practicing the Presence of Christ: *Life Together*

The book emerging from and reflecting upon the experiment in Christian communal living at Finkenwalde, *Life Together*, could be considered as Bonhoeffer's antidote to the "positivism of revelation" and conservative restorationism which he perceived to be infecting the Confessing Church. *Life Together* was written over a span of four weeks in September and October of 1938, one year after the closing of the seminary at Finkenwalde by the Gestapo. The book appears to have been of special importance to Bonhoeffer, as evidenced not only by the intensive single-minded effort he

---

140. Godsey, "Barth and Bonhoeffer," 25.

141. Northcott has drawn attention to the similarity between the spirituality of the desert fathers and their conceptions of human interiority and those of Dietrich Bonhoeffer in "'Who Am I?,'" 25–7.

142. *AB* (*DBWE* 2), 134.

put into writing it, but also in the recollections of Bonhoeffer's fiancé Maria von Wedemeyer. Wedemeyer recalls that when she admitted to Bonhoeffer that she was struggling to work her way through his books, he "claimed that the only one of concern to him at that moment was *Life Together*, and he preferred that I wait until he was around to read it."[143]

Life Together is a constructive theological proposal intended to stimulate a conversation about the shape of the life of the church in an increasingly post-Christendom context. Bonhoeffer makes his intentions quite clear in his preface to *Life Together* where he remarks, "We are not dealing with a concern of some private circles but with a mission entrusted to the church."[144] The opening pages of *Life Together* make clear that this mission is not a retreat from the world into the friendly and comfortable confines of "the seclusion of a cloistered life," but rather it involves the practice of authentic Christian community within the world "in the midst of enemies."[145] *Life Together* is concerned with the question of the spiritual formation of the people of God under the conditions of diaspora, so that they may be "the seed of the kingdom of God in all the world."[146]

Bonhoeffer's conception of Christian community can be summarized as "life together under the Word," for it is the presence of the person of Jesus Christ which distinguishes Christian community from all other types of community.[147] This means that the Christian community is not founded upon common piety, shared spiritual experiences, Church growth methods, or evangelistic techniques rooted in emotional manipulation.[148] Nor is it founded upon "emotion fired by aggressive and exclusionist objectives," like that which underlay the Nazi attempts to form *Volksgemeinschaft* (national community).[149] True Christian community is a spiritual or pneumatic reality whose basis is the truth of the Word of God in Jesus Christ. This Word always comes to us from the outside (*extra nos*), but God has graciously put the Word in the mouth of human beings. For this reason Christians need fellow believers to speak God's Word to them; they recognize that "the Christ in their own hearts is weaker than the Christ in the word of other

---

143. Wedemeyer-Weller, "Other Letters," 416.

144. *LT* (*DBWE* 5), 25.

145. Ibid., 27.

146. Ibid., 28.

147. Ibid., 27.

148. These are simply aspects of what Bonhoeffer calls "psychic" reality—the self-centered existence of fallen humanity. *LT* (*DBWE* 5), 38–41. It is interesting to note the resonances between Bonhoeffer's description of "psychic" reality in *Life Together* and his later discussion of "religion" in *Letters and Papers from Prison*.

149. Moses, *Reluctant Revolutionary*, 137.

Christians."[150] Bonhoeffer's emphasis upon the *extra nos* and the "alien righteousness" which comes to the community places him squarely within the Lutheran tradition, as does, in a different way, his assertion that "Christian community is not an ideal we have to realize, but rather a reality created by God in Christ in which we may participate."[151]

The Christian community which shares life together under the Word is a liturgically ordered community. The form that this worship takes will vary according to the composition and needs of the community, but in all contexts it will include: "the *word of Scripture, the hymns of the church, and the prayer of the community.*"[152] With regards to the latter, Bonhoeffer sought to recover a practice that was very important to him in his personal devotional life, namely, the liturgical practice of praying the psalms.[153] Bonhoeffer understood the Psalter to be "the great school of prayer."[154] Through praying the Psalter, Christians learn that prayer is nothing less than participation through the Holy Spirit in the prayer of Jesus Christ who intercedes for humanity before the throne of the Father.[155] Just as Christians must learn to pray through participating in the prayer of Christ in praying the Psalter, they must also learn the Scriptures, so that they may discover their lives have been taken up in the saving story of Jesus Christ.[156] Between the corporate services of worship which bookend the day, the community shares in table fellowship with one another and the risen Lord. In each meal that is shared, Christians are bound to one another and to their Lord as "they recognize their Lord as the true giver of all good gifts," and also as "the true gift, the true bread of life itself, and finally as the one who calls them to joyful banquet in the reign of God."[157]

The shared life in community stands in a dialectical relationship with the individual member's life of solitude.[158] This is reflected in Bonhoeffer's

---

150. LT (DBWE 5), 32.

151. Ibid., 38.

152. Ibid., 52–53.

153. In a letter of May 15, 1943, sent from prison to his parents, Bonhoeffer writes, "I am also still reading the Psalms daily as I have done for years. There is no other book that I know and love as much" (LPP (DBWE 8), 81).

154. LT (DBWE 5), 55.

155. Ibid., 55–57.

156. Ibid., 62.

157. Ibid., 73.

158. As Bonhoeffer stressed in *Discipleship*, the call of the Mediator both separates the disciple from the masses and the crowds, making the disciple into a genuine individual *and* engrafts the disciple into a new community. See the chapter entitled, "Discipleship and the Individual" in D (DBWE 4), 92–99.

famous aphorism: "Whoever cannot be alone should beware of community. Whoever cannot stand being in community should beware of being alone."[159] While the life of the community is characterized by speech, the Christian individual's life of solitude is marked by silence.[160] Silence, for Bonhoeffer, is always for the sake of the Word.[161] Bonhoeffer insists that every Christian should observe a daily period of time alone for the purpose of meditation upon the Scriptures, prayer and intercession.[162] Whereas the communal reading of the Bible will consist of relatively large chunks of Scripture, the time of personal meditation will focus upon a particular verse or even within that upon a single word or phrase with the hope of hearing "God's Word for me personally."[163] Reflecting his overarching theological concerns, Bonhoeffer insists that intercessory prayer must engage with the concrete demands of life within the community paying heed to the particular needs and struggles of specific individuals.[164] In addition to the daily period of meditation, most Christians will find themselves alone for many hours at work in the world. This time of work and service in the world will reveal whether the Christian's life in community and time of meditation has been merely a subtle evasion of the world through clothing oneself in religious garments, or whether it has allowed them to enter more deeply into the reality of the world reconciled in Jesus Christ.[165]

As we have just seen, the life of the community which lives together under the Word is oriented towards God in worship. This vertical axis of the community's life is complemented by the horizontal axis of the shared communal life of the Christian community's members which takes the form of mutual service. Just as we saw in the previous chapter that the vertical and horizontal dimensions of Bonhoeffer's Christology cannot be abstracted from one another, in the same way, within the life of the community worship and mutual service go hand in hand. The life of a community which lives by the grace of God will take the form of service.[166]

159. *LT (DBWE* 5), 83.

160. Ibid.

161. Ibid., 85.

162. Ibid., 86.

163. Ibid., 87. This spiritual discipline helped to sustain Bonhoeffer throughout his long internment in prison, as is evidenced by the frequent references to the *Daily Texts* scattered throughout his prison correspondence. E.g., *LPP (DBWE* 8) 139, 239, 241, 264, 292, 326, 342, 378, 400, 422, 485, 511, 514.

164. *LT (DBWE* 5), 91.

165. Ibid., 92.

166. This had been a central point for Bonhoeffer since his doctoral dissertation where he characterized the church as a community which through the vicarious

Bonhoeffer highlights four particular ways that the life of service will manifest itself within the community: 1) listening to others, 2) active helpfulness, 3) bearing with others in their freedom and in their sin, and 4) the proclamation of the free word between individuals.[167] The first three forms of service prepare the way for the fourth and ensure that the service of the Word does not become oppressive. The free word shared between friends is the starting place for church discipline. It is here that words of fraternal correction can first be risked, and indeed, if one truly cares for their brother or sister, must be risked. For as Bonhoeffer observes:

> Nothing can be more cruel than that leniency which abandons others to their sin. Nothing can be more compassionate than that severe reprimand which calls another Christian in one's community back from the path of sin. When we allow nothing but God's Word to stand between us, judging and healing, it is a service of mercy, an ultimate offer of genuine community.[168]

The discovery of the presence of sinners in the church-community is not an abnormality, but is, in fact, the normal course of affairs. Before God every human being is a sinner and in the presence of Jesus Christ every pious pretense is brought to an end, with the result that individuals no longer need to keep up appearances, but are allowed to be the sinners that they truly are. Only in this way may they be really helped. The community of faith lives by the forgiveness of sins. This is a concrete reality that is lived out within the community as the followers of Jesus act upon the authority that he has bestowed upon them "to hear the confession of sin and to forgive sin in Christ's name."[169] In the confession of sin, the Gospel becomes an existential event in the life of the believer. The brother or sister who hears our confession stands in Christ's place, which means that in the presence of the confessor one encounters the tangible presence of both God and the entire church-community and thereby receives true assurance. "Confession," Bonhoeffer asserts, "is conversion."[170] Consistent with this asser-

---

representative action of Christ is enabled to "live *one* life, *with each other* and *for each other*" (SC (*DBWE* 1), 184).

167. *LT* (*DBWE* 5), 98–105. Bonhoeffer maintains that these four forms of service are the marks of genuine spiritual authority. However, "the genuine authority of service appears to be too insignificant" to the church infected by worldliness, which pines instead for charismatic leaders and dynamic personalities (106).

168. Ibid., 105.

169. Ibid., 109. The personal confession of sin occupied a key place in Bonhoeffer's theological agenda going right back to his doctoral dissertation where he first stressed the importance of recovering the practice for the life of the church. *SC* (*DBWE* 1), 248.

170. *LT* (*DBWE* 5), 112.

tion, Bonhoeffer's account of confession includes the treatment of aspects of conversion that have been traditionally addressed under the headings *mortificatio* and *vivificatio*. First, "by confessing actual sins the old self dies a painful, humiliating death, before the eyes of another Christian."[171] Second, as concrete sins are confessed and brought into the light, "the power of sin is broken" and "the Christian gains one victory after another."[172] For these reasons, Bonhoeffer is led to pronounce that "confession is following after [Nachfolge]," or, in other words, discipleship.[173] Bonhoeffer first introduced the practice of the personal confession of sin at Finkenwalde in conjunction with the preparation for the celebration of the Lord's Supper on the sixth Sunday after Easter in 1935.[174] This connection between confession and the Lord's Supper remains prevalent in the pages of *Life Together*.[175] Bonhoeffer ends his reflections on life together under the Word with a note of joyous eucharistic celebration. The Lord's Supper is an appropriate point for Bonhoeffer to conclude his reflections on Christian community. It is at the table of the Lord that the Christian community reaches its goal. "The community of the holy Lord's Supper," Bonhoeffer writes, "is above all the fulfillment of Christian community."[176]

PART 2: THE ECCLESIOLOGY OF STANLEY HAUERWAS

Background to Hauerwas's "Popular" Ecclesiology Writings

It was during his tenure as a professor at Notre Dame that Stanley Hauerwas's theological project came to acquire its mature form. The fruit of this maturation is on display in *The Peaceable Kingdom*, Hauerwas's "primer in Christian Ethics" published in 1983. The pages of the book reflect the landscape traversed by Hauerwas in his "journey from quandary to the Church (via character, narrative and community)."[177] Although Hauerwas's theology would continue to materially develop over the course of his career, it appears that with the publication of *The Peaceable Kingdom* all of his formal

---

171. Ibid., 111.

172. Ibid., 112.

173. Ibid. In both *Discipleship* and *Life Together* Bonhoeffer cites the *Larger Catechism* where Luther states, "Therefore, when I urge you to go to confession, I am simply urging you to be a Christian" (D (*DBWE* 4), 271; *LT* (*DBWE* 5), 114; quoting Tappert, *The Book of Concord*, 460).

174. Kelly, editor's introduction to *LT* (*DBWE* 5), 16.

175. *LT* (*DBWE* 5), 117–18.

176. Ibid., 118.

177. Wells, *Transforming Fate*, 61.

commitments were in place.[178] While Notre Dame may have been the site of Hauerwas's theological maturation, it was only after he came to Duke Divinity School that his work was introduced to a broad readership, as a result of his writing partnership with William Willimon.[179] In the pages that follow, *Resident Aliens* and its sequel, *Where Resident Aliens Live*, both co-authored with Willimon, will serve as the catalyst for exploring Hauerwas's unique ecclesial vision.[180]

Resident Aliens owes as much to the friendship between Hauerwas and Willimon, as it does to the larger surrounding culture of Duke Divinity School itself. At Duke, Hauerwas found himself back in a Protestant context, for the first time teaching students preparing for ministry in the Methodist church. Like other mainline denominations in the 1980s the United Methodist Church found its influence waning and its numbers in decline.[181] While the mainline churches were struggling to remain relevant to the surrounding culture, often by identifying themselves with progressive social agendas, the 1970s witnessed the rise of the "New Religious Right" which sought in its own way to preserve a Christian influence upon America.[182] This movement came to a crescendo with the election of Ronald Reagan in 1980 and continued to exercise its influence over the course of Reagan's ensuing presidential term. The 1980s also witnessed the rise to prominence of the Church Growth Movement, which sought to apply marketing

178. Hauerwas himself shares this intuition, reflecting in his memoir: "I suspect it is all 'there' in *The Peaceable Kingdom*. Most of what I have said since, I said there. But if so, then everything remains to be done, insofar as everything is projected toward the future" (*HC*, 136).

179. *Resident Aliens*, the first of several collaborative projects between the two men, went on to sell over 100,000 copies. See http://authors.simonandschuster.com/William-Willimon/39001662.

180. Examining these works introduces the problem of co-authorship. This leads to questions such as, How do we know who is responsible for what? In our case, we might be tempted to ask whether we are getting pure, undiluted Hauerwas in these works. But to ask such a question is to betray our enthrallment to the Enlightenment conception of the great mind or solitary genius. For Hauerwas, theology can never be "a unique activity that is the product of a creative genius" (*IGC*, 52). Rather, theology is merely the attempt to think with and for the church, which means that faithfulness is more important than originality and that one only comes to know what they know in conversation with their friends and opponents. Hauerwas, "Testament of Friends," 212. Seen from this perspective, the co-authorship arising from his friendship with Willimon is simply the embodiment of Hauerwas's own theological convictions. Furthermore, the fact that Hauerwas has fully claimed the two titles as his own is sufficient reason for them to be taken seriously by anyone investigating Hauerwas's theology.

181. Between 1965 and 1985 the United Methodist Church lost 17 percent of its members. Noll, *History of Christianity*, 468.

182. Ibid., 445.

techniques in an attempt to prove the church's continuing relevance to the contemporary individual. Amidst these developments, Hauerwas and Willimon sensed that there was something deeply wrong with the church in America. Their intuition was reinforced through their contact with divinity students and pastors who were disillusioned with the church and deeply confused about the nature of their pastoral vocation. It was with these servants of the church in mind that *Resident Aliens* was originally written. We will now turn our attention to an exploration of Hauerwas's ecclesiological convictions through an engagement with *Resident Aliens*, at times drawing upon some of Hauerwas's other more "scholarly" ecclesiological writings for additional clarification.

The Twilight of Christendom

The opening sentence of *Resident Aliens* makes the dramatic claim that "sometime between 1960 and 1980, an old, inadequately conceived world ended, and a fresh, new world began."[183] What Hauerwas and Willimon have in view is the expiration of Christendom and with it the demise of the Constantinian mindset that has plagued the church for centuries. Hauerwas's conception of Constantinianism is largely shaped and informed by the work of John Howard Yoder.[184] Following Yoder, Hauerwas employs the term Constantinianism to describe the deep shift or reversal in the relationship between the church and the world which occurred when the Emperor was received into the church.[185] In the span of a century, Christianity went from being a repressed movement embraced by only a small percentage of the population, to being the official religion of the Empire.[186]

This turn of events has had various lasting and deleterious effects on the life of the church. With the establishment of Christianity as the religion of the Empire, conviction was no longer required to be a Christian.[187] As a result the meaning of the term "Christian" underwent significant lexical

---

183. *RA*, 15.

184. Constantinianism is a recurring theme in Yoder's work. Many of Yoder's essays in the collection *The Royal Priesthood* either address Constantinianism directly or touch upon it in passing. Also of note is Yoder's essay "The Constantinian Source of Western Social Ethics," in *Priestly Kingdom*, 135–47.

185. *CET*, 181. Hauerwas's employment of the term "Constantinianism" has no particular investment in the man Constantine or the specific events in his life and rule. As Reno has observed, Hauerwas most often uses the term "to denote the ways in which Christian truth becomes innocuous and weightless" ("Stanley Hauerwas," 310).

186. Yoder, *Priestly Kingdom*, 135–36; *CET*, 181.

187. Yoder, *Priestly Kingdom*, 136.

change. Under the conditions of establishment, to be a subject of the Empire was synonymous with being a Christian. "This shift," Yoder observes, "called forth a new doctrinal refinement, namely the doctrine of the invisibility of the true church."[188] This doctrine assures that there continue to be true believers even though they remain a minority and may not be identifiable. As a consequence, "the church thus no longer signified an identifiable people, but came to mean primarily the hierarchy and sacramental institution, with the consequence that faith and Christian life primarily were understood in inward terms."[189] This shift toward inwardness represented the obfuscation of the apocalyptic character of the Christian faith, as according to this new understanding it became impossible to conceive of the church as a people engaged in a very real struggle with cosmic forces and powers aligned against God.[190] Under the conditions created by the Constantinian Synthesis, the church lost sight of the apocalyptic reality that the world is ruled by the slain lamb upon the throne and came to equate the success or failure of the civil authority with the triumph or defeat of God's cause. As a result of this shift, the figure of the ruler came to be the model for ethical deliberations and the church assumed the role of chaplain to those in power.[191] Faithfulness to the particular tradition generated by the Gospel was replaced as the driving force of ethical deliberations by the attempt to determine "how much Christian ethics Caesar can be induced to swallow without choking."[192] A morality shaped around the "naturally apparent" demands of office, station, or vocation, as opposed to the teaching of Jesus now formed the basis of the ethical council given to the ruler and beyond that to the nominally Christian mass. This was accompanied by the conviction that Christians have a sacred responsibility to ensure that history turns out right—namely in favor of whatever ruling regime is determined to be on the side of the angels. This mindset opened the door to the Christian use of violence and participation in war, which is a troubling development for both Yoder and Hauerwas. As Yoder frames the matter, "What the churches accepted in the Constantinian shift was what Jesus had rejected, seizing godlikeness, moving *in hoc signo* from Golgotha to the battlefield."[193] The ironic result of this Constantinian attempt to transform the world into the kingdom through the exercise of the strong arm of the state was that rather

188. Ibid.
189. Rasmusson, *Church as Polis*, 222.
190. *WRAL*, 33.
191. *CET*, 181.
192. *RA*, 72.
193. Yoder, *Priestly Kingdom*, 145.

than making the world Christian, the church became worldly. The result is tragic both for the accommodated church of Christendom which lives by "holding to the outward form of godliness but denying its power" and for the world which on account of the witness of this church is inoculated against a true form of Christianity.[194]

Although the Holy Roman Empire has long since crumbled, Constantinian habits are hard to break. Hauerwas explains:

> With the Renaissance and Reformation, "Christendom" was replaced by the nation-state. Christians, however, did not respond to this change by maintaining the cosmopolitanism of the Holy Roman Empire, but rather now maintained that Christian societies could wage war on one another in the name of preserving their Christian culture. With the Enlightenment, the link between church and state was broken, but the moral identification of Christians with the state remained strong.[195]

Perhaps nowhere has this moral identification of Christians with the state remained stronger than in the United States of America. It is with respect to tracing the implications of Constantinian habits of thought upon the church in late twentieth-century America that Hauerwas begins to move beyond simply introducing Yoder's theologically informed cultural analysis to a broader audience towards making his own distinct contribution. The shift towards understanding the Christian faith in terms of inwardness provoked by the Constantinian settlement was further sharpened following the Enlightenment on account of the modern tendency to bifurcate life into public and private realms or spheres. Christianity came to be understood as a matter of "holding certain 'beliefs' that were then described as 'private.'"[196] On the other hand, the workings and machinations of the burgeoning nation-state were quite obviously "public."

Amidst this state of affairs, there arose in the twentieth century another strand of Christian piety in America that rebelled against the modern relegation of Christianity to the private sphere and sought to go public with its faith. Walter Rauschenbusch and his fellow social gospelers stand, for Hauerwas, as the tragic heroes of this development in Christian ethics. Rauschenbusch and his companions are heroes for Hauerwas because through their engagement with the Hebrew prophets they "discovered an old truth that had been lost through centuries of Christian accommodation with the status quo—namely that the essential characteristic of the Christian

---

194. *RA*, 90. The quotation at the beginning of the sentence is from 2 Tim 3:5.
195. *CET*, 182.
196. *HC*, 160.

religion is its insistence on organic unity between religion and morality, theology and ethics."[197] They are tragic figures in that in their desire to christianize the social orders they continued in a Constantinian outlook that could conceive of no public of significance other than the nation-state.[198] Hauerwas argues that for Rauschenbusch and his fellow social gospelers "democracy was seen as the institutionalized form of Christianity."[199] In fact, Hauerwas believes that this conviction has largely been taken for granted by the majority of those writing in the area of Christian ethics in the United States in the twentieth century.[200] Both the Christian left and right in America are caught up in the same Constantinian outlook; namely, "both assume wrongly that the American church's primary social task is to underwrite American democracy."[201] The result of these Constantinian assumptions is that for both the Christian left and right in America the gospel cannot help but be transformed into civil religion.[202]

The predominant approach to Christian social strategy in America finds itself on precarious footing for it is "caught in a fateful ambiguity—namely, Christians claim that Christianity, or at least religion, should be more present in public life yet they want to make government itself religiously neutral."[203] Under such conditions, as society becomes increasingly secular and pluralistic, Christians, with theologians at the forefront, discover that if they are going to continue to have any impact in shaping public policy and sharing in power they must learn to translate their particular theological commitments into universally accessible principles, maxims, and strategies that can be accepted by any person of goodwill, regardless of their religious commitments.[204] This development can be looked upon as a

---

197. *AN*, 28.

198. Airhart's telling of the story of the United Church of Canada in *Church with the Soul of a Nation* could be plausibly read as a case study of the ecclesial effects of this phenomenon in a Canadian context.

199. *CET*, 177.

200. Hauerwas identifies the following prominent theological ethicists as sharing in this conviction: Reinhold Niebuhr, *CET*, 177; John Courtney Murray, *CET*, 177–78; Paul Ramsey, *AN*, 35. Even Jerry Falwell, according to Hauerwas's judgement, was not able to escape from operating under this set of assumptions. *RA* 69–71; *WRAL* 115–16.

201. *RA*, 32. It is for this reason that the political outlook of conservative Christians tends to be so difficult to distinguish from that of the Republican Party, while the social outlook of the mainline church generally reflects the values of the Democrats (38).

202. *CET*, 180. In reflecting upon the context in which Hauerwas has lived out his theological vocation, Wells observes that it is "hard to speak of Church in America, because America is Jesus. America has become the embodiment of the way God overcomes evil and brings life" ("Difference Christ Makes," 13–14).

203. *CET*, 183.

204. *AN*, 32, 38.

variation of Schleiermacher's theological project, at least as it is commonly understood. Whereas Schleiermacher's "cultured despisers" were German idealists and those enthralled by romanticism, Americans tended towards pragmatism. Hence, in America, theologians tended to become ethicists; replacing specific theological language with more universal, but highly abstract, concepts such as freedom, justice, and human rights in the attempt to prove their enduring relevance to an increasingly skeptical society.[205]

This confusion of the story of America with the Christian story, and the accompanying acceptance of liberalism as a social strategy by Christians in America, has had many variegated and deleterious effects on the life and witness of the church. In adopting the assumptions of liberalism, Christians allowed their faith to be relegated to the private realm and in the name of "responsibility" willingly sacrificed the visibility of the church in order to "leaven the whole of society."[206] The attempts to translate theological convictions into generally accessible principles which accompanied this acquiesce to modernity's relegation of religion to the private realm, further reinforced the notion that Christian faith is about giving intellectual assent to a set of beliefs or propositions rather than a life lived in the presence of the Messiah Jesus, who is never without his Messianic people. The separation of Christian beliefs from Christian practices has contributed to the erosion of distinctive Christian habits, a disastrous development for Protestantism which was largely dependent upon the taken-for-granted Christian habits developed over the centuries prior to the Reformation for its continuing intelligibility and viability.[207] Lacking such habits, the church is especially susceptible to being further swept up in the currents of the reigning cultural ideology.[208] As a result, the church appears to be largely compromised in many aspects of its life and suffering from much confusion about its identity and mission. Immersed in the "vast supermarket of desire," which is liberal capitalistic society, and lacking the resources to resist, it is not surprising that the church often comes to think of itself as a "helping institution," that is, "one more consumer-oriented organization, existing to encourage individual fulfillment."[209] "The called church," Hauerwas remarks, "has become

---

205. *AC*, 31.

206. Wells, *Transforming Fate*, 110.

207. *BCCE*, 48.

208. The rise of historical-criticism and fundamentalism as predominant and mutually antagonistic approaches to reading Scripture is evidence of the church's infection by the ethos of liberalism. Both approaches presume that the Bible is accessible to anyone apart from the transformation that occurs through participation in the life of the church. *US*, 35.

209. *RA*, 32–33.

the voluntary church, whose primary characteristic is that the congregation is friendly."[210] This identity crisis within the church results in corresponding confusion amongst the clergy. As Hauerwas and Willimon put it, "when the church lacks confidence in what it is, clergy have no earthly idea what they are doing here."[211] These anchorless pastors then find themselves pulled in every direction by the insatiable needs of a people who are "not trained to want the right things rightly, but rather [are] a people who share the liberal presumption that all needs which are sincerely felt are legitimate."[212] The result is the replacement of true Christian ministry with a sentimentality that is unable to do more than help people adapt to the status quo. When that status quo is a civil religion built upon the sacrifices of war, the very identity of the church and its ability to witness to the Gospel is called into question, with terrifying implications for the world.[213]

The Church as a Colony of Resident Aliens

In the twilight of Christendom, Hauerwas and Willimon assert that Christians are faced with what is essentially a political challenge; namely, the recovery of the distinctive character of the church's life as a community of disciples gathered by and around Jesus.[214] Quite simply, truth matters for Hauerwas, hence his great concern for the truthfulness of the church's life and witness. However, truth is not an idea, principle or a piece of empirical data. The rational character of Christian faith is not to be secured by a *theory* of truth. Rather truth is the person of the crucified and risen Messiah of Israel; therefore truthfulness involves being drawn into His life and conformed to His image. As the community of the eschatological Israel which participates in the body of the Jewish Messiah Jesus, the church's life and witness can be no less concrete or corporeal than the chosen people of Israel whom God entered into covenant with at Sinai.[215] The church, as the body of Christ, is as much a public and empirical reality as the body of Jesus which hung upon the cross on the hill outside of Jerusalem. "There is," Hauerwas writes, "no ideal church, no invisible church, no mystically existing univer-

---

210. *AC*, 94.

211. *RA*, 127.

212. Ibid., 121.

213. It is the burden of Hauerwas's collection of essays, *War and The American Difference* to demonstrate that America is united by a civil religion which gains its intelligibility from the sacrificial economy of war.

214. *RA*, 24, 30.

215. *IGC*, 31.

sal church more real than the concrete church with parking lots and pot luck dinners. No, it is the church of parking lots and potluck dinners that comprises the sanctified ones formed by and forming the continuing story of Jesus Christ in the world."[216] *Resident Aliens*, then, much like Hauerwas's larger theological project emerges from the ruins of the spiritualized church of modernity and the legacy bequeathed to it from the Constantinian shift as the attempt to reclaim the public and political character of the Church.[217]

As a means of emphasizing and exploring the concrete and corporate nature of the life of the church, Hauerwas and Willimon introduce the metaphor of "a colony of resident aliens."[218] The metaphor of a colony of aliens, previously used by Bonhoeffer in his discussion of the church in *Discipleship*,[219] emphasizes the diasporic character of the church's existence in the time between Christ's ascension and *parousia*. Disciples of Jesus never quite find themselves at home in this world, for through the waters of baptism they have become citizens of the heavenly commonwealth and, as a result, discover themselves to be out of sync with the surrounding cultures that live according to a variety of truths other than the Truth which is Jesus.[220] As a colony of resident aliens, the church is "a beachhead, an outpost, an island of one culture in the middle of another, a place where the values of home are reiterated and passed on to the young, a place where the distinctive language and life-style of the resident aliens are lovingly nurtured and reinforced."[221] Hauerwas's and Willimon's model of a colony of resident aliens serves to reinforce the crucial distinction between the church and the world which is so prevalent in the pages of the New Testament, and which so often seemed to be lacking in mainstream Protestantism. The metaphor of a colony of resident aliens stresses the concrete nature of the church as an identifiable people in the world and reflects the way that people are formed in their faith and develop character as embodied, timeful human beings.

As a colony of resident aliens, outnumbered and surrounded on all sides, it is not the responsibility of the church "to *make* the world the kingdom, but to be faithful to the kingdom by showing what it means to be a

---

216. *PK*, 107.

217. *HC*, 160.

218. The biblical roots of the metaphor can be traced to 1 Pet 2:11 which refers to Christians relating to the surrounding social order as "aliens and exiles" (*WRAL*, 95). Phil 3:20 also refers to the church as, according to Moffat's vivid translation, "a colony of heaven" (*RA*, 11).

219. *D* (*DBWE* 4), 250; *WRAL*, 95.

220. *RA*, 12.

221. Ibid., 12.

community of peace."[222] In this way, the metaphor of the church as a colony of resident aliens resonates with two of Hauerwas's most famous ecclesial affirmations: "the first social ethical task of the church is to be the church" and "the church does not have a social ethic; the church is a social ethic."[223] The insistence that the church *is* a social ethic calls into question the reigning paradigm of modernity's definition of the political and the bifurcation of life into private and public spheres or realms. The church is neither apolitical nor must it struggle to find a way to go public by entering into the politics of the nation-state. Hauerwas clarifies, "For the church to *be* a social ethic, rather than to *have* a social ethic, means the church must be (is) a body polity."[224]

Politics, for Hauerwas, is not about pulling the levers of power or executing shrewd backroom deals. Rather politics is "about the conversation necessary for a people across time to discover goods that they have in common."[225] As the body politic of the crucified and resurrected Messiah Jesus, the church can be understood as "the lively argument, extended over centuries and occasioned by the stories of God's calling of Israel and of the life and death of Jesus Christ."[226] Here Hauerwas's debt to the philosopher Alasdair MacIntyre and his conception of a living tradition lies quite close to the surface.[227] However, it is to Augustine that Hauerwas will turn to distinguish the church from the politics instantiated in all other living traditions, particularly the modern nation-state. Hauerwas observes that Augustine, in his discussion of the two cities in *The City of God*, argues that "Rome is not a commonwealth, because a commonwealth is determined by justice—that is, where each gets his or her due—and because Rome does not give God his due, Rome cannot be a society. Only the Christian community offers sacrifice to the true God, and it is a sacrifice that only Christ could make possible."[228] Apart from such a proper orientation to the true telos

222. *PK*, 103.
223. Ibid., 99.
224. *IGC*, 26.
225. Ibid., 6.
226. *CET*, 102.

227. MacIntyre defines a living tradition as "an historically extended, socially embodied argument, and an argument precisely in part about the goods that constitute that tradition" (*After Virtue*, 222). Hauerwas's appropriation of MacIntyre's understanding of traditions has exposed him to some criticism. Healy argues that MacIntyre's definition requires significant theological thickening, if it is to be truly ecclesiologically useful. *Hauerwas*, 104–9. Mangina expresses the concern that understanding the church as an argument may reflect an overly intellectualized conception of the faith which also sits uneasily with the New Testament's view of conflict. "Church, Cross, and Caritas," 445–49.

228. *AC*, 41.

of creation and a corresponding formation in the truth, truthful politics is impossible. For this reason, "the church's first political task is to worship the true God truly."[229]

The assembly of the congregation on the Lord's Day to worship the King, Hauerwas and Willimon suggest, is something akin to a political rally.[230] On Sunday morning in the midst of the *ekklēsia*, the proclamation of the story of God with us and for us in Jesus Christ and the enactment of that same story in the celebration of the sacraments clashes with the other narratives that seek to shape and claim our lives.[231] Worship, quite simply, *is* the church's politics. In this vein, Hauerwas elaborates on the significance of the sacraments:

> These rites, baptism and eucharist, are not just "religious things" that Christian people do. They are the essential rituals of our politics. Through them we learn who we are. Instead of being motives or causes for effective social work on the part of Christian people, these liturgies *are* our effective social work. For if the church *is* rather than has a social ethic, these actions are our most important social witness. It is in baptism and eucharist that we see most clearly the marks of God's kingdom in the world. They set our standard, as we try to bring every aspect of our lives under their sway.[232]

If the worship of the church is its politics, then for Hauerwas, its constitution is the Sermon on the Mount.[233] The Sermon is not special counsel for a religious elite,[234] nor is it law meant to drive us to the point of recognizing our need for forgiveness,[235] nor is it guidance for relationships between individuals that must be transcended by a more "realistic" approach when it comes to the systems and structures of society.[236] All of these approaches fail to take account of the eschatological reality of what God has done in Christ

---

229. *DT*, 182.

230. *WRAL*, 45.

231. Ibid., 50.

232. *PK*, 108. "Because the Christian story is an enacted story, liturgy is probably a much more important resource than are doctrines or creeds for helping us to hear, tell, and live the story of God" (26).

233. *US*, 67. References to the Sermon on the Mount pervade Hauerwas's corpus, however his most concentrated treatments of the Sermon are found in: *RA*, 69–92; *US*, 63–77; *Mt*, 58–92.

234. *US*, 64.

235. Ibid., 65; *Mt*, 59–60.

236. *RA*, 76. Hauerwas and Willimon have in mind Reinhold Niebuhr's influential book *Moral Man and Immoral Society*.

in reconciling the world to Himself and calling into existence a people of the new age.[237] The Sermon is intended to be lived.[238] Jesus has inaugurated the new age making it possible for his people to live in accordance with the Sermon and he himself is the pioneer whose "life is but a commentary on the sermon, and the sermon is the exemplification of his life."[239] So in learning to turn the other cheek, to go the extra mile, to love one's enemies and pray for one's persecutors, the Christian community is learning to live in accordance with "the grain of the universe," because the Sermon shows us what God is like. Disciples who follow Jesus in the midst of a world that does not acknowledge his Lordship cannot help but appear to be visibly different from those around them. They do not "seek to be subversives; it just turns out that living according to the Sermon on the Mount cannot help but challenge the way things are."[240] By provoking such opposition for those who order their lives according to its precepts, the Sermon on the Mount creates a people who must learn to depend on God and one another for their survival.[241]

Objections to Hauerwas's "Colonialism"

Hauerwas's emphasis upon the political character of the church as a living, breathing, visible community distinguished from the world on account of its allegiance to Jesus has sparked both appreciative inquiry and vehement protests. In what follows, we will consider three areas of objection that arise with respect to Hauerwas's understanding of the church as a "polis" and the title metaphor of *Resident Aliens*.

First, the metaphor of a colony of resident aliens could be construed in terms that are too static to depict the full reality of the identity and mission of the church. Immigrants who arrive in a new country and attempt to create, in the midst of their new surroundings, an enclave of the home country they left behind, find themselves radically bound to the past. While life in the old country continues, those in the colony are often left attempting to create a way of life based upon the culture they left behind as it was five, ten, or even twenty years ago or more. For this reason, the metaphor of a colony of resident aliens may not be dynamic enough to capture the reality of the life of the people of God. Christians are indebted to the past, but they are not

237. *RA*, 87.
238. *US*, 66.
239. *Mt*, 92.
240. Ibid., 81.
241. Ibid., 91.

enslaved to it. The events upon which the Christian colony is founded—the cross, resurrection, and pouring out of the Holy Spirit—are the eschatological irruptions of God's future in the midst of this passing world. The Christian colony, then, is defined not by the values of the Old World, but of the world to come. This means that the colony cannot be construed in static terms for they are a people on the move travelling between the ages.[242] The recurring motifs of pilgrimage, journey and adventure in Hauerwas's writings serves to complement and correct a static misconception of the colony metaphor of *Resident Aliens*.[243] Like the unlikely fellowship of humans, hobbits, dwarves and elves in J. R. R. Tolkien's *The Lord of the Rings* trilogy, which found themselves propelled on a quest to save Middle Earth when the ring of power providentially came into the possession of Frodo Baggins, so the members of the Christian community find themselves on "an adventure we didn't know we wanted to be on."[244]

Second, the metaphor of a colony of resident aliens can suggest a defensive posture characterized as a retreat into a sectarian enclave. Perhaps the most famous criticism along these lines came from Hauerwas's former teacher, James Gustafson, who charged Hauerwas with being a "sectarian, fideistic, tribalist."[245] Hauerwas has aptly defended himself against these charges and has also received ample support from various allies.[246] It is not necessary to rehash those arguments here; rather it is sufficient to highlight three of Hauerwas's primary convictions. First, as a concrete and corporeal community of human beings, the church is never faced with the question of

242. Richard Hays has observed that "the metaphor of pilgrimage emerges again and again in Hauerwas's work as the most apt description of the church's experience" (*Moral Vision*, 258). This emphasis on pilgrimage further establishes the inseparable bond between the church and the people of Israel on their journey with God.

243. See for example *RA*, 49–68; and "Christianity: It's Not a Religion: It's an Adventure," in *HR*, 522–35.

244. *HR*, 531. The depiction of Christianity as an "adventurous journey" also has an apologetic function within the context of de-storied Western post- or hyper-modernity in which life often appears to be "just-one-damn-thing-after-another" (*RA*, 51, 67). Tolkien's trilogy includes: *Fellowship of the Ring*; *Two Towers*; and *Return of the King*.

245. Gustafson, "The Sectarian Temptation." The phrase "sectarian, fideistic, tribalist" is not actually employed by Gustafson, but rather appears to be Hauerwas's own short-hand summary of the charges, which he delights in repeating in various places and sometimes in differing word order. E.g., *DF*, 18; *BH*, 23; *SU*, 51, 165; *CSCh*, 154; *CDRO*, 10; *HC*, 208; *WAD*, 118 n. 6; *AE*, 70, 92.

246. *HR*, 90–110; *CET*, 1–21; *AN*, 1–10; *BH*, 23–34; Rasmusson, *Church as Polis*, 231–47; Wells, "Stanley Hauerwas' Theological Ethics," 431–48. Stephen Fowl goes so far as to describe the charge of sectarianism against Hauerwas as being so patently false that it is "the scholarly equivalent of the claim that Barack Obama is a Muslim" (Review of *Unsettling Arguments*, 322).

whether to be in or out of the world. The church is always in the world; the question that faces the church is "*how* to be in the world, in what form, for what purpose."[247] This raises, secondly, the question of politics. Hauerwas's ecclesiology can be considered sectarian if and only if "it is assumed that the secular state has the right to determine what will and will not count as political."[248] If the cross and resurrection of Christ and the sending of the Holy Spirit leads to the creation of an eschatological community that bursts the boundaries of modernity's bifurcation of human life into the private and public spheres, then the charge of sectarianism is misplaced. Third and finally, in contrast to the church which in its catholicity crosses all borders and encompasses people of every race, tribe and tongue, it is the modern nation-state which is revealed to be the true manifestation of tribalism. "Tribalism," Hauerwas and Willimon decry, "is the United States of America which sets up artificial boundaries and defends them with murderous intensity."[249]

Finally, there is the possibility that the metaphor of resident aliens could place the church into a relationship where its identity is negatively determined by the surrounding culture, or where being weird or different becomes a virtue in and of itself. Criticism along these lines has been raised by several scholars, but has perhaps been most vigorously prosecuted in recent years by Nathan Kerr in his book *Christ, History and Apocalyptic*.[250] Since the argument advanced in this book represents the most developed and nuanced form of this line of criticism of Hauerwas's work up to his point, we will take a moment to consider the nature of the charges raised by Kerr. Kerr rightly recognizes Hauerwas to be a theological descendent of Karl Barth, who is frustrated by what he perceives to be the inadequacy of Barth's ecclesial politics. While Kerr shares Hauerwas's concern, he believes that Hauerwas has wrongly attempted to redress the problem by "shifting the doctrinal locus of apocalyptic from Christology to ecclesiology."[251] This strategy results in no shortage of ecclesial concreteness, but runs the risk of effacing Jesus's historicity and making Jesus captive to the church. Under these conditions, mission becomes a matter of self-preservation, as the church seeks to preserve its own internal identity over against the world.[252]

247. *RA*, 43. See also *WRAL*, 30.

248. *CET*, 12.

249. *RA*, 42.

250. Others who have criticized Hauerwas on this score include: Matthewes, "Appreciating Hauerwas," 343–60; and Reno, private letter to Douglas Harink, quoted in *PTF*, 236.

251. Kerr, *Christ, History and Apocalyptic*, 93.

252. Ibid., 171.

Kerr maintains that this development is "determined from the outset by Hauerwas's anti-liberal agenda and that his concern to secure a certain fixed narrative and linguistic 'identity' for the church forces him into a structurally imperialistic and functionally 'ideological' articulation of the church's political and missionary existence in the world."[253] This comes to the fore in Hauerwas's development of the concept of the church-as-*polis* which stands in contradistinction to the modern liberal nation-state.[254] The ecclesiology which emerges from this overly-determined relationship to modern liberalism suffers from a deformed conception of mission. Kerr elaborates, "the primary objective of Christian mission ceases to be thought of as the ongoing 'conversion' to the singular lordship of Christ as embedded within the evernew particularities and contingencies of history, and rather becomes thought of as 'conversion' *into* a particular narrative community, as the meaning and reality of Christ's lordship over history is now recognized as embedded within this particular community's culture, language, and practices."[255]

Kerr's critique of Hauerwas's ecclesiology brings to the fore several important issues that merit careful consideration.[256] First, Kerr is quite right to highlight the danger of construing the identity of the church by means of an oppositional relationship to some other reality. Although, in distinction from Kerr, it does not seem to me to be immediately problematic to speak of the church-as-*polis*, I would agree that when the language-use shifts in such a way that the church is construed in terms of being a counter-*polis* that one is now skating on theological thin ice. Hauerwas himself has recognized this danger and at the beginning of the millennium acknowledged that his work has at times been seemingly more determined by his opponents, as evidenced by the frequent polemical rather than constructive character of his writings.[257] Instructive, however, is his engagement with the command placed before all Christians to love their enemies, found in the opening paragraph of *A Better Hope*. On the one hand, the command to love our enemies "is not a strategy to guarantee all enmity can be overcome, but a reminder that for Christians our lives must be determined by our loves,

---

253. Ibid., 93.

254. Ibid., 118–19.

255. Ibid., 121.

256. Hauerwas has graciously and patiently responded to Kerr's criticisms in a recent essay entitled, "Beyond the Boundaries: The Church Is Mission," in *WAD*, 167–81. For a less conciliatory engagement with Kerr's work, see Jenson, Review of *Christ, History and Apocalyptic*, 310–12.

257. *BH* 9–10; *PTF* 14–15.

not our hates."[258] On the other hand, the command to love our enemies is a reminder to Christians that the faithful proclamation of the Gospel will create enemies.[259] As Hauerwas has correctly identified, theological work is always occasional, in that "bound up in its own conception of its own calling is a certain reading of the circumstances in which it speaks."[260] Therefore any ecclesial theology which proceeds as if no enemies exist betrays both the occasional nature of theology and the eschatological character of the Gospel. To flesh this out in terms of the debate between Hauerwas and Kerr, one must ask whether Kerr's characterization of Hauerwas's project as "anti-liberal" problematically grants modern liberalism normative status while failing to account for modern liberalism's distinctive anti-Christian origins.[261] In other words, is Hauerwas "anti-liberal" or does his work exemplify the faithful execution of the task of Christian theology according to its occasional character through his cognizance of the enemies the gospel has created in his particular time and place? The question is likely not answerable in either/or terms with respect to Hauerwas's corpus as a whole, but is probably best pursued in a concrete analysis of particular texts, which I suspect would sometimes result in the former conclusion, but more often in the latter.

Second, although Kerr has correctly flagged the danger of construing the identity of the church solely in terms of being "counter" to some other cultural reality, one cannot help but wonder what assumptions are at work in his framing of the missionary imperative in such a way that it necessitates a choice between conversion to the Lordship of Christ and initiation into the church as a particular narrative community. The very logic of the New Testament suggests that to attempt to tell the story of this particular man, Jesus of Nazareth, apart from the story of the church is no longer to tell the story of this man, but another.[262] The apocalyptic irruption which is the concrete historicity of Jesus of Nazareth gives birth to a community which embodies a concrete history constituted by its walking in both obedience to and disobedience of the Holy Spirit. For this reason the tradition of the church cannot be reified or deemed infallible, however, neither can it be completely ignored or disregarded. Kerr's emphasis upon the "independence" of Jesus is both helpful and necessary and could be understood to be way of restating

---

258. *BH*, 9.

259. For a fuller treatment of this theme, see "No Enemy, No Christianity: Preaching between 'Worlds,'" in *STT*, 191–200.

260. *PTF*, 22 n. 19, quoting Webster, *Word and Church*, 4.

261. This point is raised in Lee, Review of *Christ, History and Apocalyptic*, 250.

262. For one example of a biblical text that points strongly in this direction see the risen Christ's address of Saul, "Saul, Saul, why do you persecute me?" (Acts 9:4).

the Reformation slogan *semper reformanda*. However, the "independence of Jesus" cannot be emphasized in such a way that it threatens to negate the promise of the risen Lord to never leave or forsake his church.[263] It would be an act of hospitality directed towards Kerr and those who are similarly inclined if Hauerwas, in light of his strong emphasis upon tradition, were to offer a fuller explanation of how reformation is possible and to explicate the periodic necessity for Spirit-directed speaking against the tradition.[264] Of course, this request is somewhat ironic, in light of the fact that Hauerwas's call for the church to be the church is premised upon the assumption that the reformation of the church is both desirable and possible.

The Church in the Economy of Salvation

As we have already begun to see, for Hauerwas, the visibility of the church in its concrete locality is a necessity for the church's ordained role in the economy of salvation. The existence of the church as an historical, corporeal community is essential for two interrelated purposes. Borrowing from Hauerwas's lexicon, we could describe these two purposes as: 1.) sanctifying disciples in the truth,[265] and 2.) helping the world to understand that it is the world.[266]

In order to consider these two aspects of the church's place in the economy of salvation, it is first necessary to pause to consider Hauerwas's understanding of salvation. Put most simply, salvation is, for Hauerwas, nothing other than the reign of God.[267] Salvation for the Christian involves

---

263. Unfortunately, this is exactly what seems to occur in *Christ, History and Apocalyptic*, where the church as a concrete and historical community appears to have evaporated following the lightning strike of the apocalyptic irruption of the particular historicity of Jesus. In denying the continuing historic, corporeal existence of the body of Christ, Kerr risks reducing such favorite terms as "historicity" and "particularity" to empty ciphers.

264. Hays and Healy are among those who have questioned how Scripture can stand over and against the church in Hauerwas's theology. Hays, *Moral Vision*, 263–66; Healy, *Hauerwas*, 59–61.

265. This is derived from the title of Hauerwas's collection of essays *Sanctify Them in the Truth*, which in turn is taken from the high-priestly prayer of Jesus in John 17:17.

266. Variations of this phrase appear throughout Hauerwas's writings. E.g., *TT*, 140; *PK*, 100; *CET*, 102; *RA*, 94; *WRAL*, 46, 59. This is closely related to Hauerwas's repeated claim that "without the church the world would have no history" (*CET*, 61); *IGC*, 33; cf. *AC*, 36.

267. *HR*, 533. Rasmusson offers the following concise definition, "Salvation means that God creates a people as the social manifestation of the new alternative history determined by the kingdom of God that has come in Jesus Christ" (*Church as Polis*, 190).

being taken up in the story of God's creation, reconciliation, and redemption of the world in Jesus Christ. When this happens, "the little story I call my life is given cosmic, eternal significance as it is caught up within God's larger account of history."[268] There is the danger that this emphasis upon narrative could be understood in liberal existentialist terms, which understands the salvific importance of the category of story to be found in the way it provides "meaning" for my life, or also in gnostic terms, which equates salvation with the knowledge of the story.[269] Hauerwas attempts to combat these two distorted conceptions of the way the Christian story functions in the economy of salvation in an important essay entitled, "The Church as God's New Language."[270] In the essay, written in honour of his former teacher Hans Frei, Hauerwas combines a sermon for the Day of Pentecost with methodological commentary as a way to offer an important corrective to the burgeoning narrative theology movement. Hauerwas cautions that any emphasis upon narrative that does not take account of its ecclesial context is simply an abstraction. In other words, it must be remembered that, in the words of a simple phrase that signals the ecclesial turn which characterizes Hauerwas's later theology, "the narrative does not refer but rather people do."[271] The Christian story cannot be separated from the questions of where the story is told, how the story is told, and who tells the story.[272] The story of Pentecost points to the eschatological irruption of the new creation as the Spirit calls into existence a people who on account of Christ's work are able to live peaceably in the midst of a violent world. The church lives by the *anamnesis* of the apocalyptic work of Jesus of Nazareth, but in so telling and enacting the story the church finds that it "cannot tell that story without becoming part of the tale."[273] Hauerwas insists, "The church as witness to God's work for us in Israel and Jesus of Nazareth means that here the teller and the tale are one."[274] As the community of the new humanity reconciled to God and one another, the church is not only the means of mediating salvation, but is itself also the goal of salvation.[275] For this reason,

---

268. *RA*, 55.

269. Appeals to narrative qua narrative could also be understood as an attempt to instantiate a new form of foundationalism. See Wells's discussion of the place of "narrative from below" and "narrative from above" in Hauerwas's corpus in *Transforming Fate*, 40–61.

270. *CET*, 47–65.

271. Ibid., 59.

272. Ibid., 61.

273. Ibid., 54.

274. Ibid.

275. Ibid., 65 n. 23. See also Hauerwas's discussion of John Milbank's ecclesiological presuppositions in an informative footnote to his essay "Why There is No Salvation

Hauerwas is elsewhere able to unabashedly affirm, "The church's politics is our salvation."²⁷⁶

"To be saved is to be sanctified."²⁷⁷ This terse formulation at once captures one of the central thrusts of Hauerwas's project and at the same time reflects the influence of his Methodist heritage. Although the writings of John Wesley are rarely the explicit subject of theological reflection in Hauerwas's corpus, it is from Wesley that Hauerwas has inherited a teleological conception of the Christian life and the concomitant interest in recovering the importance of sanctification.²⁷⁸ For Hauerwas, there can be no sanctification of individuals apart from the existence and life of a sanctified people. The Christian community is essential for the formation of Christians because the church "is the only community formed around the truth, which is Jesus Christ, who is the way, the truth, and the life."²⁷⁹ It is through being initiated into the living tradition arising from the story of Jesus Christ and being trained in its peculiar habits and customs that individuals come to be sanctified in the truth. It is only through immersion in the life of the storied community of Jesus Christ that disciples acquire the skills necessary to identify and name the powers which seek to rule over their lives through fear and falsehood. The ability to name these powers is the beginning of the Christian's emancipation from them.²⁸⁰ Those living under the illusion that they are the authors of their own story cannot help but be forced into a state of self-deception when confronted by personal failure, tragedy, or other wrongs they can't make right, furthering their complicity in the powers' cosmic reign of terror. The Christian story which narrates God's refusal to abandon us to our sin and is embodied in such practices as confession, forgiveness, and reconciliation provides "us a way to go on in a lie-shaped world."²⁸¹ Through worship, Christians receive training in being a forgiven people, which is essential if they are to be a people who are able to speak the truth to one another without destroying themselves. Set free for the truth by the liberating power and practices of forgiveness, the church is a polity "unlike any other insofar as it is formed by a people who have no reason to fear the truth."²⁸²

---

outside the Church," in *AC*, 169 n. 23.

276. *IGC*, 8.
277. *STT*, 6.
278. For explicit engagement with Wesley see *CCL*, 188–202; *STT*, 123–42.
279. *RA*, 77.
280. *TT*, 88; *HR*, 112, 524; *IGC*, 8.
281. *DT*, 28.
282. *PK*, 102.

The truth of the Christian story which comes to us *extra nos* identifying us as sinners who are beloved and reconciled to God in Christ can only be received as a gift. This gift takes the threefold form of the gift of the body of Christ: Jesus of Nazareth, the church, and the Eucharist.[283] Through the ongoing reception of this gift, believers are enabled to receive the entirety of their lives as gifts from God as they learn to live "out of control" in dependence upon the faithful God who promises to give His people everything they need to follow Him.[284] Having already beheld the end of the story in the cross and resurrection of Jesus Christ, the church is freed from the desperate impulse of self-preservation and anxious attempts to make the story turn-out right, which inevitably lead to violence, in order to "gladly give itself over to the long, patient labor of becoming a sacrament of Christ's peaceable presence."[285] This directs us towards the organic and inseparable connection in Hauerwas's thought between the existence of the church as a sacramental people and as a holy people. For Hauerwas, the sacraments are "sanctifying ordinances" through which the character of Christians is formed according to the image of Christ.[286] This indissoluble connection between the sacraments and holy living is reflected in Hauerwas's enumeration of the marks which help to identify the church. Hauerwas states, "The church is known where the sacraments are celebrated, the word is preached, and upright lives are encouraged and lived."[287] Only through immersion in the life of a community defined by the practices of the politics of Jesus, through which we encounter living exemplars of the faith in the form of the saints—past and present—are we able to make the Christian story our own. The entire life of the church, and not just what occurs in the Sunday school classroom, must be looked upon as "a form of education that is religious" through which Christians are sanctified in the truth.[288] Through the shaping of their vision, Christians are trained "to desire the right things rightly."[289]

---

283. BCCE, 16–18.

284. For an introduction to the theme of "living out of control," see *PK*, 105–6.

285. *PTF*, 97. Hence Rasmusson's observation that Hauerwas's eschatological convictions free Christians "to do the good thing even if it seems presently ineffective" (*Church as Polis*, 329).

286. The term "sanctifying ordinance" is Willimon's, but it is cited approvingly by Hauerwas. *PK*, 168 n. 10, quoting *Service of God*, 125.

287. *PK*, 107.

288. *CET*, 103. One cannot but help hear resonances with Calvin's conception of the church as a school from which we will not be dismissed "until we have been pupils all our lives" (*Institutes*, 4.1.4).

289. *CET*, 103. This is a fairly direct allusion to Augustine.

For this reason, "the church is crucial for Christian epistemology."²⁹⁰ There can be no sanctification of the individual in the truth apart from the sanctified people who truthfully worship the true God.

This brings us to the second aspect of the church's role in the economy of salvation. It is the presence of this sanctified community in the midst of the world that presents to the world the possibility of its salvation. Hauerwas and Willimon insist:

> The world needs the church because, without the church, the world does not know who it is. The only way for the world to know that it is being redeemed is for the church to point to the Redeemer by being a redeemed people. The way for the world to know that it needs redeeming, that it is broken and fallen, is for the church to enable the world to strike hard against something which is an alternative to what the world offers.²⁹¹

Apart from the proleptic presence of the peaceable Kingdom embodied in the life of the Church, the world would have no way of knowing that it is God's good creation, reconciled in Jesus Christ, and heading towards its consummation in the Spirit. Accordingly, Hauerwas insists that "the church is, therefore, an ontological necessity if we are to know rightly that our world is capable of narrative construal."²⁹²

The emphasis upon the church as the embodied presence of God's story in the world quite naturally leads to Hauerwas's famous epigram: "The first task of the church is not to make the world just. The first task of the church is to make the world the world."²⁹³ Although we have already received hints pointing towards the answer, the epigram does beg the question as to just what exactly Hauerwas means when he uses the term "the world." Like the New Testament usage of the term *kosmos*, "the world" has polyvalent significance for Hauerwas, such that the meaning of a particular usage must be determined with reference to the context in which it appears.²⁹⁴ In some places Hauerwas uses the world as a simple synonym for the created realm, but more frequently Hauerwas uses the term world to denote "all that

---

290. *RA*, 94. Elsewhere, Hauerwas cites Yoder's claim, "The church precedes the world epistemologically. We know more fully from Jesus Christ and in the context of the confessed faith than we know in other ways" (*Priestly Kingdom*, 11, quoted in *AC*, 37).

291. *RA*, 94.

292. *CET*, 61.

293. The epigram is frequently quoted by Hauerwas in talks and presentations and appears with some minor variations in wording throughout his writings. This particular wording is from: "Faith Fires Back," para. 14.

294. Rasmusson, *Church as Polis*, 211.

in God's creation have taken the opportunity of God's patience not yet to believe in him."[295] The distinction between the church and the world, then, is not an ontological distinction but rather is a distinction between agents arising from how they respond to the eschatological irruption of the Kingdom in the person of Jesus Christ.[296] Nor is it an attempt to separate insiders from outsiders, a pure church from a contaminated world, for those who are being sanctified in the truth will recognize that the line dividing church and world cuts through the center of each human heart.[297] As a result, the description "world" encompasses such things as "the modern story of the self-fabricated individual" who lives under the illusion of being in control, and places, such as the Pentagon, "where the principalities and powers are organized against God for the most noble of reasons."[298]

The primary calling of the church is to be the church. This assertion is neither anti-world nor a desperate attempt to ensure ecclesial survival, rather it is a matter of supreme missional and evangelistic importance.[299] Just as the separation of the person and work of Christ cannot help but fail to lead to grave distortions in Christian life, in a similar way the identity and mission of Christ's body, the church, cannot be separated. The church must be itself; God's life-giving gesture given on behalf of a broken and needy world.[300] Hauerwas can therefore write, "The call for the church to be the church is meant as a reminder that the church is in the world to serve the world."[301] The church first and foremost serves the world by being a people who worship the true God in Spirit and in truth. This returns us full circle, for once again the interrelation between the sanctification of the saints and the Church's witness to the world is on full display. The Gospel presents human beings with the gift of salvation in Christ. The reception of this gift takes the form of the journey of discipleship. Though this journey the community of disciples, as it continues to rely on the good gifts of God, is conformed to the truth of the One they worship and becomes God's gift to the world.

---

295. *BCCE*, 21.

296. *PK*, 101; *CET*, 102. See also Rasmusson's discussion of "church and world" in *Church as Polis*, 211–12.

297. *WRAL*, 82.

298. Ibid., 82, 78; *PK*, 101.

299. Kenneson puts it well when he writes, "the church must attend to the character of its embodied life because that embodied life *is* its witness to the world" (*Beyond Sectarianism*, 2).

300. *CET*, 101–10.

301. *PTF*, 231.

Hauerwas's Ecclesiological Criticism of Barth

Hauerwas's strong affirmation of the patristic slogan *extra ecclesiam nulla salus* brings us to the heart of his criticism of the theology of Karl Barth. As we have seen in previous chapters, the work of Karl Barth has had a tremendous influence upon Hauerwas's theological formation. Hauerwas considers himself to be a member of the Barthian camp and Barth frequently appears as the hero when Hauerwas attempts to tell the story of theology in the twentieth century.[302] However, Hauerwas's long-standing admiration for Barth has not led to uncritical acceptance of his work. In fact, over the course of his entire academic career Hauerwas's appropriation of Barth's thought has been accompanied by an ever-evolving subtle critique of the Swiss theologian's work.[303] These criticisms find their most developed expression in Hauerwas's 2001 Gifford Lectures, *With the Grain of the Universe*, which we will now consider.

In *With the Grain of the Universe*, Hauerwas advances the counter-intuitive argument that Karl Barth was the great Gifford lecturer of the twentieth century—the natural theologian *par excellence*. Natural theology done in Lord Gifford's vein is not theology at all, for the God of Abraham, Isaac and Jacob is not a logical deduction stemming from empirical observation, but rather the living Lord and creator of all that is. To fail to understand this is to make God "part of the metaphysical furniture of the universe."[304] True natural theology, on the other hand, "simply names how Christian convictions work to describe all that is as God's good creation."[305] The pre-eminent example of such natural theology in modern times, Hauerwas avers, is nothing other than the fourteen volumes of Barth's unfinished *Church Dogmatics*. While lauding Barth's brave and compelling theological witness in *Church Dogmatics*, Hauerwas worries that Barth may not have sufficiently developed the material conditions necessary "to sustain the witness that he thought was intrinsic to Christianity."[306]

"Put simply," Hauerwas states, "and no doubt too simply, the question is whether, when all is said and done, Barth is sufficiently catholic."[307] In

---

302. For examples of Hauerwas's self-identification as a Barthian see *STT*, 37; "Faculty Forum," 70; *HC*, 87. For three different narrations of the story of theology in the twentieth century in which Barth plays the leading role see *RA*, 19–29; "On Doctrine and Ethics," 21–40; and *WGU*, 141–204.

303. *CCL*, 129–78; *DFF*, 58–79; *WRAL*, 20–21.

304. *WGU*, 28.

305. Ibid., 142.

306. Ibid., 39.

307. Ibid., 145.

framing the dilemma in terms of ecclesiology, Hauerwas is drawing upon and continuing the line of questioning raised by theologians such as Reinhard Hütter, Nicholas Healy, and Joseph Mangina.[308] This ecclesiological criticism also includes the recognition that previous charges against Barth of occasionalism stemming from his actualism may have, in fact, been misplaced.[309] Citing Mangina, Hauerwas asserts that the criticism of those who questioned Barth on this score in the past is:

> better stated as a *pneumatological* worry and specifically a worry about the role played by the church in the economy of salvation. In brief, is the church merely a human echo or analogy of Christ's completed work, as in Barth? Or is it also somehow the herald of new activity in which God is engaged between now and the eschaton?[310]

As we have already seen in the preceding section, Hauerwas would affirm the latter and suggests that Barth's own thought has been over-determined by his reaction to the anthropologically-driven agenda of Protestant liberalism to the extent that it is "difficult for him to acknowledge that through the work of the Holy Spirit, we are made part of God's care of the world through the church."[311] Barth's desire to preserve the priority of divine agency over human agency and the distinction between the two, perhaps most clearly evidenced in his treatment of the sacraments, results in a strange bifurcation of the church between its essential character as the body of Christ on the one hand, and the constellation of practices which characterize the life of the church as a human community, but which appear to be merely incidental to its identity, on the other.[312] In other words, as Hauerwas puts it, "Barth never quite brings himself to explain how our human agency is involved in the Spirit's work."[313] Approvingly citing Mangina once more, Hauerwas asserts that "an adequate account of the role of the Spirit in faith not only involves 'the glad acceptance of the church's preaching, but acceptance of the church itself as the binding medium in which faith takes place.

---

308. Hütter, *Bound to be Free*, 24–28, 46–48, 78–94; Healy, "Logic of Barth's Ecclesiology"; Mangina, "Bearing the Marks." It should be noted that Healy has subsequently offered a more appreciative reading of Barth's ecclesiology in "Barth's Ecclesiology Reconsidered."

309. *WGU*, 188, 194–95.

310. Ibid., 195 n. 46, quoting Mangina, "Bearing the Marks," 282.

311. *WGU*, 145.

312. The "bifurcation" of the church in Barth's ecclesiology is a theme sounded by Healy, "Logic of Karl Barth's Ecclesiology," 258–59. For Barth's final treatment of baptism see *CD* 4/4.

313. *WGU*, 145.

The medium is, if not the message, the condition of possibility of grasping, the message in its truth."[314]

In light of his own meager employment of Spirit-talk, it could appear that Hauerwas's charges against Barth are simply a case of the pot calling the kettle black. However, *With the Grain of the Universe* can be looked upon as Hauerwas's attempt to address his own pneumatological deficiency by locating the life and ministry of the church within a more explicitly trinitarian framework.[315] "Just as the Son witnesses to the Father," Hauerwas writes, "so the Spirit makes us witnesses to the Son so that the world may know the Father."[316] If the Spirit did not raise up such witnesses, then the Christian story of the God who created and redeemed the world out of the eternal communion of love shared between Father, Son, and Holy Spirit would not be true. Hauerwas draws upon the work of Bruce Marshall in advancing the pragmatic thesis that "successful practice on the part of the Christian community and its members helps to *justify* the community's central beliefs."[317] In arguing for such a pragmatic understanding of the truth of Christian convictions Hauerwas is not asserting that the Christian community is free to construct its own version of reality simply by bearing down and embodying a particular type of lifestyle. Nor is he claiming that the Holy Spirit provides additional proof for the truth of the Gospel through the witnessing community, for "there can be no 'evidence' for beliefs beyond the totality of beliefs to which any contested claims might be brought."[318] Rather, what Hauerwas intends to affirm by advancing this pragmatic thesis is that if the Christian story is a truthful, comprehensive account of the way things are, then there must be people who order their lives according to its truth. The Christian story is not a matter of mere intellectual beliefs or principles, but rather is the story of the God who in sending His Son into the world and the Spirit of His Son into our hearts makes us participants in the divine life itself and hence claims the entirety of our lives. Hauerwas's pragmatic construal becomes clear when he pauses to consider the witness of the martyrs: "that

---

314. Ibid., 145, quoting Mangina, "Bearing the Marks," 294–95.

315. Many scholars sympathetic to Hauerwas have commented upon his implicit, but underdeveloped pneumatology, often in association with observations surrounding the underdeveloped character of Hauerwas's sacramentology. See for example: Mangina, "Bearing the Marks of Jesus," 292; Rasmusson, *Church as Polis*, 179; Thomson, *Ecclesiology of Stanley Hauerwas*, 214–15; Wells, *Transforming Fate*, 97–98. Hauerwas has very recently begun to address some of these pneumatological concerns, see "How to Be Caught by the Holy Spirit."

316. *WGU*, 207.

317. Marshall, *Trinity and Truth*, 202, quoted in *WGU*, 213.

318. *WGU*, 214.

martyrs die for their faith does not *prove* that Jesus is risen; on the other hand, that some people have assented to a totality of belief that includes the belief that Jesus is risen surely means that martyrs will die for their faith."[319] Witnesses, in living according to Christian convictions, or even dying for their faith as in the case of the martyrs, show us what the world is really like.[320] Without the eloquent testimony of the lives of witnesses, the world would have no way of knowing that its existence is the result of the gracious creating and redeeming activity of God. In a statement which summarizes the main thrust of his argument and could reasonably be seen to encapsulate a significant emphasis of his broader theological project, Hauerwas asserts that "Christianity is unintelligible without witnesses, that is, without people whose practices exhibit their committed assent to a particular way of structuring the whole."[321] It is at this very point that Hauerwas must look beyond Barth for additional resources. Hauerwas maintains that Barth's failure to specify the material conditions necessary for sustaining the church's witness gives his work the character of "a stunning intellectual performance" which "can too easily give the appearance of springing from the head of Zeus."[322] In the context of his Gifford Lectures, Hauerwas turns to the figures of John Howard Yoder and Pope John Paul II to advance his case.[323] Although Hauerwas's argument turns out to be surprisingly effective, it is to two earlier works that we will turn to explore his presentation of the material conditions necessary for sustaining the church's witness.

---

319. Ibid.

320. Hence, Yoder's claim from which the title of Hauerwas's Gifford Lectures is derived: "people who bear crosses are working with the grain of the universe" ("Armaments and Eschatology," 58, quoted in *WGU*, 6).

321. *WGU*, 214.

322. Ibid., 216. Pushing back against Hauerwas and others who have taken issue with the lack of concreteness in Barth's ecclesiology, Bender enriches the conversation by directing readers to Barth's own discussion of "the basic forms" of the church's ministry in *CD* 4/3.2:865–901. *Confessing* Christ, 55–9.

323. *WGU*, 215–30. Echoing Kallenberg, one cannot help but wonder whether in light of the argument he has advanced Hauerwas would not have been better served by directly drawing attention to the witness of Christian communities, rather than indirectly doing so by focusing attention on these two significant figures. "Strange New World," 212. Hauerwas has successfully made such a move in other contexts, which has included: drawing attention to the villagers of Le Chambon in *AN*, 87–8; discussing the Masai people of Tanzania in *PK*, 110–11 and *BCCE*, 7–9; and telling the story of the monks of Tibhirine in *CSC*, 31–3.

The Practices of a Disciplined Community

Many of the ecclesiological themes developed in *With the Grain of the Universe* already appear in nascent form in Hauerwas's and Willimon's sequel to *Resident Aliens*: *Where Resident Aliens Live*. Present is the emphasis upon the importance of faithful witnesses,[324] the identification of the truth of the Gospel as a truth that is only known through the practices of the worshipping community,[325] the identification of Karl Barth as the great liberator from Protestant liberalism,[326] and the corresponding criticism of Barth's deficient ecclesiology.[327] As its subtitle, *Exercises for Christian Practice*, suggests, *Where Resident Aliens Live* is an attempt to specify the material conditions necessary for sustaining the type of community of faithful witness that was put forward in *Resident Aliens*. If the church is to be a community of disciples that faithfully witnesses to the truth of Jesus Christ then it must be a disciplined community. This is also a central presumption of an essay which appeared in Hauerwas's first solo publication following *Resident Aliens*, entitled "How We Lay Bricks and Make Disciples."[328] The argument presented in this essay serves as a helpful supplement to the exploration in *Where Resident Aliens Live* of the question "What would it mean for our church to be a disciplined community?"[329]

In order to help the Christian community catch a glimpse of what it might mean for the church to exist as a disciplined community Hauerwas turns in his essay to the craft of bricklaying and then in the book coauthored with Willimon to the marine training camp at Parris Island. The first will come as no surprise to those familiar with Hauerwas's biography.[330] The second is a somewhat surprising choice considering Hauerwas's pacifist commitments, but both examples clearly do the work for which they are intended. In order to learn to lay brick, one must undergo a period of instruction and training as an apprentice in the service of a master craftsman. Such an apprenticeship is necessary, because one cannot simply be told how to lay brick, rather "you must learn a multitude of skills that are coordinated into the activity of laying brick—that is why before you lay brick you must

---

324. *WRAL*, 17.
325. Ibid., 18.
326. Ibid., 20.
327. Ibid., 20–21.
328. *AC*, 111.
329. *WRAL*, 102.
330. *HC*, 27–33.

learn to mix the mortar, build scaffolds, joint, and so on."[331] These distinct practices do not stand alone, but are immersed in the matrix of the peculiar language of bricklaying which reciprocally forms and informs these skills. Expressions such as "frogging mud" and "klinkers" are as intricate a part of the craft as knowing how to hold a trowel. As Hauerwas puts it, "You cannot learn to lay brick without learning to talk right."[332] Learning how to properly speak the language and acquiring the skills intrinsic to brick-laying results in the transformation of the self and hence necessitates the guidance of one who has him- or herself been transformed through the internalization of the standards of excellence associated with the craft. Being apprenticed to a master is essential because what often seems good to a novice, may not actually be the best according to the accumulated wisdom of the tradition.[333] The master is one who "knows how to go further, using what can be learned from tradition afforded by the past, so that he or she can move toward the telos of fully perfected work."[334] To be initiated into the craft of bricklaying by a master requires discipline, but this discipline is experienced as joy as one acquires the habits and virtues necessary to become a skilled bricklayer oneself. Hauerwas insists that learning to lay bricks is not only an analogy for becoming moral, but that bricklaying itself is decisive moral formation.[335]

The marine training camp at Parris Island is similarly highlighted by Hauerwas and Willimon as another site of decisive moral formation.[336] The slogan of Parris Island, "Where the Difference Begins," encapsulates the transformative agenda of the marine camp. Over the course of 11 weeks, recruits undergo a process of "cultural indoctrination" through which they are initiated into "the Marine way of talking, walking, and thinking."[337] Recruits are initiated into a web of practices, which includes the marines' own peculiar nautical language, a ban on the use of the first person in speech, and their own "casualty cadence" which could be considered as a type of hymnody.[338] At the conclusion of their extended citation of the article, Hauerwas and Willimon offer their own commentary: "Note what the Marines did to

331. *AC*, 101.
332. Ibid.
333. Ibid., 105.
334. Ibid., 106.
335. Ibid., 107.
336. Hauerwas and Willimon allow an article from *The Wall Street Journal*, which is cited at some length, to make the case for them. Thomas E. Ricks, "'New' Marines Illustrate Growing Gap between Military and Society," quoted in *WRAL*, 74–76.
337. *WRAL*, 74.
338. Ibid., 75–76.

their new recruits: They put them in a group, they moved them through a perilous ordeal, they taught them a new language, they gave them the skills to analyze what was wrong with their former life."[339]

The initiation of apprentices into the craft of bricklaying and the basic training of marines at Parris Island provide lenses that allow us to look upon the church's formation of disciples in a new light. In a way that is similar to what is experienced by the apprentices and recruits, Hauerwas and Willimon write, "In baptism, the church inculcates in us a set of practices whereby we become disciples."[340] At the head of this list of practices stands the discipline of learning the language of the Christian faith. Proponents of accomodationist strategies for attracting seekers and boosting weekly church attendance figures have failed to understand that "the church's language is not a natural language, but it is a language that requires the self to be transformed to be part of that language."[341] Learning to speak the Christian language opens up new vistas for perceiving and hence inhabiting the world. This language is first and foremost learned through the practice of prayer, which must be learned from those who have learned to pray well.[342] Learning to pray cannot be divorced from the larger complex of disciplines which must be learned in order to worship God and it is through worship that we learn to acknowledge that we are creatures and that we are sinners. For this reason, Hauerwas insists that such an acknowledgement must be understood to be a "theological and moral accomplishment," which is inseparable from the Christian practice of concretely confessing sins to one another.[343] As is apparent from the practice of the confession of sins, inherent to Christian discipline is the posture of vulnerability. To be discipled or disciplined—the two are synonymous for Hauerwas—one must become vulnerable to the truth which takes the form of submission to proper authority and the opening of one's life to others. "To be disciplined," write Hauerwas and Willimon, "means to make our lives vulnerable to friends."[344]

Conversion occurs as one is immersed in this matrix of practices and relationships and comes to develop habits which profoundly alter one's way of being in the world. The habits which are developed empower the Christian for life and service in the world by allowing them to take the right things for granted and ruling out from the beginning certain alternatives.

339. Ibid., 76.
340. Ibid., 77.
341. Ibid., 59.
342. Ibid., 42.
343. *AC*, 108.
344. *WRAL*, 111.

Christian discipline is therefore not a burden or oppressive law that must be dialectically qualified by the Gospel, rather it is of the Gospel itself. It is through being inculcated in the truthful practices of the church that we are given the means to name the powers that seek to claim our lives and the power to order our lives in conformity with the Gospel.[345] Discipline is a joy because it provides the church with "power for service" and develops the habits "through which we would not do anything other than what we are delightfully doing."[346] The church not only teaches disciples how to pray, but through learning how to pray disciples become prayerful, and come to reflect the image of Jesus Christ, "the Father's prayer for the world."[347]

PART 3: ECCLESIOLOGICAL CONCLUSIONS

In what follows, the traditional creedal notes of the church—one, holy, catholic, apostolic—will provide a framework for bringing to light the shared ecclesiological convictions emerging from each thinker's profound christological concentration and for considering areas of divergence where one may offer a helpful correction to the other.[348] The creedal notes are received by the church as both gift and calling. They are calling because they are first gift. Furthermore, since the notes are predicates of the reality which is the church, the conceptual borders between the notes are naturally fluid, with each note overlapping with and flowing into the others.

The Church is "One"

There is widespread agreement throughout the Christian tradition that the church is one on account of the unity of the one God who calls the church into existence and graciously sustains it.[349] The ecclesiological sensibilities

---

345. While he continues to stand by his co-authored works with Hauerwas, Willimon has expressed the concern that the language of "practice" in contemporary Christian theology and spirituality is often shorn of its theological content, essentially becoming an anthropologically-centered Pelagianism. "Too Much Practice," 23–25.

346. *AC*, 107; *WRAL*, 112.

347. *PTF*, 153.

348. While the traditional creedal notes of the church will provide the framework for this section, extended discussion and detailed analysis of the historical interpretation of the *notae ecclesiae* notes lies beyond the scope of the chapter. For a survey of patristic understandings of the notes, see Di Berardino, *One Holy Catholic and Apostolic Church*, 54–86. For two contemporary introductions to the notes of the church as they appear in the Nicene and Apostles' Creeds respectively, see, Abraham, "I Believe"; and Wood, "Holy Catholic Church."

349. Williams, *Tokens of Trust*, 126.

of Bonhoeffer and Hauerwas are no different from the broader Christian theological tradition in this regard. For both Bonhoeffer and Hauerwas, the church is one because there is one Lord Jesus Christ. Underlying both of their theological projects is a christological realism which understands the church to truly be Christ's body. The church is a reality of revelation. Now to be sure both authors speak according to their own distinctive theological dialects, but nonetheless, both in their own way make this affirmation.[350]

The difficulty arises for both Bonhoeffer and Hauerwas, as it does for the tradition, with respect to how to understand this unity in the face of the messy, empirical reality of the church. As Protestant theologians, the strand in Roman Catholic theology which identifies the unity of the church with the institutional hierarchy is not a live option for either Bonhoeffer or Hauerwas.[351] On the other hand, Protestant attempts to ground unity in agreement in doctrine are equally problematic for both men—beyond the fact that the achievement of doctrinal consensus between Protestant churches has proven to be quite elusive.[352] Doctrine is to serve Christian unity, but it is not the foundation for unity, because the church is a theological and social reality which precedes doctrine.[353] This does not mean that matters of doctrine can be ignored. Both Bonhoeffer and Hauerwas have no time for conceptions of unity rooted in facile pluralisms which do not take the question of truth seriously. This is evident in Hauerwas's ongoing critique of liberalism and also in Bonhoeffer's frustrations with the ecumenical movement of his day, which he perceived to be lacking an adequate theological foundation.[354] While some theologians have sought to escape from the intractable dilemmas presented by the concrete life of the empirical church through appeals to an ideal or invisible church, both Bonhoeffer and Hauerwas, on account of the incarnation, stand opposed to such metaphysical flights of fancy.[355]

For both Bonhoeffer and Hauerwas any conception of Christian unity which neglects the centrality of the life of the local congregation is seriously deficient. The local congregation is the site where the Gospel is concretely

---

350. For Bonhoeffer, this perhaps comes across most clearly in his designation of the church as "Christ existing as church-community." One place where Hauerwas's insistence on the church as a reality of revelation is apparent is in the essay "The Church as God's New Language," where he asserts that with respect to the church's telling of the story of Jesus of Christ, ultimately, "the teller and the tale are one" (*CET*, 54).

351. Dulles, *Models of the Church*, 118–19.

352. McGrath, *Christian Theology*, 391–92.

353. *ATE*, 107 n. 22; *DBWE* 11:282–90.

354. *DBWE* 11:356–72.

355. Dulles, *Models of the Church*, 135–36.

lived out in the daily life of its members and it is within the context of the gathering of the congregation that Christ is tangibly present through the preaching of the word and the administration of the sacraments. The proclaiming of the Word creates *koinōnia* which finds it goal in sharing in the *koinōnia* of the body of the Lord Jesus Christ at His Table.[356] Although neither author has provided a detailed sacramental theology, both clearly suppose the real presence of Christ in the Eucharist. In this way, the ecclesiologies of both Bonhoeffer and Hauerwas could be considered to be nuanced explications of the patristic maxim *ubi Christus, ibi ecclesia*.[357]

The presence of the risen Christ in the local congregation stands as a gracious invitation for the community to look beyond itself and discover the unity they share in Christ with other communities gathered around the risen Lord.[358] Bonhoeffer's reception of this invitation took the form of involvement in the nascent international ecumenical movement prior to the outbreak of the Second World War. It appears that Bonhoeffer thought that the ecumenical movement could act as the one church of Jesus Christ, if it summoned the courage to proclaim the clear word of Christ to the world. In the late 1930s Bonhoeffer perceived this to be the command prohibiting another world war.[359] Despite his frustrations with the ecumenical movement of his day, Bonhoeffer's participation in the World Alliance and his hope that it would summon the courage to utter the clear and unambiguous Word of Christ indicate that Bonhoeffer was open to some type of conciliar expression of intra-denominational unity.[360] For Bonhoeffer, an ecumenical

---

356. For an example of this liturgical or sacramental theo-logic in the work of each author, see *DBWE* 14:435–46; *IGC*, 33–49.

357. "Wherever Christ is, there is the church."

358. Hauerwas approvingly cites Rowan Williams in this vein: "The entire Church is present in every local church assembled around the Lord's Table. Yet the local church alone is never the entire Church. We are called to see this not as a circle to be squared but as an invitation to be more and more lovingly engaged with one another" ("Presidential Address," quoted in *WAD*, 161).

359. See Bonhoeffer's lecture "On the Theological Foundation of the World Alliance" delivered at the International Youth Peace Conference in Czechoslovakia in 1932. "The work of our World Alliance—consciously or unconsciously—is grounded in a very distinct conception of the church. The church as the one church-community of the Lord Jesus Christ, who is the Lord of the world, has the task of speaking his word to the entire world. The range of the one church of Christ is the entire world. There are local boundaries for the proclamation of each individual church, but the *one* church has no boundaries around it" (*DBWE* 11:359).

360. Bonhoeffer never gave up hope for the ecumenical church, as is evident from the farewell message he asked his fellow prisoner Payne Best to transmit to his friend, the Anglican Bishop, George Bell: "Tell him that this is for me the end, but also the beginning—with him I believe in the principle of our Universal Christian brotherhood

council would stand as a concrete gathering in the power of the Holy Spirit of representatives of the scattered congregations of Christ, through which the risen Christ would proclaim his Word to his whole Church. Bonhoeffer's commitment to conciliarism is also reflected in his involvement in the Church Struggle in Germany and his unswerving allegiance to the Council of Brethren and the pronouncements of the synod of Barmen and Dahlem. Bonhoeffer was firmly convinced that God had spoken through the synods of Barmen and Dahlem with the result that for Christians in Germany there was no getting around or behind their proclamations.[361]

Hauerwas does not share Bonhoeffer's interest in conciliarism, but has in recent writings taken to describing himself as a "congregationalist with Catholic sensibilities."[362] According to Hauerwas's own logic, this self-designation does not stand in self-contradiction, because, "for Christianity, particularity is constitutive of universality and is, therefore, appropriately called catholic."[363] The various particularities which are constitutive of universality are held together through the office of the bishop.[364] "The office of the bishop," Hauerwas writes, "is an office of hospitality, for it is the bishop's duty to share the stories of particular Eucharistic assemblies to ensure that when we move from one parish to another we can have some assurance that we are worshipping the same God."[365] The office of bishop ensures that the necessary conditions for communication exist between congregations. The ministry of the bishop allows congregations to expand their understanding of the Gospel as they are encountered by new readings of Scripture arising from the reception of the Gospel in different contexts. These encounters between congregations across both time and space, facilitated by the bishop, become not only the opportunity for expanding theological horizons within the local congregation, but may also serve as the impetus for calling communities to reform and renewal through repenting of distorted ways of telling and enacting the story of Jesus.

Both Bonhoeffer's understanding of an ecumenical conciliarism and Hauerwas's conception of congregationalism with bishops provide forums for distinct congregations to encounter one another in a personal way. Such personal encounters are necessary if the church is to be led into all truth,

---

which rises above all national hatreds, and that our victory is certain—tell him too that I have never forgotten his words at our last meeting" (*DBWE* 16:468–69).

361. *DBWE* 14:667–69, 694.
362. *ATE*, 102.
363. *WAD*, 153 n. 7.
364. *ATE*, 112.
365. *WAD*, 160 n. 28.

for the truth that is Jesus is inherently personal. Where there is no concern for truth there can be no unity, for as Bonhoeffer writes with Hauerwas's approval, "There can only be a community of peace when it does not rest on lies and injustice."[366] The space for personal encounter with the truth that is Jesus that is opened up in both theologians' attempts to conceive of trans-congregational unity means that the unity to which the church is called may very well necessitate repentance as the appropriate response to the encounter between congregations and/or denominations. The church must, as Hauerwas frames the matter, "confess its fallibility, which requires that claims of the church's indefectibility must be given up."[367] Bonhoeffer offers a concrete example of what such penitence might look like in the ecclesial confession of guilt found within the *Ethics* manuscript, "Guilt, Justification, Renewal."[368] While unity may ultimately be a gift that awaits its fulfillment in the eschaton, this should in no way diminish or normalize the scandal of the divided church.[369] The in-breaking of the eschaton in the crucifixion of Christ impels the church to bear its divisions with contrition and humility under the sign of the cross.[370] The confession of guilt may very well be the form that unity takes in this period of the church's pilgrimage between the ages.[371]

The Church is "Holy"

The adjective "holy" when applied to the church has often been understood as an attribute that sets the church apart from the peoples which surround them. At times this holiness has been identified with the unique character of the institutional hierarchy and the sacramental means of grace.[372] Other

366. Bonhoeffer, *No Rusty Swords*, 168; quoted in *PTF*, 13.

367. *ATE*, 108. I do wonder whether Hauerwas in this quotation has elided a subtle distinction that should be maintained between infallibility and indefectibility. While the church should acknowledge its fallibility, the indefectibility of the church, as I understand it, does not rest on the church's own capacity to remain without error, but rather upon the promise of Christ that "the gates of Hades will not prevail against it" (Matt 16:18).

368. *E* (*DBWE* 6), 134–45.

369. *ATE* 109 n. 27; *DBWE* 15:445.

370. "Division is to be carried as a cross, believing that God [has] called it as *una sancta*" (*DBWE* 11:330).

371. Jennifer McBride has drawn upon Bonhoeffer's thinking surrounding confession of sin and repentance in formulating a theology of public witness in a non-triumphalist mode for Protestant churches in North America. See "Thinking within the Movement," and *Church for the World*.

372. Dulles, *Models of the Church*, 119.

times holiness has been identified with the moral standing or purity of the church's members—as either an empirical, imputed, or eschatological possession.[373] For Bonhoeffer and Hauerwas, however, holiness does not name an attribute but a relation. The character of the church as a holy people is rooted in the person of the living Lord Jesus Christ, who calls disciples into his company, and the Holy Spirit who conforms the community of disciples to their Master. Hence, the attribute holy does not designate a status, but rather names the dynamic reality of a life lived within the pilgrim community of radical discipleship that is on the road with Jesus. As the eschatological polis of God, the church is the corporate presence of the new humanity in the midst of the passing world. As it enacts the politics of the Kingdom, the concrete shape of the life of the Christian congregation distinguishes it from the surrounding world. Occupying a central place in this unique mode of ecclesial existence is the Sermon on the Mount. The New Testament scholar Joachim Jeremias once observed that "the Sermon on the Mount is not Law, but Gospel"[374]—a phrase which would surely earn a hearty "Amen!" from both Bonhoeffer and Hauerwas. The Sermon characterizes the shape of Kingdom life as it has been definitively established and exhibited in the life of the King himself. Discipleship entails becoming like Jesus, for the community of disciples recognizes that the way that Jesus is the Way is not disposable, but is intrinsic to the salvation offered in His name. As a result both Bonhoeffer and Hauerwas recognize that the church is both a gracious community and a disciplined community. It is, in fact, a gracious community to the extent that it is a disciplined community.

A consideration of the disciplined life of the community involves speaking of the specific rhythms and practices which characterize the life of this people and provide the occasion for the risen Christ to encounter His people and take form within them. Such formation takes the shape of *mortificatio* and *vivificatio* in the life of the disciple, for in encounter with the living Christ disciples inevitably discover how far they are from being like Jesus. For this reason, both Bonhoeffer and Hauerwas stress the centrality of the confession and absolution of sins to the life of the church. For both, the church lives by the forgiveness of sins, not as an abstract principle, but as a dynamic, living reality within the life of the community as the power of falsehood is broken as particular sins are truthfully acknowledged and forgiven in the name of Jesus Christ and genuine community with God and one another is restored. The church then is the site of an unfolding drama as Christ encounters his people through the preaching of the word,

---

373. McGrath, *Christian Theology*, 394.
374. Jeremias, *Sermon on the Mount*, 32, quoted in Ziegler, "Not to Abolish," 288.

the administration of the sacraments and the web of practices and relationships that make up the ongoing life of the community. As this occurs, the community of disciples is drawn into the life of Christ and conformed to His image, so that in the church the world may encounter the form of the One who is its life.

While Bonhoeffer and Hauerwas are in general agreement that through the sanctifying work of the Holy Spirit the community of disciples is drawn into conformity with Jesus Christ, a potential impasse arises with respect to how to best speak of this work of conformation in the life of the disciple. Hauerwas employs virtue language as a way of speaking of the disciple's conformation to Christ. Bonhoeffer, however, appears to be somewhat reluctant to use such conventions for speaking of the work of the Holy Spirit in conforming disciples to the image of Christ.[375] Although Bonhoeffer does not provide an explicit treatment of the virtues, he does at various points express concerns about them. Perhaps the most well-known of the aspersions cast by Bonhoeffer towards an ethics of virtue occurs in the famous prologue to *Letters and Papers from Prison*, the essay "After Ten Years."[376] In this essay, Bonhoeffer reflects upon how the rise of the Third Reich has revealed the inadequacy and ineptness of the reigning ethical paradigms. The standards of reason, principles, conscience, freedom, and virtuousness were all unable to withstand the "huge masquerade of evil" which befell Germany in the 1930s and 1940s.[377] In turning to the paragraph in which Bonhoeffer addresses virtuousness it becomes apparent that what he has in mind is one who divides life into public and private spheres and attempts to preserve personal purity and blamelessness by taking flight from the realm of public life and retreating into the realm of what he calls "private virtuousness."[378] What Bonhoeffer appears to be criticizing here is a type of sectarian withdrawal that abandons the world to its own devices in the name of preserving clean hands. Those who mistakenly charge Hauerwas with being a sectarian might see some purchase in applying this passage

375. Jennifer Moberly has recently contributed a significant exploration of the affinities between Bonhoeffer's *Ethics* and what is commonly referred to as virtue ethics. While Bonhoeffer's ethics may not simply be equated with virtue ethics, Moberly does conclude that "it is possible to claim that Bonhoeffer is bringing together Thomist virtue ethics and Barthian divine command ethics, in a distinctive ethic for his own context" (*Virtue of Bonhoeffer's Ethics*, Loc. 7643). Moberly does acknowledge early on that Bonhoeffer would not have identified himself as a "virtue ethicist" (Loc. 1368). However, as Moberly rightly recognizes, one cannot be content to stop with simple labels or formal ascriptions but must press on to examine Bonhoeffer's material convictions themselves.

376. *LPP* (*DBWE* 8), 37–52.

377. Ibid., 38–40. A parallel passage is found in *E* (*DBWE* 6), 80.

378. *LPP* (*DBWE* 8), 40.

to the Texan theological ethicist. However, for Hauerwas virtue is never a private matter, rather character is a way of speaking of the human agent in a holistic manner which attempts to overcome the modern division of life into private and public realms.[379]

The far more significant constellation of concerns expressed by Bonhoeffer about the virtues arises in the pages of *Discipleship*. While in this book Bonhoeffer does in many ways offer a significant correction to the Lutheran tradition of his day, he nonetheless retains a characteristically Lutheran nervousness surrounding the language of virtue. This is evident for example in his reflections upon Matthew 5:16, where he states that the good works of the disciples which lead people to ascribe glory to God cannot be human virtues, for "if the good works were all sorts of human virtues, then the disciples, not the Father, would be praised for them."[380] Bonhoeffer appears concerned that speaking of virtue could in some way imply that through their own virtuousness human beings come to have righteousness as their own possession and hence are no longer dependent upon the righteousness of God that always comes to the sinner *extra nos*. The danger becomes that in their desire to see something of their own developing inherent righteousness the disciple will lose sight of the One who is forever their righteousness and always goes before them on the way.[381] Talk of the virtues, appears for Bonhoeffer, to always stand in danger of making discipleship an all too human self-realization project, which in place of the grace of the Gospel that liberates human beings to be truly for one another, propagates the basest narcissistic and triumphalistic tendencies within the fallen human being.[382]

To counter these concerns, Bonhoeffer emphasizes the hidden nature of the Christian life.[383] There is a self-forgetfulness to being a disciple that Bonhoeffer believes to be incongruent with an emphasis on the virtues.[384]

---

379. *CET*, 191.

380. *D* (*DBWE* 4), 114. This is reminiscent of how Bonhoeffer first came to the personal attention of Karl Barth by quoting in Barth's seminar "Luther's statement that the curses of the godless sometimes sound better to God's ear than the hallelujahs of the pious" (Bethge, *Dietrich Bonhoeffer*, 176).

381. *D* (*DBWE* 4), 279.

382. Moberly suggests that Bonhoeffer's own unique employment of virtue-ethical themes charts a course beyond the dangers of Pelagianism and problematic self-love which often seem to accompany accounts in which virtue plays a central role. *Virtue of Bonhoeffer's Ethics*, Loc. 7809.

383. To this end, Bonhoeffer frequently refers to Matthew 6:3: "do not let your left hand know what your right hand is doing."

384. "It is clear that because it is hidden love, it cannot be a visible virtue, a human *habitus* [attitude]. Beware—it says—that you do not mistake genuine love for the virtue of kindness or for a human 'quality'! It is self-forgetting love in the most genuine sense

True disciples never see themselves, because their gaze is always focused on Jesus.[385] Any construal of the Christian life that would tempt the disciple to turn their eyes from the One who goes before them or believe that they have moved beyond their utter and complete need of the crucified One must be rejected. Wannenwetsch offers a Bonhoefferian critique of the limits of employing virtue theory for understanding the life of discipleship in a paragraph that deserves repeating:

> Discipleship, understood properly, is unlike virtue habituation through emulation. In fact, when Jesus sends his disciples to preach in the villages, to heal or to cast out demons, they do this as those who travel under the auspices of Jesus' own *exousia*—his powerful authority that he sends along with them; the disciples are, strictly speaking, doing "his deeds" rather than their own. Accordingly their 'moral' aim must be to simply stay within the sphere of their calling and do what comes to hand, instead of aiming at perfecting their vocational skills through exercise so as to eventually rival or transcend their master's own virtuosity in them.[386]

The concerns raised by Bonhoeffer about the virtues are serious, but not, I believe, ultimately debilitating for Hauerwas's project. As was argued in the previous chapter, Hauerwas has increasingly made his theological commitments more explicit, which has included locating his Christology within a more substantial Trinitarian framework. This development should help to assuage the fears of Protestants by assuring them that Hauerwas understands Luther's insistence that "the chief article and foundation of the gospel is that before you take Christ as an example, you accept and recognize him as a gift, as a present that God has given you and that is your own."[387]

While Hauerwas has provided a tremendous service to the church in helping to recover the place of the virtues in Christian ethical discourse, he must also continue to work to ensure that the discourse surrounding the virtues remains subservient to the Gospel. The language of Athens must not be allowed to eclipse or efface the language of Jerusalem.[388] As Hauerwas

---

of the word" (*D* (*DBWE* 4), 151–52).

385. Ibid., 108.

386. Wannenwetsch, "Whole Christ," 88.

387. Luther, *Basic Theological Writings*, 105. See also Wannenwetsch, "Whole Christ," 88–89.

388. Healy seems to believe that something along these lines is, in fact, the case in Hauerwas's work. Healy asserts that Hauerwas needs to provide "an account of the virtues and practices that makes far clearer how Aristotle's account is radically deficient" (*Hauerwas*, 129).

himself acknowledges, Christians have no particular investment in the virtues per se.[389] Rather, the virtues are useful only to the extent that under the discipline of the Gospel they assist in the explication and understanding of the Christian life. After all, as Hauerwas succinctly put it, while commenting on Matthew 6 in dialogue with Bonhoeffer: "Christians are not called to be virtuous. We are called to be disciples."[390]

If, however, the starting point for Christian ethics truly is, as Bonhoeffer insists, "the formation of the church according to the form of Christ," then it would appear that there must be a place for something along the lines of Hauerwas's account of the virtues.[391] For if, as Bonhoeffer suggests, the community of disciples truly are transformed into the image of the One they look upon, there must be some way of describing this transformative work that takes into account the historicity of human existence.[392] Furthermore, if the Holy Spirit actually does bring forth real and tangible fruit in the life of the church-community, which can only be discerned to the extent that they are reliable and recurring patterns of behavior and ways of relating to one another, then what is in view is in fact some type of "a community of character."[393] As a result, Hauerwas has ample ground for insisting that Bonhoeffer's claim that the hidden love of the disciple cannot be a visible virtue or human habit is overstated.[394] Hauerwas appears to be correct in detecting a whiff of the docetism Bonhoeffer otherwise so vehemently opposes in his refusal to countenance the bodily reality of the virtues. The development of virtues is quite simply a consequence of embodied human existence. Every social body inculcates virtues in its members.[395] The question is not whether to have virtues, but "which virtues we acquire, how they are acquired, and what they tell us about the kind of social order in which we exist."[396]

---

389. *CAV*, 55.

390. *Mt*, 75.

391. *E* (*DBWE* 6), 97. Moberly expresses a similar judgment with respect to Bonhoeffer's relation to virtue ethics in general, observing that "the notion of formation is more closely related to character and virtue ethics than any other mode of ethical thought" (*Virtue of Bonhoeffer's Ethics*, Loc. 4373).

392. *D* (*DBWE* 4), 288.

393. Rasmussen has drawn a similar conclusion noting that Bonhoeffer's ethic is essentially a *Gesinnungsethik* (an ethic of disposition) because what counts most for Bonhoeffer is the formation of the moral agent into Christ's form. *Reality and Resistance*, 158.

394. *Mt*, 75 n. 2.

395. For evidence of this, one need look no farther than how the procedural virtues of tolerance, sincerity and fairness have been enshrined in modern liberal societies. *CET*, 191.

396. Ibid., 192.

Hauerwas agrees with Bonhoeffer that "those who would follow Jesus can be characterized by a kind of forgetfulness," yet suggests that this forgetfulness is commensurate with developing the habits necessary for acquiring the virtues.[397] "There is a kind of forgetfulness to being so formed," Hauerwas argues, "because virtuous persons are virtuous for no other reason than that they would not desire to be other than they are."[398] Properly understood, the development of the virtues need not be associated with narcissistic preoccupation, but rather should be seen as the liberation from our over-powering sense of self which is the consequence of being caught up in the grand adventure of the dawning Messianic Kingdom. For this reason an emphasis on the virtues should also not be associated with works-righteousness, for the virtues which characterize the life of the disciple do not arise of independent human initiative. Rather, the virtues of the disciple are the result of the radical transformation of the self that occurs on account of being drawn into the life of the Triune God. Hauerwas helpfully clarifies the matter by proposing that:

> becoming truly virtuous is more like a moment of felicity—like something that comes as a gift—than something we do. Moreover, it is crucial that this gift, like character, be preserved. Otherwise, we have no sense of transcendence which makes us too likely to become self-righteous, or worse, such communities of virtue risk becoming ends in themselves rather than having virtues that render them open to the God that has called them into existence.[399]

Hauerwas's employment of the term "felicity" and his talk of being rendered open to God in the preceding paragraph suggest a way that the concept of the virtues could be incorporated into Bonhoeffer's project that is congruent with his overall theological outlook. This paragraph clarifies that the virtues refer not to the *vita activa* of the rebellious human being, but rather speak of a type of *vita passiva*, which is the posture of the newly (re)created human being before God. This would appear to open the door for a construal of the virtues that would perhaps be more congenial to Lutherans like Bonhoeffer than the traditional Catholic understanding informed by Aquinas. It suggests that alongside of charity, there may be a way to understand faith as the form of the virtues.[400]

397. *Mt*, 74.
398. Ibid., 75.
399. *CET*, 196.
400. For a recent proposal that emphasizes the inseparability of faith, hope and love and attempts to rehabilitate a certain priority for faith in the theologically virtuous life,

The Church is "Catholic"

The adjective "catholic" when spoken of as a note of the church is often understood to mean universal or worldwide.[401] While both Bonhoeffer and Hauerwas freely affirm that the church of Jesus Christ transcends all racial, ethnic and national boundaries, the descriptors universal and worldwide lack the necessary density to accurately portray the catholic character of the church in their theologies. The origins of the word catholic in the Greek phrase *kath' holou* ("referring to the whole"),[402] begin to point us towards a conception of catholicity that is congruent with what is expressed in the ecclesiologies of Bonhoeffer and Hauerwas. In both of their theologies, the catholicity of the church could be understood to be a function of the church's situatedness with respect to the whole of reality. Reality, for both men, cannot be understood apart from the incarnation of the Son of God and the reconciliation of God and man accomplished in the cross and resurrection of Jesus Christ. To try to conceive of reality in any other way is to fall into the realm of abstraction.[403] The church is the community that has emerged from the waters of baptism immersed in the reality of the Triune God with the commission to live from the depths of this reality in every aspect of its life in the world.

The catholic character of the church as pertaining to the whole of reality is inherent in the decision made by both men to describe the birth of the church at Pentecost in terms of a new creation.[404] In describing the church as a new creation, they rule out any notions that the church might simply be a religious entity, pertaining to only certain spheres or realms of existence. Rather, "*catholic*," Bonhoeffer states in a manner that would surely win Hauerwas's approval, "[is a] predicate of the church that concerns its worldliness."[405] The church as the body of Christ is the place within the world where worldly life is wholly reoriented to its true origin in creation and its proper end in the Kingdom of God.[406] Caught up in the reconciliation of God and the world in Jesus Christ, the church becomes the site for the reintegration of fragmented human existence.

---

see O'Donovan, *Self, World, and Time*, 97–112.

401. Grenz et al., "Catholic," 24.

402. McGrath, *Christian Theology*, 395.

403. *E (DBWE 6)*, 54.

404. *DBWE* 14:441–43; *CET*, 53.

405. *DBWE* 11:330.

406. *E (DBWE 6)*, 53.

The community which has found itself taken up within the reality of the world reconciled to God in Jesus Christ is commissioned to realize its catholicity under the guidance of the Holy Spirit in ever new circumstances. At this point, Bonhoeffer's distinction between the eternal realization of the church in Jesus Christ and the actualization of the church in time by the Holy Spirit is apropos.[407] Also pertinent is Hauerwas's insistence that "in Jesus Christ God has occupied space in the world and continues to do so through the work of the Holy Spirit's calling the church to faithfulness."[408] Spiritual discernment therefore becomes a crucial aspect contributing to the realization of the church's catholic character in the world. In each particular context the church has the responsibility of discerning how the concrete ordering of its liturgical and communal life, which cannot be divorced from its ethical witness before the world, is best shaped in accordance with reality in Jesus Christ. Through its varying responses to the Spirit's continuing invitation to participate in the reality of Christ in the world the church acquires a history. The web of practices, structures, and relationships which emerge from the church's response to the call to bring all aspects of its life under the acknowledged Lordship of Jesus Christ provides the church with a certain density in the world. This process of spiritual discernment, which involves the ongoing testing of the church's convictions in relation to the particular contexts in which it finds itself, gives rise to a tradition of metaphysical, aesthetical, and ethical reflection within the church.[409] The church, therefore, as a catholic people exists within time and space, which for Bonhoeffer and Hauerwas is quite simply an implication of the incarnation of the Son of God.

Differences, however, arise between Bonhoeffer and Hauerwas as to how to conceive of the temporal and spatial nature of the church's existence in the world. With respect to the question of temporality, Hauerwas's advocacy of what I will call an "evangelical casuistry" brings to light some confusion in Bonhoeffer's thought surrounding moral deliberation and the historicity of the church. Casuistry, for Hauerwas, is the means by which the church-community in conversation with the living tradition tests the

---

407. *SC* (*DBWE* 1), 139, 144, 157; *DBWE* 11:305–6

408. *PTF*, 48.

409. While both Bonhoeffer's and Hauerwas's christological metaphysics and ethics have received a fair amount of attention, the significant place of aesthetics in their work is frequently overlooked. Writing from prison, Bonhoeffer suggests to Bethge that recovery of authentic "aesthetic existence" might only be possible within the church. *LPP* (*DBWE* 8), 268. For one of Hauerwas's more explicit treatments of aesthetics see "Suffering Beauty: The Liturgical Formation of Christ's Body," in *PTF*, 151–65.

practical implications of its fundamental convictions.[410] Such an evangelical casuistry arises not on account of a desire to replace the command of God or to supersede His judgement, but rather out of the desire of God's people to live most faithfully according to the divine will.[411] The employment of casuistry in this manner would seemingly fulfill Bonhoeffer's own words of instruction, when he insists that, "in order to discern what the will of God may be, the entire array of human abilities will be employed."[412] However, the word casuistry seems to exist only as a by-word for Bonhoeffer. For this reason, I have intentionally made use of the adjective qualifier evangelical to distinguish the type of casuistry practiced by Hauerwas from the kinds of casuistry that Bonhoeffer seems to have been familiar with and regarded with justifiable suspicion. When Bonhoeffer speaks of casuistry he seems to have in mind a type of Catholic moral theology that has lost sight of the particular person of Jesus Christ and now speaks according to seemingly universal laws and principles under the rubric of natural law.[413] Such a formal system jeopardizes both the freedom of the Christian and the freedom of the Christian's sovereign Lord and runs the perennial risk of denigrating into legalism.[414]

There does, however, seem to be room within Bonhoeffer's understanding of spiritual discernment and moral deliberation for an evangelical casuistry which would occupy an analogous place to the practice of theology within the life of the church-community.[415] For Bonhoeffer, "theology is the memory of the church."[416] It stands between past and future preaching, existing for the purpose of assisting the preacher to proclaim the Gospel. Through its contribution to the formation of dogma, theology rightly stands as the presupposition of preaching. However, since the subject matter of theology is the living God of the Gospel who can never be captured within a system of objective thought, theology can only properly be practiced as an ecclesial discipline within the church "where the living person of Christ is

---

410. *CET*, 70.

411. Ibid., 68–69.

412. *E* (*DBWE* 6), 324.

413. *E* (*DBWE* 6), 99–100.

414. Ibid., 386; 395–96; *LPP* (*DBWE* 8), 120 n. 11. Hauerwas is also concerned about these developments within what he calls the "old morality" of Catholic moral theory. *PK*, 117–18; 55–57; *CET*, 70; *BCCE*, 45.

415. This would seem to be implied in Bonhoeffer's declaration in *Ethics* that "The *subject matter of a Christian ethic is God's reality revealed in Christ becoming real [Wirklichwerden] among God's creatures,* just as the subject matter of doctrinal theology is the truth of God's reality revealed in Christ" (*E* (*DBWE* 6), 49).

416. *AB* (*DBWE* 2), 130.

itself present and can destroy this existing thing or acknowledge it."[417] This description of the place of theology in the life of the church seems to open the door for understanding a parallel place for evangelical casuistry as the ethical memory of the church. Just as theology serves the preacher in identifying the God of the Gospel out of the recognition that God has definitively revealed himself in the person of Jesus Christ, an evangelical casuistry assists the members of the church in discerning whether their action is in accordance with the reality of that same Christ. Similarly, as theology occupies a place between past and future preaching, casuistry would occupy a place between past and future Christian action. It is only as it exercised within the context of the life of worship and prayer of the local congregation, where it is made vulnerable to the interruptive presence of the living God, that casuistry can avoid the temptation of falling into a stagnant system of rules which seeks to take the living Lord in hand. For a truly evangelical casuistry does not simply reason on the basis of Jesus Christ, as if he is now absent from the scene, but rather reasons in service and responsiveness to its Living Lord.[418] The practice of a certain type of casuistry is therefore congruent with Bonhoeffer's own theological presuppositions and is, in fact, an evangelical necessity.[419] Hauerwas affirms as much, when he states, "The church is that community pledged constantly to work out and test the implications of the story of God, as known through Israel and Jesus Christ, for its common life as well as the life of the world."[420]

As a catholic people, the church not only exists across time, but also exists as a visible people in the world. Hauerwas has helpfully drawn attention to the significant place of the recovery of the visibility of the church within Bonhoeffer's work in an essay entitled, "Dietrich Bonhoeffer's Political Theology."[421] For the sake of the world, the church must recover the concrete character of its corporate pilgrimage. As Bonhoeffer wrote and Hauerwas approvingly cites, "it is essential to the revelation of God in

417. Ibid., 131.

418. Wannenwetsch offers an important correction along these lines to Christian moral reasoning that attempts to take Christ in hand: "Christ is not the *foundation* of our moral knowledge, but the *interlocutor to* our moral discourse; he is not the one to assure us, but the one to challenge us, not the one who *is* near, but the one who *comes near*: Christ, the mediator" ("Whole Christ," 96).

419. Rasmussen has identified the presence of a line of "neo-casuistic" reasoning within Bonhoeffer's work itself, which is perhaps most prominently displayed in the *Ethics* manuscript on "The Natural Life." *Reality and Resistance*, 27; cf. E (*DBWE* 6), 171–218.

420. *PK*, 131–32.

421. *PTF*, 33–54.

Jesus Christ that it occupies space within the world."[422] While Hauerwas has provided a generous gift to Bonhoeffer studies by drawing attention to Bonhoeffer's interest in recovering the public character of the church in the face of the corrosive influence of modernity, there is a dialectical character to Bonhoeffer's understanding of the visibility of the church that is largely absent from Hauerwas's work.[423] This dialectical understanding of the (in)visibility of the church stems directly from Bonhoeffer's christological convictions. In his Christology lectures, Bonhoeffer gave voice to his conviction that Christ's coming to us incognito, in the likeness of sinful flesh, "is the central problem of Christology."[424] Christ's coming under the conditions of history and entering into the reality of fallen human existence necessitates the presence of faith if the One who was crucified outside of the city walls is to be recognized as the Lord of Glory. As the following quotation from *Discipleship* makes clear, the problem of Christ's presence in sinful flesh and the corresponding faith required to recognize his true identity in no way diminishes the corporeal existence of the body of Christ, but it does introduce a nuanced dialectal understanding of its visibility:

> the incarnation does entail the claim to space on earth, and anything that takes up space is visible. Thus the body of Christ can only be a visible body, or else it is not a body at all. Our human eyes see Jesus the human being; faith knows him as the Son of God. Our human eyes see the body of Jesus; faith knows him as the body of God incarnate. Our human eyes see Jesus in the flesh; faith knows him as bearing our flesh. 'To this human being you shall point and say "Here is God" (Luther).[425]

Similarly, the church, as the bodily presence of Christ on earth in the time between the resurrection and the *parousia*, is a visible body whose true identity must be discerned through faith.[426] It is only in faith that the divine reality of the peculiar sociology which is the church is recognized for what it truly is—the body of Christ. As a result, there is a place for speaking of invisibility as a proper predicate of the church. To speak of the invisibility of the church is not to affirm the eclipse of the church as a distinctive sociology that has occurred in modernity, but rather is a way of preserving the identity

---

422. E (*DBWE* 6), 68, quoted in *PTF*, 48.

423. Richardson has noted this difference but frames it in a slightly different way, asserting that Hauerwas's ecclesiology "is even more radically empirical than that of Bonhoeffer" ("*Sanctorum Communio*," 110).

424. *DBWE* 12:356.

425. D (*DBWE* 4), 225.

426. SC (*DBWE* 1), 127.

of the church as the creation of Word and Spirit. In his well-intentioned desire to combat the former misunderstanding of the invisibility of the church, Hauerwas seems to have lost sight of the importance of the latter proper place for speaking of the invisibility of the church. "Hauerwas," an ally and insightful commentator observes, "can get so involved in the social and linguistic media of revelation that the sovereign power of the Revealer is neglected."[427] This neglect opens the door to various misunderstandings of Hauerwas's project and introduces potential difficulties into his work.[428] Hütter has observed that if Hauerwas's ecclesiological axiom "'the church is a social ethic' is not unfolded pneumatologically, the alternative becomes overpowering, namely, to approach the church's vocation in the mode of managerial production and bureaucratic engineering which sees the church as needing to 'realize' programmatically its 'ethical nature,' which is to be planned, programmed, and implemented by administrative elites through bureaucratic means."[429] At this point the limits of Hauerwas's employment of brick-laying and particularly the marine training camp at Parris Island as analogies for discipleship become apparent. While such examples are extremely useful for demonstrating the importance of discipline, authority, and tradition within a counter-cultural community for the formation of people of character, apart from a robust account of the Spirit's work in and through such practices, there is the risk that such accounts could be propagating "nothing else than works-righteousness under the conditions of modernity."[430] The example of Parris Island raises further questions when one looks upon the concrete life of local congregations today. For example, how do we account for the apparent reality that the immersion of people in the life and practices of the local congregation does not always produce elite spiritual warriors but sometimes results in nominal, self-satisfied, or confused Christians? Furthermore, is there a word of grace for those who despite their best efforts and involvement in the life of the church still find themselves unable to consistently march in time with the cadence of the Spirit? Nicholas Healy touches on these pastoral concerns in an essay highlighting a trend within "the new ecclesiology" which he terms "the danger of misplaced concreteness."[431] Healy observes that an emphasis on the practices of the church in and of themselves is insufficient to account for the ac-

427. Wells, *Transforming Fate*, 80.

428. E.g., Healy's recourse to the hiddenness of the Christian's true identity in Christ in the context of his criticisms of Hauerwas's emphasis on visibility. *Hauerwas*, 106–7.

429. Hütter, "Ecclesial Ethics," 434–35.

430. Ibid., 435.

431. Healy, "Practices and the New Ecclesiology," 296. Healy has further expanded this line of criticism in *Hauerwas*, 73–99.

tual spiritual formation, or malformation, as the case may be, of the church's members. For example, Healy observes that practices performed by agents with inappropriate intention or according to a misinformed construal of what Christianity is all about and the place of the practice within the faith contribute not to the formation of Christian character, but rather to its deformation.[432] Hauerwas routinely acknowledges the importance of proper intention when speaking at the formal level of the formation of persons of virtue, but up to this point, he has had relatively little to say about the place of intention in the formation of Christians with respect to specific church practices.[433] Healy continues his critique by arguing that church practices also suffer from mis-performance or even the absence of performance at the congregational level, something that Hauerwas's "theologically-informed social theory" fails to fully account for.[434] Hauerwas's account of the practices of the church can at times sound overly idealistic.[435] For instance, anyone who has attended a handful of congregational annual meetings might have reason to pause upon hearing Hauerwas's declaration that "the church's politics is our salvation."[436] While Healy's criticisms do not discredit the important contribution that Hauerwas has made to our ecclesiological understanding, Hauerwas's account would surely be strengthened by providing a more robust account of how the Holy Spirit works in and through, and perhaps even sometimes in spite of the practices of the church to sanctify those gathered in Christ's name.[437] The rehabilitation of the proper theo-

---

432. Healy supplies the example of the Roman Catholic practice of dipping one's fingers into holy water and crossing oneself upon entering the church. Such a practice may contribute to one's inculturation into the Roman form of Christianity, however it could also contribute to the formation of a non-Christian identity if routinely performed with the superstitious understanding that by doing so one "will ward off accidents and other evils during the coming week" ("Practices and the New Ecclesiology," 294).

433. "The just person is not one who does this or that action, but does what he or she does in the way in which a just person does them—which means that they must know what they are doing, that they must do what they do for no other reason then what they do is what a person of justice does, and that they must do what they do from a firm and unchanging character" (*Mt*, 75). Hauerwas is drawing upon Aristotle's *Nicomachean Ethics* at this point (§1105a30–b10).

434. Healy, "Practices and the New Ecclesiology," 301.

435. Healy scathingly, and perhaps somewhat unfairly, remarks, "Hauerwas's church is the one he worships in, but he seems to prefer, and talk more about, the one he constructs" (*Hauerwas*, 10).

436. *IGC*, 8.

437. This would seemingly involve unfolding the dialectical affirmation that the Holy Spirit has freely bound Spirit-self to the practices of the church, while at the same time affirming that in doing so the Spirit does not become a prisoner or possession of the church.

logical means of speaking of the invisibility of the church would seem to go hand-in-hand with responding to the concerns articulated by Healy. It is possible that in Bonhoeffer, Hauerwas might find the resources for just such a recovery. As we have seen, Bonhoeffer, like Hauerwas, was particularly concerned about recovering the sociological visibility of the church. However, Bonhoeffer recognized that the proper response to the reigning ecclesiological docetism of his day was not to advocate a reactionary ecclesiological ebionism, but rather to speak of the church in a robustly Chalcedonian manner. As a result, Bonhoeffer was able to speak of divine agency in the ecclesiological sphere without in any way diminishing the truly human character of the community or falling into an ecclesiological Nestorianism which threatened to separate the visible from the invisible.[438] A more explicit articulation of something resembling Bonhoeffer's approach towards a properly theologically informed understanding of the invisibility of the church would help Hauerwas in addressing some important criticisms of his ecclesiology without in any way impeding or obstructing his concerns for the concrete life of the local congregation.[439]

The Church is "Apostolic"

The Christian tradition has generally understood the apostolicity of the church to be a matter of the church's continuity with the apostles.[440] The differences between the various Christian communions and denominations begin to emerge with regards to how this continuity is to be understood. Some communions, particularly those within the Catholic, Orthodox, and Anglo-Catholic traditions, place a heavy emphasis upon understanding apostolicity in terms of the apostolic succession of bishops and pastors.[441]

---

438. Illustrative is a quote from *Sanctorum Communio* where Bonhoeffer writes: "We do not believe in an invisible church, nor in the Realm of God within the church as coetus electorum [company of the elect]. Instead we believe that God has made the concrete, empirical church [Kirche] in which the word is preached and the sacraments are celebrated to be God's own church-community [Gemeinde]" (*SC* (*DBWE* 1), 280).

439. It should be noted that Hauerwas's own work is not without examples pointing in this direction. For example, in exploring why the Creed insists that Christians confess belief in the "one holy catholic and apostolic church," Hauerwas writes, "That we do so is a recognition that the church, catholic and apostolic, is not our but God's creation. Moreover, it is not a creation that God did at one point in time and does not need to do again. Rather, it is our belief that what God did at Pentecost he continues to do to renew and sustain the presence of the church so that the world might now there is an alternative to Babel" (*CET*, 54).

440. McGrath, *Christian Theology*, 398.

441. Dulles, *Models of the Church*, 119–20.

Within Protestant traditions apostolicity is often understood to refer to continuity with and conformity to the testimony of the apostles.[442] For Bonhoeffer and Hauerwas it would appear that the apostolicity of the church is a predicate of the church's identity as the body of Christ. The church is apostolic because it participates in the life and mission of "the Apostle."[443] This understanding of the apostolicity of the church is not without relation to the apostolic testimony. It could be said that both Bonhoeffer and Hauerwas are interested in reforming the church within their particular contexts on the basis of the apostolic testimony in order to restore the apostolic character of the church as a sent or missional community.

The church that clings faithfully to the apostolic testimony to Christ will find that its allegiance to its Lord sets it apart in various ways from the people who surround them. However, they must not seek to minimize the difference Christ makes in order to become custodians of the prevailing culture, for their life as a peculiar people is necessary if the world is to know that it has not been abandoned. The existence of such a community of witness is necessary, for the Gospel is not a universally available piece of data. Rather it is the news of God's contingent, yet decisive, action within history to redeem the cosmos through the cross and resurrection of Jesus Christ. Such news must be shared if it is to be known, however, the Gospel can only be proclaimed within the eschatological space where the proclamation has already been received and taken hold of in faith. This brings us full circle to our earlier discussion of the church as a reality of revelation. However, now we must note that for both Bonhoeffer and Hauerwas the epistemological priority of the church is a correlate of the church's apostolicity. The truth which the Gospel attests can only be grasped within the church-community, which has itself been seized by the One who is the Truth. There is no neutral position from which one can assess the truth claims inherent to the Gospel. This does not mean that the church has a monopoly on truth or has nothing to learn from encountering those outside its bounds. However it does entail, as Bonhoeffer wrote in his doctoral dissertation, that *"there is no relation to Christ in which the relation to the church is not necessarily established as well. The church, therefore, logically establishes its own foundation in itself; like all revelations, it can be judged only by itself."*[444] Or, to express the matter in Hauerwasian terms: "in a world without foundations all we have is the

---

442. Migliore, *Faith Seeking Understanding*, 203.

443. The letter to the Hebrews describes Jesus as "the apostle" (3:1), but the nomenclature also fits with the Johannine portrayal of the Son as the one sent by the Father, who in turn sends the church. John 20:21.

444. SC (*DBWE* 1), 127.

church."[445] Recognizing this priority of the Church for the Christian way of knowing should have implications for the practice of theology. Bonhoeffer elaborates, "In order to establish clarity about the inner logic of theological construction, it would be good for once if a presentation of doctrinal theology were to start not with the doctrine of God but with the doctrine of the church."[446] Since Hauerwas's entire project could be considered to be one possible unfolding of Bonhoeffer's thesis, it is not surprising that Hauerwas himself enthusiastically cites this quote, referring to it as evidence of Bonhoeffer's increased willingness to risk "being Catholic" in his ecclesiology in comparison to his theological mentor Karl Barth.[447]

Apostolicity refers not to an aspect of the church's life, such as evangelistic efforts or world missions, but rather qualifies the entirety of the church's existence. Hauerwas reflects such an understanding when he asserts that "the church does not have a mission, but rather *is* mission."[448] Bonhoeffer reflects a similar sentiment in the *Ethics* manuscript he was working on at the time of his arrest: "the church-community, precisely by seeking to be merely an instrument and means to an end, has in fact become the goal and center of all that God is doing with the world."[449] The church is an apostolic people because its origins, its goal, and its continuing existence are all located within the *missio Dei*. At this point it is once again necessary to return to the christological center of both theologians' work and build upon that foundation in order to clarify our understanding of how the church is mission. The doctrine of the hypostatic union affirms that the identity of the man Jesus is constituted by the Father's sending of the Son and the Son's consent to being sent by the Father. As a result of this sending and consent to being sent, Jesus of Nazareth exists. This means that, to put it in a phrase whose simplicity risks betraying its profundity, Jesus *is* mission. This crucial insight derived from the *missio Dei* naturally enriches the emphasis that both Bonhoeffer and Hauerwas place upon the inseparability of the person and work of Christ. Salvation is not something that is achieved above or beyond the person of Jesus Christ. To put it plainly in terms both men would endorse: Jesus *is* salvation. The advent of Jesus Christ marks the apocalyptic entrance of the God of Israel into the very midst of His creation as a creature to heal and restore His wayward creation from the inside. Therefore in Jesus Christ one encounters both the reconciling God and the reconciled human

---

445. *IGC*, 33.
446. *SC* (*DBWE* 1), 134.
447. Hauerwas, "Bonhoeffer and Yoder," 208 n. 4.
448. *WAD*, 168.
449. *E* (*DBWE* 6), 404.

being.[450] Although Bonhoeffer and Hauerwas have their own characteristic ways of speaking, they both point to this same eschatological reality. For Bonhoeffer, Jesus Christ brings to birth a new humanity in his very own body in which sinful human beings who were formerly turned in upon themselves are turned inside out by the love of Christ so that they live for God and for one another in the fellowship of the Holy Spirit. The so-called vertical and horizontal dimensions of salvation are inseparable for Bonhoeffer, for as he put it in his doctoral dissertation, "community with God by definition establishes social community as well."[451] Hauerwas prefers to speak of Jesus as the one who proclaims and enacts the Kingdom of God in the face of the powers that seek to keep us in bondage through violently and deceptively manipulating us through our fear of death. "Salvation," Hauerwas writes, "is the reign of God."[452] As such, salvation is inherently social and political. However, this salvation is not separable from Jesus himself, as if Jesus were merely instrumental to the dawning of the Kingdom. Rather, Jesus is the *autobasileia*, the personal presence of the Kingdom. Salvation therefore entails coming under the life-giving rule of the Messiah Jesus as one is granted a foretaste of the coming Kingdom through being engrafted into the life and practices of his body "that save us from those powers that would rule our lives making it impossible for us to truly worship God."[453] Cyprian's dictum—*extra ecclesiam nulla salus*—rings true in the ecclesiologies of both Bonhoeffer and Hauerwas. Both understand that soteriology is inseparable from ecclesiology and that both soteriology and ecclesiology are properly predicates of Christology.

We are now in a better position to understand how apostolicity names not a function, but rather characterizes the entirety of the existence of the new creation community called into existence through the Father's sending of the Son and the Spirit of the Son into the world. "That salvation is ecclesial," Hauerwas explains, "is why the church does not *have* a mission but by being faithful to the gospel *is* mission."[454] As a result, attempts to separate the identity and mission of the Church are the ecclesiological equivalent of attempting to separate the person and work of Christ. We could say then that the mission of the church is quite simply to be the church. Properly understood, this is not a formula for internally-focused, narcissistic pre-

---

450. These are two of the central "christological aspects" of Barth's magisterial treatment of the doctrine of reconciliation. *CD* 4/1:128–32.

451. *SC* (*DBWE* 1), 63.

452. *HR*, 533.

453. *IGC*, 8.

454. *WAD*, 175.

occupation on the part of the church, but rather the transcending of the very assumptions that presume that the church's internal life can be neatly divided from its external witness. Bonhoeffer gestures in this direction in his introduction to *Life Together*. Whereas many would be tempted to read *Life Together* as being concerned with a discrete subset of the Christian life known as spiritual formation and, hence, pertaining to the internal identity of the church, Bonhoeffer insists that in this book, "We are not dealing with a concern of some private circles but with a mission entrusted to the church."[455] The work of the Holy Spirit in drawing the church into conformity with its Lord, is not merely an internal ecclesial matter, but is of central missional significance. Apart from the Spirit's sanctifying work in establishing such a community of witness, the world would have no way of knowing of the victory of Jesus Christ over all that threatens to separate the creation from the love of God. The recognition of the inseparability of the identity and mission of the church signals the end of the troubling binary logic of modernity which has so influentially infiltrated the contemporary church, falsely suggesting that congregations must decide between focusing their energies on worship *or* mission, discipleship *or* evangelism, spiritual formation *or* outreach. Rather the church is "at its missionary best when it does those things that make it a faithful witness to the gospel of Jesus Christ."[456] The up-building of the Christian community, therefore, is for the sake of the world, for it is the means by which the church is drawn into conformity with the One who in complete obedience to His Father offered up his life for the life of the world. The apostolic character of the church's existence is therefore ultimately located in the apostolicity of Jesus Christ. This means that Bonhoeffer was quite right to insist that the church is "a distinct domain . . . an end in itself, which consists precisely in its being-for-the-world."[457] The question of how the church exercises its mission in the world through the enactment of its concrete identity will be the topic of exploration in the next chapter.

---

455. *LT* (*DBWE* 5), 25.
456. *WAD*, 170.
457. *E* (*DBWE* 6), 406–7.

4

For the Life of the World
Church and World

The preceding chapter demonstrated how the christological concentration of both Dietrich Bonhoeffer and Stanley Hauerwas funded the development of concrete ecclesiologies, which situate the church internal to the Gospel of Jesus Christ. The renewed clarity about the identity and mission of the church found in the work of both men allows them to avoid the "atomizing pathology" that has characterized much of modern Protestant theology and church life.[1] This pathology tends to lose sight of the church as a corporate body and focusses upon how the individual Christian is to act in the secular realm. It is often accompanied by a truncated doctrine of sin, which fails to take into account the comprehensive effects of sin upon the entirety of creation and therefore tends to result in a conception of Christian witness and ministry in the world which could be described as "redemption by osmosis."[2] This outlook has proven to be especially vulnerable to co-option by the "rulers of this age"; as under these conditions, "the church is easily reduced to being a voluntary association of religious, pious individuals whose true allegiance lies elsewhere—namely, with such fallen principalities as the state or the market."[3]

While Bonhoeffer and Hauerwas are no less concerned about the world than their modern precursors, the combination of the ecclesiological

---

1. Cavanaugh introduces the description "atomizing pathology" in his description of some prominent twentieth-century political ecclesiologies. "Church," 401.
2. Stringfellow, *Ethic for Christians*, 58, 76.
3. Harper and Metzger, *Exploring Ecclesiology*, 130.

density of their theologies and their staunch commitment to christologically-shaped visions of reality provide resources for envisioning a church which is free from captivity to the world for the very sake of service in the world. The writings from the period of Dietrich Bonhoeffer's involvement in the conspiracy and subsequent imprisonment (1940–1945) will provide the impetus for exploring Bonhoeffer's understanding of the church-world relationship. The new millennium marked a self-professed turn towards a "more constructive engagement with the social order called America" for Stanley Hauerwas.[4] It is the writings that follow this turn, particularly Hauerwas's engagements with Dietrich Bonhoeffer, Romand Coles, and Jean Vanier that will provide the material content for the exploration of Hauerwas's understanding of the church's witness to the world. The chapter will then be brought to a close with a concluding section which seeks to bring the two theologians into dialogue around the themes addressed over the course of the chapter.

PART 1: CHURCH AND WORLD IN THE THEOLOGY DIETRICH BONHOEFFER

Background to the Writings of 1940 to 1945

Between October 1940 and his arrest on April 5, 1943, Dietrich Bonhoeffer covered over thirty-thousand miles in his travels as a *V-Mann* (a confidential agent) within the *Abwehr*, the foreign office of Military Intelligence.[5] During this period, Bonhoeffer essentially functioned as a double agent, using his international ecumenical contacts to travel abroad and inform representatives of the Allied nations of the conspiracy with the intention of securing guarantees of peace following the anticipated coup d'état. Bonhoeffer's involvement with the conspiracy introduced him to a new circle of contacts beyond the academic and ecclesial realms he had largely inhabited up to that point. Although only some of the conspirators were Christians, the character and courage of these men left a deep impression on Bonhoeffer.[6] The self-sacrificial, being-for-others, exhibited by members of the conspiracy, stood for Bonhoeffer in stark juxtaposition to the Confessing Church, which in the years immediately preceding the war often seemed to be preoccupied with struggling for its own existence. Bonhoeffer became increasingly disillusioned and depressed by the failures of the Confessing Church,

---

4. *PTF*, 15.
5. Schlingensiepen, *Dietrich Bonhoeffer*, 247.
6. Rasmussen, *Reality and Resistance*, 55.

which included: the majority of pastors swearing an oath of allegiance to Hitler, the failure to stand as a united front in the face of the offer of pastoral security through legalization, and the silence of the church following the organized violence against the Jews of *Kristallnacht*.[7] While Bonhoeffer's increasing dissatisfaction with the Confessing Church and his immersion in the conspiracy must surely have influenced his worldly theological reflections, it would be a mistake to think that the writings from this period mark a sharp break with what came before. On the intellectual level: ethics was an interest of Bonhoeffer's going back to his days as an assistant pastor in Barcelona,[8] an interest in worldliness and the character of the created realm featured prominently in his writings in 1932,[9] and the cosmic Christ of *Ethics* and the *theologia crucis* of the prison letters were, as we have seen, already firmly established in his Christology lectures. Although Bonhoeffer increasingly found himself in secular contexts during the last years of his life, he was not entirely removed from ecclesial circles. Before being released by the Council of Brethren of the Old Prussian Union in November of 1940 for the purpose of academic work, Bonhoeffer was involved in visiting the Confessing congregations in East Prussia. Following his release from official ministerial duty, Bonhoeffer continued to serve as a theological resource for the Confessing Church authoring various theological position papers upon request.[10] Furthermore, it must not be forgotten that the majority of Bonhoeffer's international contacts were ecumenical colleagues and that he drafted a significant portion of his *Ethics* manuscripts at the Benedictine monastery at Ettal. Bonhoeffer also continued to function as a pastor to his former seminarians. The circular letters he sent throughout the war years to his young charges, many of whom were stationed and ultimately fell at the front, are amongst the most poignant readings in the Bonhoeffer corpus.[11] In a letter to Manfred Roeder, the judge responsible for investigating the case against him, Bonhoeffer himself points to the continuity in his work, suggesting that *Ethics* was to be the long-awaited follow-up to *Discipleship*

7. Schlingensiepen, *Dietrich Bonhoeffer*, 212–17.

8. See Bonhoeffer's ambitious congregational address, "Basic Questions of a Christian Ethic," in *DBWE* 10:359–78.

9. See for example Bonhoeffer's address, "'Thy Kingdom Come! The Prayer of the Church-Community for God's Kingdom on Earth," in *DBWE* 12:285–97, and his theological exposition of the opening chapters of Genesis published as *Creation and Fall*.

10. See for example "A Theological Position Paper on the Question of Baptism, 1942," in *DBWE* 16:551–72; and "A Theological Position Paper on the *Primus Usus Legis*," in *DBWE* 16:584–601.

11. Many of these circular letters can be found in *DBWE* 15 and *DBWE* 16. A more complete collection of the materials circulated amongst the dispersed Finkenwalde community has recently been published as Bethge et al., *Die Finkenwalder Rundbriefe*.

which would provide "the explication of a 'concrete Protestant ethic.'"[12] Clifford Green succinctly captures the essence of the divergence between the two works when he states, "*Ethics* differs from *Discipleship*, however, in looking beyond the Church Struggle and beyond the war to the tasks of peace and reconstruction; it focuses on society and history, and the responsibility of Christians and the church in that public world."[13] In light of this focus on the reconstruction of society, the *Ethics* manuscripts written between September 1940 and April 5, 1943 tend to be characterized by somewhat of a Constantinian or Christendom outlook. This judgement is further reinforced when one of Bonhoeffer's potential titles for *Ethics* is taken into account: "Foundations and Structure of a (Future) World Reconciled with God." Within the working note, this "future world" is more clearly identified as "a united West."[14]

On April 5, 1943, Bonhoeffer was arrested at his parents' home and imprisoned in Tegel military prison. He would not have the opportunity to finish his *Ethics*. However, the clandestine seven by ten foot cell became the site of one of most intellectually productive periods of Bonhoeffer's life. He read broadly and wrote just as widely, experimenting for the first time with writing poetry and fiction. He wrestled deeply with questions surrounding the nature of faith and the future of the church in a post-Christian modern world. Some of his thoughts were preserved in the form of letters smuggled out of prison to his close friend Eberhard Bethge. This correspondence formed the core of the collection of letters which captured the imagination of so many in the theological world when they were published after the war under the title *Widerstand und Ergebung* (1951), translated into English as *Letters and Papers From Prison* (1953). To this day readers continue to be exhilarated by Bonhoeffer's fresh and creative reflections about "Jesus: the man for others," "the world come of age," and "religionless Christianity" and scholars continue to debate the meaning of these provocative and enigmatic formulations.[15]

In the sections that follow, we will engage with the writings that emerged from the periods of Bonhoeffer's involvement with the conspiracy

---

12. *DBWE* 16:417. While one might question the trustworthiness of statements made in this context, there does not appear any reason to doubt the veracity of this assertion.

13. Green, editor's introduction to *E* (*DBWE* 6), 5. It should not be overlooked that a second significant concern of the *Ethics*, as Green himself notes, involves consideration of "the ethics of tyrannicide and coup d'état" (2).

14. Ibid., 10, referring to Bonhoeffer, *Zettelnotizen für eine "Ethik,"* note No. 1.

15. For a recent study of the reception of *Letters and Papers from Prison*, see Marty, *Bonhoeffer's Letters*.

and his subsequent imprisonment in order to consider Bonhoeffer's perspectives on the life of the church in the world. In particular we will focus on three themes which occupy a prominent place in Bonhoeffer's writings from this period, namely, the relationship between church and state, the worldliness of faith, and friendship.

Church and State

Bonhoeffer's entire corpus could profitably be read as an indirect theological commentary on the relationship between church and state. This lies beyond the scope of the current project which will limit itself to considering Bonhoeffer's doctrine of the mandates. The doctrine of the mandates emerges as the fruit of Bonhoeffer's struggles with his own Lutheran theological and German cultural inheritance.[16] The Protestant Reformer Martin Luther had, in response to what he perceived as the hegemonic claims of Roman curia, distinguished in principle between the kingdom of God and the kingdom of the world.[17] Within the kingdom of God, Christ rules over all true believers in the power of the Holy Spirit. This is the spiritual government. However, since there are few true Christians, God has also ordained the temporal government which restrains the wicked through the exercise of the sword.[18] Christians are free to, and in fact, expected to assume responsibility for bearing the sword when needed. This does not contradict the evangelical counsels, which do in fact apply to each and every Christian and not simply to a spiritual elite. The tension can be resolved in the following manner: "In what concerns you and yours, you govern yourself by the gospel and suffer injustice towards yourself as a true Christian; in what concerns the person or property of others, you govern yourself according to love and tolerate no injustice toward your neighbor."[19] In making this distinction, Luther risks bifurcating the Christian life in a way that threatens to make discipleship invisible, and, in so doing, perhaps contributes to the paving of the way for the public-private distinction which has come to characterize modernity. However, Luther's notorious contribution doesn't end there. His designation of the prince as a *Notbischof*—"an emergency or substitute bishop with responsibility for maintaining oversight over the church"[20]—resulted in the

---

16. Zerner, "Bonhoeffer's Views," 146.
17. Luther, *Basic Theological Writings*, 662.
18. Ibid., 666.
19. Ibid., 670.
20. Moses, *Reluctant Revolutionary*, 6.

effective absorption of the church by the state, leaving the former with little critical capacity with respect to the latter.

Believing that he was building upon Luther's understanding of the state, the German philosopher G. F. Hegel (1770–1831) formulated a philosophy of the state, which could be read as a philosophical justification of Prussia.[21] For Hegel, the state was looked upon as the agent of God upon earth. History was understood to be the theatre of struggle between existing states in which God had ordained the domination of the weaker by the more powerful or superior. Hegel's doctrine of the power state (*Machstaat*) provided the philosophical justification for the placing of the state beyond the realm of criticism by the church, as it located the state in an independent realm, free from moral constraint. This Hegelian doctrine of the state came to hold a powerful grip over the German imagination at the beginning of the twentieth century, as many "came to believe that Germany was, in fact, the 'World Historical Nation,' effectively chosen by almighty God to dominate the world."[22] After the humiliating defeat of the first World War, however, some adjustments in this outlook were needed, which "explains the shift in direction among many Protestant pastors and theologians in Germany towards a so-called *Schöpfungstheologie*, that is, the theology of creation, according to which the world was comprised of various 'orders of creation.'"[23]

We have already seen how Bonhoeffer's focused christological convictions allowed him to identify and object to the messianic aspirations of the Nazi state. This same christological concentration also led him to chafe against the popular understandings of his day surrounding the doctrines of the two kingdoms and the orders of creation. The early 1930s witnessed Bonhoeffer's first serious forays into the murky waters that characterized

21. Ibid., 8–14.

22. Ibid., 11.

23. Ibid., 35. An example is found in the Ansbach Memorandum, a statement published in response to the Barmen Declaration and endorsed by, among others, Werner Elert and Paul Althaus. Included in the Ansbach Memorandum is the statement: "The law, 'the unchangeable will of God' . . . obligates us to the natural orders to which we are subject, such as family, people [Volk], race (that is, blood relationship)" (Ansbach Memorandum, quoted in Green, editor's introduction to *E* (*DBWE* 6), 18 n. 70). Friedrich Werner, head of the Evangelical Church of the Old Prussian Union and of the German Evangelical Church, signed and published the Godesberg declaration that called upon the orders of creation as a means of quelling participation in the ecumenical movement. "*All supra-national or international churchliness of a Roman Catholic or World-Protestant type is a political degeneration of Christianity. A fruitful development of genuine Christian faith is possible only within the given orders of creation*" (Schlingensiepen, *Dietrich Bonhoeffer*, 225, italicized material is from Visser't Hooft, *Memoirs*, 95).

the theological discourse surrounding the relationship between church and state.[24] During this period Bonhoeffer chafed against the "pseudo-Lutheran" notion that there could be areas of life removed from the lordship of Jesus Christ and called into question the established wisdom surrounding the orders of creation.[25] Bonhoeffer recognized that talk of orders of creation fails to take seriously the fallenness of the world and, furthermore, can be used to justify just about any social arrangement or state of affairs.[26] Therefore, Bonhoeffer insisted that it is more appropriate to speak of orders of *preservation*, for the orders are not ends in and of themselves, but rather are only God's means of holding the world together in the face of the forces of dissolution and chaos for the sake of the revelation in Jesus Christ.[27] During this period, Bonhoeffer envisions the church as standing as a boundary to the state. Neither church nor state may be neglected by Christians, for to ignore the former is to fall into secularism, while to disregard the latter is to retreat into otherworldliness. The church witnesses to the new life that is present through the reality of the resurrection of Christ, while the state serves to preserve life in the midst of this fallen world. Church and state are thus reciprocally related and mutually limiting.[28] In the years that followed this explosion of commentary on the relationship between church and state, Bonhoeffer made little explicit mention of the problem. However, Bonhoeffer's work during his time in London (1933–1935), at Finkenwalde (1935–1937), and with the collective pastorates (1937–1940) can be understood as his attempt to fortify a church capable of being such a limit to the omnivorous Nazi state.[29]

Explicit reflections on the relationship between church and state return to a position of prominence in Bonhoeffer's writings upon his return to Germany from America in 1939. Bonhoeffer's work alongside of his fellow co-conspirators, who were presented not only with the challenge of removing a reigning tyrant, but also of envisioning the rebuilding of the nation following the war, naturally presented an impetus for further reflection on the relationship between church and state.[30] It is within this context

24. See *DBWE* 11:356–70; *DBWE* 12:285–97, 361–70; *CF* (*DBWE* 3), 139–40.

25. *DBWE* 11:358–63.

26. Ibid., 363.

27. Ibid., 364; *CF* (*DBWE* 3), 139–40.

28. *DBWE* 12:294.

29. Lovin advances a similar argument in "Christian and the Authority of the State," 35.

30. For example, Bonhoeffer was involved in some of the preliminary stages of the process which eventually led to the Freiburg memorandum, a document drafted by various distinguished scholars and professionals which presented detailed proposals

that Bonhoeffer revisited his understanding of the "orders of preservation" and introduced in their stead his new formulation of the doctrine of the mandates. The mandates emerge from a similar set of concerns to those that Bonhoeffer wrestled with in the early 1930s. Bonhoeffer remained committed to resisting any way of thinking that attempts to make the concern of Christ merely "a partial, provincial affair within the whole of reality."[31] As a result, Bonhoeffer is convinced that the church can neither retreat from the world into a sacred realm, as found in the medieval flight to the monastery, nor completely accommodate itself to the world as cultural Protestantism had done.[32] Luther recognized and embodied this reality in his return from the monastery into the world. The teaching of the Reformation sought to preserve Luther's insight through its teaching on the orders, estates, and offices. While Bonhoeffer held the substance of these Reformation doctrines in considerable esteem, he recognized that over the centuries the use of the terminology had ossified in distorted patterns which were perhaps beyond rehabilitation. The language of order had become static and could too easily be used to sanction the current state of affairs. The term estate suffered from obscurity and seemed to suggest elements of favoritism and privilege. The concept of office had, in Bonhoeffer's opinion, "become so secularized and so closely connected to institutional-bureaucratic thinking that it no longer conveys the solemnity of the divine decree."[33] Bonhoeffer's introduction of the concept of mandates represents his attempt to reclaim the insights of the Reformation doctrines, while at the same time avoiding the terminological pitfalls associated with them and establishing them upon a more solid biblical foundation. The mandates first appeared in Bonhoeffer's writings in 1941 and he continued to refine and develop the concept right up to and even beyond his arrest, with references to the mandates occurring in several of the early prison letters.

Bonhoeffer's doctrine of the mandates seems to appear for the first time in an essay entitled "State and Church," which was likely written sometime following Bonhoeffer's stay at Ettal in April 1941.[34] Bonhoeffer

---

for the reorganization of Germany following the anticipated removal of Hitler from power. Bethge, *Dietrich* Bonhoeffer, 775–77.

31. *E* (*DBWE* 6), 57.

32. Ibid., 57.

33. Ibid., 390.

34. *DBWE* 16:502–28. The text bears stylistic and structural resemblance to theological position papers that Bonhoeffer wrote during this period for the Confessing Church, however the exact dating of the essay, in addition to the occasion for writing and its intended audience have not been definitely ascertained. *E* (*DBWE* 6), 68 n. 75; *DBWE* 16:502 n. 1.

begins "State and Church" by drawing a conceptual distinction between "state" and "government." "State," Bonhoeffer writes, "means an ordered commonwealth; government is the power that creates and upholds the order."[35] Bonhoeffer insists that it is the latter that is the interest of the New Testament; hence there is no definitive form of state prescribed in the Bible. Introducing themes that he will further develop in later *Ethics* manuscripts, Bonhoeffer asserts that government is "the vicarious representative action of God on earth" and that it "can only be understood from above."[36] The attempt to establish government by grounding the state in human nature, as in classical antiquity, Catholic theology, and modern Lutheranism, is deficient according to Bonhoeffer because it ultimately ends up dissolving the concept of government and reconstructing it from below.[37] Lacking a proper sense of the authority of government, the state proves to be omnivorous in its appetite as it seeks to digest all spheres of life into itself. The Reformation tradition fares somewhat better in Bonhoeffer's opinion, as it preserves the understanding of government as a power established and ordained by God. Rather than viewing the state as the highest expression of human nature, the Reformers understood government as a divine institution made necessary by the fall. Echoing Karl Barth's criticism of the Reformation teachings on the state, Bonhoeffer calls not only those who attempt to ground the state in human nature, but also the Reformers to task for offering an abstract account of the state that seems to exist in isolation apart from the revelation of God in Jesus Christ.[38] A proper understanding of government must be established upon a christological foundation. Alluding to the opening chapter of Colossians, Bonhoeffer insists that Jesus Christ is the one "through whom" all things have been created, "in whom" all things hold together, and "toward whom" everything created is oriented, who has reconciled "all things" to God.[39] Therefore to speak of government apart from Jesus Christ is to flee from reality into the realm of abstraction. It is only through grounding government in Jesus Christ that one is able to move beyond grounding the state in natural law, which is inherently conservative and can, with a little imagination, be used to establish and justify any existing social order.[40]

35. *DBWE* 16:503. The editors of *DBWE* rightly draw attention to the fact that term translated as "government" is the German word *Obrigkeit*, which Luther employed to translate the Greek biblical term *exousía* ("authority") (503 n. 5).

36. Ibid., 504.

37. Ibid., 505–8.

38. Ibid., 510; cf. Barth, "Church and State," 102–4.

39. *DBWE* 16:510–13.

40. Ibid., 512.

Bonhoeffer's high view of government is apparent in the next section of the essay in which he explicates the divine character of government. The frequent references to Romans 13 and 1 Peter 2 in this section indicate the formative role that these passages appear to have played in shaping Bonhoeffer's reflections on the theme. According to Bonhoeffer, government in its being is a divine office, which is connected with a divine task, and hence exercises the claim of God upon the governed. The divine dignity of government is independent of how any party or individual comes to a position of governing. "The being of government," Bonhoeffer writes, "stands beyond its earthly origination; for government is an order of God not in its origination but in its being."[41] Government exists for the sake of service to Jesus Christ. This does not mean that the governing authorities will seek to create a Christian state. Rather, through the proper exercise of the sword, government seeks to maintain an external righteousness by punishing the wicked and commending the good, and in so doing, preserves space for the church to exercise its ministry of proclamation.[42] The second table of the Decalogue provides the standard by which governing authorities should evaluate their actions. The government becomes aware of these standards through the preaching of the church. However, in countries without a Christian presence, God has ordered things in such a way that "a providential correspondence exists between the contents of the second table and the law inherent in historical life itself."[43] The claim of government is understood by the Christian as the claim of God and therefore is to be obeyed "up to the point where the government forces them into direct violation of the divine commandment."[44] At this point the government must be disobeyed for the sake of conscience, but this cannot be generalized into a principled rejection of the government *in toto*, for the government in error remains the government. The decision for disobedience can only be freely ventured within the context of each concrete historical circumstance.

Bonhoeffer next turns his attention to the relationship between government and the divine orders in the world. It is in this section that Bonhoeffer introduces his doctrine of the mandates. His use of the terms "orders" and "mandates" alongside of one another, at this point, indicates that he has not yet achieved the level of terminological consistency that will later become apparent. Government presumes and depends upon the existence of God's creation. It is entrusted with preserving the created order,

---

41. Ibid., 513.
42. Ibid., 515.
43. Ibid.
44. Ibid., 516–17.

but it has no creative capacity in and of itself. However, as government goes about exercising its commission, "it discovers two orders through which God the Creator exercises creative power and upon [which] it is therefore by nature dependent: *marriage* and *work*."[45] Unlike government, marriage and work are supra-lapsarian realities that continue to exist after the fall as "divine orders of discipline and grace."[46] Both marriage and work are creative, in that they both bring forth something new in dependence upon God's original *creatio ex nihilo*. Therefore, the existence of the family and the responsibility of raising children is implicit within Bonhoeffer's understanding of the mandate of marriage, which in later writings will sometimes even be referred to as "marriage and family," or as simply "family."[47] Work, for Bonhoeffer, "encompasses the whole realm from agriculture, through trade and industry, to science and art (cf. Gen. 4:17ff)."[48] Government exercises regulative oversight over marriage and work, but at no time can government become the subject of marriage and work.[49]

Bonhoeffer devotes the next section of the essay to exploring the mutual claims that government and church have upon one another and their mutual responsibility for one another. Although government exists to serve the reign of Christ, this does not mean that the church is to rule over the government. Rather the government provides indirect service to the church by creating the external conditions which allow the church-community to live a "quiet and peaceable life."[50] The government claims the obedience of all Christians. In doing so it does not place Christians under a foreign authority, for the authority of the government is a form of the authority of Christ.[51] The government may not interfere in the work of the pastoral office, however, "insofar as the pastoral office is a publicly practiced office, government is entitled to oversee that everything happens in good order—i.e., in accordance with outward justice."[52] This does not imply that the government is responsible for propagating the gospel. On the contrary,

---

45. Ibid., 518–19.

46. Ibid., 519. Grobien has suggested that a supra-lapsarian case for government could possibly be constructed on the basis of the commission given to human beings to exercise dominion over all the earth in Gen 1:26–28. "Lutheran Understanding," 219.

47. *DBWE* 16:549–50; *E* (*DBWE* 6), 380, 388.

48. *DBWE* 16:520.

49. Bonhoeffer also emphasizes that since the so-called "order of the people [*Volk*]" lacks an origin in paradise or an explicit divine mandate it should not be understood to be an order at all. Ibid., 521.

50. 1 Tim 2:2, quoted in *DBWE* 16:521.

51. *DBWE* 16:522.

52. Ibid.

government should remain religiously neutral. Christians who serve in government must not in misplaced zeal confuse their task, but instead must soberly remember that the gospel advances not by the tip of the sword, but only by the Word. However, Bonhoeffer writes, "if there should be a particular state of church crisis, then it would lie within the responsibility of Christians in government to make their power available at the request of the church to restore healthy conditions."[53] Although Bonhoeffer's proviso does specify that government intervention must be requested by the church (in contradistinction to the meddling of the Nazi government in church affairs) and seems to be concerned with the ordering or structuring of the church, it does seem to conjure the unfortunate specter of heretics being handed over in previous ages to the state for execution. Considering the reciprocal dimension of the relationship, without the church the government would have no understanding of the reason for its existence. The church, then, does not call upon the government to enact Christian politics; rather it simply demands that the government be genuine government in executing its limited, but important role. The church claims before the government the right to proclaim the Gospel freely and unhindered. Even when the government refuses to hear this claim, it continues to serve its Lord, by creating the conditions for the church to bear witness to Christ through martyrdom. In response to the government's claim upon it, the church bears the threefold responsibility toward society of: 1.) naming and warning of the dangers of sin; 2.) bearing witness to the reign of Christ; 3.) preserving outward justice among its own members. The various connections and differentiations that define the relationship between church and government comprise a dynamic reality that cannot be captured in any ideal or programmatic set of principles.[54]

Although Bonhoeffer is not overly concerned about the particular form of the state, he does propose some general criteria to provide assistance in determining the "relatively best form of the state."[55] These include: 1.) a form of state in which it is obvious that the authority of government is derived "from above"; 2.) the maintenance of justice and the proper respect of the mandates of marriage, work and church; 3.) the expression of solidarity between those who govern and the governed.[56] The first criterion provides the theological rationale for the ambivalence that Bonhoeffer expresses elsewhere towards liberal democracy. Bonhoeffer's suspicions towards liberal

---

53. Ibid., 524.
54. Ibid., 526.
55. Ibid., 527–28.
56. Ibid., 528.

democracy were not without experiential validation. Bonhoeffer had come to the conclusion, as Moses explains, that:

> the Nazi regime could succeed in Germany essentially because the Weimar Republic had opened the floodgates to a fateful political pluralism, the by-product of the false doctrine of the sovereignty of the people as enshrined in the Weimar Constitution. This radical departure from the doctrine of the sovereignty of God that was expressed in the divine-right monarchy allowed the formation of numerous political parties whose platforms appealed to the ignorant and uncultured, all competing in the Reichstag for power. It was an open invitation for the flourishing of unprincipled demagoguery.[57]

Bonhoeffer recognized that democracy in and of itself was no safeguard against tyranny. Rather, as the ecumenist Visser't Hooft expressed in a document drafted in consultation with Bonhoeffer, "Democracy can only grow in a soil which has been prepared by a long spiritual tradition."[58] For this reason, Bonhoeffer was opposed to the idea of imposing a democratic parliamentarian form of government upon Germany following the war and hoped instead for the establishment of "an authoritarian 'Rechsstaat.'"[59]

Bonhoeffer would continue to develop his doctrine of the mandates throughout the period leading up to his arrest on April 5, 1943. However, in his understanding of the relationship between church and state he would not depart from the basic foundation laid in "State and Church." In what follows, we will conduct a brief survey of these developments as they pertain to the issue at hand.

The manuscript "Christ, Reality and Good," originally drafted in the fall of 1940, contains a significant insertion on the topic of the mandates, which appears to be based on "State and Church."[60] This addition offers some clarifications of the concepts introduced in "State and Church" and also sees Bonhoeffer developing a greater degree of terminological consistency. The use of the language of orders has been largely phased out and in its place the terminology of the mandates is consistently utilized. Whereas in "State and Church" Bonhoeffer had spoken of marriage and work as being *under* a divine mandate, he now speaks of work and marriage, alongside

---

57. Moses, *Reluctant Revolutionary*, 189–90.

58. Visser't Hooft, "On William Paton's Book *The Church and the New Order*," in *DBWE* 16:536.

59. *DBWE* 16:220.

60. *E* (*DBWE* 6), 47–75; the inserted material appears on pp. 68–74.

of government and church, simply *as* divine mandates.[61] Although Bonhoeffer, oddly, never explicitly discusses the etymology of the word "mandate" (*Mandat*), its origins are certainly implied in the rationale Bonhoeffer provides for his use of the term.[62] Bonhoeffer writes, "We speak of divine mandates rather than divine orders, because thereby their character as divinely imposed tasks [Auftrag], as opposed to determinate forms of being, becomes clearer."[63] Through his use of the term mandate, which refers not to any historic instantiation, but rather to the divine commission behind them, Bonhoeffer is able to avoid the pitfalls of orders language which often end up sanctioning the status quo. It could be said that, for Bonhoeffer, the mandates are the theatre where the Christian life is played out. They are where "the relation of the world to Christ becomes concrete."[64] Each human being has been placed under all four mandates, which overlap with one another. This is not a formula for competing loyalties and ceaseless fragmentation for the whole of life has been taken up and claimed by Jesus Christ. This reality is only known in the church, which therefore must bear witness to the world "that all the other mandates are not there to divide people and tear them apart but to deal with them as whole people before God the Creator, Reconciler, and Redeemer—that reality in all its manifold aspects is ultimately *one* in God who became human, Jesus Christ."[65]

References to the mandates continue to appear in many of the manuscripts emerging in the period between the insertion into "Christ, Reality, and Good" and Bonhoeffer's arrest in 1943. We will limit our discussion to exploring three developments from this period that are of particular significance for Bonhoeffer's doctrine of the mandates. These developments include: 1.) the explication of the concepts "above" and "below"; 2.) the indication of the significance of vicarious representative action (*Stellvertretung*) for the mandates; 3.) the clarification of the interrelation of the mandates.

Bonhoeffer's employment of the spatial metaphor of above and below (*Oben und Unten*) is one of the more controversial and misunderstood aspects of his writing from the period of his involvement with the conspiracy.[66] Although Bonhoeffer does use the metaphor of above and below with

---

61. *DBWE* 16:419; *E* (*DBWE* 6), 68.

62. "The term 'mandate' is derived from the Vulgate Latin translation, *mandatum*, of the Greek term ἐντολή 'commandment,' e.g., John 13:34" (*DBWE* 16:519 n. 85). Perhaps Bonhoeffer simply assumed that the background of the term would be familiar to his intended audience.

63. *E* (*DBWE* 6), 68–69.

64. Ibid., 68.

65. Ibid., 73.

66. Earlier English translations of *Ethics*, which rendered the phrase as "superior

several different nuances, what is often overlooked is how each of the uses emerges from the general theological orientation that Bonhoeffer has inherited from Karl Barth's theology of revelation. Like Barth, Bonhoeffer was convinced that the movement of the Gospel does not consist of humanity ascending to divine heights, but rather is the divine interruption created by the free condescension of God to us in Christ. If one is to truly speak theologically, one must be governed by the logic of the Gospel and the divine movement of the Word from above to below. Hence, Bonhoeffer insists:

> The divine mandates depend solely on God's *one* commandment as it is revealed in Jesus Christ. They are implanted in the world from above as organizing structures—"orders"—of the reality of Christ, that is, of the reality of God's love for the world and for human beings that has been revealed in Jesus Christ. They are thus in no way an outgrowth of history; they are not earthly powers, but divine commissions. Church, marriage and family, culture, and government can only be explained and understood from above, from God.[67]

Bonhoeffer not only draws upon the imagery of above and below when discussing how the origins and content of the divine mandates must be understood, he also uses the terminology in an analogous way to describe relationships of authority which are brought into being by the mandates.[68] These relationships of authority, such as those of parent-child and teacher-student, provide the context and authorization for ethical discourse.[69] Bonhoeffer acknowledges that his affirmation of these authority structures cannot help but be offensive to the modern mind, but he observes that the modern project's attempt to formulate formal ethical principles apart from these concrete contexts have simply resulted in abstractions which have contributed to the atomization of genuine human community.[70] Furthermore, Bonhoeffer insists:

---

and inferior" served to further confuse the matter. Green, editor's introduction to *E* (*DBWE* 6), 23.

67. *E* (*DBWE* 6), 390. Note that in this manuscript from 1943 Bonhoeffer uses the term "culture" to describe the mandate he elsewhere speaks of as "work."

68. As a result, Krötke charges Bonhoeffer with advancing an "authoritarian conception of the mandates." "Bonhoeffer and Luther," 79.

69. There are some obvious points of contact here with Hauerwas's emphasis upon the significance of the master-apprentice relationship for ethical formation. See *AC*, 93–111.

70. *E* (*DBWE* 6), 372–73.

ethical chaos is already breaking in, wherever one no longer dares to be above and where one 'considers oneself too good' to be below, where being above seeks its rationale entirely from below—that is, where parents derive their authority from the trust of the children or a government's authority derives from its popularity—and, correspondingly, where being below is always seen merely as waiting in line for being above, that is, as what explodes any being above at all.[71]

Bonhoeffer does seem to recognize that his use of the language of "above and below" is vulnerable to commandeering by those whose agendas are not congruent with his own. As a result, he attempts to stave off this threat through providing some necessary qualifications of the terminology. First, Bonhoeffer explains, above and below must not be simply equated with existing power relations. The divine mandates do not provide license for the strong to rule over the weak, or the rich to exploit the poor. Rather, "it is part of the nature of the divine mandate to correct and order the earthly power relations in its own way."[72] Second, the divine mandate creates not only the above, but also the below, which "belong together in an inseparable and mutually delimiting relationship."[73] Third and finally, being above or below must be understood within the context of the divine commission. The language of above and below says nothing of personal or subjective value, but pertains solely to the responsibilities inherent to the offices and relationships constituted by the mandate. Failure to recognize the grounding of being both above and below in the divine mandate will inevitably lead to abuses by those above, as well as by those below.[74]

The nexus of relationships established by the divine mandates provides the context for genuine ethical activity. Genuine ethical activity involves freely accepting responsibility for others in accordance with the reality of Jesus Christ's bearing and incorporation of all human beings within himself. "All human responsibility," Bonhoeffer asserts, "is rooted in the real vicarious representative action of Jesus Christ on behalf of all human beings."[75] The person appointed to bear the divine mandate not only stands as a vicarious representative of God to those below, but through the exercise of his or her office is presented with opportunity to accept responsibility for those

71. Ibid., 376.
72. Ibid., 391.
73. Ibid.
74. Ibid., 392.
75. Ibid., 232.

placed under his or her authority.[76] For example, a man who has become a father, can no longer act as if he is a solitary individual, as he bears the responsibility for his entire family in each of his actions and activities.[77] Bonhoeffer stresses that responsibility is not the sole purview of those in authority. "Obedience and responsibility are interwoven," he writes, "so that responsibility does not merely begin where obedience ends, but obedience is rendered in responsibility."[78] There is no contradiction between obedience and free responsibility because Jesus Christ is the truly free human being who has demonstrated his freedom in his obedience to the will of the Father. Therefore, both those above and those below are free to be mutually responsible for one another.

As the bearer of the mandate to proclaim the revelation of God in Jesus Christ, the church stands in a relationship of responsibility for the world. Those who receive the word of Christ in faith "stand vicariously in the place [stellvertretend dastehen] of all other human beings, of the whole world."[79] It is the responsibility of the church "to witness to the world concerning its faith in Christ, to work on removing any offense, and to make room for the gospel in the world."[80] The exercising of this responsibility will bring the church into direct contact with the other mandates. In this encounter, the church must not abandon its own divine commission to proclaim the Gospel, through appealing instead to natural law, universal human rights, or some other meta-discourse.[81] Rather, the church must address the government, or for that matter any of the other mandates, only on the basis of the revelation of God in Jesus Christ. The church must not cease being the church, for, "only by fulfilling its own mandate can it legitimately question the government about its mandate."[82] This brief sketch of the church's responsibility towards government is illustrative of Bonhoeffer's formal understanding of the proper interrelationship of the mandates as characterized by the recurring refrain "being with-one-another [Miteinander], for-one-another [Füreinander], and over-against-one-another [Gegeneinander]."[83] Bonhoeffer insists that the mandates exist alongside of one another, not as

76. Ibid., 389; 221.
77. Ibid., 221.
78. Ibid., 287.
79. Ibid., 403.
80. Ibid., 357.
81. Ibid., 356.
82. Ibid., 399.
83. Ibid., 393. See also ibid., 380; 402–3. The terminology employed here is reminiscent of the personalist language Bonhoeffer used in his doctoral dissertation to describe the relations between members of the church-community. SC (*DBWE* 1), 178.

isolated entities, but rather they are oriented to one another, through which they also become the boundary or limit to one another.[84] In contradistinction to the prevailing cultural realities of Nazi Germany, Bonhoeffer insists that it is the commandment of Jesus Christ which rules over the mandates of church, family, culture and government. In contrast to the tyrannical rule of Hitler, the rule of Christ is a liberating, life-giving rule which sets human beings free to enter into the fullness of life in all its dimensions. Bonhoeffer writes, "Jesus Christ's claim to rule as it is proclaimed by the church simultaneously means that family, culture and government are set free to be what they are in their own nature as grounded in Christ. Only through this liberation, which springs from the proclaimed rule of Christ, can the divine mandates be properly with-one-another, for-one-another, and against-one-another, as we will have to discuss at a later point."[85] Unfortunately Bonhoeffer's completion of the manuscript was pre-empted by his arrest by the Gestapo on April 5, 1943. However, in his various comments upon the relationship between church and state, he has left us with a reasonably clear indication of how the being for-, with-, and against-one-another of the divine mandates would have been fleshed out.

There is much to appreciate in Bonhoeffer's attempt to overcome his cultural and theological heritage through his formulation of the doctrine of the mandates. He quite rightly rejects the static realm thinking which emerges from the ossification of the Two Kingdoms doctrine. He is to be commended for his clear recognition that both the retreat of pietism into other-worldliness and the capitulation of cultural Protestantism to the world fail to reckon seriously with Christ's entrance into and claiming of the world for Himself. His refusal to grant autonomous standards to the mandates apart from the divine commandment in Jesus Christ is also to be admired. Bonhoeffer's emphasis on the dynamic character of the mandates and the way they become the venue for the ever-fresh encounter with the Word of God and for the living out of the Christian life in freedom and responsibility is also to be commended.[86] Without diminishing these positive aspects it must be acknowledged that Bonhoeffer's doctrine of the mandates, much like his *Ethics* in general, remained a work in progress. In spite of its experimental character, it does seem that Bonhoeffer remained in some sense limited by the theological framework he inherited from the Lutheran tradition.[87]

84. *E (DBWE* 6), 393–94.
85. Ibid., 402–3.
86. Brock, "Bonhoeffer and the Bible," 7–29; Heuser, "Cost of Citizenship," 49–69.
87. Hence Zerner's assessment that in this realm Bonhoeffer remained "a synthesizer,

Bonhoeffer himself seemed to remain to some extent dissatisfied with his articulation of the doctrine of the mandates.[88] He returned to the topic of the mandates in the early stages of his correspondence from prison with Eberhard Bethge. Bethge's marriage to Bonhoeffer's niece, Renate, had served as the impetus for an exchange of thoughts between the two men on the relationship of marriage and friendship.[89] Through this exchange Bonhoeffer comes to realize that friendship, as well as culture and education, cannot be neatly subsumed under any of his previously formulated mandates. Of friendship, culture, and education, Bonhoeffer writes:

> They belong not in the sphere of obedience but rather in the sphere of freedom [Spielraum], which encompasses all three spheres of the divine mandates. Someone who doesn't know anything of this sphere of freedom can be a good parent, citizen, and worker, and probably also be a Christian, but whether such a person is a full human being (and thus also a Christian in the fullest sense) is questionable to me.[90]

This quotation is important, for it points to the central intention lying behind Bonhoeffer's doctrine of the mandates, namely the freeing of the human person to enter into the fullness of life as a genuine human being. Bonhoeffer would continue to explore this theme throughout his time in prison, leading to memorable reflections upon the worldliness of faith, religionless Christianity and the polyphony of life. In the following section we will trace the trajectory of this theme of worldliness from *Ethics* through *Letters and Papers from Prison*.

The Worldliness of Faith

In the letter that was quoted above, Bonhoeffer goes on to suggest that the "ethical" person, who is by definition preoccupied with the prohibitions that are found at the boundaries of life, cannot "light-heartedly make music, nurture friendship, play, and be happy."[91] Rather, it is the church that must cultivate the sphere of freedom where these activities may thrive and grow. In airing this view, Bonhoeffer is returning to convictions he had earlier articulated in the *Ethics* manuscript, "The Ethical and the Christian as a

---

not an innovator" ("Bonhoeffer's Views on the State," 150).

88. Dumas, *Dietrich Bonhoeffer*, 157; Pangritz, *Karl Barth*, 68.
89. *LPP* (*DBWE* 8), 183, 224, 247–48, 267–69.
90. Ibid., 268.
91. Ibid.

Topic."[92] In this manuscript, Bonhoeffer set out to recover a sense of the continuity of life, in the face of the work of some ethicists which could give the impression that life is simply a series of crises. Bonhoeffer asserts that it is the commandment of God revealed in Jesus Christ that "prevents life from disintegrating into innumerable new beginnings, but instead gives it a clear direction, an internal steadiness, and a firm sense of security."[93] The ethical is encompassed by the commandment, but the commandment itself is much broader, embracing the entirety of life. The divine commandment is distinguished from all other laws in that its content is freedom. "The commandment of God," Bonhoeffer writes, "is permission to live before God as a human being."[94]

Bonhoeffer roots his concern for living authentically as a human being in his Christology. His reformulation of the soteriological axiom of the Church Fathers—"Human beings become human because God became human"[95]—clearly and concisely demonstrates the interrelationship between Christology and theological anthropology in his thought.[96] The incarnation, at one and the same time, overcomes both religious escapism and attempts to deify the world.[97] As a result of God's becoming human in Jesus Christ, human beings are set free to be what they are before God, namely human beings. For Bonhoeffer, being a Christian means being a human being in the truest sense of the term. As Bonhoeffer would later write to Bethge from Tegel prison, "The Christian is not a *homo religiosus* but simply a human being, in the same way that Jesus was a human being."[98] The theme of worldliness that Bonhoeffer would develop throughout the "theological letters" beginning in April 1944 finds its roots here in this simple, but profound christological conviction. The seeds that would later flower in the tantalizing reflections from prison are already present in nascent form in *Ethics*, as the following extended quotation demonstrates:

---

92. *E (DBWE* 6), 363–87.

93. Ibid., 381.

94. Ibid., 382.

95. Ibid., 96. The patristic axiom can be articulated in the following manner: "God became human in order that humanity might become divine." For one patristic expression of this sentiment, see Athanasius, *On the Incarnation*, 93.

96. Zimmerman rightly recognizes that Bonhoeffer's understanding of the truly human "derives from a Trinitarian, incarnational Christology." As a result, he argues that we should recognize that "Bonhoeffer's Christological humanism is a repristination of patristic humanism" ("Being Human," 30).

97. Feil, "Bonhoeffer's Understanding of the World," 248.

98. *LPP (DBWE* 8), 485.

The cross of reconciliation sets us free to live before God in the midst of the godless world, sets us free to live in genuine worldliness [Weltlichkeit]. The proclamation of the cross of reconciliation frees us to abandon futile attempts to deify the world, because it has overcome the divisions, tensions, and conflicts between the "Christian" and the "worldly," and calls us to single-minded action and life in faith in the already accomplished reconciliation of the world with God.[99]

These seminal formulations burst into the full light of day in the letter of April 30, 1944 and continued to sprout and grow throughout the duration of the prison correspondence.[100] In this letter, Bonhoeffer raises the central question which would dominate his thinking for the rest of his life: "What keeps gnawing at me is the question, what is Christianity, or who is Christ actually for us today?"[101] As we have seen, the question of the identity of Jesus Christ has been central to Bonhoeffer's thought throughout his academic and pastoral career. What is new and is encapsulated in the word 'today' is Bonhoeffer's growing conviction that the world, or more accurately what has historically been understood as Western Christendom, had entered into a new age or epoch. "We are approaching a completely religionless age," Bonhoeffer writes, "people as they are now simply cannot be religious anymore."[102] Bonhoeffer's conviction that the age of religion is past is the flip side of his assessment, which he later introduces, of a "world that has come of age."[103] The employment of the term "world come of age" does not represent a value judgement on Bonhoeffer's part, but rather is a descriptive term that seeks to encapsulate the historical development which has culminated in the autonomous, completely secular human being of late modernity.[104] Bonhoeffer describes this historical process in the following way:

99. *E (DBWE 6)*, 400.

100. A mistranslation of the German word *"weltlich"* as "secular" rather than "worldly" in the original English translation of *Letters and Papers from Prison* spawned a variety of aberrant interpretations of Bonhoeffer in the early years of his work's reception in the English-speaking world. Green, "Sociality, Discipleship, and Worldly Theology," 86. Green notes that the word *"säkular"* makes only one appearance in Bonhoeffer's prison correspondence (86 n. 52).

101. *LPP (DBWE 8)*, 362.

102. Ibid., 362.

103. The phrase is introduced for the first time in the letter of June 8, 1944. Ibid., 426.

104. Harvey rightly warns against reading Bonhoeffer's comments on "a world come of age" as "an uncritical endorsement of its relationships and institutions" ("Narrow Path," 110). Plant has suggested that Bonhoeffer when he spoke of "a world come

> The movement toward human autonomy (by which I mean discovery of the laws by which the world lives and manages its affairs in science, in society and government, in art, ethics, and religion), which began around the thirteenth century (I don't want to get involved in disputing exactly when), has reached a certain completeness in our age. Human beings have learned to manage all important issues by themselves, without recourse to "Working hypothesis: God."[105]

As human knowledge has progressed, God has been pushed further and further out of the world and away from the center of daily life. In the face of advancing human knowledge, Christians have attempted to preserve space for God at the boundaries of human knowledge and at the liminal experiences of human life. Tracing this development, Bonhoeffer observes, "God's being pushed out of the world, away from public human existence, has led to an attempt to hang on to God at least in the realm of the 'personal,' the 'inner life,' the 'private' sphere."[106] The attempt to read the Bible in this light and to cast the Christian faith in these terms are the marks of religious interpretation. Religious interpretation means "to speak metaphysically, on the one hand, and, on the other hand, individualistically."[107] In several places, Bonhoeffer refers to metaphysics as a mark of religiousness, but the term itself is left undefined. However, it is unlikely that Bonhoeffer is expressing a disdain for metaphysics *in toto*, for at no point does he retreat from the distinct christological metaphysics upon which his *Ethics* is constructed, which understands Christ to be the "origin, essence, and goal" of all things.[108] It seems more likely that what Bonhoeffer has in mind when he speaks of metaphysics is a type of otherworldliness which fragments life, by making "the beyond" the sole concern of Christian life. In a letter written just two days before the failed coup attempt at the *Wolfsschanze*, Bonhoeffer further clarifies the nature of religion and its relation to faith: "the 'religious act' is always something partial, whereas 'faith' is something whole and involves one's whole life."[109]

---

of age" may have primarily had in mind "a small, educated, Western élite such as his family and co-conspirators" (*Bonhoeffer*, 145).

105. *LPP* (*DBWE* 8), 425–26.

106. Ibid., 455.

107. Ibid., 372.

108. *E* (*DBWE* 6), 226, 251, 253, 259–60, 268–70, 402. See also Ott, *Reality and Faith*, 46.

109. *LPP* (*DBWE* 8), 482. For further engagement with Bonhoeffer's understanding and critique of "religion," see Green, *Theology of Sociality*, 258–69; Rasmussen, *Reality and Resistance*, 81–82; Feil, *Theology of Dietrich Bonhoeffer*, 167–77; Pangritz, *Karl*

Bonhoeffer's initial question of "Who is Christ for us today?" is followed in the same letter with the question, "How do we go about being 'religionless-worldly' Christians, how can we be ἐκ-κλησία, those who are called out, without understanding ourselves religiously as privileged, but instead seeing ourselves belonging wholly to the world?"[110] While Bonhoeffer's diverse prison reading undoubtedly shaped his understanding of "the world come of age," it was his daily engagement with the Old Testament Scriptures which seem to have most profoundly influenced his understanding of religionless-worldly faith.[111] In the Old Testament, Bonhoeffer encountered a worldly faith that affirms creaturely existence in all of its dimensions. Human strength, health and happiness are not to be despised, as if only the weak and despairing could be Christians. Rather, they may be freely affirmed under the Old Testament category of blessing. "This blessing," Bonhoeffer writes, "is the addressing and claiming of earthly life for God, and it contains all [God's] promises."[112] The Old Testament concept of blessing cannot be opposed in principle by the cross or else one denies the contingent character of suffering within God's economy.[113] The world affirming dimension of the Christian story is obscured, however, when the story of Christ is divorced from the Old Testament and read instead in the light of the myths of the ancient near East. When this occurs, Christianity begins to be construed as a religion of otherworldly redemption. This deferral of hope to the beyond, Bonhoeffer objects, is not the true Christian hope of resurrection. Disciples of Jesus Christ have no "escape route" into eternity, but rather as a result of the resurrection are referred back to their life on earth "in a wholly new way, and more sharply than the OT."[114] The following excerpt from the first "theological" letter explains how the modern conception of transcendence is entirely reframed in the light of the Old Testament:

Barth, 87–94; Bethge, "Bonhoeffer's Christology," 66–68; Ott, *Reality and Faith*, 151–57.

110. *LPP* (*DBWE* 8), 364. Green has observed how Bonhoeffer employs the terms "religionless" and "worldly" throughout the prison writings to describe his proposal. The former functions as Bonhoeffer's "negative and polemical description" of the project, while the latter is his "positive and affirmative description." Hence, at times, as in the above quotation, Bonhoeffer can employ the terms together. "Sociality, Discipleship, and Worldly Theology," 87.

111. Dumas, *Dietrich Bonhoeffer*, 154; Pugh, *Religionless Christianity*, 50; De Gruchy, editor's introduction to *LPP* (*DBWE* 8), 24–25; De Gruchy, "Bonhoeffer as Christian Humanist," 20–21.

112. *LPP* (*DBWE* 8), 492.

113. Ibid., 492.

114. Ibid., 447.

> Belief in the resurrection *is not* the "solution" to the problem of death. God's "beyond" is not what is beyond our cognition! Epistemological transcendence has nothing to do with God's transcendence. God is the beyond in the midst of our lives. The church stands not at the point where human powers fail, at the boundaries, but in the center of the village.[115]

While the religious person looks to God for deliverance when their strength or knowledge runs out, the Christian enters fully into the earthly life, keeping watch with Christ in the hour of his pain. In the words of Bonhoeffer's renowned formulation, "The human being is called to share in God's suffering at the hands of a godless world."[116] True repentance consists of being drawn out of oneself and made a participant in the messianic event of Jesus's being-for-others. As Bonhoeffer would later succinctly state in his outline for a book which, sadly, was never written, "Jesus' 'being-for-others' is the experience of transcendence!"[117] Therefore, faith may quite simply be understood as a participation in this being of Jesus.[118]

Less than a month after the "new theology" burst onto the scene, in a letter of May 20, 1944, Bonhoeffer introduced the evocative musical metaphor "the polyphony of life" as an aid to conceptualizing his developing religionless-worldly understanding of the Christian faith. It should not be surprising that Bonhoeffer would employ such a musical term for he was an avid musician who at one point appeared destined for a career in music.[119] When the recipient of the letter, Bonhoeffer's friend, confidante, and frequent musical collaborator Eberhard Bethge, is taken into account, the naturalness of the decision to employ musical terminology is even more apparent.[120] Bonhoeffer had previously drawn upon the acoustic image

---

115. Ibid., 367.

116. Ibid., 480.

117. Ibid., 501.

118. Ibid. Perhaps somewhat counter-intuitively, Bonhoeffer's religionless-worldly understanding of Christianity opens up at this point a vista for understanding the patristic conception of deification. Zimmerman explains, "Deification means becoming divine according to the divine kenosis in the Incarnation. Becoming like God meant becoming more Christ-like and thus becoming more truly concerned about others. True humanity means becoming like God in his downward movement toward man" ("Being Human," 39).

119. Bethge, "Reflections," 33; Marsh, *Strange Glory*, 16.

120. A recollection by Bethge's wife, recorded by de Gruchy, gives texture to this dimension of the friendship between the two men: "when Bonhoeffer and his close friend Franz Hildebrandt met they invariably talked theology, but when Bonhoeffer and Bethge met they invariably made music, Dietrich playing the piano to accompany Bethge's singing" (*Daring, Trusting* Spirit, 17).

of Bach's famous, unfinished *Art of the Fugue* as a way of reflecting upon the meaning of life in a time of great personal and social fragmentation.[121] However, with respect to the polyphony of life Bonhoeffer's interest lies not so much in understanding and overcoming the fragmentariness of life in a time of war and chaos, but rather in understanding the richly variegated and multi-dimensional reality of human life. The term first arises in the context of brotherly advice offered by the prisoner Bonhoeffer to the recently married Bethge:[122]

> there is a danger, in any passionate erotic love, that through it you may lose what I'd like to call the polyphony of life. What I mean is that God, the Eternal wants to be loved with our whole heart, not to the detriment of earthly love or to diminish it, but as a sort of cantus firmus to which the other voices resound in counterpoint. One of these contrapuntal themes, which keep their *full independence* but are still related to the cantus firmus, is earthly love.[123]

The term "polyphony" is derived from Greek and literally means "many sounds" or "many voices." Its usage in musical parlance is somewhat varied and can mean: "music in more than one part, music in many parts, and the style in which all or several of the musical parts move to some extent independently."[124] From the context of its usage in the letter, where Bonhoeffer also refers to contrapuntal themes, it is apparent that the third definition is what Bonhoeffer intends when he speaks of polyphony. The type of polyphonic composition which Bonhoeffer had in mind involved adopting an existing plainsong or secular tune as the *cantus firmus* (lit. "fixed melody") and adding over it other contrapuntal (from the Latin *contrapunctum*, "against note") voices.[125] The addition of these musical lines adds depth and texture to the composition and for Bonhoeffer points towards the multi-dimensionality of truly human life in Christ. In a follow-up letter dated May 29, 1944, in which he once again picks up the imagery of polyphony, Bonhoeffer tells Bethge that Christianity "puts us into many different dimensions of life at the same time; in a way we accommodate God and the whole world within us."[126] While the Christian life is polyphonic,

121. *LPP* (*DBWE* 8), 306.
122. For the circumstances leading to this letter, see Bethge's letter of May 5, 1944. Ibid., 370.
123. Ibid., 393–94.
124. Frobenius, "Polyphony," 70.
125. Kemp, "Polyphony of Life," 145.
126. *LPP* (*DBWE* 8), 405.

the contrapuntal themes are only truly free to develop to the extent that the *cantus firmus* remains strong and robust. Smith elaborates on the functioning of the *cantus firmus*:

> the *cantus firmus* must not be construed as an artificial limit on the resulting polyphony. Instead of acting as a controlling force, the *cantus firmus* informs the composition and provides a foothold in the midst of confusion. The point, in other words, is not to impose some external order on a multidimensional and polyphonic life but rather to point a Christian to her firm foundation.[127]

Bonhoeffer draws upon the language of the Chalcedonian Definition—"undivided and yet distinct"—to highlight the nature of the relationship between the *cantus firmus* and counterpoint. He inquires of Bethge, "Is that perhaps why we are so at home with polyphony in music, why it is important to us, because it is the musical image of this christological fact and thus also our *vita christiana*?"[128] "To deny the cultivation of polyphonic existence, that is, to deny the worldliness of Christian commitment," Smith correctly deduces, "would be to dismiss the Chalcedonian Definition in favor of a docetic discipleship and ecclesiology."[129]

It has been observed that the musical metaphor of the polyphony of life stands at a key transitional period in Bonhoeffer's thought between the emerging "new theology" and what had gone before.[130] It is interesting to note that in the letter of April 30, 1944 and those following, Bonhoeffer makes no further explicit mention of the mandates.[131] This is not necessarily to say that Bonhoeffer has abandoned the doctrine, only that he had perhaps not yet had the opportunity to consider how the mandates could be integrated, if at all, within his new understanding of the world come of age. Although they don't cover exactly the same terrain, nor are they necessarily mutually exclusive, I would suggest that Bonhoeffer's metaphor of the polyphony of life provides a more helpful and hopeful way forward around the obstacles presented by the doctrine of the mandates. Despite Bonhoeffer's best effort to overcome the static understanding of the orders through

---

127. Smith, "Bonhoeffer and Musical Metaphor," 201.
128. *LPP* (*DBWE* 8), 394.
129. Smith, "Bonhoeffer and Musical Metaphor," 202.
130. Ibid., 204; Day, "Conviviality and Common Sense," 215.
131. Certainly some type of understanding of the mandates is implied in the poem, "The Friend." *LPP* (*DBWE* 8), 526–30. However, the intellectual origins of the guiding themes and images of this poem are found in correspondence dating back to January 1944 (248, 267–69).

the introduction of the terminology of mandates and his insistence on their dynamic interrelatedness, his doctrine of the mandates could not escape the spatial language (realms, spheres, etc.), which threatens to fragment life and make discipleship invisible. The musical metaphor of the polyphony of life points a way forward beyond the mandates, by overcoming the limitations of the spatial imagery inherent to the mandates. David Ford comments upon the significance of this breakthrough: "The imagery of sound allows much more clearly and without inappropriate paradox for a simultaneity in which one theme can be more 'constant' while yet being in essential reciprocity with others."[132] The metaphor of the polyphony of life provides a vehicle for affirming the multi-dimensionality of worldly life in all its fullness, while at the same time ensuring that that existence is grounded in the *cantus firmus* of the love of Christ.

Friendship

Letters and Papers from Prison stands as a testament to the friendship shared between Dietrich Bonhoeffer and Eberhard Bethge. The mere existence of the book testifies to the loyalty of Bethge in faithfully, diligently, and creatively carrying out his responsibilities as the executor of his friend's literary estate. The contents of the book itself, centered as they are in the correspondence between Bonhoeffer and Bethge, exude the stuff of friendship. The reader encounters numerous reminiscences and recountings of various shared experiences and events. In these pages, the publicly staid and emotionally-reserved pastors express uncommon expressions of affection and appreciation for one another.[133] It is not without warrant when one commentator states that "friendship must be understood as the central theme of the book."[134]

132. Ford, *Self and Salvation*, 260 n. 53.

133. De Gruchy, *Daring, Trusting Spirit*, 63. I confess to being at somewhat of a loss as to how to best understand Marsh's recent depiction in *Strange Glory* of Bonhoeffer as romantically smitten with the younger Bethge. Some of the most insightful commentary on Marsh's reading of the Bethge-Bonhoeffer relationship has, in my opinion, been offered by Wesley Hill. Hill observes, "But what emerges most clearly from that close attention is not a homoerotically inclined Bonhoeffer to the exclusion of a 'quite normal' one (to use Bethge's designation for his friend) but a Bonhoeffer whose zeal for intimacy and filial, spiritual closeness complicates and overflows the categories by which we often classify such things. I think here of Rowan Williams' conclusion that romantic love and the love of same-sex friendship are best understood as 'different forms of one passion—the passion for life-giving interconnection'" ("Full This-Worldliness," para. 12).

134. Scott, "'From the Spirit's Choice," 53."

The most explicit discussion of friendship as a topic in and of itself occurs in the correspondence of late 1943 and early 1944. The conversation is sparked by Bethge's comment: "Marriage is what remains stable through all passing relationships."[135] Bonhoeffer latches onto this passing remark, affirming its content, but then in a question that perhaps bears the mark of a degree of personal insecurity, asks, "But don't we also count a good friendship among the things that remain stable?"[136] Bethge objects, observing that friendship lacks the external recognition which is granted by the world to marriage. As a case in point, he draws attention to the difficulty he has had in getting the Bonhoeffer family to pass Dietrich's letters on to him and the low priority status he has been afforded with respect to securing a permit to visit his friend in prison. This is because, as Bethge's father-in-law has described the situation to him, friendship has no *necessitas*.[137] These comments spark Bonhoeffer's most sustained reflection on friendship. Bonhoeffer acknowledges that friendship has no *necessitas*. It belongs not to the realm of obedience, but rather to the realm of freedom which characterizes true human existence. Bonhoeffer writes:

> Precisely because friendship belongs within the scope of this freedom ("of the Christian person"!?), we must defend it confidently against all "ethical" existences that may frown upon it—certainly without claiming for it the "*necessitas*" of a divine command, but by claiming the "*necessitas*" of *freedom*! I believe that, within this realm of freedom, friendship is by far the rarest—where it is still found in our world, which is defined by the *first three* mandates?—and the most precious good. It is beyond comparison with the benefits we have from the mandates; over against them it is sui generis, but belongs together with them like the cornflowers belong to the field of grain.[138]

The cornflower in the field of grain would become the central image of the poem, "The Friend," that Bonhoeffer would later compose in honor of Bethge's birthday.[139] Reflecting upon the second verse, where Bonhoeffer introduces the image, Bethge observes that "he characterizes the sheer and wonderful 'uselessness' of friendship, in which its love lives, just as the cornflower lives uselessly in the middle of the useful cornfield."[140] The im-

---

135. *LPP (DBWE* 8), 211.
136. Ibid., 224.
137. Ibid., 248.
138. Ibid., 268–69.
139. Ibid., 526–30.
140. Bethge, *Friendship and Resistance*, 102.

age of the cornflower amidst the grain is Bonhoeffer's acknowledgement that he is unable to locate friendship within or under the purview of the divine mandates. Instead, friendship, along with other aspects of life such as culture and education, belongs to the sphere of freedom. Reflecting on his own cultural location, Bonhoeffer observes:

> Our "Protestant" (not Lutheran!) Prussian world is so strongly defined by the four mandates that the whole sphere of freedom has been pushed into the background. I wonder whether—it almost seems so today—it is only from the concept of the church that we can regain the understanding of the sphere of freedom (art, education, friendship, play). This means that 'aesthetic existence' (Kierkegaard) is not to be banished from the church's sphere; rather, it is precisely within the church that it is founded anew.[141]

It is fitting that Bonhoeffer should turn to the church as the site for the cultivation of the sphere of freedom in which friendship may develop and thrive. Although at this point it seems to simply be an instinctual move, the connection of friendship and the church resonates deeply with the Christology which both informs Bonhoeffer's soteriology and undergirds his ecclesiology. Jesus is pre-eminently, for Bonhoeffer, the friend of sinners. Jesus is the *Stellvertreter*; the one who stands in my place. In his very ontological constitution, he is *pro me*. He is the One who lays down his life for his friends.[142] In doing so, Christ brings into existence a new humanity liberated from the incurvature of sin to be freely with and for one another. The site of this new humanity is the body of Christ, the church-community. Although I am not aware of Bonhoeffer himself using the following terminology, it would be quite in keeping with what we have just rehearsed to describe this new humanity as a community of friends.

The relationship between Bethge and Bonhoeffer can be considered to be paradigmatic of the friendship that is made possible within the life of the church. Although it is true that Bonhoeffer and Bethge came to share many common judgments on matters of musical and artistic taste, their friendship was ultimately grounded in a much deeper spiritual reality—namely, their shared calling to serve the church of Jesus Christ. It was at the illegal Confessing Church seminary at Zingst that they first met and their common hope in Christ would continue to provide the foundation of their friendship. Even a cursory reading of the letters exchanged between the two men during the time of Bonhoeffer's imprisonment makes plain the

---

141. *LPP* (*DBWE* 8), 268.
142. John 15:13; cf. *D* (*DBWE* 4), 125.

way their friendship is permeated by prayer.[143] Over the course of the correspondence Bethge continues not only to be Bonhoeffer's friend, but also his pastor, resuming the responsibility he first assumed as Bonhoeffer's confessor in the House of Brethren at Finkenwalde.[144] The intense friendship shared between the pastor (Bethge) and his parishioner (Bonhoeffer) on the one hand, and the professor (Bonhoeffer) and his student (Bethge) on the other, goes against the grain of much of the common wisdom stemming from professionalized conceptions of ministry and academia which dismiss the possibility of genuine friendship between pastors and parishioners and professors and students.[145]

While the friendship between Bonhoeffer and Bethge may helpfully exemplify the friendship that is possible within the church, Bonhoeffer's relationships with members of the conspiracy are suggestive for understanding the possibility of construing the church's relationship to the world through the lens of friendship. Within the conspiracy, Bonhoeffer encountered like-minded men who were willing to take the risk of acting decisively on behalf of others and, if necessary, to suffer on account of this action. In being willing to risk this venture of free responsibility, these conspirators in many ways stood closer to the reality of Jesus Christ, "the man for others," than the Confessing Church which often seemed to be preoccupied with mere self-preservation.[146] As Bonhoeffer had put the matter in *Ethics*, "To live as a human being before God, in the light of God's becoming human, can only mean to be there not for oneself, but for God and for other human beings."[147] This interaction with his high-minded, self-sacrificially committed, but not necessarily Christian, fellow conspirators undoubtedly factored largely in Bonhoeffer's developing interest during this period in what he termed "unconscious Christianity."[148] Bethge, who was drawn into the circle of conspirators through his friendship with Bonhoeffer, has observed that,

---

143. Sallie McFague's comments on the relationship of friendship and intercessory prayer seem particularly appropriate in the context of the friendship shared between Bonhoeffer and Bethge: "Just as betrayal is the sin of friendship in which one hands over the friend to the enemy, so intercessory prayer is the rite of friendship in which one hands over the friend to God" (*Models of God*, 180).

144. *LPP* (*DBWE* 8), 170; De Gruchy, *Daring Trusting Spirit*, 28–35.

145. See for example Barnes, "Pastor, not Friend."

146. *LPP* (*DBWE* 8), 500.

147. *E* (*DBWE* 6), 400.

148. Unfortunately, all that survives on this theme from Bonhoeffer's own hand are a few occurrences of the term in notes and a passing reference to his increasing interest in the topic in a letter to Bethge. Ibid., 170 n. 111; *LPP* (*DBWE* 8), 489, 491.

"the time of the conspiracy created even stronger relationships of trust than the years of the church-struggle."[149]

Bonhoeffer reflects upon this phenomenon at an ecclesial level in the *Ethics* manuscript "Church and World I."[150] He observed that the time of Nazi tyranny created a strange alliance between Christians and the defenders of liberal-humanist values who had previously stood at odds with the church. Finding themselves to be in a state of cultural homelessness, the classic liberal-humanist concepts of "reason, culture, humanity, tolerance, autonomy" began to make their way home, seeking refuge in the site of their origin—the church.[151] The church to which they returned was not the liberal church of cultural Protestantism which sought an easy alliance with the world, but the Confessing Church, within which, as a result of the Church Struggle, "the central Christian tenets were being emphasized in their sternest, most uncompromising, and most offensive form to reason, culture, humanity, and tolerance."[152] In its concrete historical existence, the Confessing Church had experienced the reality of the dialectical interplay of the two sayings of Christ, "Whoever is not against us is for us" and "Whoever is not for me is against me."[153] On the one hand, over the course of its struggle against the German Christians, the Confessing Church began to understand the threat to the church posed by those who sought to remain in a position of neutrality with respect to the Church Struggle. On the other hand, the Confessing Church came to recognize its affinity with people of honor and goodwill outside of its ranks who sought the refuge and protection of the church. The two sayings of Christ cannot be separated. Neglect of the former leads to fanaticism and sectarianism, while neglect of the latter leads to secularization and accommodation to the world. Bonhoeffer states the counterintuitive reality, "The more exclusively we recognize and confess Christ as our Lord, the more will be disclosed to us the breadth of Christ's lordship."[154] When the church is truly and properly devoted to its Lord, Bonhoeffer seems to be telling us, it will discover friends and allies in the strangest of places. Exclusive allegiance to Christ is not the recipe then for sectarianism, but is in fact the only way that the church can truly be for the world.[155] In fact, the church is called to continually encounter

---

149. Bethge, *Friendship and Resistance*, 83.
150. *E* (*DBWE* 6), 339–51.
151. Ibid., 340
152. Ibid.
153. Mark 9:40; Matt 12:30, quoted in *E* (*DBWE* 6), 342–43.
154. *E* (*DBWE* 6), 344.
155. Reflecting upon the Church Struggle, de Gruchy observes, "The confession

the world in the spirit of friendship, irrespective of whether that friendship is reciprocated by the world. This reality is most tantalizingly hinted at in the outline Bonhoeffer sketched while he was in prison for a short book he intended to write.

Near the beginning of August 1944, Bonhoeffer sent the outline of the book to Bethge.[156] For the next two months this work preoccupied Bonhoeffer. It is believed that he took the manuscript with him when he was transferred to the prison at Prinz-Albrecht-Strasse, but it has never been recovered.[157] The outline sent to Bethge suggests that Bonhoeffer intended to compose three chapters which he described in the following way: "1. Taking Stock of Christianity; 2. What is Christian faith, really? 3. Conclusions."[158] The contents of the book, particularly the first two chapters, appear to be largely anticipated by the ideas formulated in the "theological letters" Bonhoeffer had exchanged with Bethge. For our purposes it is sufficient to draw attention to one comment from the outline of each of the first two chapters before proceeding to a closer examination of the third chapter, which is essentially an ecclesiological proposal. The quotation from the sketch of the first chapter appears in a subsection on "The Protestant church" and reflects Bonhoeffer's highly critical evaluation of the Confessing Church of his day. Here Bonhoeffer jots down the short phrases: "Decisive: Church defending itself. No risk taking for others."[159] This is incisive criticism in light of the way Bonhoeffer will go on to speak about faith in the notes for the second chapter. There Bonhoeffer writes, "our relationship to God is a new life in 'being there for others,' through participation in the being of Jesus."[160] A church that has turned in upon itself and is not willing to take risks for others has separated itself from the source of its life in Christ. For this reason Bonhoeffer begins the outline of his conclusions in chapter 3 with the verdict: "The church is church only when it is there for others."[161] The sketch for this chapter reads as follows:

---

of Christ and the struggle for the 'true church' was not for the sake of theological correctness and ecclesial purity but for the sake of the world for which Christ had died. To surrender the truth of the gospel, to deny Christ, meant denying humanity, denying the victims of Nazism, and denying all that was good and great in German culture. To affirm the truth of the gospel, by contrast, meant affirming humanity, expressing solidarity with the victims of injustice, and affirming the good and great in culture" ("Bonhoeffer as Christian Humanist," 14).

156. *LPP* (*DBWE* 8), 499–504.
157. Bethge, *Dietrich Bonhoeffer*, 862.
158. *LPP* (*DBWE* 8), 499.
159. Ibid., 500.
160. Ibid., 501.
161. Ibid., 502.

As a first step it must give away all its property to those in need. The clergy must live solely on the freewill offerings of the congregations and perhaps be engaged in some secular vocation [Beruf]. The church must participate in the worldly tasks of life in the community—not dominating but helping and serving. It must tell people in every calling [Beruf] what a life with Christ is, what it means "to be there for others." In particular, *our* church will have to confront the vices of hubris, the worship of power, envy, and illusionism as the roots of all evil. It will have to speak of moderation, authenticity, trust, faithfulness, steadfastness, patience, discipline, humility, modesty, contentment. It will have to see that it does not underestimate the significance of the human "example" (which has its origin in the humanity of Jesus and is so important in Paul's writings!); the church's word gains weight and power not through concepts but by example. Further: revision of the question of "confession" (Apostolikum); revision of apologetics; revision of the preparation for and practice of ministry.[162]

In this brief paragraph, Bonhoeffer provides us with a glimpse into his emerging vision for a post-Christendom church in a world come of age.[163] That what Bonhoeffer has in mind is a church that has relinquished its Constantinian privileges is apparent from his insistence that the church no longer be supported by the state and that it should give away its property and subsist solely on freewill offerings. Furthermore, the humble posture of helping and serving in the worldly tasks of life is in keeping with a post-Christendom church that has renounced its aspirations to dominate and rule. It will be necessary for such a church to cultivate a particular set of virtues: "moderation, authenticity, trust, faithfulness, steadfastness, patience, discipline, humility, modesty, contentment."[164] It is surely no coincidence that the virtues required for a community of disciples in a world come of age are the very building blocks of true and enduring friendships. This listing of virtues is followed by an observation about the importance of human example which is completely in keeping with Bonhoeffer's conception of the Christian faith as not simply a set of doctrines to be affirmed, but a life to be lived in the presence of God. This also ties in with the short phrase "revision

162. Ibid., 503–4.

163. Drawing upon the observation that Bonhoeffer largely draws upon exilic and post-exilic Old Testament texts when discussing religionless-worldly Christianity, Harvey intriguingly suggests that Bonhoeffer was beginning to recognize a typological connection between the life of Israel during and after the Babylonian exile and the life of the church he was envisioning. "Narrow Path," 115–23.

164. *LPP* (*DBWE* 8), 503.

of apologetics." It would be a mistake to think that Bonhoeffer's reflections upon Christianity in a world come of age were an apologetic endeavor to make Christianity palpable to people that had learned to live quite well without it.[165] Instead Bonhoeffer's concern was with discerning and declaring the Lordship of Christ over the entire world. From this perspective the best apologetics, if one can call still use the term, are lives lived in conformity to the Gospel.[166] Bonhoeffer concludes his outline for the chapter by speaking of the need for "the revision of the preparation for and practice of ministry."[167] This had been a passionate concern of Bonhoeffer's since at least the mid-1930s. When he speaks of the need for the revision of the preparation for ministry one cannot help but think of Bonhoeffer's own experiments with theological, spiritual, and communal formation with the seminarians at Finkenwalde. Surely these experiences were not far from Bonhoeffer's own mind as he penned these words. The life shared amongst the members of the community at Finkenwalde—a life shaped around corporate worship, prayer, meditation, study, and recreation—cultivated a sphere of freedom in which true friendships were realized, as the brothers learned to live with and for one another.[168] This brings us to the importance of the "arcane discipline" to Bonhoeffer's vision of the church. Although the term is not mentioned in the outline for the chapter and is only mentioned relatively rarely throughout the prison correspondence, the concept remains central to Bonhoeffer's theological outlook.[169] De Gruchy clearly explicates the central significance of the arcane discipline to Bonhoeffer's prison reflections in a paragraph that warrants reciting at length:

> If Jesus exists only for others, so too the church must not seek its own self-preservation but be "open to the world" and in solidarity with others. This does not mean that the church must surrender its own identity, for that would simply be another example of "cheap grace," or a confusion of the penultimate and the

---

165. Bethge has observed, that throughout his prison reflections, Bonhoeffer's "elaborations on this theme, from the very beginning, never entered the sphere of apologetics" (*Dietrich Bonhoeffer*, 865).

166. A more "Hauerwasian" thought is hardly imaginable.

167. *LPP* (*DBWE* 8), 504.

168. The intention is certainly not to idealize the community life at Finkenwalde. The community did experience its own internal problems unique to its particular context. For instance, there appears to have been some resentment amongst members of the community to the increasingly close friendship that was developing between Bonhoeffer and Bethge. De Gruchy, *Daring Trusting Spirit*, 17–18. However, these struggles made it all the more necessary that the practice of the confession of sin should stand at the heart of community life.

169. Bethge, *Dietrich Bonhoeffer*, 881.

ultimate. It is necessary for the church to recover the "discipline of the secret" (*disciplina arcanum*), whereby the mysteries of the faith are protected from profanation (ibid., 286). Prayer, worship, the sacraments, and the creed, remain at the heart of the life of the church, but they must not be thrust upon the world in some triumphalist manner.[170]

Bonhoeffer himself continued to practice the arcane discipline throughout the time of his imprisonment. On the one hand, he continued to observe the Christian year, he immersed himself deeply in the Scriptures, he reflected upon the hymns of his church, particularly those of Paul Gerhardt, and he persevered in prayer. On the other hand, he refused to prey upon the emotional vulnerability of his fellow prisoners by attempting to thrust the Gospel upon desperate men during air raids and instead simply sought to be present to them during times of crises.[171] The arcane discipline ensures that being in and for the world is not equivalent to being of the world. At the same time, the practice of the *arcanum* is not an insular or inward-focused activity. As the practice of the presence of Jesus, it can only direct the disciple towards the world which has been reconciled to God in Christ. Bethge explains, "In the *Arcanum* Christ takes everyone who really encounters him by the shoulder, turning them around to face their fellow human beings and the world."[172] The church can only be for the world to the extent that it stands with Jesus and participates in the life of the One who stands on behalf of others before the Father. As the community of friends surrounding the friend of sinners, the church is the community that extends the gracious offer of divine friendship as it stands in solidarity with the world Christ loves. When Bonhoeffer was arrested on April 5, 1943, a working note remained upon his desk, inscribed with the title, "Existing for the World."[173] The phrase not only provides a haunting commentary on the last phase of Bonhoeffer's life, but in this concise formulation we are directed towards the compelling ecclesiological vision which captured Bonhoeffer's imagination during those dark days in Tegel Prison.

---

170. de Gruchy, "Dietrich Bonhoeffer," 250. The internal reference is to the 1971 English translation of *Letters and Papers*.

171. *LPP* (*DBWE* 8), 276.

172. Bethge, *Dietrich Bonhoeffer*, 883.

173. Ibid., 720.

PART 2: CHURCH AND WORLD IN THE THEOLOGY OF STANLEY HAUERWAS

Stanley Hauerwas in the New Millennium

"It may happen that a church that praises its freedom as a possibility offered by the world succumbs to the world to a particular degree, that is, a church that is free in this way may be secularized faster than a church that does not possess freedom as a possibility."[174] Stanley Hauerwas was born less than a year after Bonhoeffer penned these words following his final visit to the United States. The situation that Bonhoeffer had warned against would be the ecclesial context for Hauerwas's life and writing. From very early on in his academic career, Hauerwas recognized that the church which had been granted formal religious freedom in the United States, had "succumbed to the world to a particular degree" and now found its imagination captured by the gospel of America.[175] Throughout the 1980s and 1990s Hauerwas came to see with increasing perspicuity the depths of the church's captivity to America; a development which he did not shy away from energetically denouncing.[176] As a result it was somewhat ironic when *Time* magazine, as part of a series identifying "America's best" in a variety of fields, identified Hauerwas as "America's best theologian."[177] The issue of *Time* hit newsstands on September 10, 2001. The next day hijackers flew planes into the two towers of the World Trade Center in New York. In a certain sense, one could say that 9/11 became one of the defining moments of Hauerwas's life.[178]

The days following September 11 witnessed a remarkable groundswell of patriotism within the United States. Hauerwas was particularly troubled by the identification of "God and country" which accompanied this patriotic surge.[179] Hauerwas took the opportunity to comment on the troubling

---

174. *DBWE* 15:449.

175. For some of Hauerwas's preliminary thoughts pointing in this direction see: "Theology and the New American Culture," in *VV*, 241–60.

176. See, for example, *ComC*, 72–86; *AN*, 122–31; *CET*, 171–90; *US*, 29–38; *IGC*, 199–216; *WW*, 32–47.

177. Elshtain, "Christian Contrarian," 74–75. In public lectures, Hauerwas frequently shrugs off the acclamation by observing that "best" is not a theological category. However, the fact that Hauerwas in his memoir rephrases the designation from "America's best theologian" to "best theologian in America" suggests something of the tension inherent for him in being so named. The irony of being named "America's best theologian" is further compounded when it is recalled that the Pentecostal, prosperity-gospel preacher T. D. Jakes was named "America's best preacher" in the same issue.

178. *HC*, 264.

179. *DT*, 175. The rhetoric of President George W. Bush frequently displayed this

national developments in one of his first public lectures following 9/11 at the University of Virginia on October 1, 2001. In the address Hauerwas directly called into question the idolatrous conflation of God and country:

> Red is a color of the Christian tradition. It's Pentecost. White is a color of the Christian tradition. It's Easter. Blue is the color for our mother who gave birth to Jesus. In the church, we never put them together. That red, white, and blue have now become Christian colors is an indication the church has been captured by a very different narrative than the story of Jesus' birth.[180]

Hauerwas's lecture ruffled the feathers of several former colleagues and was followed a short time later by a very public falling out with the neo-conservative theological journal *First Things*, on whose editorial board Hauerwas had been serving up to that point.[181] On the eve of American military action against Iraq, *Time* magazine approached him about writing an article on the morality of the impending war. In the article, Hauerwas denounced the rhetoric of evil as it was being applied to the regime of Saddam Hussein on the basis that it "threatens to turn war into a crusade."[182] He identified the linguistic mistakes involved in designating the events of September 11 as an "act of war" and the ensuing declaration of a "war on terrorism" and warned of the potentially dire consequences. Finally, in the most straightforward manner, he boldly proclaimed, "The identification of cross and flag after Sept. 11 needs to be called what it is: idolatry."[183]

The timing of 9/11 is also rather interesting in the way that it corresponded with a significant shift that Hauerwas was attempting to make with respect to the tone of his work. In the introduction to his last collection of essays published before the attack on the World Trade Center,

---

confusion of God and country. For instance, Bush described American ideals as "the hope of all mankind" which "shines in the darkness" and ascribed "power—wonder-working power" to "the goodness and idealism and faith of the American people." For the former see Bush, "President's Remarks to the Nation," para. 13. For the latter, see Bush, "State of the Union Address," para. 48. The phrase "there is power, power, wonder working power" is found in the refrain of Lewis E. Jones' hymn, "There is Power in the Blood" (1899). For further consideration of the identification of "God and country" in the United States following 9/11, see Northcott, *Angel Directs the Storm*; and Hughes, *Christian America*.

180. Hauerwas, "September 11," para. 4.

181. The essay which ignited the controversy is: Neuhaus and Nuechterlein, "In a Time of War." In response, Hauerwas penned the essay: "In a Time of War: An Exchange." Hauerwas's account of the situation appears in *HC*, 268–69. Hauerwas has since resumed submitting contributions to *First Things*.

182. Hauerwas, "War Would Not Be Moral," 45.

183. Ibid., 45.

Hauerwas had written, "*A Better Hope* is my attempt to make the 'for' more determinative than the 'against.'"[184] Despite his intentions to write a more positive book, Hauerwas himself would later observe that for the most part, "*A Better Hope* seemed more determined by my criticisms of 'liberalism' than by any attempt to provide a constructive alternative."[185] The publication of *Performing the Faith: Bonhoeffer and the Practice of Nonviolence* in 2004 marked Hauerwas's recommitment to a "more constructive engagement with the social order called America."[186] Hauerwas's decision to turn at this point for the first time to Bonhoeffer is significant and certainly understandable when one considers the broader ecclesial and political contexts.[187] Similarities between Nazi Germany and post 9/11 America must not be overstated; on the other hand, neither should they be casually dismissed. Michael Northcott, for example, has drawn attention to the chilling parallels between the suppression of individual liberties and the maintenance of concentration camps under the Nazi regime, "with the Patriot Act, with Guantanamo Bay, and also with the incarceration of 'illegal' refugees in America."[188] Beyond whatever similarities there may be between the national and international climates in which Bonhoeffer and Hauerwas found themselves, the two are even more closely connected through their painful firsthand experience with churches that lacked the formation and internal resources to say "No!" to states determined to go to war. Although explicit engagement with Bonhoeffer occurs only in the introduction and first two chapters, Hauerwas claims that *Performing the Faith* as a whole can be understood "as an ongoing commentary on Bonhoeffer's claim that a community of peace can only exist if it does not rest on lies and injustice."[189] The most important gift, then, that the church can offer to the world is its very existence as a community capable of speaking truthfully to one another and to the world.

184. *BH*, 9.

185. *PTF*, 15. Hauerwas does evaluate the essays "Enduring: Or, How Rowan Greer Taught Me to Read," and "Captured in Time: Friendship and Aging" with Laura Yordy to be notable exceptions to this trend. *BH*, 163–72, 173–87.

186. *PTF*, 15. The subtitle of the book, *Bonhoeffer and the Practice of Nonviolence*, is somewhat misleading in that Bonhoeffer is only explicitly engaged in the introduction and first two chapters.

187. Hauerwas acknowledges that although this is the first time he was written on Bonhoeffer, he has long been influenced by the German pastor-theologian. Bonhoeffer's influence upon Hauerwas extends back to an encounter with *Discipleship* during his time in seminary. Ibid., 35.

188. Northcott, "Angel Directs the Storm," 148–49.

189. *PTF*, 20. Bonhoeffer made this claim in an address delivered at the Youth Peace Conference in Czechoslovakia in 1932. *DBWE* 11:365.

In the years that followed 9/11, Hauerwas was drawn into fruitful dialogue with the radical democratic theorist and activist Romand Coles. Hauerwas's ongoing conversation with Coles sparked a fresh re-appropriation of the life and thought of Jean Vanier and the L'Arche movement. Recent years have also witnessed Hauerwas engaging with topics of broad societal interest such as the university and the place of war in the American national mythos and ethos.[190] In what follows, I will draw upon the writings from Hauerwas's self-professed "constructive" turn, particularly those in which he engages with Dietrich Bonhoeffer, Romand Coles, and Jean Vanier, to explore Hauerwas's alternative approach to the modern problematic of church and world, with a particular focus on the themes of church and state, the radical ordinary, and friendship.

Church and State

One searches throughout Hauerwas's vast corpus in vain to find his theory of the state. This absence of a theory of the state is not an error of omission, but is in fact by design.[191] Hauerwas believes that it is a theological misunderstanding stemming from Constantinian presumptions that causes Christians to think they must provide an account of the state.[192] Such an account cannot help but provide ideological legitimation to the state in its current existing form, in effect establishing its immunity from the claims of the gospel.[193] Instead, Hauerwas insists, "A more realistic view [of the State], one more in accordance with the New Testament, is that the State simply exists."[194] This statement reflects the deep and continuing influence of John Howard Yoder on Hauerwas.[195] A brief foray into Yoder's thought at this point will helpfully illuminate the presumptions upon which Hauerwas's understanding of the state is grounded.

In a chapter entitled, "Theoretical Understandings of the State" within his book *The Christian Witness to the State*, Yoder directs attention towards the interpretation of Romans 13 within the Christian tradition. Historically,

---

190. For Hauerwas's reflections on the university see: *The State of the University*; for his reflections on war and America see: *War and the American Difference*.

191. *PTF*, 50.

192. Hauerwas, "On Learning Simplicity," 136.

193. *PTF*, 196.

194. Hauerwas, "On Learning Simplicity," 136.

195. In his first essay on Yoder, Hauerwas had criticized the Mennonite theologian on this very score, but he has since come to share Yoder's perspective. *VV*, 213–21; cf. *SU*, 154.

Yoder argues, the text has been interpreted in one of two ways. He refers to these two ways of interpretation as positivistic and legitimistic. The positivistic interpretation finds its home in the Lutheran tradition and draws "the conclusion that whatever state now exists in any given time and place is the state which God desires to exist then and there."[196] The legitimistic interpretation finds in Romans 13 and other biblical texts a catalogue of prescriptions and conditions that the state must fulfill in order to be considered legitimate. This way of thinking sprouts from the soil of the Reformed tradition. Both the positivistic and legitimistic interpretations share the assumption that God has providentially instituted the state in either its' empirical or ideal form; an assumption which may be foreign to the text of Romans itself. Yoder elaborates:

> More careful recent analysis, both exegetical and systematic, has given good reason to doubt whether the intention of Paul in this passage was at all to provide this sort of metaphysic or ontology of the state. Paul was simply arguing that the Christians in Rome should not rebel even against a government which threatened to mistreat them. They could be confident that God was using the powers in and behind the state within his providential purpose. The state is not instituted, i.e., established, but rather accepted in its empirical reality, as something that God can overrule toward His ends. Paul therefore does *not* mean that in the divine acceptance of the state there is implied any ratification of its moral standards or political purposes, or any theory of the proper state.[197]

It is the account of the state that Yoder has offered here and elsewhere in his writings which informs Hauerwas's refusal to provide a theory of the state. Yoder's influence is also evident in the following formulation penned by Hauerwas:

> Modesty requires, however, that Christians resist the temptation to legitimate the structures the New Testament identifies as the "powers." Such powers do not need legitimating. Rather in order to be and remain modest these structures require a people capable of saying "no" when those who rule do so in a manner that goes beyond the limited task they have been given.[198]

---

196. Yoder, *Christian Witness*, 74.
197. Ibid., 75.
198. *SU*, 171.

The above quotation reflects Yoder's apocalyptic outlook, but also intimates that Hauerwas has some conception of the responsibility to which the state is called. In this regard, Hauerwas can sound rather traditional.[199] Like Bonhoeffer, Hauerwas insists that only the church knows why the state actually exists.[200] Reflecting the way that his thought has also been influenced by the work of Karl Barth, Hauerwas affirms that the true test of any polity or social order is whether it allows for the free preaching of the Gospel.[201] Hunsinger has called into question the apparent Constantinian character of such an assumption.[202] While Hauerwas's assertion could understandably be read in a Constantinian way, it takes on a rather different character when it is remembered that for Hauerwas the church which knows the true reason for the state's existence has no coercive power over the state and can only call the state to account on the basis of its own vulnerable witness to the Crucified One.

While Hauerwas is insistent that the state, whether it acknowledges it or not, exists for the sake of the gospel, he remains decidedly agnostic about what might be the ideal form of government. However, this does not require that Christians must retreat from any attempt to discern between relatively better and worse societies.[203] Hauerwas, for his part, has been quite critical of the Western liberal-democratic instantiation of the state which he has known and experienced in the United States. Hauerwas's suspicion of the Western liberal state can be traced back to some of his earliest essays. Many of Hauerwas's most incisive criticisms of the liberal state are already present in the essays, "Politics, Vision and the Common Good" (1974) and "The Church and Liberal Democracy: The Moral Limits of Secular Polity" (1981).[204] In the first of these essays Hauerwas poses a question that, although lacking the facility with words that will come to characterize his later writings, will continue to animate his challenge to liberal democratic societies throughout his career. "The crucial question for us today," he suggests, "is how to make efficacious a substantive notion of the common good within a democratic framework."[205] When there is no place for addressing questions of the common good, justice must be reduced to a mere matter

---

199. Rasmusson, *Church as Polis*, 226.

200. At this point, Hauerwas is once again following Yoder's lead. *SU*, 171 n. 17; cf. Yoder, *Christian Witness*, 16.

201. Hauerwas, "On Learning Simplicity," 136; *BH*, 259 n. 17; *PTF*, 56.

202. Hunsinger, "To Hauerwas," 255.

203. *SU*, 152.

204. *VV*, 222–40; *ComC*, 72–86.

205. *VV*, 229.

of procedure, which leads to the rise of the increasingly complex forms of bureaucratic organization necessary to adjudicate and attend to the competing and ultimately irreconcilable interests of individuals.[206] Founded upon the illusion that it is possible to have a just polity without a just and virtuous people, liberalism ends up producing the kind of people it presumes we already are, namely, self-interested consumers.[207]

A quick glance at the footnotes of "Politics, Vision and the Common Good" reveals the significant influence that the political theorist Sheldon Wolin had upon Hauerwas's earliest evaluations of the Western liberal democratic project. Recent developments, including his interaction with Romand Coles, have led Hauerwas to revisit and re-articulate what he has learned from Wolin. "In particular," Hauerwas observes, "Wolin's last chapter [of *Politics and Vision*], 'The Age of Organization and the Sublimation of Politics,' convinced me that liberal political theory ironically too often legitimates the substitution of organizational manipulation for genuine politics."[208] In this chapter, Wolin gives voice to sentiments that will profoundly influence Hauerwas's own reading of the modern state. At one point Wolin observes that modern society's fascination with organization reflects the conviction that "man could accomplish great things without himself becoming great, without developing uncommon skills or moral excellence."[209] This resonates with Hauerwas's ongoing criticism of modern liberal society, including his identification of the parasitic nature of liberal societies. According to Hauerwas, modern Western liberal societies are dependent upon habits and virtues being shared among their members which cannot be accounted for by liberal theory and are ultimately undermined and eroded by liberal practice.[210] Under Wolin's influence, Hauerwas came to the conclusion that liberalism is the attempt to avoid the arguments constitutive of truly democratic politics.[211] Constitutional democracies are not immune from the sublimation of the political, for, as Wolin explains, "As in theories of organization and method, constitutionalism relied on rules and procedures to the virtual exclusion of the art of politics."[212] For this reason, Hauerwas insists, Christians would be further ahead if they were to recognize that institutional democracy is not really the "rule of the people,"

---

206. *ComC*, 79.
207. Ibid., 73, 79.
208. *PTF*, 227.
209. Wolin, *Politics and Vision*, 340.
210. *PTF*, 226.
211. *SU*, 148.
212. Wolin, *Politics and Vision*, 349.

but rather is best understood as a mechanism for attempting to ensure that the elites who in fact rule are in some way accountable to the people.[213] If Christians were to recognize this they would be in a better position to "learn how to make fruitful use of the self-justification language of rulers who always claim to be our benefactors."[214]

Hauerwas's recent reengagement with Wolin also coincides with the publication of a newly expanded edition of *Politics and Vision*. In the new chapters, Wolin particularly emphasizes how the political imagination of the people in contemporary liberal democracies has been so profoundly shaped by the strictures and discipline of the market that it is now almost impossible for people to think that the economy could be organized in any other way.[215] Hauerwas draws upon Wolin to critique Jeffrey Stout's project, insisting that Stout's narration of the current state of political participation amongst American citizens is deficient to the extent that it does not "deal with the subversion of politics by capitalism."[216] This is not an entirely new theme in Hauerwas's work. Rasmusson has highlighted how this assumption stands at the heart of Hauerwas's criticism of neoconservatives, namely, that their emphasis upon "the capitalist economy and the freedom of the individual as the supreme value undermine[s] the sort of traditional values they defend."[217] What does seem to come to the fore in a new way in Hauerwas's writings from the past decade is an increasing awareness of the perils and challenges for politics posed by globalization. In attempting to understand this development, he finds assistance that is quite congenial with the musings of Sheldon Wolin in Rowan Williams's reflections upon emerging "market states." Summarizing Williams, Hauerwas writes:

> such states are now servants of global capitalism, which means that they are unable to be the focus for conversations necessary to discover goods in common. Rather, market states derive their legitimacy by trying to provide insurance to voters who seek maximum possible freedom without the corresponding risks. Such states push "politics towards a consumerist model, with the state as the guarantor of 'purchasing power,' it raises

213. *SU*, 155–56.

214. Ibid., 155. At this point Hauerwas is drawing upon Yoder's treatment of Luke 22:25 in *Priestly Kingdom*, 151–71.

215. Wolin, *Politics and Vision*, 578.

216. *SU*, 149 n. 12. In a recent article, Stout seemingly concedes this point when he acknowledges that "so much power has recently accumulated in the hands of the managerial elite that all holders of political office who are not themselves billionaires are now beggars beholden to billionaires" ("Spirit of Democracy," 5).

217. Rasmusson, *Church as Polis*, 255.

short-term expectations. By raising short-term expectations, it invites instability, reactive administration, rule by opinion poll and pressure."[218]

Hauerwas's collaboration with the radical democratic theorist and activist Romand Coles gives rise to perhaps his most cogently articulated and compelling criticisms about the current "state" of affairs. Hauerwas and Coles depict contemporary Western society as dominated by a constellation of forces (what Wolin has described as Superpower) involved in what could be called a conspiracy against contingency.[219] "Empire, global capitalism, the megastate, and even many forms of cosmopolitanism," Hauerwas and Coles assert, "name systems of power that frequently proliferate death in the name of a life that would be free of it."[220] This denial of death results in configurations of political power which are deeply determined by death.[221] The result is a "politics of glory" which must attempt to secure some form of immortality against the encroachment of death.[222] Such a politics, in its desire to erect a lasting monument in the face of death, becomes fixated with results and hence is determined by the criteria of speed and efficiency.[223] The effect of these commitments is the radical depersonalizing of politics, which is further reinforced by the effacing of the importance of time and place by the constellation of powers surrounding the market, state, and empire. Under the conditions of the death-determined politics of our time, not

---

218. *PTF*, 27–28. The internal quotation is attributed to Williams, "Dimbleby Lecture, 2002."

219. "As an ideal type, Superpower might be defined as a system of power that accepts no other limits other than those it chooses to impose on itself. Its system blends the political authority of the 'democratic' state, *de jure* power, with the powers represented by the complex of modern science-technology and corporate capital. The distinctive element that these *de facto* powers contribute to Superpower is a dynamic (from the Greek *dynameis*, or powers), a driving force. They are cumulative, continually evolving into new forms, self-revivifying. Their effect is to change significantly the lives not only in the 'homeland' but in near and distant societies as well" (Wolin, *Politics and Vision*, xvi–xvii).

220. *CDRO*, 3. There are echoes here of Hauerwas's earlier and oft-stated conviction that liberalism names the attempt to secure agreement between individuals who share nothing in common save their fear of death. E.g., *HR*, 353, 608; *WAD*, 18. This is also connected with the aphorism frequently employed by Hauerwas which states that Americans are determined to "get out of life alive." One particular employment of the phrase is found in *PTF*, 208.

221. It would be fascinating to bring Pope John Paul II's understanding of the "culture of death" as presented in the encyclical *Evangelium Vitae* into dialogue with Hauerwas at this point.

222. *CDRO*, 1–3, 23–30.

223. Ibid., 4, 318.

only is it assumed that "we do not have the time to take the time to listen to one another or to remember the dead," but there is no place for a true encounter with those who are different.[224] The conflict which may ensue from such an encounter threatens to topple the tenuous tower which has been constructed as a hedge against death.[225] From Hauerwas's and Cole's perspective this conspiracy against contingency results in the denial of politics, for ultimately, "politics is about relationships between people dead and alive, relationships that are as painful as they are unavoidable."[226] The word "democracy" is frequently invoked in contemporary contexts to conceal the sublimation of politics that has occurred under the influence of "the hegemony of global capital, the megastate in pursuit of militarized empire, and cultural matrixes that are increasingly produced in ways that fall into line with both."[227] Where then is hope to be found? It is certainly not be found, Hauerwas and Coles tell us, in efforts to place leaders in positions of power within the existing political-economic system. Not only would very few be able to understand a leader proclaiming an alternative politics to the politics of death, Hauerwas and Coles also assert that "holding positions of power in the economic polity is a lot like wearing Tolkien's ring. The systemic forces of corruption dig deep into the soul and are enough to overwhelm most who—with good intentions—assume positions within the systems of power."[228] Rather than storming the White House, what is needed is concrete communities which live out in their ordinary day-to-day lives a true politics which in its radical receptivity of the other provides an alternative to the politics of death. Hauerwas and Coles put the matter simply, "We are without hope if there are no examples of an alternative politics to the politics of death."[229]

This emphasis upon the necessity of examples of alternative politics brings Hauerwas to an obvious place of intersection with Coles which opens up the possibility for fruitful dialogue. As we have observed in the previous chapter, Hauerwas has long maintained that the church is such an alternative politics. Although Hauerwas has had much to say about the political arrangements of the modern liberal nation-state, he has always been insistent that his primary concern is not the liberal democratic state as such, but with

---

224. Ibid., 4.
225. *WAD*, 18.
226. *CDRO*, 2.

227. Ibid., 113. The formulation is Coles's, reflecting the influence of Wolin, *Politics and Vision*, 601, but it is in keeping with Hauerwas's own reading of the situation.

228. *CDRO*, 7.
229. Ibid., 7.

"Christians who have confused Christianity with liberalism."[230] Contrary to the objections of his cultured despisers, Hauerwas has never advocated for social withdrawal on the part of Christians, rather he has only questioned the seemingly widespread assumption among Christians that they "must become liberals or, at least, accept liberal political principles and/or practices in order to be of service in America."[231] In a letter to Romand Coles, Hauerwas elaborates upon the ecclesiocentric character of his writing as it pertains to questions relating to the world:

> That I seem so "churchy," that I write first and foremost about the church, is not because I have no interest in the "world." Rather I emphasize the significance of the church because I fear that the devastated character of the church in our time will be unable to produce the Will Campbells, the Ella Bakers, the Martin Luther Kings, the Bob Moseses. But it is never a question of church or world. Rather it is a question of having a people so captured by the worship of God that they can be for the world what the world so desperately needs.[232]

The Extraordinariness of the Ordinary

The dialogue shared between Hauerwas and Coles in *Christianity, Democracy, and the Radical Ordinary* is marked by a generous receptivity, which is characterized by careful reading and listening that seeks to learn from the other while at the same time openly acknowledges difference and is therefore unwilling to silence points of contention.[233] In order to fruitfully engage with the conversation between Hauerwas and Coles, it is first helpful to come to some type of understanding of what is meant by the phrase "radical democracy." The fugitive character of radical democracy presents difficulties for the interpreter at this point, for radical democracy is not so much an object in the world, as it is a way of inhabiting the world. The adjective "radical" is necessary to distinguish radical democracy from the impotent and emasculated forms of democracy which characterize political life in modern Western societies.[234] Seen in this light, radical democracy can

230. *PTF*, 232. See also *CSChu*, 148.
231. *BH*, 24.
232. *CDRO*, 111–12.
233. That such an exchange could take place between America's most famous "sectarian, fideistic, tribalist" and a non-Christian radical democrat, such as Coles, casts additional doubt upon the accuracy of the (in)famous ascription.
234. *CDRO*, 114.

be understood as "the intermittent and dispersed traditions of witnessing, resisting, and seeking alternatives to the politics of death wrought by those bent on myriad forms of immortality-as-conquest."[235] In contrast to "the dominant forms of 'disengaged liberal democracy' currently identified with the nations of the West," radical democracy recognizes that politics is ultimately about personal involvement and therefore is inherently relational, embodied, and inseparable from the particularities of place and memory.[236] Central to Coles's construal of radical democracy is Sheldon Wolin's notion of "tending." "Tending" refers to an intensely personal way of relating to another, as in tending to a garden or tending to one who is sick. "Tending" is contrasted with the impersonal and instrumental politics of "intending," which seek to capture and mobilize individuals for pre-established political goals and objectives in accordance with anti-democratic modes of power.[237] Wolin's conception of tending, contributes to radical democracy's understanding that there can be no depersonalizing of politics. As a result, a good political end or outcome cannot be divorced from the means by which it is achieved. Specific liturgies or bodily practices are necessary for cultivating the habits of generous receptivity necessary for engaging with others in a truly democratic fashion. A posture of generous receptivity stands at the heart of the radical democratic ethos, but such a posture must be carefully inculcated for it does not come naturally to those who find themselves within a world bent toward the criteria of speed and efficiency. As Coles and Hauerwas explain, "Listening not only takes time, but it also requires a trained vulnerability that does not come easily. Vulnerability means that our life is not under our control, which means that we must learn to trust others if we are not only to survive but flourish."[238] Among those whom radical democrats must learn to trust and listen to are those whom the systems of worldly power attempt to render mute and invisible, for politics is not simply about "'doing something' for the poor and marginalized, but [is rather] about learning to *be with* the poor and marginalized."[239] Such

---

235. Ibid., 3.

236. Ibid., 18. Hauerwas at this point is summarizing a section from Coles's work *Beyond Gated Politics*, x.

237. CDRO, 151. Coles draws particular attention to Wolin's book *Presence of the Past*, 87–93. The politics of intention are perhaps most clearly exemplified in the political machinery surrounding elections in the United States that seeks to manipulate voters into supporting one of the two parties and, when they have done so, seeks to convince them that by virtue of having spent their brief stint in the voting booth that they have done their political duty.

238. *CDRO*, 5.

239. Ibid., 13; italics mine.

a politics will inevitably find itself immersed in the quotidian rhythms of everyday life, hence the phrase inscribed within the title of the book: "the radical ordinary."[240] It is the politics of the everyday, or the politics of small achievements, that provides the most appropriate context for the tending to and cultivation of ongoing relationships.

It should come as no surprise that Hauerwas would be drawn to Coles's articulation of radical democracy for it in many ways resonates with the theo-political vision which animates his ecclesiology. Hauerwas not only shares with Coles a similar diagnosis of the maladies that plague modern Western societies, but also shares some substantive convictions with respect to the shape that a true alternative to the politics of death should take. Hauerwas and Coles observe, "Both radical democracy and Christianity are lived pedagogies of hope inspirited and envisioned through memories of the 'good, at its best.'"[241] In this way, the anthropology of radical democracy fits naturally with Hauerwas's own emphasis upon the historically and communally situated nature of the self and the corresponding importance of character, the virtues, and narrative than does the atomistic and ahistorical individual of modern liberalism. The politics of the church and of radical democracy both take time, which means that patience is a key virtue for radical democrats much in the same way that Hauerwas understands it to be central to the Christian life. Patience is made possible, from Hauerwas's perspective, by the apocalypse of the God of Israel in the life, death and resurrection of Jesus Christ. This may sound counterintuitive to those who equate the word apocalypse with doomsday meteors or escapist rapture theology, however, Hauerwas insists that "the apocalyptic character of the Gospel paradoxically makes possible the everyday."[242] Furthermore, "the apocalyptic character of our faith not only makes the everyday possible but also enables us to see how extraordinary it is."[243] It is this apocalyptic outlook that has funded the ongoing emphasis prevalent throughout Hauerwas's corpus upon the significance of what could be called the "radical ordinary."[244] This emphasis is perhaps most paradigmatically on display in the 1988 essay, "Taking Time for Peace: The Ethical Significance of the

---

240. In a later collaborative effort, Hauerwas and Coles suggest that "'Tending to ordinary life' is a phrase that gestures to the heart of the case we tried to make in *Christianity, Democracy, and the Radical Ordinary*" ("Long Live the Weeds," 350).

241. CDRO, 3.

242. DT, 8.

243. HC, 246.

244. Cavanaugh suggests that the "conviction that the mystery of God is found in the trivia of everyday life" is also reflected in Hauerwas's own passionate engagement with the trivial ("Stan the Man," 26).

Trivial."²⁴⁵ In this essay, Hauerwas argues that in the face of the totalitarian powers that attempt to tyrannize our lives (the threat of nuclear annihilation stands at the fore in this particular essay), one of the most politically significant things we can do is to take the time for peace by engaging in such seemingly trivial activities as raising lemurs, playing baseball, and having children. Christians can enter into these activities because, Hauerwas writes, "it is our belief that God has given us the time and space to be people who can rest and enjoy our creation as creatures."²⁴⁶ To inhabit the world in such a way is a mode of eschatological existence which Hauerwas first learned to articulate with the help of John Howard Yoder. Yoder convinced Hauerwas that nonviolence is essential for genuine politics, because it is the commitment not to kill the other that creates the space for the conflict and conversation necessary for discerning goods in common. Furthermore, from Yoder Hauerwas came "to see how the church could make a genuine contribution to American political life by being 'itself,' that is, a community that refuses to come to judgment without hearing the voice of the 'weakest member.'"²⁴⁷ The parallels between these aspects of Hauerwas's ecclesiological vision and Coles's vision of radical democracy are rather obvious, and perhaps should not be entirely surprising when it is recognized that Coles himself is a sympathetic reader of Yoder. The relational character of radical democracy made manifest in its posture of generous receptivity also resonates with Hauerwas's conviction that "the gospel requires vulnerability if it is to be true to itself."²⁴⁸ As a result, the politics which is the church should never be non-dialogical or impervious to the other. Rather, Hauerwas maintains, "Vulnerability must be at the heart of such a politics just to the extent that living well requires readiness to learn from the stranger. I should like to think that vulnerability is at the heart of what it means to be Christians, because through worship we are trained to have our lives disrupted by the strangest of strangers—God."²⁴⁹

These points of contact with radical democracy allow Hauerwas to identify himself, in a carefully qualified sense, as a "radical democrat."²⁵⁰ This does not mean that Hauerwas is without questions for Coles and radical democracy, or conversely, that Coles has no concerns with the vision of Christianity articulated by Hauerwas. At the center of this tension are

245. *CET*, 253–66.
246. Ibid., 257.
247. *PTF*, 227.
248. *CDRO*, 333.
249. Ibid., 112.
250. *SU*, 163.

questions surrounding the person of Jesus and the place of faith. Hauerwas is concerned that, in finding such a congenial and sympathetic conversation partner in Coles, Christians could be tempted to overlook his unbelief.[251] This is closely associated with the corresponding risk for the church that in entering into partnership with radical democratic movements the practices of the Christian faith could end up being instrumentalized in the service of radical democracy.[252] However, the question remains as to whether radical democracy is ultimately either coherent or tenable apart from the God who raised Jesus Christ from the dead. Coles himself appears to be haunted by this possibility. Referring to the lives of the activists and organizers which he finds so compelling, men and women such as Ella Baker, Bob Moses, Amzie Moore, Septima Clarke, and Medger Evans, Coles asks, "Are they ultimately stories of Christian characters who, because they were Christian, provided the patience without which such practices I call radical-democratic could not have transpired?"[253] Hauerwas believes that the church is required for the formation of a people of character who are capable of staring down death, which is the necessary condition for a truthful politics which stands as an alternative to the politics of glory and immortality.[254]

It is perhaps appropriate at this point to highlight Coles's suspicion of what he calls Christians' jealousy for Jesus. Coles worries that the exclusive allegiance Christians owe to Christ risks short-circuiting the conditions necessary for genuine dialogue and renders them less than vulnerable to those outside the community.[255] This concern about Christian jealousy for Jesus is intricately connected with concerns Coles has about the place of orthodoxy in Hauerwas's work. Drawing on the criticisms raised by Peter Dula and Alex Sider, Coles questions whether a commitment to orthodoxy and the corresponding affirmation of some form of institutional authority is ultimately compatible with radical democracy.[256] Hauerwas responds that orthodoxy, as opposed to being an obstacle to the type of generous receptivity required by democracy, is actually the necessary precondition for such a posture of vulnerability.[257] Orthodoxy names the hard-fought

251. *CDRO*, 12.
252. Ibid., 111.
253. Ibid., 35.
254. Ibid., 28–29.
255. Ibid., 21–22.
256. Dula and Sider, "Radical Democracy," 482–504.

257. In an analogous way, Coles himself seems to acknowledge the significance of orthodoxy when he suggests that the epical character of Wolin's work is a helpful correction to radical democracy's own reluctance to generate theory. Coles writes, "This reluctance renders democracy too inarticulate at key junctures, such that it tends to

wisdom of the church which exists to direct the gaze of the faithful towards the vulnerable love of God made manifest in the cross. "Therefore," Hauerwas writes, "rather than being the denial of radical democracy, orthodoxy is the exemplification of the training necessary for the formation of a people who are not only capable of working for justice, but who are themselves just."[258] Hauerwas turns the tables by suggesting that radical democracy, with its refusal to recognize the historical gifts given to communities, such as orthodoxy and the episcopate in the case of the church, appears to have a problem with concrete community. As a result, radical democracy will face distinct challenges when it comes to cultivating the virtues it professes to admire.[259]

Although Hauerwas does appear to have staved off the challenge, in the process of responding to Coles's worries about Christianity's jealousy for Jesus, Hauerwas makes an offhand remark about theocracy that raises additional concerns for Coles. Hauerwas suggests that Coles is right to recognize the exclusive allegiance that is owed by Christians to Christ. However, this should not be a worry for Coles, because those who affirm the confession "Jesus is Lord!" cannot be sectarians. On the contrary, Hauerwas asserts, "We are rather theocrats. It is just very hard to rule when you are committed to nonviolence. But we are willing to try. 'Try,' however, means that politics is always a matter of persuasion."[260] This is not the first time that Hauerwas has identified himself as a theocrat. It appears that the origins of the designation can be traced back to Michael Cartwright's "Afterword" to *The Hauerwas Reader* (2001) where Cartwright wrote of Hauerwas, "If as he argues, the common good for Christians is rightly understood as God, then it would be more apt to charge Hauerwas with being a theocrat without a state."[261] The charge stuck, at least in Hauerwas's own mind, and he has been identifying himself as a theocrat in his writings and in public appearances ever since.[262] Hauerwas's self-designation raises warning flags for Coles, as does Hauerwas's talk about being willing to try to rule. Coles's anxieties are not assuaged by Hauerwas's talk about a nonviolent rule, for many of the anti-political powers and forces which capture the imaginations of modern

---

become too vulnerable in some bad ways and not vulnerable enough in some ways that are key to the vitality of democracy" (*CDRO*, 115). The word "analogous" was deliberately chosen, as Hauerwas would surely consider it a mistake to univocally equate doctrine with theory.

258. *CDRO*, 30.
259. Ibid., 345.
260. Ibid., 22 n. 5.
261. Cartwright, afterword to *HR*, 638.
262. *PTF*, 68; *CSChu*, 154.

Western men and women could be considered to be nonviolent in some sort of way.[263] Coles, I think rightly, suggests that language of being "willing to rule" should at least cause Hauerwas pause for thought. Democracy, from Coles's perspective, reflecting the influence of Wolin, "is not another form of 'ruling over'—or a mere substitution of a few leaders by rule of the many, but rather the effort to replace ruling with another kind of power."[264] Hauerwas's insistence that "politics is always a matter of persuasion" is helpful in mitigating this concern at some level, but his continuing use of the language of "willingness to rule" suggests that the church might ultimately be interested in playing the same tune as the ruling powers of this world, only transposed into a slightly different key. Hauerwas is correct to understand that "Jesus is Lord!" is an imperialistic claim embracing the totality of creation. However, the fact that Jesus is a Lord who rules from the cross, radically calls into question any facile or immediate claims on the part of Christians about being willing to rule. Rather than making bold statements about being a theocrat, Hauerwas would perhaps be better to lend his ear once more to John Howard Yoder and hear afresh the radical christological claim that "people who bear crosses are working with the grain of the universe."[265] Participating in the reign of Christ, is not about learning how to become a nonviolent Caesar, but rather involves the call to, as Bonhoeffer came to recognize, "share in God's suffering at the hands of a godless world."[266]

It's not that Hauerwas doesn't recognize this cruciform reality, but there are times, as commentators have noticed, when his language seems over-determined by his opponents and under-determined by the disruptive logic of the cross.[267] Hauerwas's insistence upon referring to himself as a theocrat is one such example. Another occurs in the context of the conversation with Coles that concludes *Christianity, Democracy, and the Radical Ordinary*. During this conversation Hauerwas refers to the dehumanizing character of liberalism which causes us to forget the dead and ignore those involved in everyday work in the name of a grand civilizational project. In

---

263. As an example, Coles draws attention to shopping malls, noting that "shopping malls (if you exclude the sweatshops . . . which you of course can't) are nonviolent, I suppose, but hell-bent on absorbing every corpuscle of flesh-desire that enters them, to largely, though not simply—odious ends" (*CDRO*, 39). For an interesting exegesis of the formative liturgies of the shopping mall, see Smith, *Desiring the Kingdom*, 93–103.

264. *CDRO*, 139.

265. Yoder, "Armaments and Eschatology," 58 cited in *WGU*, 6, 17.

266. *LPP* (*DBWE* 8), 480.

267. Dula and Sider, "Radical Democracy," 495; Reno, personal correspondence cited in *PTF*, 236; Kerr, *Christ, History and Apocalyptic*, 116–26.

contradistinction to those pressures, Hauerwas suggests that he and Coles share a common commitment to looking for "smaller politics."[268] Coles quickly corrects Hauerwas, noting that the politics they both aspire to is actually a much more expansive politics than the politics identified with the modern liberal nation-state. While the politics of the modern liberal nation-state are profoundly amnesiac and are circumscribed by lines drawn on a map, Coles notes that the politics envisioned by himself and Hauerwas freely transgress these temporal and geo-political boundaries through their willingness to remember the dead and participate in "transnational networks of indigenous peoples who live locally *and* organize and cultivate relations with other traditions and localities."[269] In a sense, Coles is reminding Hauerwas of the theological reality of catholicity, a reality which does not simply stand in opposition to the social imaginary of the modern liberal nation-state, but rather transcends its categories entirely. Once again, this is not news to Hauerwas, however the interaction with Coles does at times seem to serve as a type of speech-therapy which helps Hauerwas to purge from his vocabulary expressions that are overly-determined by their negative relationship to liberalism and the modern nation-state. Central to this development is Coles's engagement with the work of Rowan Williams. In Williams's reading of the Jesus story, Coles discovers an elegant and suggestive articulation of a politics free of all territorialism. This vision finds paradigmatic expression in Williams's insistence that "Jesus did not come here to be 'a competitor for space in this world.'"[270] This engagement with Williams, via Coles, provides resources for a way of speaking about the church's engagement with the world that moves beyond some of the binary oppositional ways of speaking that sometimes creep into Hauerwas's speech. This in no way nullifies a provisional, eschatological dualism, which is in keeping with the apocalyptic character of the Gospel, but it does prevent the falling back into and ossification of the antinomies which characterize the world which has been done away with in the cross and resurrection of Christ.[271] Coles and Hauerwas recognize this reality by acknowledging that aspiring to be non-competitors for space in this world does not result in the abolition of enemies. Rather, they note, "insofar as a person or group struggles against

268. *CDRO*, 340.
269. Ibid., 341.
270. Ibid., 14, internal quotation is found in Williams, *Christ on Trial*, 6.

271. For an intriguing exposition of the apostle Paul's understanding of the old antinomies which characterized the fallen world (e.g., Jew/Greek, slave/free, male/female) and the new antinomies introduced by the Father's apocalyptic sending of the Son and the Spirit (e.g., Spirit/Flesh, death of Christ/Law) see Martyn, *Theological Issues*, 111–23.

particular practices or persons, there is a profound sense in which we are always competitors against particular patterns of territoriality."[272] Hauerwas and Coles then proceed to make a crucial terminological distinction, noting that being competitors against particular patterns of territoriality does not necessarily lead to and, in fact, should be distinguished from being competitors for space in this world.[273] Coles proves to be a helpful conversation partner for Hauerwas as a result of, among other things, his ability to call Hauerwas to account when he is in danger of slipping into either sectarian or theocratic ways of speaking. Cavanaugh has similarly observed that "radical democracy does seem to have given Hauerwas ways of more adequately conceptualizing how the church might enact the politics of Jesus without needing to adopt any position at all vis-à-vis 'wider society.'"[274] One of the important fruits emerging from Hauerwas's dialogue with Coles, according to Cavanaugh, is a conception of the complexity of political space which allows Hauerwas to articulate how "those forms of church can be seen as doing more than resisting or participating in the dominant society, and how they can be seen as participating in other networks of connectivity that leave the imagination of a dominant society behind."[275] Cavanaugh suggests that if Hauerwas is able to continue in this way of speaking and writing, the charges of sectarianism raised against him might finally be laid to rest once and for all.

Friendship

The life and witness of Jean Vanier and the L'Arche movement occupies a central place in the conversation between Hauerwas and Coles. The L'Arche movement began in 1964 in Trosly-Breuil, France, when Jean Vanier invited two men suffering from developmental disabilities to live and share life with him.[276] What began as one man's faithful response to the summons of the God of the Gospel quickly became an international movement.[277] References to Vanier and L'Arche occur in numerous places in Hauerwas's work, however the writings from this later period represent his most sustained engagement

---

272. *CDRO*, 15.
273. Ibid., 16.
274. Cavanaugh, "Politics of Vulnerability," 106.
275. Ibid., 106.
276. *LGVW*, 23–24.
277. Today over 140 L'Arche communities can be found spread over 40 different countries. L'Arche Canada, "What is L'Arche?," para. 4.

with and reflections upon the L'Arche movement.[278] This renewed engagement with the ministry of L'Arche culminated with a two-day conference at the University of Aberdeen where Hauerwas was invited to join with Vanier in reflecting upon the intersection of theology and disability.[279]

In L'Arche, Hauerwas discovered a community with friendship at its core that is sustained by liturgies of celebration. The liturgical life of the community includes daily community meals, celebrating the birthdays of each and every member, funerals, and other special events, integrated with the rhythm of the weekly celebration of the Mass on Sunday evening.[280] In Vanier, Hauerwas found a fellow Aristotelian who, through the transformative impact of the Gospel, had been led to practice friendship in a way that transcended anything Aristotle would ever have thought possible. Aristotle believed that true friendship, as opposed to friendships of mere usefulness or pleasure, was only possible between equals.[281] As a result, it would have been inconceivable to Aristotle that friendship could be shared between the mentally disabled and those who are not. Yet, as Hauerwas notes, "Vanier believes that friendship is what L'Arche is about."[282] Vanier puts it as follows:

> The vision Jesus came to share is about meeting people and trusting people. Faith in Jesus is trust that we are loved. It is knowing that deeper than being part of a group, religious or otherwise, there is the fundamental experience of becoming a friend of truth, a friend of Jesus, a friend of God. But I can't do this alone. I need community. I need friends.[283]

Beyond the shared understanding which both men have inherited from Aquinas that salvation is ultimately friendship with God, Hauerwas is particularly taken by Vanier's injunction that we must learn to be "friends of time."[284] For Hauerwas, the call to be "friends of time" rests upon a chris-

---

278. Hauerwas's most extensive reflections upon L'Arche prior to this period are found in the essay "Timeful Friends: Living with the Handicapped," in *STT*, 143–56. The work of Jean Vanier also informs a prayer which Hauerwas offers as a conclusion to an important essay responding to the events of 9/11 found in *DFH*, 188–89 and *PTF*, 209–10.

279. The fruit of these discussions is found in the essays written by Hauerwas and Vanier which comprise the book *Living Gently in a Violent World*.

280. *CDRO*, 104.

281. *CAV*, 34–38.

282. *CDRO*, 203.

283. *LGVW*, 73.

284. Vanier, *Community and Growth*, 3, quoted in *STT*, 143. Becoming "friends of time" is the central theme of Hauerwas's earlier reflections upon L'Arche found in *STT*, 143–56.

tological, and hence, eschatological basis. In the incarnation, the One who stood beyond time entered into time to befriend us and in so doing has redeemed time. The resurrection stands as the definitive pledge of the ultimate triumph of the One who bore the cross. As a result of God's presence with us in time in the person of Jesus Christ and the assurance that God will bring the creation to its proper end in Christ, Christians are released from all imperial ambitions to make history come out right and freed to live as "friends of time" who are truly present to one another in the present moment. Hauerwas explains, "We live by slowing down and saying with our lives that the world will not be saved by frantic activity. If time has already been redeemed by Jesus, we learn to wait on the salvation of the Lord by taking time to listen to our weakest members."[285] Becoming "friends of time" engenders the patience necessary for befriending, being with, and learning to listen to the mentally disabled. What distinguishes the ethos of L'Arche from that of modern social services agencies and organizations is the fundamental distinction Vanier draws between "doing for" and "living with."[286] Assistants do not come to L'Arche out of a desire to be helpful or effective, but rather simply to be with the intellectually disabled. Life at L'Arche is slow and often repetitive. However, the ordinariness of the day-to-day routines and activities of L'Arche communities is the site of a quite extraordinary political reality that can easily be missed by those trained to measure results with such modern metrics as size, speed, and efficiency. Those who look upon the world through such lenses might be tempted to say that nothing ever happens at L'Arche, but this is of no concern to Vanier, who is of the conviction that "love doesn't mean doing extraordinary or heroic things. It means knowing how to do ordinary things with tenderness."[287] This quote from Vanier points towards the significant gift which Hauerwas believes L'Arche offers to both the church and the world, namely, an instantiation of the politics of gentleness. Through enacting this peculiar politics of befriending, L'Arche recalls the church to its true calling and serves as a sign to the world that "gentleness is constitutive of any politics that would be just."[288]

L'Arche holds before the church the vulnerable politics of the crucified, through whose befriending it has been given the gift of time necessary for befriending those who are different. In this encounter, the able-bodied are confronted by the vulnerability of the mentally disabled, which in turn

285. *LGVW*, 45.
286. Vanier, *Community and Growth*, 106, quoted in *STT*, 143.
287. Vanier, *Community and Growth*, 220, quoted in *CDRO*, 195.
288. *CDRO*, 195.

reveals the vulnerability and brokenness of those who are often tempted to think of themselves as invulnerable and whole. This recognition frees L'Arche from the politics of glory which tempts modern societies with the false promise of immortality and allows the community to receive each individual, whether abled or disabled, as a gift through whom each member of the community is, in turn, enabled to receive their own life as gift. "L'Arche is the reality at the heart of the church," Hauerwas insists, "insofar as it reminds us that we have all the time we need in the world in a world of the deepest injustice to care for one another."[289] Through its deep rootedness in the realities of place and time stemming from the shape of its daily liturgies, L'Arche stands as "a prophetic sign of what the church needs to see if we are to avoid the world of speed and placelessness."[290] Learning to listen to the mentally disabled takes time, particularly when some may only communicate by imprecise gestures and inarticulate groans. For this reason, Hauerwas insists that "L'Arche embodies the patience that is absolutely crucial if we are to learn to be faithful people in our world."[291] The witness of L'Arche "helps the church find the gospel," but in doing so it cannot help but reveal where the church has lost its way.[292] For example, the politics of gentleness enacted at L'Arche exposes the harshness of what often passes for politics in many local congregations and denominational structures. In these contexts the mechanism of voting, frequently pursued in the name of democracy, becomes a way of avoiding the time and effort necessary to discern the voice of the Spirit speaking through the weakest member. At one point in his conversation with Coles, Hauerwas confesses that he is haunted by Vanier:

> I am haunted by Vanier because my strident polemics on behalf of the church seem so hollow when juxtaposed against the confident, joyful work L'Arche represents. I suspect Vanier would remind me, however, that such confidence is but the overflow of love found through the worship of the Father, Son, and Holy Spirit. To worship such a Lord, a King, who rules from a cross, is to learn to live by surprise, because you never know where or how such a God is going to show up.[293]

An openness to being similarly haunted by L'Arche, could be a sign of the Spirit's leading the church in North America beyond its anxious quest

289. *LGVW*, 54–55.
290. Ibid., 54.
291. Ibid., 45.
292. Ibid., 57.
293. *CDRO*, 105.

for self-preservation amidst the crumbling ruins of Christendom into a new day of free, joyful and confident service of the God who rules from the cross.

Before moving on to consider the important witness that L'Arche offers to the world, it is important to acknowledge that although Hauerwas clearly has deep respect and appreciation for Jean Vanier and the ministry of L'Arche, this does not stop him from offering words of fraternal counsel to them. Welcoming the stranger is an essential element of the ethos of L'Arche. Stemming from this understanding, L'Arche communities have begun to welcome people of different faiths, with Christians in some L'Arche communities living alongside Muslims and, in other contexts, Hindus.[294] Hauerwas does not object to such radical hospitality; however he does caution the L'Arche movement that they must not lose sight of what has been their animating center—the person of Jesus Christ, who makes such welcome possible.[295] In issuing this warning, Hauerwas may be looking beyond Vanier to the future of L'Arche and the next generation of leaders who will surely be tempted by the sirens of the liberal values of tolerance and inclusion which masquerade as substitutes for the radical hospitality of Christ.[296] Hauerwas urges these future leaders to remember the God who has made the work of L'Arche possible. Hauerwas cautions, "If L'Arche loses its theological voice, I think it will be a loss not only for L'Arche, but for any politics—and in particular those determined by liberal political arrangements—in which L'Arche exists."[297]

The world would suffer a loss if L'Arche lost its theological voice, because the world could never have dreamt up such a community on its own. In a world hell-bent on denying the contingencies of human existence, there is no alternative but to eliminate the mentally disabled in the name of progress, in order to eliminate the suffering they represent.[298] Accordingly,

---

294. Ibid., 223.

295. Vanier recognizes that it is Jesus who makes radical hospitality and interfaith dialogue and relations possible. Vanier observes, "The more we are called to be open to others and encourage the gift of God in them, the more we must be rooted in our own faith, growing in a personal relationship with Jesus. And the more we become one with Jesus, the more we open up to others and begin to see and love them as Jesus loves them" (*Drawn Into the Mystery*, 215, quoted in *CDRO*, 224).

296. In a footnote, Hauerwas confesses, "I fear some may confuse Vanier's Christian humanism with a secular humanism that is the antithesis of the Gospel" (*CDRO*, 319 n. 26).

297. Ibid., 206.

298. *LGVW*, 52. The problem that suffering presents for modern society has been a recurring theme in Hauerwas's work. For his most extended treatment see *God, Medicine and Suffering*. Hauerwas has also spent considerable energy exploring the unfortunate intersection of modernity's desire to eliminate suffering with the "problem" of the mentally disabled. See for example the essays collected under the heading "'Caring'

Hauerwas believes that "Vanier's great gift, the gift of L'Arche, is to teach us to see pain, to enter into the pain of others, without wanting to destroy those who suffer."[299] However, to be made capable of receiving this gift one must be "gentled into being" through the timely and timeful friendship of the mentally disabled. Cultivating the trust which sustains such a friendship takes time and hence becomes the context within a world of speed "in which we can learn the patient habits necessary for peace."[300] Hauerwas, therefore, understands L'Arche to be a concrete sign of peace planted among the nations whose fear of one another fuels mutual suspicion and violence. Similarly, the existence of a community in which members vulnerably entrust themselves to one another in the bond of friendship stands as a shining alternative to the depersonalized politics of liberalism which envisions self-sufficient individuals freed from the need to trust in or depend on anyone.[301] L'Arche is essential for the well-being of the world, "for without examples like L'Arche, we will assume that there is no alternative to the politics of distrust that derives from the wound of our loneliness."[302]

This theme of friendship as an alternative politics that stands at the heart of the church's life emerges in several other essays written after Hauerwas's self-professed "constructive turn." In "Captured in Time: Friendship and Aging" written with Laura Yordy, Hauerwas explores how the enacting of friendships across generational divides within the church can stand as an alternative to the predominant narrative of aging in America, which contributes to the elderly becoming increasingly alienated from others and themselves.[303] The anonymous deaths suffered by the elderly are the fruit of a society which places such a high premium on autonomy.[304] Through inculturation in the Gospel of Jesus Christ, believers are liberated from the myth of the autonomous, self-made individual and enabled to receive their lives as gifts. In the church, Christians do not merely discover that they get by with a little help from their friends, but rather that their lives are constituted by friendships they would not have chosen for themselves. Through friendship with the elderly, the young are given the gift of truth in the presence of the aged who are able to serve as agents of memory responsible for

---

for the Mentally Handicapped," in *SP*, 159–217, and also the essays, "Killing Compassion" and "The Church and the Mentally Handicapped: A Continuing Challenge to the Imagination," in *DFF*, 164–76, 177–86.

299. *CDRO*, 314.
300. Ibid., 311.
301. Ibid., 203; *LGVW*, 50–51.
302. *CDRO*, 204.
303. *BH*, 173–87.
304. Ibid., 176.

narrating the story of God's faithfulness to His people through time and teaching the young what it means to die in Christ. The young challenge their elderly friends to think and grow in new ways and serve as a reminder to them that "for Christians there is no 'Florida,' even if they happen to live in Florida."[305] Hauerwas and Yordy conclude the essay by noting, "In such friendships do we become church; in church are such friendships possible."[306]

In the essay "Friendship and Freedom: Reflections on Bonhoeffer's 'The Friend,'" Hauerwas argues that the friendship the church makes possible stands as an alternative to the politics of the omnivorous nation-state.[307] Many of the themes from Hauerwas's discussions of friendship with the elderly and at L'Arche resonate throughout the essay, as is particularly apparent in the following quotation:

> Trust, the trust made possible by friendship, is for Bonhoeffer not a retreat into the private, but rather an alternative politics to the privatization of the self and friendship that is the natural breeding ground for totalitarian politics. Friendship is not a safe-haven from the struggle, but rather the source of the truthfulness necessary to challenge the despair produced by the betrayal of trust.[308]

Hauerwas's reflections upon the friendship shared between Bonhoeffer and Bethge yield several further interesting observations. Commenting upon an extended reminiscence shared between the two pastors in the prison correspondence, Hauerwas observes that friendship "and in particular the friendship between Bonhoeffer and Bethge, can only be captured by a story to be told, retold, and revised."[309] It is also for this reason that Hauerwas insists that Bonhoeffer said more than he realized when he lamented to Bethge about how difficult it was to find a "substitute" friend. "Of course a substitute is not possible," Hauerwas explains, "because no one else has shared their history. What can be hoped for rather is that such a friendship opens the friends to new friendships that their history requires."[310]

The best place to look for the clearest exhibition of Hauerwas's politics of friendship may not actually be in his body of writings, but rather, simply in his body. Friendship has been deeply inscribed into Hauerwas's life. He is,

305. Ibid., 185.
306. Ibid., 187.
307. *WWW*, 270–85.
308. Ibid., 282–83.
309. Ibid., 281.
310. Ibid.

as a former graduate student who wrote his dissertation with Hauerwas has observed, "a man whose loyalty and generosity to his friends is legendary."[311] This generosity even extends to the strangers who take the time to write him, as Hauerwas has long made a practice of spending an hour a day responding to correspondence.[312] Hauerwas's graduate students invariably comment upon how they have been the beneficiaries of being claimed as a friend by the Texan bricklayer-turned-theologian.[313] It is, in fact, the numerous graduate students that Hauerwas has trained and mentored that, when all is said and done, may ultimately prove to be his most enduring legacy.[314] For this particular network of friends, represents, if not Hauerwas's success in teaching his students to think like him, then at least, his success in teaching them to think enough like him to make for meaningful disagreement. It was the friendship Hauerwas shared with his graduate students that brought him into contact with Romand Coles and ultimately made possible their somewhat unlikely friendship.[315] This development bears witness to the truth of Hauerwas's contention that "friendship opens the friends to new friendships that their history requires."[316] It also validates an assertion made much earlier that although Christians can never make peace with the world, "frequently we discover in what we are wont to call 'the world' strangers who speak to us as friends."[317] One would be hard-pressed to read Hauerwas's memoir without coming to recognize that his life has been constituted by friendship. In an epilogue appended to the paperback edition of *Hannah's Child*, Hauerwas confesses that he was tempted to subtitle the book "A Testimony to Friends."[318] The frequently recurring concerns which are raised about Hauerwas's ambiguous ecclesial status could perhaps in some way be alleviated by recognizing the centrality of friendship to Hauerwas's

---

311. Waddell, "Friendship," 266.

312. *HC*, 247–49; Cavanaugh, "Stan the Man," in *HR*, 26; Nation, "Stanley Hauerwas," 33. Paul Johansen, a Toronto-area pastor, has been the recipient of this generosity. Johansen has told me of how he received a gracious written response to a letter and sermon he had sent to Hauerwas.

313. For example, see Pinches et al., introduction to *Unsettling Arguments*, xvii; Waddell, "Friendship," 265; Sider, "Friendship, Alienation, Love," 86; Cavanaugh, "Stan the Man," in *HR*, 28.

314. Hauerwas has directed more doctoral dissertations (approximately 75) than any other professor at Duke University. Wells, "Difference Christ Makes," 26.

315. *CDRO*, x.

316. *WWW*, 281.

317. *CAV*, 85.

318. *HC*, 286.

life.[319] While acknowledging that an ambiguous ecclesial status is in some sense the fate of all Protestant Christians in modernity and with no reason to question Hauerwas's self-identification as a Methodist communicant in the Episcopal Church, the recognition of the centrality of friendship to Hauerwas's life and work could go some length towards reframing this concern. Hauerwas's diverse and numerous friendships could be understood as the concrete instantiations of his participation in the church catholic. For, as Hauerwas himself has written, "In such friendships do we become church; in church are such friendships possible."[320]

PART 3: CONCLUDING THOUGHTS ON CHURCH AND WORLD

The intense christological focus and the corresponding concrete ecclesiologies of both Dietrich Bonhoeffer and Stanley Hauerwas provide an invaluable point of departure for considering how the church best serves the world over the course of its earthly pilgrimage. The later writings of both writers, characterized as they are by a profound interest in worldly matters, demonstrate how the church's faithful negotiation of its relationship to the world is essential for the very life of the world. As a means of synthesizing what has been learned from Bonhoeffer and Hauerwas, and in order to facilitate further dialogue between their theologies, this chapter will conclude by exploring how their respective emphases upon the worldliness of Christian faith and the radical ordinary present the building blocks for an authentic Christian humanism. This will open up a vista for bringing their shared convictions and differences in opinion regarding the relationship between church and state into focus. The chapter will then conclude with a final consideration of the church-world problematic from the christological perspectives promoted by Bonhoeffer and Hauerwas.

Towards a True Christian Humanism

The dawning of the new age in the cross and resurrection of Christ and the pouring out of the Holy Spirit gives human beings all the time necessary to make music and play baseball; in short, to live a truly human life.

---

319. Among those who have raised the issue of ecclesial ambiguity are: Cavanaugh, "Can't We Just Argue?," 9; Byassee, "Becoming Church," 32; and Reno, "Hauerwas and the Liberal Protestant Project," 325.

320. *BH*, 187.

The revelation of the ultimate, transcendent eschatological reality does not lead to spiritual escapism or otherworldliness, but immerses one most profoundly in the realities of life in the world. The Christian faith should not create people who are "so heavenly minded that they are of no earthly good," but rather it should liberate people to enter into the multi-dimensionality of genuine human existence in the world. In this way, Bonhoeffer and Hauerwas both stand within an intellectual trajectory that began with the Protestant Reformers and extends into modern times that philosopher Charles Taylor has identified as "the affirmation of ordinary life."[321] This "affirmation of the ordinary" is one of the contributing factors to the default worldview of modern individuals. In a more recent work, Taylor has introduced the phrase "the immanent frame" to describe this worldview.[322] According to Taylor this immanent frame stands on its own independent of the transcendent and can be "spun" in such a way that is either open or closed to the transcendent world beyond.[323] Both Bonhoeffer and Hauerwas seek to move beyond these modern understandings of the world through their employment of a robust christological metaphysics which explodes the very categories of immanence and transcendence. As a result of the incarnation—the coming of the Transcendent One to dwell with us in the immanence of the flesh—any attempts to speak of transcendence and immanence must now be submitted to christological discipline. Hauerwas in a review essay of *The Secular Age*, co-authored with Romand Coles, criticizes Taylor on this very score. "For Christians," Hauerwas asserts, "immanence first and foremost names that God became man that we might participate in the very life of God. So nothing can be more immanent than God with us."[324] The line of theological reflection that Bonhoeffer took up in prison anticipates Hauerwas's response to Taylor, as evidenced in this short excerpt:

---

321. Taylor, *Sources of the Self*, 13. "According to traditional, Aristotelian ethics, this has merely infrastructural importance. 'Life' was important as the necessary background and support to 'the good life' of contemplation and one's action as a citizen. With the Reformation, we find a modern, Christian-inspired sense that ordinary life was on the contrary the very centre of the good life. The crucial issue was how it was led, whether worshipfully and in the fear of God or not. But the life of the God-fearing was lived out in marriage and their calling. The previous 'higher' forms of life were dethroned, as it were. And along with this went frequently an attack, covert or overt, on the elites which had made these forms their province" (13–14).

322. Taylor, *Secular Age*, 539–93.

323. Ibid., 549.

324. *WWW*, 175. In a response to Hauerwas and Coles, Taylor concedes their point and expresses his own reservations about the distinction he draws between the immanent and transcendent in *A Secular Age*. "Challenging Issues," 410–13.

> Our relationship to God is no "religious" relationship to some highest, most powerful, and best being imaginable—that is no genuine transcendence. Instead, our relationship to God is a new life in "being there for others," through participation in the being of Jesus. The transcendent is not the infinite, unattainable tasks, but the neighbor within reach in any given situation. God in human form!³²⁵

The incarnation directs us to the reality that transcendence is not properly an epistemological category, but is rather a moral category arising from the event of personal encounter with the living Lord Jesus Christ within the theatre of ordinary life as it is lived out within God's good creation. The voice of the Lord is encountered not only in the sermon, but also in the encouraging and correcting words of one's brothers and sisters in Christ. The body of the Lord is manifested at the Eucharist, but as a result of this meal, each and every meal receives special dignity. In vulnerable encounter with others, we are allowed to recognize the face of the Lord in our neighbors. The creation truly is the theatre of God's glory and through the incarnation of the Word every dimension of human life has been taken up into the life of God. Bonhoeffer succinctly summarizes the matter when, speaking of the Incarnate Word, he proclaims, "Nothing human is foreign to him."³²⁶ In the work of both Bonhoeffer and Hauerwas, we encounter the building blocks of a true Christian humanism.³²⁷

Such a Christian humanism arising from a commitment to the radical implications of the incarnation must not be confused with its secular off-shoot naturalism. Naturalism offers a blanket endorsement of so-called natural human desire.³²⁸ Bonhoeffer and Hauerwas avoid this danger through their recognition that incarnation is not an abstract philosophical principle, but rather is a theological qualification pertaining to the life, death, and resurrection of the particular man, Jesus of Nazareth.³²⁹ As a

---

325. *LPP* (*DBWE* 8), 501.

326. *DBWE* 12:353.

327. With respect to Bonhoeffer, this note is strongly sounded in the essays found within Zimmerman and Gregor, *Being Human, Becoming Human*. Within his contribution to the volume, de Gruchy notes that as early as 1948 Bonhoeffer had been identified by his brother-in-law Gerhard Leibholz as representing a version of "Christian Humanism" ("Bonhoeffer as Christian Humanist," 4, quoting foreword to *Cost of Discipleship*, 18).

328. Taylor suggests that the transposition of the Reformers' "affirmation of ordinary life" has resulted in the naturalism that characterizes the modern ethical outlook. *Sources of the Self*, 23–24, 70.

329. Hauerwas's tongue-in-cheek censure of Anglicans comes to mind at this point: "Anglicans should never use the word *incarnation* because they mean God became man

result, incarnation, for the two theologians, is never abstracted from cross and resurrection.

The cross stands as God's judgement upon the human being that through its rebellion against its Creator has fallen under the power of sin and cast the world into chaos and disarray. The cross is God's "No!" to the powerful nothingness of sin and evil, which threatens to undo God's good creature and creation. Enfolded within God's acceptance of humanity in Jesus Christ is God's refusal to accept the de-humanizing and death-dealing forms of life which arise on account of humanity's sinful attempt to live apart from God. Both theologians, therefore, recognize that the development of a theology of natural life, or even a natural theology, cannot be derived from empirical observation of the world, but rather must be firmly rooted in a robust doctrine of God.[330] As a result, the worldliness of both Bonhoeffer and Hauerwas is not simply the acceptance of the status quo. The crucifixion of the Incarnate One requires that a firm "No!" be uttered against such things as cultural Protestantism, civil religion, and the "if it makes you happy, it can't be that bad" mentality of modern liberal society.

The resurrection is the divine verdict which is pronounced over the One who was accused of being a Messianic pretender, condemned as a blasphemer, and executed as a common criminal. As such, it is the apocalyptic event *par excellence* and includes within itself the creation of a new humanity. For both Bonhoeffer and Hauerwas the apocalypse is not simply the vision of an idyllic city to come, but rather is the beginning of the end that has already been witnessed in the life, death, and resurrection of Jesus Christ. The resurrection does not encourage pious otherworldliness by mapping an escape route to a life beyond this world, but rather "refers people to their life on earth in a wholly new way."[331] The resurrection opens up a new way of inhabiting the world for the new creation people who have been called into existence through the life, death, and resurrection of Jesus Christ. Freed from the oppressive need to constitute their own identity and secure their own existence, the life of this new creation people is character-

and said, 'Hmm, this is pretty good.' You can't tell the difference between a Unitarian and an Anglican in Boston, because they're both humanist and get along very well without God" (*DT*, 199).

330. "Natural Life" is the title of one of Bonhoeffer's *Ethics* manuscripts. *E* (*DBWE* 6), 171–218. *With the Grain of the Universe* is Hauerwas's attempt to develop of a natural theology based upon the christological metaphysics of Karl Barth. Plant has also observed the similarities between the attempts of both theologians to recover a theological understanding of the natural on christological grounds. *Bonhoeffer*, 88.

331. *LPP* (*DBWE* 8), 447. Hauerwas approvingly cites Bonhoeffer's assertion that "belief in the resurrection *is not* the 'solution' to the problem of death" (*PTF*, 47, quoting *LPP* (*DBWE* 8), 367).

ized by gratitude and joy. Through the community's enactment of its resurrectionary politics, the community stands as "an alternative immanence to the immanence of the world."[332] In Bonhoeffer's terms, "the church of Jesus Christ is the place [Ort]—that is, the space [Raum] in the world where the reign of Jesus Christ over the whole world is to be demonstrated and proclaimed. The space of the church does not, therefore, exist just for itself, but its existence is already always something that reaches far beyond it."[333] The church is called to be today what the world can and one day will be, namely a people who are fully and truly human.[334] The church is the site of the only genuine humanism, for it is there that men and women are made participants in the life of the Triune God as they are engrafted into the body of, and correspondingly conformed to the life of, the one true human being, the Lord Jesus Christ.[335] Those who find themselves rapt into the Messianic event of the apocalypse of Jesus Christ find themselves, as result of their union with this same Christ, placed firmly back within the world to enact a better worldliness for the sake of the world. As those joined to the body of the incarnate, crucified, and risen Christ, they participate in the life of the age to come, in the very midst of their being taken, blessed, broken, and given for the life of the world.

Church and State

The christologically-shaped visions of reality forwarded by both Bonhoeffer and Hauerwas result in broad agreement between the two theologians with respect to the question of church and state. This general agreement makes the areas where they part company all the more conspicuous. Following a brief summary of the vast areas of agreement between the two men on the question of church and state, I will turn to a more detailed consideration of where their thoughts diverge.

---

332. *WWW*, 181 n. 10.

333. *E* (*DBWE* 6), 63.

334. The first part of this sentence is a gloss on a statement Hauerwas makes defending himself and Yoder against charges of sectarianism in *SU*, 153.

335. For this reason Bonhoeffer can write such things as: "Christian life means being human [*Menschsein*] in the power of Christ's becoming human, being judged and pardoned in the power of the cross, living a new life in the power of the resurrection. No one of these is without the others" (*E* (*DBWE* 6), 159). "The Christian is not a *homo religiosus* but simply a human being, in the same way that Jesus was a human being" (*LPP* (*DBWE* 8), 541). Hauerwas also does not shy away from speaking about a Christian humanism which arises from the one true human being Jesus Christ: "Christian humanism is determined by the Father's sending of the Son to be one of us. So humanism must always begin with Jesus' humanity" (*LGVW*, 53; see also *Mt*, 99–100).

In terms of agreement, both Bonhoeffer and Hauerwas are convinced that the allegiance of Christians to the Lord Jesus Christ is ultimate and trumps the demands and claims of the state whenever and wherever they come into conflict. The claims of the state are relativized and exposed as petty and provincial in light of the catholicity of the church of Jesus Christ which transcends the boundaries of time and space. The confession of Jesus as Lord, then, is not simply a matter of private or personal opinion, but rather is the statement of a cosmic reality. As a result, both Bonhoeffer and Hauerwas refute any conceptions that the state exists in an independent realm or sphere, separate from the commands and claim of the Gospel. The state exists to provide an external order that allows for the free preaching of the Gospel. This does not mean that the state will be Christianized or that Christians must rule, however it does mean that only the church knows why the state exists.[336] As such the church best serves the state by being a people who live according to the truth of the Gospel of Jesus Christ and who are unafraid to address the state in the name of this truth. To this end, the work of both men can be understood to be directed towards the sustaining of a church capable of acting as a limit or boundary to the omnivorous modern nation-state; a people who are able to say "No!" to the state which has become totalitarian in its claim upon human beings. One of the ways that Bonhoeffer and Hauerwas serve the church's resistance against the totalizing claims of the fascist state and the market-state respectively is through providing accounts which attempt to complexify political space. Bonhoeffer accomplishes this work through his doctrine of the mandates and later through his further reflections on the sphere of freedom which includes culture and education. For Hauerwas, this complexification of political space is most apparent in his interactions with Romand Coles and radical democracy. Friendship also occupies a central place in both of their theologies and serves to further contribute to the creation of political space which refuses to be mastered by the hegemonic appetite of the modern-nation state.

It is with respect to the doctrine of the mandates that Hauerwas significantly parts ways with Bonhoeffer. Hauerwas raises his criticisms of Bonhoeffer's doctrine of the mandates in his otherwise favorable treatment of "Dietrich Bonhoeffer's Political Theology."[337] While greatly appreciative of Bonhoeffer's efforts to retrieve the significance of the visibility of the church in *Sanctorum Communio* and the writings of the Finkenwalde period, Hauerwas believes that Bonhoeffer, in his conception of the mandates,

---

336. A conviction which may emerge from their shared Barthian inheritance. See Barth, "Church and State," 140.

337. *PTF*, 33–54.

remains trapped within the social imaginary of Protestant Christendom. "Bonhoeffer's attempt to rethink the Lutheran two-kingdom theology in the light of his Christological recovery of the significance of the visible church, I think," Hauerwas suggests, "failed to escape from the limits of the habits that have long shaped Lutheran thinking on these matters."[338]

It appears to me that Hauerwas is correct in his judgement. I would suggest that there are three particular areas where the influence of Protestant Christendom thinking upon Bonhoeffer's doctrine of the mandates is apparent. The first occurs in Bonhoeffer's handling of Rom 13:1–7 and 1 Pet 2:13–17, the *loci classici* for the Magisterial Reformers' understanding of the state.[339] These texts seemingly provide the basis for Bonhoeffer's understanding of the being and purpose of the state. Recent biblical and theological studies have called into question the assumption that the apostles were providing a theology of providence or laying a metaphysical foundation for the state in these passages. Harink encapsulates some of these findings when he states, "In their texts Peter and Paul do not give us a theory of the providential purpose of secular government or civil order, or of the Christian's responsibility in or for the political order, or of the proper spheres and roles of 'church and state.'"[340] In a similar vein, John Howard Yoder comments, "God is not said to *create* or *institute* or *ordain* the powers that be, but only to *order* them, to put them in order, sovereignly to tell them where they belong, what is their place."[341] These avenues of interpretation do not seem to have been open to Bonhoeffer. Acknowledging Bonhoeffer's theological pedigree and cultural situatedness, Hauerwas sympathetically remarks, "Understandably it does not occur to Bonhoeffer that he does not need to provide an account in principle of what the state is or should be."[342] Further evidence of the influence of Bonhoeffer's Lutheran heritage upon his exegesis of these texts is evident in the way he consistently presents the obligation of the Christian towards the state to be that of obedience. This understanding rests on a historic mistranslation of the Greek verb *hupotassō*, which occurs in both passages. Yoder, summarizing the work of C. E. B. Cranfield, draws the following important exegetical conclusions:

> It is not by accident that the imperative of 13:1 is not literally one of *obedience*. The Greek language has good words to denote

338. Ibid., 51.
339. Luther discovered a "sound basis for the civil law and the sword" in Rom 13 and 1 Pet 2. *Basic Theological Writings*, 659–60.
340. Harink, *1 and 2 Peter*, 79.
341. Yoder, *Politics of Jesus*, 201.
342. *PTF*, 50.

obedience, in the sense of completely bending one's will and one's actions to the desires of another. What Paul calls for, however, is sub*ord*ination. The verb is based upon the same root as the *ordering* of the powers of God. Subordination is significantly different from obedience. The conscientious objector who refuses to do what the government demands, but still remains under the sovereignty of the government and accepts the penalties which it imposes, or the Christian who refuses to worship Caesar but still permits Caesar to put him or her to death, is being subordinate even though not obeying.[343]

The language of subordination, as opposed to obedience, casts the relationship of the Christian to the state in a somewhat different light.

The second area where the influence of Protestant Christendom seems to impinge upon Bonhoeffer's doctrine of the mandates is with respect to his understanding of the task or role of government. Government is commissioned with the task of preserving justice through the power of the sword and the law. Against those who attempt to ground their understanding of justice in natural law, Bonhoeffer is insistent that government is grounded in the divine commandment of God in Jesus Christ. However, in the absence of any exploration of the material implications of this claim, Bonhoeffer's grounding of government in Jesus Christ risks becoming an empty formal principle. If Jesus is, in fact, God's justice and if the clearest representation of true exercise of government is to be found in Christ's royal rule then surely there must be implications for a Christian understanding of government. Bonhoeffer's recourse to the second table of the Decalogue as the standard for government action not only fails to resolve these issues, but opens further lines of questioning. One wonders, for instance, whether it is theologically legitimate to separate the second table of the Decalogue from the first and whether the second table of the Decalogue presents a standard of justice that exists apart from Jesus Christ?[344] This complex of questions emerges from the problematic severing of the connection between the Torah and the people of Israel in Christendom contexts. When this occurs the Law either comes to be understood as a universal morality for all people or the particular nation or people-group comes to be identified as the chosen

---

343. Yoder, *Politics of Jesus*, 208–9.

344. Bonhoeffer himself in the manuscript "On the Possibility of the Church's Message to the World" insists that the second table of the Decalogue cannot be divorced from the first. *E* (*DBWE* 6), 358, 360. With respect to governing according to the second table of the Decalogue, one is confronted with the perplexing dilemma of determining how to legislate against coveting. In our contemporary context in North America legislation against coveting would certainly have fascinating implications for the advertising industry.

people. In both of these scenarios, the election of Israel as God's own peculiar people and the necessity for faith are overlooked and obscured. Hence Hauerwas's concern that "Bonhoeffer's account of the mandates can invite the distinction between the private and public, which results in Christian obedience becoming invisible."[345]

Finally, we could say that Bonhoeffer's doctrine of the mandates suffers from the flattened, overly-realized eschatology that plagues Christendom in general. The decision to place the church as a mandate alongside of marriage, government, and work seems to reflect a vision of a total Christian society. However, Bonhoeffer never specifies why the church, an aspect of the order of redemption, should be designated as a mandate alongside of the other mandates which were earlier designated as orders of preservation.[346] In making this move, Bonhoeffer obfuscates the eschatological character of the church and grates against the better impulses of his ecclesiology.[347] From the beginning of his academic career, Bonhoeffer has identified the church as the site of the eschatological in-breaking of the new humanity which has been realized in Christ and is actualized by the Holy Spirit.[348] This theme continues right through Bonhoeffer's writings into the last *Ethics* manuscript, where Bonhoeffer emphasizes that the church not only has a divine mandate of proclamation, but that through the exercise of this mandate a community is constituted which "is the place where the world fulfills its own destiny; the church-community is the 'new creation,' the 'new creature,' the goal of God's ways on earth."[349] If Bonhoeffer were to be more consistent with this central christological-ecclesiological thrust of his work, then it seems he should argue that the mandates receive the proper orientation to their christological telos within the life of the church. It would then be possible to speak of something like the transfiguration of life within the church-community. If the church truly is the new humanity then surely it is within this community that the mandates will be exercised according to their true character and goal. Bonhoeffer, however, in his doctrine of the mandates was unwilling, or perhaps unable due to the social imaginary he inherited from Lutheran Christendom, to proceed down this

---

345. *PTF*, 51.

346. This may be evidence of the continuing influence of Luther upon Bonhoeffer. Luther identifies the commandment prohibiting eating from the tree of the knowledge of good and evil in Genesis 2:16 with the establishment of the church. *Lectures on Genesis*, 103–6.

347. Similar assessments are expressed in Bretherton, *Christianity and Contemporary Politics*, 208 n. 97, and O'Donovan, *The Ways of Judgement*, 254.

348. *SC* (*DBWE* 1), 134–41.

349. *E* (*DBWE* 6), 404–5.

path. In a brief, but suggestive footnote, Hauerwas expresses his puzzlement that Bonhoeffer never explored the Pauline doctrine of the principalities and powers in connection with his treatment of the mandates. Recourse to the doctrine of the powers, "could have provided Bonhoeffer with a way to think through the perversions of the mandates as well as their christological *telos*."[350] Certainly, an engagement with the Pauline doctrine of the powers could have been of great assistance to Bonhoeffer in this regard. However, in Bonhoeffer's defense, the theological discourse surrounding the principalities and powers did not truly emerge in its own right until the years following the Second World War.[351]

The Church in the World

The christological construals of reality present in the work of Bonhoeffer and Hauerwas provide the basis for a potentially fruitful way of approaching the question of the church's missional calling in post-Christendom contexts. The major contours of this shared christologically-informed vision of the world can be summarized as follows. The world is God's good creation, created through Christ, held together in Christ, for the sake of Christ. The creation is fallen, as reflected in the New Testament use of the term "the world" (most pre-eminently in the Johannine writings) to describe the elements of creation which have fallen away from God and refuse to acknowledge the Lordship of Christ. Both Bonhoeffer and Hauerwas recognize that, used in this sense, "the world" is not an ontological designation, for all that is remains God's good creation. The world, though fallen, has been reconciled to God through the cross of Jesus Christ. The church, as the new creation community, lives in the power of the Spirit who raised Christ from the dead as a witness to the resurrection for the sake of the world which has not acknowledged, as of yet, its Reconciler and Lord. Through its common life and witness the church stands as a beacon of truth in the midst of a world enshrouded in the shadows and darkness of falsehood, until the day when all will be brought to light in the day of Christ's glorious appearing. Not only does this shared christological construal of reality provide the necessary building blocks for the development of a post-Christendom missional

---

350. *WWW*, 276 n. 21.

351. Hendrik Berkhof's important work *Christus en de Machten* was published in Dutch in 1953. The work appears in English translation as *Christ and the Powers*. Karl Barth adopted a similar orientation to the powers in his reflections on the Christian life, published posthumously as *The Christian Life*, 213–33.

theology, agreement in these central convictions also allows for the emergence of a potential area of tension between the two theologians.

This area of tension involves the question of whether the understanding of the church's relationship to the world in Bonhoeffer's writings from the period of his involvement with the conspiracy and his subsequent imprisonment, which culminates in the memorable phrase "the church is the church only when it exists for others,"[352] is ultimately compatible with Hauerwas's position famously articulated in such aphorisms as, "the first social ethical task of the church is to be the church" and "the church is not to make the world more just but to make the world the world."[353] To rephrase the question, is there an irresolvable tension between Bonhoeffer's conception of the calling of the church to be for others and Hauerwas's understanding of the church's calling to be itself? Certainly, Bonhoeffer and Hauerwas have at times been read in ways that place them in conflict with one another. One need only refer to those who put Bonhoeffer forward as the champion of secularity and others who insist on labeling Hauerwas as a sectarian. However, as has hopefully become apparent, neither reading does justice to either the scope or central emphases of the two theologians' work. I would propose that what is reflected in the expressions "the church is the church only when it exists for others" and "the first social ethical task of the church is to be the church," is not a substantial difference, but rather a difference in accent arising from the particular contexts in which each theologian was operating.

The Bonhoeffer who penned the phrase "the church is the church only when it exists for others" had lived through the tumultuous days of the Church Struggle and witnessed the same Confessing Church, which had raised its voice so vociferously against state intervention into matters of church government, remain deafeningly silent with respect to those outside of its ranks who were suffering persecution under the Nazi regime. In a sermon, written for the baptism of his god-son Dietrich Bethge, Bonhoeffer lamented, "Our church has been fighting these years only for its self-preservation, as if that were an end in itself."[354] Several months later in his outline for a book, he would concisely summarize the matter in the following manner: "Decisive: Church defending itself. No risk taking for others."[355] Just as years earlier, in his contribution to the Bethel Confession, he had called for a church which stood in radical solidarity with the Jews, Bonhoeffer, as

352. *LPP (DBWE 8)*, 503.
353. *PK*, 99; *PTF*, 14.
354. *LPP (DBWE 8)*, 389.
355. Ibid., 500.

he neared the end of his short life, continued to envision a church that had moved beyond concerns about preserving its own existence to truly existing for the sake of the world.[356]

Whereas Bonhoeffer confronted a church that had turned in upon itself in the desperate quest for self-preservation, Hauerwas encountered a Protestant Church in America which had so confused its mission with the American project that it had become completely secularized. The problem with the church Hauerwas addressed was not that it existed for itself, but that it existed for America in the mode and manner of citizens of the United States. For a church that had largely confused civil religion with the Gospel, Hauerwas's insistence that "the first social ethical task of the church is to be the church," was a clarion call summoning the church to faithfulness.

It is Bonhoeffer's and Hauerwas's readings of their different contexts that result in the different accents present in their work. However, both theologians are convinced that the church exists for the sake of the world and the way the church best lives out its worldly calling is by being the church. Just as the work of Christ cannot be separated from his person, in the same way the mission and identity of the church cannot be severed. For both men, the church is the body of the living Lord Jesus Christ which exists to bear witness to His life-giving royal rule. In offering this testimony, in word and deed, before a watching world the church does not simply exist for itself, but serves the world. Hauerwas clarifies his famous aphorism by asserting that "for the church to be the church, therefore, is not anti-world, but rather an attempt to show what the world is meant to be as God's good creation."[357] Bonhoeffer expresses a similar conviction in the *Ethics* manuscript "Christ, Reality and Good," where he writes, "the church of Jesus Christ is the place [Ort]—that is, the space [Raum]—in the world where the reign of Jesus Christ over the whole world is to be demonstrated and proclaimed."[358] A few sentences later, in a sentence that includes a clause that sounds remarkably similar to Hauerwas's claim that "the first task of the church is not to make the world more just but to make the world the world,"[359] Bonhoeffer attempts to nuance his use of spatial terminology by writing, "The space of the church is not there in order to fight with the world for a piece of its territory, but precisely to testify to the world that it is still the world, namely, the world

---

356. The section in which Bonhoeffer summoned the Confessing Church to stand in radical solidarity with the Jews, much to Bonhoeffer's dismay, did not survive the revisionary process. Scharffenorth, editor's afterword to *DBWE* 12:498. See also Nicolaisen, "Concerning the History of the Bethel Confession" in *DBWE* 12:509–13.

357. *PK*, 100.

358. *E* (*DBWE* 6), 63.

359. *PTF*, 14.

that is loved and reconciled by God."[360] If the church were in the business of fighting for a piece of the world's territory than it would reproduce the modern division of life into sacred and secular realms that Bonhoeffer was so interested in overcoming. So Bonhoeffer continues:

> The church can only defend its own space by fighting, not for space, but for the salvation of the world. Otherwise the church becomes a "religious society" that fights in its own interest and thus has ceased to be the church of God in the world. So the first task given to those who belong to the church of God is not to be something for themselves, for example, by creating a religious organization or leading a pious life, but to be witnesses of Jesus Christ to the world.[361]

Hauerwas seems to understand that his call for "the church to be the church" could be understood in such a self-serving way, so he immediately qualifies it by specifying that the church is "the servant community."[362] That being said, Hauerwas's own use of spatial metaphors have not always been immune from giving the impression that he was interested in creating the type of sectarian enclave Bonhoeffer wished to avoid.[363] As we have observed earlier in this chapter, Hauerwas's engagement with Romand Coles and the latter's appropriation of Rowan Williams's presentation of a Jesus who is "not a competitor for space in this world," has provided Hauerwas with a way of speaking of the church's politics in a non-territorial manner. Bonhoeffer's insistence that the church is not there to fight for space in this world not only challenges some of Hauerwas's earlier formulations, but also some of his own earlier assertions. However, Bonhoeffer's comments about the space of the church during this latter period must not be read as renunciation of the earlier ecclesiology of *Discipleship*, but rather as a helpful clarification.[364] This is evident from what he writes in "Christ, Reality, and Good" shortly after the sentences quoted above: "Of course, it is presupposed that such a witness to the world can only happen in the right

---

360. E (*DBWE* 6), 63.

361. Ibid., 64.

362. *PK*, 99.

363. Wells, *Transforming Fate*, 141.

364. While an earlier generation of Bonhoeffer scholarship tended to focus on the elements of discontinuity between Bonhoeffer's Finkenwalde writings and *Ethics*, as well as *Letters and Papers from Prison*, there are now an increasing number of voices highlighting the profound continuity between these works. See, for example, Schmitz, "Reading Discipleship and Ethics"; Plant, "The Sacrament of Ethical Reality"; Harvey, "Narrow Path"; Nation et al., *Bonhoeffer the Assassin?*, 125–220.

way when it comes out of sanctified life in God's church-community."³⁶⁵ The following assessment of Bonhoeffer's political theology offered by Hauerwas therefore accurately pertains to the entire Bonhoeffer corpus: "Put as starkly as possible, Bonhoeffer clearly saw that the holiness of the church is necessary for the redemption of the world."³⁶⁶

Bonhoeffer's emphasis, then, on the church being for others in no way implies "surrendering either its identity or the profound mystery of its faith in Christ, for that would simply be another example of 'cheap grace,' or a confusion of the penultimate and the ultimate as he distinguished them in *Ethics*."³⁶⁷ The church can only truly be for the world to the extent that it remains rooted in its christologically-derived identity. Bonhoeffer's continuing interest in the "arcane discipline" at both the ecclesial and personal-practical levels reflects his enduring commitment to the necessity of holiness for the church's mission in the world.³⁶⁸ For Hauerwas, the increasingly central place that the liturgy has come to occupy in his work represents his ongoing commitment to this core conviction. Interestingly, the book which Hauerwas thinks comes closest to representing his work as a whole is *The Blackwell Companion to Christian Ethics*. This book was written by his friends and ordered according to the shape of the liturgy so that "readers of the book will be able to see the connections between common acts of worship and how we must be formed to rightly think of questions of racial reconciliation, beauty, poverty, and practical rationality."³⁶⁹ Both Bonhoeffer and Hauerwas understand that the church lives by the forgiveness of sins. For this reason the practice of the confession and absolution of sin is central to both of their ecclesiologies. It is, therefore, quite appropriate that Hauerwas begins *Performing the Faith* with a quotation from Bonhoeffer that includes the following sentences: "There can only be a community of peace when it does not rest on lies and injustice. . . . There is a community of peace for Christians only because one will forgive the other his sins."³⁷⁰ A people who live by the forgiveness of sins have no reason to fear the truth and hence are free to speak the truth to one another and to the world.

The church must dare to speak truthfully to the world, but it does so not on the basis of a constructed meta-discourse or a so-called universal

---

365. *E (DBWE* 6), 64.

366. *PTF*, 44.

367. de Gruchy, editor's introduction to *LPP (DBWE* 8), 29.

368. For Bonhoeffer's reflections and questions about the ecclesial importance of the arcane discipline, see *LPP (DBWE* 8), 365, 373. For references to his own personal life of prayer and devotion, see *LPP (DBWE* 8), 63, 81, 167, 179, 189, 201, 220.

369. *CSChu*, 154.

370. *PTF*, 13; citing Bonhoeffer, *No Rusty Swords*, 168–69.

language, but solely on the basis of the Word of God.[371] This does not mean that the church withdraws from worldly problems, but only that it engages them from its own unique starting point given in the revelation of God in Jesus Christ.[372] This is not a recipe for social irrelevance, for as Bonhoeffer insists, "The more the church holds to its central message, the more effective it is."[373] Hauerwas, who could have easily written the previous sentence, has attempted to provide such a service to the world by engaging worldly problems from a distinctive Christian perspective. In his recent writings, this service to the world is exemplified in his treatment of friendship with the elderly, his continuing interest in the mentally disabled, his engagement with radical democracy, his reflections upon the university, and his analysis of America as a sacrificial system built on war. Lest the wrong impression be given, it must be stated that the church does not address the world like a coach barking out instructions to his team from the sidelines, but who is nonetheless separated from the fray. Rather, Christians will work side-by-side with all people of goodwill in seeking "the welfare of the city."[374] As Bonhoeffer prescribes in his outline for the short book that was never completed, "the church must participate in the worldly tasks of life in the community—not dominating but helping and serving."[375] For the Christian faith "is not simply a set of propositions to be accepted by the intellect,"[376] but rather, as John Paul II observed, "is a *truth to be lived out*."[377] For this reason, Bonhoeffer also speaks of the importance of recovering the significance of human example, observing that "the church's word gains weight and power not through concepts but by example."[378] What the church has to offer the world is not simply truthful verbal proclamation, although that certainly is important, but also lives which have become eloquent through their conformity to the truth who is Christ. The community of saints makes

---

371. *E* (*DBWE* 6), 356–57.

372. Bonhoeffer writes, "Since Jesus brings the redemption of human beings, rather than the solution to problems, he indeed brings the solution to all human problems—'all these things will be given'—through from a completely different vantage point" (*E* (*DBWE* 6), 354). Hauerwas, for his part, affirms, "Contrary to critics who accuse me of tempting Christians to withdraw from the world, my concern has always been to help Christians understand we cannot and should not avoid engagement with the world. I, of course, have tried to remind Christians that there is no reason to privilege the terms the world tries to set for such an engagement" (*PTF*, 14).

373. *E* (*DBWE* 6), 132.

374. Jer 29:7.

375. *LPP* (*DBWE* 8), 503.

376. *WGU*, 229.

377. John Paul II, *Veritatis Splendor*, sec. 89, par. 2, 747, quoted in *WGU*, 229.

378. *LPP* (*DBWE* 8), 504.

present within the world an alternative to the dominion of death that would be otherwise unimaginable. The lives of the saints are God's gift to the world in that they stimulate the imagination to perceive new ways of being in the world that resonate with the One who entered the world as the fullness of life and truth. It is the saints, the friends of God, who are, in fact, the true friends of the world.

5

Conclusion

SUMMARY

The theologies of Dietrich Bonhoeffer and Stanley Hauerwas provide the contemporary Western church with invaluable resources for negotiating its way amidst the crumbling ruins of Christendom. As has been demonstrated in the preceding chapters, the intense christological focus of both Bonhoeffer and Hauerwas has allowed each to recover a robust conception of the identity and mission of the Church. The concrete ecclesiologies which emerge from their distinctly evangelical christological convictions allows them to address questions surrounding the relationship between church and world from a much different perspective than that which has dominated much of theology and church life in modernity.

Put quite simply, what sets Bonhoeffer and Hauerwas apart is their unwavering conviction that Jesus matters.[1] This christological impulse, originally inherited from Karl Barth, has been rigorously prosecuted by both men with admirable consistency throughout the entirety of their work. For both Bonhoeffer and Hauerwas there can be no leaving Jesus behind and no separating of Christ's person from his work. For both men

---

1. A reader provided some resistance to this point, noting that by definition Jesus matters for all Christians and Christian theology. In light of this criticism, it would be more precise to say that what sets Bonhoeffer's and Hauerwas's work apart is the way that Jesus matters. That being said, I think Bonhoeffer and Hauerwas would also be quick to point out that in practice there are both contemporary theologians and ecclesial communities for whom Jesus simply does not appear to make much of a difference.

the Chalcedonian definition stands as a necessary safe-guard to the mystery of the incarnation. However, Chalcedon should not open the door to abstract metaphysical speculation, but rather should direct the gaze of the church towards the glorious particularity of her Lord, Jesus Christ. In him, the church recognizes the revelation of the true God, but also humanity reconstituted in the image of God. This new humanity is both vicarious, in that Christ does for humanity what fallen human beings are unable to do for themselves, and participatory, in that through the work of the Holy Spirit human beings now find themselves incorporated into the body of Christ and hence taken up into his mission. Those who heed the call of the Lord Jesus Christ find themselves in the midst of an eschatological drama, travelling between the ages in the company of the eschatological Messiah of Israel and the new creation people he has gathered around himself. Through their de-theorizing of Christology and focus upon the unique identity of Jesus Christ, both Bonhoeffer and Hauerwas are able to reclaim the ethical and political character of the Christian faith in the face of the individualizing, intellectualistic and gnostic currents of modernity. Their emphasis upon the concrete person of Jesus Christ is accompanied by a corresponding characterization of the believer's relationship to Christ as pre-eminently one of discipleship. It is this emphasis upon discipleship which emerges organically from their christological convictions which allows the thought of both men to transcend many of the dichotomies that have plagued post-Reformation Protestant theology and church life, such as: faith and works, justification and sanctification, and theology and ethics.

The christological concentration of Bonhoeffer and Hauerwas provides both men with a perspective from which they are able to insightfully diagnose the ecclesial maladies afflicting the churches of their day. In the face of culturally accommodated forms of Protestantism, in which the church is frequently understood to be simply an add-on or accessory to the Gospel, both Bonhoeffer and Hauerwas recognize that the church is a necessary implicate of the person and work of Christ. Reflecting upon Bonhoeffer's ecclesiology, Hauerwas writes, "As Christ was in the world so the church is in the world."[2] The church, for both men, can be no less bodily, no less visible, than the body of the young Palestinian rabbi which hung upon the cross at Golgotha. Admittedly, this is a special visibility in that only through the eyes of faith does one truly perceive the salvation of the world in the form of the figure hanging upon the tree. The church therefore cannot be reduced to a merely material or social reality, but at the same time neither can the divine reality of the church be separated from the daily

2. *PTF*, 45.

life of the empirical church-community. As a result, both Bonhoeffer and Hauerwas worked tirelessly to recover the public, political, and communal character of ecclesial life. In so doing, they sought to restore the place of holiness in the self-understanding of the contemporary church. The church, for both Bonhoeffer and Hauerwas, is a holy people called out and set apart from the world, and sent back into the world for the life of the world. In contrast to the understanding of the modern market-state, the church is not a voluntary association in which individuals come together on account of their religious preferences. Rather, it is a disciplined community of the called, whose life together of worship and mutual service is organized according to its unique identity and purpose in Christ. The church is the site of transformative encounter with the risen Lord as through the preaching of the Word, the celebration of the sacraments, and the fellowship of the community, disciples are drawn up into the life of the Triune God. Although Bonhoeffer and Hauerwas differ with respect to how to best describe the effects of this transformative encounter, both are insistent that within the church disciples truly are conformed to the image of the Lord Jesus Christ. The church is a beacon of truth planted amidst the nations from which the light of the love of God in Christ shines forth, piercing the darkness of the world. The holiness of the church, therefore, is essential to its mission. Like the people of Israel, the church is a blessing to the world only to the extent that its members remember who they are, or better, whose they are. This means that the identity of the church is of supreme missional significance. There can be no separating the identity of the church from its mission. The church both proclaims the Kingdom of God and itself proleptically participates in the reality of that same Kingdom. The One whom the church declares to the world as Lord is savingly present in the midst of the church, exercising his royal rule. As a result, the church, for both Bonhoeffer and Hauerwas, is both a means to an end and an end in itself. It is at this point, in sounding the note of *extra ecclesiam nulla salus*, that both Bonhoeffer and Hauerwas display how they have learned to think both with and beyond their theological mentor, Karl Barth.

The christological concentration and the corresponding concrete ecclesiologies of Bonhoeffer and Hauerwas provide an invaluable point of departure for considering how the church ministers to the world over the course of its earthly pilgrimage. Both Bonhoeffer and Hauerwas understand that the church is in the world to serve the world. However, the way that the church best serves the world is by being the church. The demise of Christendom presents the church with the opportunity of being released from its generations of indentured servitude to the state. In this way, the oft-lamented end of Christendom actually presents a tremendous opportunity for the church. With nothing left to lose, the church is freed to truly be the church, loving extravagantly, taking bold risks in faith, and living by its wits as the peculiar people of God scattered throughout the nations. As it embraces its true identity in Christ, the church makes present within the world an alternative to the dominion of death that would otherwise be unimaginable. Only such a community is capable of acting as limit or boundary to the omnivorous modern nation-state and forming people who are able to say "No!" to a state which demands the allegiance which rightfully belongs only to Christ. This does not mean that Christians won't be found working for the good of society, but they will do so from a posture of humility, not ruling, but serving alongside men and women of goodwill. Christians will not abandon their convictions in order to serve in this way, for there are no spheres of life that do not fall under the Lordship of Jesus Christ. Both Bonhoeffer and Hauerwas recognized that the incarnation explodes the categories of transcendence and immanence, making ordinary life the theatre of encounter with the living Lord Jesus Christ. The Christian faith therefore frees human beings to enter into the multi-dimensionality of human existence to enact within the world a better worldliness for the sake of the world. This better worldliness is the witness offered by those who have allowed all aspects of their lives to be re-configured and re-ordered to the life-giving reign of Christ. In submitting to the royal rule of Christ and being conformed to his image, the church discovers that like its Lord, it exists for others. The disciples of Jesus Christ are the true friends of the world, for as they travel the Way of the One who went to the cross for the life of the world, they too find themselves rapt up by the Spirit into the Messianic event of being taken, blessed, broken and given for the life of the world.

FOR FURTHER CONSIDERATION

As theologians who recognized, following in the footsteps of Karl Barth, that theology is rightly an ecclesial discipline to be exercised in service of the church, it seems appropriate to place before the theologies of both Bonhoeffer and Hauerwas the question placed before theologies by pastors of all times and places: "How does it preach?"[3] This is not to suggest that works of theology should be immediately transferrable to the pulpit; as if

---

3. Although in one of his recent collections of sermons Hauerwas, drawing upon John Marsh's preface to Barth's *Deliverance to the Captives*, suggests that the question may be somewhat malformed. The better question to ask, he insists, is "What sort of preaching lies behind this kind of theology?" (*CSChu*, 14, quoting *Deliverance to the Captives*, 8).

a preacher might rise on a Sunday morning and read aloud excerpts from *Act and Being* in place of a sermon. Rather it is to ask how these theologies serve the proclamation of the church? Or, to put it another way, what type of preaching do these theologies support, encourage, and promote? While it is conceivable that there may be other preachers who more faithfully reflect the influence and embody the logic of Bonhoeffer's and Hauerwas's theology in their preaching, the most obvious place to turn for an answer to these questions is to the sermons of the two men themselves. By this time there is now a considerable pool of sermons written by both men that are available to the reading public.[4] These sermons warrant further study. In an age of insipid preaching they offer much-needed encouragement to preachers seeking to recover their theological nerve. Furthermore, they also provide an important avenue into the heart of both figures' theologies. Preaching was never an add-on or afterthought to the academic work of either man, but rather was considered by both to be amongst the most important activities in which they engaged.[5] The seriousness with which both Bonhoeffer and Hauerwas approached the task of preaching suggests that fruitful possibilities could exist for reading their academic work through the lens of their sermons. The case that I have attempted to make at several points over the course of the dissertation about the important place of their works of "popular theology" could easily be extended to include their sermons. Perhaps some recurring criticisms would be abated, some new questions brought to birth, and their theologies perceived in a different light, if their work was to be read in a way that gives their sermons priority of place.[6]

   4. It is rather difficult to produce an exact total of the number of sermons available in print by both authors. The difficulty for Bonhoeffer pertains to determining whether meditations, devotions, children's homilies, sermon outlines, etc., count towards the total. A very conservative estimate would be that there are over seventy of Bonhoeffer's sermons available in English translation. Thirty-one of these sermons have been collected and published in a single volume entitled *The Collected Sermons of Dietrich Bonhoeffer*. By my count, over eighty of Hauerwas's sermons have been published in his books. However, this number does not include sermons published elsewhere or sermons embedded within other essays. Hauerwas's sermons are largely concentrated in *US, DT, CSC, CSChu, WWW, WA*.
   5. In the introduction to his most recent collection of sermons, Hauerwas confesses, "I find preaching to be theologically the most fertile work I do" *(WA*, xii). Similar comments reflecting the importance Hauerwas attaches to his sermons are found scattered throughout his works. E.g., *DT*, 3; *CSChu*, 9. Bethge writes of Bonhoeffer: "Preaching was the great event for him [Bonhoeffer]. His severe theologizing and critical love for his church were all for its sake, for preaching proclaimed the message of Christ, the bringer of peace. For Bonhoeffer nothing in his calling competed in importance with preaching" (*Dietrich Bonhoeffer*, 234).
   6. Philip Ziegler has raised a similar question with respect to the Bonhoeffer corpus. "And what if texts such as these [the array of scriptural expositions], rather than

Another complex of issues that has emerged over the course of this study that warrants further investigation pertains to the person and work of the Holy Spirit in the theologies of both Bonhoeffer and Hauerwas. Perhaps it is simply their fate as heirs of the Western theological tradition, and Barthians (of some sort) to boot, that questions surrounding pneumatology would surface surrounding their work.[7] Now to be sure, their criticisms of Barth and their attempt to think with and beyond him involve a substantial pneumatological dimension. The shared vision of the church as a worshipping community of radical discipleship, gathered around the Word and sacraments, overcoming sin through truth-telling and absolution, and being drawn into conformity with the Lord Jesus Christ, points towards the presence of a substantial pneumatology which is operative at the heart of their ecclesiologies. However, this pneumatology remains largely implied and for the most part not explicitly developed. There are some good reasons for the lack of Spirit-talk in the works of both men. For one, both Bonhoeffer and Hauerwas share with Barth an almost allergic-type reaction to anything that hints of either pietism or theological liberalism; two contexts where talk of the Holy Spirit is easily confused or conflated with talk of the human spirit.[8] Secondly, there is something correct about not wanting to say too much about the Holy Spirit. After all, the Holy Spirit is what could be called the self-effacing member of the Trinity, whose mission within the economy of salvation is to bear witness to the Son. This suggests that pneumatology cannot be developed apart from Christology. Furthermore, talk of the Holy Spirit must be governed by a proper reticence or else it

---

say the earlier dissertations or the final *Letters and Papers from Prison*, were taken to be the centre of gravity in the whole corpus, how would our understanding of the whole be affected?" ("Dietrich Bonhoeffer," 590). Healy, however, is rather dismissive of the importance of Hauerwas's sermons for his work as a whole, suggesting they don't add much to Hauerwas's "ordinary, non-sermonic academic productions, and may possibly even diminish the latter's good effects" (*Hauerwas*, 12). Healy does not engage in any close readings of Hauerwas's sermons to substantiate this claim.

7. Numerous sources could be cited at this point, but perhaps the most prominent criticism of Barth's pneumatological deficiency remains: Jenson, "You Wonder Where the Spirit Went."

8. In the later stages of his career, Barth came to acknowledge that his speech (or lack thereof) about the Holy Spirit may have been overdetermined by his polemical relationship to liberalism. In response to a student's question about the absence of the Spirit in his doctrine of "revealed Word," Barth replied, "If I had made much of the Holy Spirit, I am afraid it would have led back to subjectivism, which is what I wanted to overcome. Today I would speak more of the Holy Spirit" (*Karl Barth's Table Talk*, 27, quoted in Bender, *Confessing Christ*, 50). See also Barth's comments about the legitimacy of attempting to formulate a "Christian anthropocentrism" as an approach to the third article of the Creed in *Humanity of God*, 24.

risks domesticating the sovereign wind which blows where it chooses.[9] As Bonhoeffer has reminded us with respect to Christology, the proper pneumatological question must also always first and foremost be, "Who?" A "pneumatological positivism" would be a poor substitute for the reality of the church of Jesus Christ alive in the power of the Holy Spirit. While acknowledging the importance of all that has just been said, it nonetheless does still seem as though both Bonhoeffer's and Hauerwas's accounts would be strengthened by providing a fuller account of the person and work of the Holy Spirit.[10] The Ignatian emphasis upon *ubi Christus, ibi ecclesia*, which is so prominent in their work, receives its necessary supplementation in the Irenaean affirmation, "Where the Spirit of God is, there is the Church and every grace."[11]

A more explicit statement of the pneumatological presuppositions inherent within the theologies of Bonhoeffer and Hauerwas could further the contribution their work has to make to contemporary theology. In particular, the work of both Bonhoeffer and Hauerwas could enrich, and in turn be enriched, by entering into the contemporary conversations surrounding apocalyptic theology and communion ecclesiology. The eschatological character of both Bonhoeffer's and Hauerwas's work, which goes hand in hand with their christological concentration, positions their theology to make a significant contribution to the developing conversation surrounding the recovery of the apocalyptic character of the Gospel.[12] This recent interest in apocalyptic is highly indebted to the work of New Testament scholar J. Louis Martyn, but is also influenced by the work of earlier apocalypticists like Ernst Käsemann, and even the early dialectical theology of Karl Barth.[13] However, like the work of the early Barth, the contemporary apocalyptic theology movement faces serious questions surrounding how to account for the continuity of the human subject and the historicity of the church. In the hands of some contemporary apolocalypticists the church appears to evaporate amidst the smoke rising from the crater left behind by the divine

---

9. John 3:8.

10. In a recent essay entitled, "How to Be Caught by the Holy Spirit," Hauerwas attempts to respond to the pneumatological concerns surrounding his work by drawing on Rogers's book *After the Spirit*.

11. Irenaeus, *Against Heresies*, 3.24.1, quoted in Dulles, *Models of the Church*, 50.

12. Ziegler and Harink have already begun to mine the potential of Bonhoeffer and Hauerwas respectively for this emerging field of theological discourse. Ziegler, "Dietrich Bonhoeffer," 579–94; Harink, *Paul Among the Postliberals*, 67–103.

13. The importance of Martyn's magisterial commentary on *Galatians* to this emerging discussion cannot be underestimated. For a collection of essays that represents the scope of concerns represented under the broad tent of apocalyptic theology, see Davis and Harink, *Apocalyptic and the Future of Theology*.

lightning strike of revelation.[14] Bonhoeffer's and Hauerwas's understandings of the church as a reality of revelation arising from the intersection of Christology and pneumatology are suggestive for the possibility of formulating a theology that is sensitive to apocalyptic theology's concern for preserving the priority of divine action, while at the same time preserving a place for the historicity and continuity of the human and ecclesial subjects.

There are also many obvious notes of resonance between communion ecclesiology and the ecclesiologies of both Bonhoeffer and Hauerwas. These include: an emphasis upon the church as a reality of revelation, the centrality of the Eucharist, and the church as a community sharing in human and divine fellowship.[15] Bringing the ecclesiology of Bonhoeffer and Hauerwas into explicit dialogue with communion ecclesiology could provide a way of bringing to the fore their pneumatological commitments which have remained largely implicit up to this point. Furthermore, the work of Bonhoeffer and Hauerwas could helpfully summon some practitioners of communion ecclesiology away from a proclivity towards abstract social trinitarianisms to a more concrete christological perspective. The work of both Bonhoeffer and Hauerwas reminds us that it is not the Trinity which is our social program, but rather the Kingdom of God, in which we share through our participation in the divinized humanity of Christ.[16]

Both apocalyptic theology and communion ecclesiology are ecumenical enterprises sustained by the work of the theologians from across the boundaries of numerous ecclesial traditions and church communions. That the theologies of Bonhoeffer and Hauerwas might both be enriched by and have some contribution to make to these developing schools of thought is evidence of the broad significance of their work for the ecumenical church. Although mainline Protestantism in Germany and America were the primary milieus in which both Bonhoeffer and Hauerwas struggled to recall culturally compromised and confused churches back to their true identity in Christ, their work holds great ecumenical promise. In fact, in the early years of the new millennium it appears that the work of both theologians may be positioned to receive a more thorough and significant reception in

---

14. E.g., Kerr, *Christ, History and Apocalyptic*. See also Congdon, "Eschatologizing Apocalyptic."

15. For an introduction to communion ecclesiology and the thought of some of its preeminent representatives, see Doyle, *Communion Ecclesiology*.

16. The phrase "the Trinity is our social program" has become a popular rallying cry within certain segments advocating a form of social trinitarianism. Kathryn Tanner advances an effective argument against this line of thought, which I believe is congruent with both Bonhoeffer's and Hauerwas's fundamental theological commitments. "Trinity, Christology, and Community," 56–74.

Christian traditions beyond their mainline Protestant homes. Suggestive areas of convergence between the thought of both Bonhoeffer and Hauerwas and some of the central emphases within the Evangelical,[17] Roman Catholic,[18] and Orthodox traditions await further exploration.[19] It also appears that the theologies of both Bonhoeffer and Hauerwas are open to being haunted by the Jews in a way that exceeds the capacity of many of the voices of modern theology.[20]

As a precocious fourteen year-old, Bonhoeffer proudly informed his family that he intended to become a theologian and a minister. When his siblings tried to convince him that he was settling for mediocrity in linking himself to such "a poor, feeble, boring, petty and bourgeois institution," Bonhoeffer replied, "In that case I shall have to reform it!"[21] This brief anecdote directs our gaze towards the ultimate criteria for determining the impact and influence of both Bonhoeffer's and Hauerwas's christocentric ecclesial

---

17. Burgeoning interest in Bonhoeffer amongst Evangelicals encompasses the publication of a recent bestselling biography written by an evangelical journalist, Metaxas, *Bonhoeffer*, and the claim by an evangelical theologian that Bonhoeffer "will be their church father in the future—or else evangelicals will have no future" (Huntemann, *Dietrich Bonhoeffer*, 12). See also Larsen, "Evangelical Reception." Hauerwas has also recently been gaining an increased hearing amongst Evangelicals. For example, Hauerwas has been invited to deliver keynote addresses on three separate occasions at theological conferences held at Wheaton College since the turn of the millennium (2000, 2006, 2013).

18. Roman Catholicism has played a significant role in the formation of both men, from Bonhoeffer's early trip to Rome to Hauerwas's time at Notre Dame (See Bethge, *Dietrich Bonhoeffer*, 59, 62; *IGC*, 83; *HC*, 95–121). One of the earliest and most significant systematic presentations of Bonhoeffer's thought was written by the Roman Catholic theologian Ernst Feil. See *Theology of Dietrich Bonhoeffer*. Hauerwas has served as *Doktorvater* to numerous Catholic scholars including "several who have become Catholic, influenced in part by his thinking on tradition and authority" (Johnson, "Worshipping in Spirit," 310).

19. Clements has highlighted the need for an encounter between Bonhoeffer and Orthodoxy, sketched out some areas of convergence, and anticipated lines of questioning in "Dialogue with the Orthodox World." For some preliminary engagements with Bonhoeffer from an Orthodox perspective see Brightman, "Dietrich Bonhoeffer," 261–72; Bebis, "Bonhoeffer and the Fathers," 273–79; Sopko, "Bonhoeffer: An Orthodox Ecclesiology?," 81–88. For a provocative engagement with Hauerwas from within the Orthodox tradition see Engelhardt, "The Belligerent Kingdom," 193–211.

20. The language of "haunting" is introduced by Romand Coles in his conversations with Hauerwas. *CDRO*, 103. It is employed by Bader-Saye with respect to the relation of Hauerwas's thought to the Jews. "Haunted by the Jews," 191–209. The Orthodox Jewish scholar Pinchas Lapide claimed that Bonhoeffer was "a pioneer and forerunner of the slow, step-by-step re-Hebraisation of the churches in our day" ("Bonhoeffer und das Judentum," 129, quoted in Kelly, "Bonhoeffer and the Jews," 160).

21. Bethge, *Dietrich Bonhoeffer*, 36.

theology. The success of their work ultimately lies not in book sales or in the founding of Bonhoefferian or Hauerwasian schools of thought. Rather, as theologians of and for the church, their work can be considered successful to the extent that their lives and thought contribute to the reformation of the church and spurs Christians on to live more faithfully as witnesses to the Gospel of Jesus Christ. Both Bonhoeffer and Hauerwas recognized that theology is not simply idle talk. Rather, theology is speech meant to do work. Theology is a matter of life and death; for the fruit of good theology is ultimately disciples conformed to the image of the One who "comes down from heaven and gives life to the world."[22]

---

22. John 6:33.

Appendix
The Ethics of Tyrannicide

In *Performing the Faith: Bonhoeffer and the Practice of Nonviolence* (2004), Stanley Hauerwas acknowledged his longstanding intellectual debt to Dietrich Bonhoeffer. Hauerwas went on to explain that there were two factors that had prevented him from acknowledging this debt much earlier. The first was the early reception of Bonhoeffer's work when it was first translated into English, associated as it was with the "death of God" and "situation ethics" movements.[1] The second, Hauerwas states, was that "Bonhoeffer's decision to participate in the plot to kill Hitler seemed to make him an unlikely candidate to support a pacifist position."[2] The first worry has been largely alleviated by the work of subsequent generations of Bonhoeffer scholars and the recently completed project of translating the *Dietrich Bonhoeffer Werke* for an English audience. The second worry remains unresolved. Hauerwas, for his part, appears rather reluctant to address the question or to make any type of judgment surrounding Bonhoeffer's involvement in the conspiracy. I suspect this reluctance stems from Hauerwas's deep respect for Bonhoeffer's life and witness.[3] Hauerwas opines, "How to understand Bonhoeffer's involvement with the conspiracy associated with Admiral Canaris and Bonhoeffer's brother-in-law, Hans von Dohnanyi, I think can never be determined with certainty."[4] Hauerwas even goes so far as to float

---

1. For representative works within the two streams of thought, see Robinson, *Honest to God*, and Fletcher, *Situation Ethics*, respectively.

2. *PTF*, 35.

3. Rasmussen's reflections upon the difficulties associated with critiquing Bonhoeffer's actions would appear to be relevant at this point: "Furthermore, dissecting the interior of any martyr's witness in order to expose the shortcomings smacks of something slightly perverse. It is glee only for the polemicist" (*Reality and Resistance*, 149).

4. *PTF*, 35. Although Hauerwas does seem drawn to the account provided by Nation et al. in *Bonhoeffer the Assassin?* See Hauerwas, foreword to *Bonhoeffer the*

the tantalizing suggestion that Bonhoeffer may not have even been aware that the conspirators were planning to kill Hitler, but, disappointingly, provides no evidence to support the claim.[5] Finally, Hauerwas suggests that "the secrecy required by the conspiracy means that we do not have available any texts that could help us know how Bonhoeffer understood how this part of his life fit or did not fit with his theological convictions or his earlier commitment to pacifism."[6] It is true that we have no autobiographical account in which Bonhoeffer outlines his rationale for joining the conspiracy, nor do we have a manuscript entitled, "The Ethics of Tyrannicide." To produce such documents while participating in planning for a coup d'état would be both foolhardy and irresponsible. However, there has been a fairly widespread tendency amongst Bonhoeffer scholars to read Bonhoeffer's discussion of "responsibility" within *Ethics* and *Letters and Papers from Prison*, and particularly the "borderline situation" which calls for a "freed deed of responsibility," as being particularly pertinent to Bonhoeffer's own personal involvement with the conspiracy.[7] In light of this trend, it is surprising that Hauerwas did not himself engage with these passages.[8] If he did, he would have discovered what appears to be an attempt on Bonhoeffer's part to come to a theologically-informed understanding of his participation in the con-

---

Assassin? In this book, the authors argue that the interpretation of Bonhoeffer's writings has been detrimentally influenced by unfounded assumptions surrounding the nature of Bonhoeffer's involvement in the conspiracy. In the first part of the book they argue that there is no evidence to support the conclusion that Bonhoeffer either affirmed or was "involved" in the plots to kill Hitler. In the second part, they seek to demonstrate that Bonhoeffer did not depart from his earlier christologically informed outlook for a more "realistic" position that recognized the necessity of the sanctified use of violence for the greater good. While I am sympathetic with the desire to accurately portray Bonhoeffer's rather limited role in the conspiracy in the face of prominent popular caricatures, I remain skeptical of the authors' biographical conclusions. That being said, the theological thesis of the second part of the book is largely congenial to the argument I am advancing in this chapter and within this book as a whole. See also Dean, review of *Bonhoeffer the Assassin?*

5. *PTF*, 35–36.

6. Ibid., 36.

7. See for example Bethge, *Dietrich Bonhoeffer*, 791–97; Green, *Theology of Sociality*, 304–21; Kelly and Nelson, *Cost of Moral Leadership*, 112–15; Rasmussen, "Ethics of Responsible Action," 222–23. Nation has questioned the assumptions surrounding this reading. See "A Blanket License," 150–52.

8. This omission is noted by both Green and de Gruchy in their reviews of *Performing the Faith*. De Gruchy, "What Kind of Pacifist?," 27; Green, review of *Performing the Faith*, 675. Hauerwas has more recently acknowledged the presence of these passages, but in doing so confessed that he is not quite sure how to read them in light of what Bonhoeffer had said previously in *Discipleship*. Foreword to *Bonhoeffer the Assassin?*, xiv.

spiracy. This is not to say that Hauerwas would necessarily approve of what he encountered there. Bonhoeffer's presentation of the extreme case that calls for a free act of Christian responsibility, which he attempts to ground christologically, appears to stand in conflict with Hauerwas's own christocentric understanding of the "pacifism of the Messianic community."[9]

It would be helpful, therefore, to briefly explore Bonhoeffer's understanding of responsibility. The concept of responsibility is central to Bonhoeffer's understanding of the ethical life.[10] The word used by Bonhoeffer to denote responsibility, *Verantwortung*, can also encompass the ideas of answering and being accountable. Responsibility, therefore, is a dialogical concept for Bonhoeffer. The ethical agent is constituted by the address of the other, both God and neighbor, which renders one both able to respond and accountable for responding. Perhaps the best definition of responsibility is provided by Bonhoeffer himself:

> This life, lived in answer to the life of Jesus Christ (as the Yes and No to our life), we call *"responsibility"* [*"Verantwortung"*]. This concept of responsibility denotes the complete wholeness and unity of the answer to the reality that is given to us in Jesus Christ, as opposed to the partial answers that we might be able to give, for example, from considerations of usefulness, or with reference to certain principles.[11]

Responsible human action takes the form of living selflessly for others. As we have previously seen in our considerations of Bonhoeffer's Christology, this is the form of Jesus's existence as the *Stellvertreter* or "man for others." In his very being, Jesus is *pro me*. As a result, Bonhoeffer can assert, "In this real vicarious representative action, in which his human existence consists, he is the responsible human being par excellence. Since he is life, all of life through him is destined to be vicarious representative action."[12] Up to this point, there are no necessary contradictions with Hauerwas's position.

The differences between the two theologians begin to emerge as Bonhoeffer turns his attention to discussing the "extraordinary situation" or "borderline case." Bonhoeffer seems to indicate in a letter addressed to Bethge from Tegel prison that he understood his decision to participate in the

---

9. Although coined by Yoder, the phrase "pacifism of the Messianic community" accurately reflects Hauerwas's own understanding of the inseparable connection between nonviolence and discipleship. Yoder, *Nevertheless*, 133–38.

10. Rasmussen calls it "the core theme" of Bonhoeffer's ethics. "Ethics of Responsible Action," 218.

11. *E* (*DBWE* 6), 254.

12. Ibid., 258–59.

conspiracy as having arisen from such a "boundary situation" (*Grenzfall*).[13] The fact that Bonhoeffer cast his situation in terms of a boundary situation also implies that Bonhoeffer had not abandoned the peace ethic that had featured so prominently in his writings during the 1930s. Green rightly points out "that 'pacifism' so-called is not a discrete and interchangeable part of Bonhoeffer's theology, to be replaced by something else in a different historical situation; nor is it simply a principle of nonviolence; rather Bonhoeffer's peace ethic is an ingredient and an implication of his theology as a whole."[14] This is evident in the way that the Sermon on the Mount continued to occupy Bonhoeffer's imagination as he was in the midst of writing the *Ethics* manuscripts, where he continued to assert that "the purpose of the Sermon on the Mount is to do it."[15] Furthermore, the fact that Bonhoeffer cast his discussion in terms of the extraordinary situation and not according to the terms of the just war tradition, suggests that his peace ethic was still in effect.[16] There is no indication that Bonhoeffer jettisoned the peace ethic he articulated in the 1930s — perhaps for something resembling Niebuhrian realism — for to do so would require the abandonment of his central christological convictions.[17] For Bonhoeffer, so-called "Christian realism" is neither Christian nor particularly realistic, for it trades in abstraction and fails to reckon seriously with the *Real One* — the Lord Jesus Christ.[18]

13. "In the beginning the question also plagued me as to whether it is really the cause of Christ for whose sake I have inflicted such distress on all of you; but soon enough I pushed this thought out of my head as a temptation [Anfechtung] and became certain that my task was precisely the endurance of such a boundary situation with all its problematic elements, and became quite happy with this and have remained so to this day" (*LPP* (*DBWE* 8), 180).

14. Green, "Pacifism and Tyrannicide," 34-35. Green prefers the term "peace ethic" to "pacifism" as a way of emphasizing that Bonhoeffer's peace commitment did not arise out of formal principles, but rather from his Christology, his reading of the New Testament, and his understanding of the church as a community of disciples. See also Green, review of *Reality and Resistance*, 159-62.

15. *E* (*DBWE* 6), 326. See also ibid., 230-31, 235-36, 242-43.

16. Green, "Pacifism and Tyrannicide," 42.

17. Green, review of *Reality and Resistance*, 163. See also Green, review of *Performing the Faith*, 676.

18. For Bonhoeffer's criticism of "pseudo-realism," see *E* (*DBWE* 6, 239-41). Bonhoeffer had criticized Niebuhr's theology for its christological deficiency in a report issued upon his return from the United States in 1939. *DBWE* 15, 460. Unfortunately, Bonhoeffer's concept of responsibility continues to be read in some quarters through the lens of Niebuhrian realism, rather than on Bonhoeffer's own terms. One of the most recent works to advance the narrative that Bonhoeffer converted to Niebuhrian realism is Marsh's otherwise quite commendable biography. See *Strange Glory*, 108, 277, 315, 342. For a developed critique of reading Bonhoeffer as a Niebhurian, see Nation et al., 212-20.

In terms of the main contours of their ethical thought, both Bonhoeffer and Hauerwas are united in the conviction that Jesus means peace and that under his royal rule disciples are called to lay down their swords and follow after Him in the way of the cross.[19] The tension between the two comes to the fore with the question of the *Grenzfall*.

In the manuscript "History and Good [2]," Bonhoeffer suggests that in the most unusual of cases, when the times are so out of joint that the necessities that make human life possible seem to hang by a mere thread over a sea of chaos, circumstances may demand from the Christian an extraordinary deed of free responsibility that cuts against every law and commandment. This borderline case or *ultima ratio* cannot be made into a law or principle. Rather, those called to act freely in responsibility for their neighbours in contradiction to the laws of the land and even the commandments of God must acknowledge "that here the law is being broken, violated; that the commandment is broken out of dire necessity, thereby affirming the legitimacy of the law in the very act of violating it."[20] In Bonhoeffer's own unique situation, the guilt associated with tyrannicide was to be incurred for the sake of re-establishing an external order which safe-guarded the necessities of life for all. Responsibility, therefore, includes the willingness to become guilty.[21] Bonhoeffer attempts to ground this point christologically by asserting that "because Jesus took the guilt of all human beings upon himself, everyone who acts responsibly becomes guilty."[22] The bearing of one's neighbour within the *sanctorum communio*, and particularly the bearing of the sins of the neighbour, has been a central component of Bonhoeffer's ecclesiology since his doctoral dissertation.[23] However, what appears to be new at this point is the introduction of the notion of guilt being "actively incurred for the other."[24] In other words, one becomes guilty as the result of one's own actions for the sake of the neighbour. In the personal reflection, "After Ten Years," prepared for his closest friends amongst the conspirators,

---

19. The recent popular biography written by Eric Metaxas (*Bonhoeffer*) overlooks the central connection between peace and Christology in Bonhoeffer's writings.

20. *E* (*DBWE* 6), 274.

21. Ibid., 275.

22. Ibid.

23. *SC* (*DBWE* 1), 184–90.

24. The phrase "actively incurred for the other" is a terminological distinction introduced by Schliesser in her insightful study *Everyone Who Acts Responsibly*. Among the important questions raised by Schliesser are questions surrounding Bonhoeffer's conception of freedom—namely, does Christ call the disciple to a liberty which transcends even the law of Christ?—and whether Bonhoeffer's attempt to ground the active incurring of guilt in Christology is adequate? Schliesser thinks not.

Bonhoeffer sums up his understanding of free responsibility: "It is founded in a God who calls for the free venture of faith to responsible action and who promises forgiveness and consolation to the one who on account of such action becomes a sinner."[25]

It is this conception of the boundary situation which demands a free deed of responsibility that places Bonhoeffer into conflict with Hauerwas. Since Bonhoeffer was writing years before Hauerwas, and Hauerwas does not directly address the question of responsible action in the *Grenzfall* in Bonhoeffer's work, it is the burden of the following section to bring to light both real and perceived areas of disagreement between the two.

First, Bonhoeffer casts strong aspersion towards principled pacifists who wield their commitment to nonviolence as a weapon contributing to their own self-justification. Those who are unwilling to become guilty for the sake of others "place their personal innocence [Unschuld] above their responsibility for other human beings and are blind to the fact that precisely in so doing they become even more egregiously guilty."[26] Life in Christ is life for others. Therefore, any commitment to nonviolence that places concern for one's own purity or personal righteousness ahead of the needs of one's neighbour is severely misguided. Superficial readers of Hauerwas's work sometimes presume that he is advocating such a position. However, Hauerwas himself has been insistent that Christians committed to the nonviolent way of Jesus are no less compromised by their enmeshment in the violent and sinful systems of the world.[27] According to Hauerwas's understanding, the Christian commitment to nonviolence is not part of a deluded quest by Christians to justify themselves, but rather is simply a consequence of being a disciple of the Prince of Peace. As Hauerwas frames the matter, in a version of a refrain that recurs throughout his work, "Christian nonviolence is necessary not because it promises a world free of war, but because in a world of war as faithful followers of Christ we cannot be anything other than nonviolent."[28]

The above quotation points towards differing conceptions of the Christian's relationship to history that emerges in relation to the question of acting responsibly in boundary situations. Both Bonhoeffer and Hauerwas strongly oppose gnosticizing tendencies which seek to understand the human subject as anything other than an embodied, historical creature. However, their perspectives diverge with respect to the question of

---

25. *LPP* (*DBWE* 8), 41.
26. *E* (*DBWE* 6), 276.
27. *PTF*, 26, 180.
28. Ibid., 181.

Christian responsibility for the directing of unfolding history. Bonhoeffer understands himself and his co-conspirators as being "coresponsible for the shaping of history."[29] This concept of coresponsiblity appears, for Bonhoeffer, to be outworking of the incarnation; because God became human, "we as human beings are permitted and called to live and act before God and the neighbour within the confines of our limited human judgment and knowledge."[30] Amongst these limited powers is the ability to "look into the immediate future" and to "consider the consequences of our actions."[31] This does not imply that human beings have acquired the divine attributes of omniscience or omnipotence with respect to the future. Rather, human beings remain the junior partners of the God who is capable of shaping history and bringing good out of evil over and beyond the actions of the human beings who happen to occupy the moral stage at any particular time.[32] However, Bonhoeffer warns his colleagues that it would be imprudent to ignore the "ethical significance of success."[33] At this point, Bonhoeffer is not backing off from his warnings about the dangers of idolizing success, nor is he claiming some type of Machiavellian understanding of the end justifying the means, rather he is simply observing that historical success creates the conditions under which future life must be lived.[34] The Christian, therefore, can neither play the role of the offended critic, who voices his displeasure from the sidelines, or the role of the opportunist, who completely capitulates in the face of success. Rather, according to Bonhoeffer, "the ultimately responsible question is not how I extricate myself heroically from a situation but [how] a coming generation is to go on living."[35]

From Hauerwas's perspective, this is an unhelpful way to frame the question. It is not that Hauerwas is unconcerned with how future generations are to live, but he is troubled by the underlying assumption that it is up to Christians to ensure that history comes out right. Such an assumption

29. *LPP* (*DBWE* 8), 42.

30. *E* (*DBWE* 6), 268.

31. Ibid., 268. Rasmussen recounts a conversation which took place between Bonhoeffer and Werner von Haeften, staff lieutenant in the Army High Command, at the home of Wolf-Dieter Zimmermann in November of 1942. Von Haeften had asked Bonhoeffer whether he should shoot if he had the chance to kill Hitler. Bonhoeffer responded that the question was not whether "he may" shoot, but whether "he should shoot." By doing so, Bonhoeffer was asking whether sufficient plans were in place that such an action would be responsibly undertaken with respect to the future. *Reality and Resistance*, 141.

32. *LPP* (*DBWE* 8), 42.

33. Ibid., 42.

34. *E* (*DBWE* 6), 89; *LPP* (*DBWE* 8), 41–42.

35. Ibid., 42.

can lead Christians to commit great evils in the name of being responsible.[36] The resurrection explodes notions of cause and effect and allows Christians to abandon the vain attempt to obtain "handles on history" and, instead, to follow in the footsteps of the crucified One who faithfully entrusted the effectiveness of his mission to God.[37] To learn to live in this eschatological manner is to learn to live out of control, as friends of time who "are not subjected to the temptation to believe that you have to make a difference, because you can take the time—in a world that doesn't think it has any time—to live lives in quiet humility and truthfulness."[38] Faithfulness to God's Kingdom, not worldly effectiveness is the primary goal of those who live in light of the end made present in Christ.[39] Hauerwas openly acknowledges that such a life of nonviolence may indeed be harsh. "Certainly," Hauerwas remarks, "you have to imagine, and perhaps even face, that you will have to watch the innocent suffer and even die for your convictions."[40] This does not mean that Hauerwas's messianic pacifism is passive. Hauerwas is far from advocating the "inactive waiting and dully looking on" which Bonhoeffer so clearly saw and criticized in his own church.[41] Evil must be resisted. However, it must be resisted in a mode and manner appropriate to the peaceable kingdom present in Christ, otherwise Christians risk becoming the very evil which they oppose.[42] Bonhoeffer himself seems to have struggled with this thought, as is evident from his questioning of what had become of himself and his fellow conspirators over the course of their resistance. Bonhoeffer reflects, "We have been silent witnesses of evil deeds. We have become cunning and learned the arts of obfuscation and equivocal speech. Experience has rendered us suspicious of human beings, and often we have failed to speak a true and open word. Unbearable conflicts have worn us down or even made us cynical. Are we still of any use?"[43]

For Hauerwas, the paradigmatic form of Christian resistance is embodied in the death of the martyrs, who refuse to exchange evil for evil in the name of effectiveness, but die in confidence that God will do something with their death.[44] Since the Christian community trusts in the God "who

36. CDRO, 326.
37. WWW, 92.
38. CRDO, 331.
39. PK, 105–6.
40. PTF, 206.
41. LPP (DBWE 8), 49.
42. PK, 106.
43. LPP (DBWE 8), 52.
44. CDRO, 332.

gives life to the dead and calls into existence the things that do not exist," it is never simply a matter of choosing between faithfulness and effectiveness.[45] Rather, the disciples of Jesus Christ trust that "God will use our faithfulness to make his kingdom a reality in the world."[46]

Our discussion ultimately brings us to the question of the *Grenzfall* and its legitimacy for Christian ethics. Bonhoeffer is insistent that the responsible action required in such borderline cases can never become a law unto itself, yet this is exactly how Bonhoeffer's involvement in the conspiracy is often popularly appropriated.[47] Included among these misappropriations of Bonhoeffer's life and legacy are: the attempt by the militant anti-abortion group "Missionaries for the Unborn" to justify the murder of a doctor who performed abortions,[48] the televangelist Pat Robertson's call for the assassination of Venezuelan president Hugo Chavez,[49] and George Bush's attempt to legitimate the "war on terror."[50] At the formal level, the ethical category of the *Grenzfall* runs the risk of becoming a law unto itself and suffers from a criteriological deficiency that makes it very difficult, if not impossible, for a community to determine whether it is encountering a borderline case. Perhaps the more serious charge to be raised against Bonhoeffer's conception of the *Grenzfall* occurs at the material level. Just as Hauerwas frequently turns to the work of John Howard Yoder to provide necessary theological conceptual clarification, in what follows we will draw upon Yoder's perceptive analysis of the ethical concept of the *Grenzfall* in the work of Karl Barth. Yoder observes that the *Grenzfall* functions in Barth, much as it does in Bonhoeffer's *Ethics*, to safeguard the sovereignty of God.[51] Yoder notes that such a concern for God's freedom lacks the necessary christological specificity, for, "if God's sovereignty is understood in the royal condescension of Christ rather than in speculation about pure infinity, then crucifixion (the willing abandonment of the genuine values incarnated in the one just Man) and resurrection (the triumph of love over a predictable impossibility) are the modes of the exercise of sovereign authority."[52] Bonhoeffer himself had said something very similar in his *Habilitationsschrift*, where he expressed reservations about the formalistic conceptions of freedom that he had

---

45. Rom 4:17.
46. *PK*, 105.
47. *E (DBWE* 6), 273.
48. Green, "Pacifism and Tyrannicide," 41.
49. Robertson, "Pat Robertson Clarifies," para.3.
50. Green, review of *Reality and Resistance*, 156.
51. Yoder, *Barth and the Problem of War*, 47.
52. Ibid., 51.

detected in Barth's early writings. In response to these concerns, Bonhoeffer stressed that "God is free not from human beings, but for them. Christ is the word of God's freedom."[53] If Christ is the word of God's freedom, as Bonhoeffer insisted, then an insistence on the possibility of *Grenzfall* situations does not in fact preserve God's freedom, but stands in contradiction to the God who has freely bound himself to us in Christ. Yoder puts the matter in the following way:

> If dogmatics—or for that matter any Christian communication—is possible, we cannot count on situations ever arising in which God would take back what he said in Christ, or give us commands which are not concordant with his revelation of himself in Jesus Christ. When the Christian theologian affirms with the Creeds that "Jesus Christ is the Son of God," he does not feel obliged by his respect for divine sovereignty to say at the same time that there might be extreme cases where this would not be true.[54]

Following this line of argumentation, Yoder goes on to assert that if ethics is inseparable from dogmatics as Barth and Bonhoeffer have both affirmed, then, "we must claim, within the limits of present understanding and subject to correction, the same degree of certainty and universality for ethics we are accustomed to claiming in Christology."[55] From his attempts to provide a christological mooring for the free deed of responsibility, it is apparent that Bonhoeffer himself is not entirely comfortable with the concept of the *Grenzfall* which calls for action completely divorced from the form of God's revelation in Jesus Christ. However, his line of christological reasoning which asserts that "because Jesus took the guilt of all human beings upon himself, everyone who acts responsibly becomes guilty" does not make the necessary material distinctions with respect to the mode and manner of bearing guilt.[56] Jesus Christ, the sinless one, does indeed bear the sins of the world, but he does so in complete faithfulness to the will of the Father. With respect to Bonhoeffer's ethics of responsible action in the boundary situation, it appears that Christ's being there for others has been divorced from the way of his being there for others.[57] It is somewhat of a bitter irony

---

53. *AB (DBWE* 2), 90-91.

54. Yoder, *Barth and the Problem of War*, 48.

55. Ibid., 48.

56. *E (DBWE* 6), 234. Schliesser introduces the distinction between guilt actively incurred and guilt non-actively incurred. *Everyone Who Acts Responsibly*, 180–86. Rasmussen speaks of guilt incurred through the violation of divine law in contradistinction to guilt which is forensically accepted. *Reality and Resistance*, 172.

57. Rasmussen frames the issue in a manner congruent with the argument

that one so adamantly opposed to any understanding of the ethical life in terms of principles or ideals, as Bonhoeffer was, would end up grounding his attempt to work through the ethics of tyrannicide in what appears to be a formal christological principle lacking sufficient material content.

Perhaps then McClendon and Jones are right to suggest that these final years of Bonhoeffer's life, during which he was involved with the conspiracy and subsequently imprisoned, are best understood through the lens of tragedy.[58] However, if Bonhoeffer is correct and it is possible that a *Grenzfall* may exist, then it can only be known by the person who encounters it in the concrete situation. On these grounds, we are not in a position to issue a verdict on Bonhoeffer's course of action. In either case, our only recourse is to entrust this servant of the Lord, as Bonhoeffer entrusted himself, to the mercy of the God who has demonstrated his great love for humankind in raising Jesus Christ from the dead.

---

advanced above, writing, "The pertinent ethical question is: with what *measurements* can Bonhoeffer advocate any other course of action as being obedient than that which is consistent with the general lines of Christ's form?" (*Reality and Resistance*, 153).

58. McClendon, *Ethics*, 193–212; Jones, *Embodying Forgiveness*, 3–33. Both McClendon and Jones understand Bonhoeffer's involvement in the conspiracy, ultimately resulting in his death, to be a tragedy arising within the context of the tragic failure of the German church to be a true locus of resistance to the horrors of the Nazi regime. In other words, since the church in Germany so utterly failed to be such a community of resistance, Bonhoeffer ended up turning to the only community he had left, the community surrounding his family involved in the conspiracy and it is within this context that Bonhoeffer attempted to enact his "repentance for the guilt of his church, his nation, and his class" (Jones, *Embodying Forgiveness*, 32).

Bibliography

Abraham, William J. "I Believe in One Holy, Catholic, and Apostolic Church." In *Nicene Christianity: The Future for a New Ecumenism*, edited by Christopher R. Seitz, 177–87. Grand Rapids: Brazos, 2001.

Airhart, Phyllis D. *A Church with the Soul of a Nation: Making and Remaking the United Church of Canada*. Montreal: McGill-Queen's University Press, 2014.

Althaus, Paul. *The Theology of Martin Luther*. Translated by Robert C. Schultz. Philadelphia: Fortress, 1966.

Anderson, Nigel. "Following Jesus: An Assessment of Dietrich Bonhoeffer's Theology of Discipleship." *Scottish Bulletin of Evangelical Theology* 24/2 (2006) 176–94.

Aquinas, Thomas. *Summa Theologica*. Translated by Fathers of the English Dominican Province. Claremont, CA: Coyote Canyon, 2010. Kindle.

Aristotle. *Nicomachean Ethics*. Translated by Terence Irwin. Indianapolis: Hackett, 1999.

Athanasius. *On the Incarnation*. Crestwood, NY: St. Vladimir's Seminary Press, 2003.

Badcock, Gary D. *The House Where God Lives: Renewing the Doctrine of the Church for Today*. Grand Rapids: Eerdmans, 2009.

Bader-Saye, Scott. *Church and Israel after Christendom: The Politics of Election*. Eugene, OR: Wipf & Stock, 1999.

———. "Haunted by the Jews: Hauerwas, Milbank, and the Decentered Diaspora Church." In *Unsettling Arguments: A Festschrift on the Occasion of Stanley Hauerwas's 70th Birthday*, edited by Charles S. Pinches et al., 191–209. Eugene, OR: Cascade, 2010.

Baillie, John. "Some Reflections on the Changing Theological Scene." *Union Seminary Quarterly Review* 12/2 (1957) 3–9.

Barker, H. Gaylon. "Bonhoeffer and the Church Struggle." *Concordia Journal* 35/4 (2009) 363–79.

Barnes, M. Craig. "Pastor, Not Friend." *Christian Century*, December 27, 2012. http://www.christiancentury.org/article/2012-12/pastor-not-friend.

Barnett, Victoria J. "The Bonhoeffer Legacy as Work-in-Progress: Reflections on a Fragmentary Series." In *Interpreting Bonhoeffer: Historical Perspectives, Emerging Issues*, edited by Clifford J. Green and Guy C. Carter, 93–100. Minneapolis: Fortress, 2013.

Barth, Karl. *The Christian Life: Church Dogmatics Volume IV, Part 4: Lecture Fragments*. Translated by Geoffrey W. Bromiley. London: T. & T. Clark, 2004.

———. "Church and State." In *Community, State and Church: Three Essays*, 101–48. Eugene, OR: Wipf & Stock, 1960.

———. *Church Dogmatics*. Edited by Geoffrey W. Bromiley and T. F. Torrance. 4 vols. London: T. & T. Clark, 2004.

———. *Deliverance to the Captives*. Translated by Marguerite Wieser. New York: Harper, 1961.

———. *Dogmatics in Outline*. Translated by G. T. Thomson. New York: Harper & Row, 1959.

———. *The Humanity of God*. Translated by Thomas Wieser and John Newton Thomas. Louisville: John Knox, 1960.

———. *Theology and Church: Shorter Writings 1920–1928*. Translated by Louise Pettibone Smith. London: SCM, 1962.

Barth, Karl, and John D. Godsey. *Karl Barth's Table Talk*. Edinburgh: Oliver & Boyd, 1963.

Barton, Stephen C., ed., *Holiness: Past and Present*. London: T. & T. Clark, 2003.

Bauckham, Richard. *God Crucified: Monotheism and Christology in the New Testament*. Grand Rapids: Eerdmans, 1999.

Bebis, George S. "Bonhoeffer and the Fathers of the Church: A Reply to Brightman." *Lutheran Quarterly* 24/3 (1972) 273–79.

Bell, Daniel M., Jr. "State and Civil Society." In *The Blackwell Companion to Political Theology*, edited by Peter C. Scott and William T. Cavanaugh, 423–38. Malden, MA: Blackwell, 2007.

Bender, Kimlyn J. *Confessing Christ for Church and World: Studies in Modern Theology*. Downers Grove, IL: IVP Academic, 2014.

———. *Karl Barth's Christological Ecclesiology*. Aldershot: Ashgate, 2005.

Benne, Robert. "The Lutheran Tradition and Public Theology." *Lutheran Theological Seminary Bulletin* 75/4 (1995) 15–26.

Bergen, Doris L. *Twisted Cross: The German Christian Movement in the Third Reich*. Chapel Hill: University of North Carolina Press, 1996.

Berkhof, Hendrik. *Christ and the Powers*. Translated by John Howard Yoder. Scottdale, PA: Herald, 1962.

Bethge, Eberhard. "Bonhoeffer's Christology and His 'Religionless Christianity.'" *Union Seminary Quarterly Review* 23/1 (1967) 61–77.

———. "Dietrich Bonhoeffer and the Jews." In *Ethical Responsibility: Bonhoeffer's Legacy to the Churches*, edited by John D. Godsey and Geffrey B. Kelly, 43–96. New York: Edwin Mellen, 1981.

———. *Dietrich Bonhoeffer: Man of Vision, Man of Courage*. Translated by Eric Mosbacher et al. New York: Harper and Row, 1970.

———. *Dietrich Bonhoeffer: Theologian, Christian, Man for His Times*. Edited by Victoria J. Barnett. Rev. ed. Minneapolis: Fortress, 2000.

———. *Friendship and Resistance: Essays on Dietrich Bonhoeffer*. Grand Rapids: Eerdmans, 1995.

Bethge, Renate. *Dietrich Bonhoeffer: A Brief Life*. Translated by K. C. Hanson. Minneapolis: Fortress, 2004.

———. "Reflections on My Uncle's Prison Letters." *Church and Society* 85/6 (1995) 23–33.

Bischoff, Paul O. "An Ecclesiology of the Cross for the World: The Church in the Theology of Dietrich Bonhoeffer." PhD diss., Lutheran School of Theology at Chicago, 2005.

———. "Participation: Ecclesial Praxis with a Crucified God for the World." *Journal for Christian Theological Reflection* 8 (2003) 19–36.

Bloom, Harold. *The American Religion: The Emergence of the Post-Christian Nation.* New York: Simon & Schuster, 1992.

Bockmuehl, Markus. "Ruminative Overlay: Matthew's Hauerwas." *Pro Ecclesia* 17/1 (2008) 20–28.

Boersma, Hans. *Heavenly Participation: The Weaving of a Sacramental Tapestry.* Grand Rapids: Eerdmans, 2011.

Bonhoeffer, Dietrich. *Act and Being: Transcendental Philosophy and Ontology in Systematic Theology.* Edited by Wayne Whitson Floyd Jr. Translated by H. Martin Rumscheidt. Vol. 2 of *Dietrich Bonhoeffer Works.* Minneapolis: Fortress, 1996.

———. *Barcelona, Berlin, New York: 1928–1931.* Edited by Clifford J. Green. Translated by Douglas W. Stott. Vol. 10 of *Dietrich Bonhoeffer Works.* Minneapolis: Fortress, 2008.

———. *Berlin: 1932–1933.* Edited by Larry L. Rasmussen. Translated by Isabel Best and David Higgins. Vol. 12 of *Dietrich Bonhoeffer Works.* Minneapolis: Fortress, 2009.

———. *Christ the Center.* Translated by Edwin H. Robertson. San Francisco: HarperSanFrancisco, 1978.

———. *The Collected Sermons of Dietrich Bonhoeffer.* Edited by Isabel Best. Translated by Douglas W. Stott. Minneapolis: Fortress Press, 2012.

———. *Conspiracy and Imprisonment: 1940–1945.* Edited by Mark S. Brocker. Translated by Lisa E. Dahill and Douglas W. Stott. Vol. 16 of *Dietrich Bonhoeffer Works.* Minneapolis: Fortress, 2006.

———. *The Cost of Discipleship.* Translated by R. H. Fuller. London: SCM, 1959.

———. *Creation and Fall: A Theological Exposition of Genesis 1–3.* Edited by John W. de Gruchy. Translated by Douglas Stephen Bax. Vol. 3 of *Dietrich Bonhoeffer Works.* Minneapolis: Fortress, 1997.

———. *Dietrich Bonhoeffer: Witness to Jesus Christ.* Edited by John W. de Gruchy. Minneapolis: Fortress, 1991.

———. *Discipleship.* Edited by Geffrey B. Kelly and John D. Godsey. Translated by Barbara Green and Reinhard Krauss. Vol. 4 of *Dietrich Bonhoeffer Works.* Minneapolis: Fortress, 2001.

———. *Ecumenical, Academic, and Pastoral Work: 1931–1932.* Edited by Victoria J. Barnett, Mark S. Brocker, and Michael B. Lukens. Translated by Anne Schmidt-Lange et al. Vol. 11 of *Dietrich Bonhoeffer Works.* Minneapolis: Fortress, 2012.

———. *Ethics.* Edited by Clifford J. Green. Translated by Reinhard Krauss et al. Vol. 6 of *Dietrich Bonhoeffer Works.* Minneapolis: Fortress, 2005.

———. *Fiction from Tegel Prison.* Edited by Clifford Green. Translated by Nancy Lukens. Vol. 7 of *Dietrich Bonhoeffer Works.* Minneapolis: Fortress, 1999.

———. *Die Finkenwalder Rundbriefe: Briefe und Texte von Dietrich Bonhoeffer und seinen Predigerseminaristen 1935–1946.* Edited by Eberhard Bethge et al. Gütersloh: Gütersloher, 2013.

———. *Letters and Papers from Prison.* Edited by Eberhard Bethge. Enl. ed. London: SCM, 1971.

———. *Letters and Papers from Prison*. Edited by Eberhard Bethge. Enl. ed. New York: Touchstone, 1997.

———. *Letters and Papers from Prison*. Edited by John W. de Gruchy. Translated by Isabel Best et al. Vol. 8 of *Dietrich Bonhoeffer Works*. Minneapolis: Fortress, 2009.

———. *Life Together* and *Prayerbook of the Bible*. Edited by Geffrey B. Kelly. Translated by Daniel W. Bloesch and James H. Burtness. Vol. 5 of *Dietrich Bonhoeffer Works*. Minneapolis: Fortress, 1996.

———. *London: 1933-1935*. Edited by Keith W. Clements. Translated by Isabel Best. Vol. 13 of *Dietrich Bonhoeffer Works*. Minneapolis: Fortress, 2007.

———. *No Rusty Swords: Letters, Lectures and Notes from the Collected Works (1928-1936)*. Edited by Edwin H. Robertson. Translated by John Bowden and Eberhard Bethge. London: Fount, 1977.

———. *Sanctorum Communio: A Theological Study of the Sociology of the Church*. Edited by Clifford J. Green. Translated by Reinhard Krauss and Nancy Lukens. Vol. 1 of *Dietrich Bonhoeffer Works*. Minneapolis: Fortress, 1998.

———. *A Testament to Freedom: The Essential Writings of Dietrich Bonhoeffer*. Edited by Geffrey B. Kelly and F. Burton Nelson. Rev. ed. New York: HarperOne, 1995.

———. *Theological Education at Finkenwalde: 1935-1937*. Edited by H. Gaylon Barker and Mark S. Brocker. Translated by Douglas W. Stott. Vol. 14 of *Dietrich Bonhoeffer Works*. Minneapolis: Fortress, 2013.

———. *Theological Education Underground: 1937-1940*. Edited by Victoria J. Barnett. Translated by Victoria J. Barnett et al. Vol. 15 of *Dietrich Bonhoeffer Works*. Minneapolis: Fortress, 2012.

———. *True Patriotism: Letters, Lectures and Notes from the Collected Works (1939-1945)*. Edited by Edwin H. Robertson. Translated by Edwin H. Robertson and John Bowden. London: Collins, 1973.

———. *The Way to Freedom: Letters, Lectures and Notes from the Collected Works (1935-1939)*. Edited by Edwin H. Robertson. Translated by Edwin H. Robertson and John Bowden. New York: Harper & Row, 1967.

———. *Worldly Preaching: Lectures on Homiletics*. Edited and translated by Clyde E. Fant. New York: Crossroad, 1991.

———. *The Young Bonhoeffer: 1918-1927*. Edited by Paul Duane Matheny et al. Translated by Mary C. Nebelsick and Douglas W. Stott. Vol. 9 of *Dietrich Bonhoeffer Works*. Minneapolis: Fortress, 2003.

———. *Zettlenotizen für eine "Ethik."* Supplementary vol. to *Ethik*, DBW 6. Edited by Ilse Tödt. Gütersloh: Chr. Kaiser/Gütersloher, 1993.

Bonhoeffer, Dietrich, and Maria von Wedemeyer. *Love Letters from Cell 92: The Correspondence between Dietrich Bonhoeffer and Maria von Wedemeyer*. Edited by Ruth-Alice von Bismark and Ulrich Kabitz. Translated by John Brownjohn. London: HarperCollins, 1994.

Bowlin, John. "Just Democracy, Just Church: Hauerwas and Coles on Radical Democracy and Christianity." *Scottish Journal of Theology* 64/1 (2011) 80–95.

Braaten, Carl E., and Robert W. Jenson, eds. *Marks of the Body of Christ*. Grand Rapids: Eerdmans, 1999.

———, eds. *Union with Christ: The New Finnish Interpretation of Luther*. Grand Rapids: Eerdmans, 1998.

Bretherton, Luke. *Christianity and Contemporary Politics: The Conditions and Possibilities of Faithful Witness*. Malden, MA: Wiley-Blackwell, 2010.

Brightman, Robert S. "Dietrich Bonhoeffer and Greek Patristic Theology: Some Points of Contact." *Lutheran Quarterly* 24/3 (1972) 261–72.
Brock, Brian. "Bonhoeffer and the Bible in Christian Ethics: Psalm 119, the Mandates, and Ethics as a 'Way.'" *Studies in Christian Ethics* 18/3 (2005) 7–29.
Buckley, James J., And David S. Yeago, eds. *Knowing the Triune God: The Work of the Spirit in the Practices of the Church.* Grand Rapids: Eerdmans, 2001.
Bush, George W. "President's Remarks to the Nation." Ellis Island, New York. September 11, 2002. http://georgewbush-whitehouse.archives.gov/news/releases/2002/09/20020911-3.html.
———. "Text of President Bush's State of the Union Adress." *Washington Post*, January 28, 2003. http://www.washingtonpost.com/wp-srv/onpolitics/transcripts/bushtext_012803.html.
Byassee, Jason. "Becoming Church: A Visit to the Ekklesia Project." *Christian Century*, September 7, 2004, 32–36, 38–39, 41.
Calvin, John. *Institutes of the Christian Religion.* Edited by John T. McNeill. Translated by Ford Lewis Battles. 2 vols. Louisville: Westminster John Knox, 1960.
Carter, Craig A. *Rethinking Christ and Culture: A Post-Christendom Perspective.* Grand Rapids: Brazos, 2006.
Cavnaugh, William T. *Being Consumed: Economics and Christian Desire.* Grand Rapids: Eerdmans, 2008.
———. "Can't We Just Argue? Hauerwas Troubles the Waters." *Christian Century*, August 1, 2001, 9–10.
———. "Church." In *The Blackwell Companion to Political Theology*, edited by Peter Scott and William T. Cavanaugh, 393–406. Malden, MA: Blackwell, 2007.
———. *The Myth of Religious Violence: Secular Ideology and the Roots of Modern Conflict.* Oxford: Oxford University Press, 2009.
———. "A Politics of Vulnerability: Hauerwas and Democracy." In *Unsettling Arguments: A Festschrift on the Occasion of Stanley Hauerwas's 70th Birthday*, edited by Charles S. Pinches et al., 89–111. Eugene, OR: Cascade, 2010.
———. "Stan the Man: A Thoroughly Biased Account of a Completely Unobjective Person." In *The Hauerwas Reader*, edited by John Berkman and Michael Cartwright, 17–32. Durham: Duke University Press, 2001.
———. *Torture and Eucharist: Theology, Politics, and the Body of Christ.* Oxford: Blackwell, 1998.
Chan, Simon. *Liturgical Theology: The Church as Worshipping Community.* Downers Grove, IL: InterVarsity, 2006.
Clements, Keith. "Dialogue with the Orthodox World: A Further Journey for Bonhoeffer." In *Bonhoeffer for a New Day: Theology in a Time of Transition*, edited by John W. deGruchy, 340–52. Grand Rapids: Eerdmans, 1997.
Coker, Joe L. "Peace and the Apocalypse: Stanley Hauerwas and Miroslav Volf on the Eschatological Basis for Christian Nonviolence." *Evangelical Quarterly* 71/3 (1999) 261–68.
Coles, Romand. *Beyond Gated Politics: Reflections for the Possibility of Democracy.* Minneapolis: University of Minnesota Press, 2005.
Congdon, David W. "Eschatologizing Apocalyptic: An Assessment of the Present Conversation on Pauline Apocalyptic." In *Apocalyptic and the Future of Theology: With and Beyond J. Louis Martyn*, edited by Joshua B. Davis and Douglas Harink, 118–36. Eugene, OR: Cascade, 2012.

Dahill, Lisa. "Jesus For *You*: A Feminist Reading of Bonhoeffer's Christology." *Currents in Theology and Mission* 34/4 (2007) 250–59.

———. "Probing the Will of God: Bonhoeffer and Discernment." *Dialog: A Journal of Theology* 41/1 (2002) 42–49.

Dahl, Nils. *Jesus in the Memory of the Early Church*. Minneapolis: Augsburg, 1976.

Davis, Joshua B., and Douglas Harink, eds. *Apocalyptic and the Future of Theology: With and Beyond J. Louis Martyn*. Eugene, OR: Cascade, 2012.

Day, Thomas I. "Conviviality and Common Sense: The Meaning of Christian Community for Dietrich Bonhoeffer." In *A Bonhoeffer Legacy: Essays in Understanding*, edited by A. J. Klassen, 213–36. Grand Rapids: Eerdmans, 1981.

Dean, Robert. Review of *Bonhoeffer the Assassin? Challenging the Myth, Recovering His Call to Peacemaking* by Mark Thiessen Nation et al. *Conrad Grebel Review* 32/2 (2014) 215–16.

De Gruchy, John W., ed. *Bonhoeffer for a New Day: Theology in a Time of Transition*. Grand Rapids: Eerdmans, 1997.

———, ed. *The Cambridge Companion to Dietrich Bonhoeffer*. Cambridge: Cambridge University Press, 1999.

———. *Daring, Trusting Spirit: Bonhoeffer's Friend Eberhard Bethge*. Minneapolis: Fortress, 2005.

———. "Dietrich Bonhoeffer (1906–1945)." In *The Blackwell Companion to the Theologians*, edited by Ian S. Markham, 2:233–52. Malden, MA: Wiley-Blackwell, 2009.

———. "Dietrich Bonhoeffer as Christian Humanist." In *Being Human, Becoming Human: Dietrich Bonhoeffer and Social Thought*, edited by Jens Zimmerman and Brian Gregor, 3–24. Cambridge: James Clarke, 2010.

———. "Eberhard Bethge: Interpreter Extraordinaire of Dietrich Bonhoeffer." *Modern Theology* 23/3 (2007) 349–68.

———. "What Kind of Pacifist? Bonhoeffer and the Path of Resistance." *Christian Century*, July 13, 2004, 26–27.

DeJonge, Michael P. *Bonhoeffer's Theological Formation: Berlin, Barth, and Protestant Theology*. Oxford: Oxford University Press, 2012.

———. "How to Read Bonhoeffer's Peace Statements: Or, Bonhoeffer Was a Lutheran and Not an Anabaptist." *Theology* 118/3 (2015) 162–71.

———. "The Presence of Christ in Karl Barth, Franz Hildebrandt and Dietrich Bonhoeffer." In *Dietrich Bonhoeffer Jahrbuch 4*, edited by Clifford Green et al., 96–115. Gütersloh: Gütersloher, 2010.

Di Berardino, Angelo, ed. *We Believe in One Holy Catholic and Apostolic Church*. Ancient Christian Doctrine 5. Downers Grove, IL: InterVarsity, 2010.

Doyle, Dennis M. *Communion Ecclesiology*. Maryknoll, NY: Orbis, 2000.

Dula, Peter, and Alex Sider. "Radical Democracy, Radical Ecclesiology." *Cross Currents* 55/4 (2006) 482–504.

Dulles, Avery. *Models of the Church*. Exp. ed. New York: Image, 2002.

Dumas, André. *Dietrich Bonhoeffer: Theologian of Reality*. Translated by Robert McAfee Brown. New York: MacMillan, 1971.

Elshtain, Jean Bethke. "Theologian: Christian Contrarian." *Time*, September 17, 2001, 74–75.

Engelhardt, H. Tristram, Jr. "The Belligerent Kingdom: Or: Why Authentic Christianity Is Even More Politically Incorrect Than Hauerwas Acknowledges." In *God, Truth, and Witness: Engaging Stanley Hauerwas*, edited by L. Gregory Jones et al., 193–211. Grand Rapids: Brazos, 2005.

Ericksen, Robert P. "Dietrich Bonhoeffer in History: Does Our Bonhoeffer Still Offend?" In *Interpreting Bonhoeffer: Historical Perspectives, Emerging Issues*, edited by Clifford J. Green and Guy C. Carter, 127–34. Minneapolis: Fortress, 2013.

Feil, Ernst. "Dietrich Bonhoeffer's Understanding of the World." In *A Bonhoeffer Legacy: Essays in Understanding*, edited by A.J. Klassen, 237–55. Grand Rapids: Eerdmans, 1981.

———. *The Theology of Dietrich Bonhoeffer*. Translated by Martin Rumscheidt. Philadelphia: Fortress, 1985.

Fergusson, David. "Another Way of Reading Stanley Hauerwas?" *Scottish Journal of Theology* 50/2 (1997) 242–49.

Field, David N. "Dietrich Bonhoeffer." In *Empire and the Christian Tradition: New Readings of Classical Theologians*, edited by Kwok Pui-lan et al., 389–403. Minneapolis: Fortress, 2007.

Finke, Roger, and Rodney Stark. *The Churching of America, 1776–1990: Winners and Losers in Our Religious Economy*. New Brunswick, NJ: Rutgers University Press, 1992.

Fletcher, Joseph. *Situation Ethics: The New Morality*. Louisville: Westminster John Knox, 1966.

Floyd, Wayne Whitson. "Dietrich Bonhoeffer." In *Modern Theologians: An Introduction to Christian Theology Since 1918*, edited by David Ford and Rachel Muers, 43–61. Malden, MA: Blackwell, 2005.

———. "The Search for an Ethical Sacrament: From Bonhoeffer to Critical Social Theory." *Modern Theology* 7/2 (1991) 175–93.

Ford, David F. "Bonhoeffer, Holiness and Ethics." In *Holiness: Past and Present*, edited by Stephen C. Barton, 361–80. London: T. & T. Clark, 2003.

———. *Self and Salvation: Being Transformed*. Cambridge: Cambridge University Press, 1999.

Fowl, Stephen. Review of *Unsettling Arguments: A Festschrift on the Occasion of Stanley Hauerwas's 70th Birthday*, edited by Charles R. Pinches et al. *Pro Ecclesia* 20/3 (2011) 320–25.

Franklin, Patrick. "Bonhoeffer's Missional Ecclesiology." *McMaster Journal of Theology and Ministry* 9 (2007–8) 96–128.

Frei, Hans W. *The Identity of Jesus Christ: The Hermeneutical Basis of Dogmatic Theology*. Eugene, OR: Wipf & Stock, 1997.

Frick, Peter, ed. *Bonhoeffer's Intellectual Formation: Theology and Philosophy in His Thought*. Tübingen: Mohr Siebeck, 2008.

Frobenius, Wolf. "Polyphony." In *The New Grove Dictionary of Music and Musicians*, edited by Stanley Sadie, 15:70–72. London: MacMillan, 1980.

Gaventa, Beverly Roberts. *Our Mother Saint Paul*. Louisville: Westminster John Knox, 2007.

Gaventa, Beverly Roberts, and Richard B. Hays, eds. *Seeking the Identity of Jesus: A Pilgrimage*. Grand Rapids: Eerdmans, 2008.

Gillespie, Michael Allen. *The Theological Origins of Modernity*. Chicago: University of Chicago Press, 2008.

Gingerich, Mark. "The Church as Kingdom: The Kingdom of God in the Writings of Stanley Hauerwas and John Howard Yoder." *Didaskalia* 19/1 (2008) 129–43.

Godsey, John D. "Barth and Bonhoeffer: The Basic Difference." *Quarterly Review* 7/1 (1987) 9–27.

———. "Dietrich Bonhoeffer and Christian Spirituality." In *Reflections on Bonhoeffer: Essays in Honor of F. Burton Nelson*, edited by Geffrey B. Kelly and C. John Weborg, 77–86. Chicago: Covenant, 1999.

———. *The Theology of Dietrich Bonhoeffer*. London: SCM, 1960.

Godsey, John D., and Geffrey B. Kelly, eds. *Ethical Responsibility: Bonhoeffer's Legacy to the Churches*. Toronto Studies in Theology 6. Lewiston, NY: Edwin Mellen, 1981.

Green, Clifford J. *Bonhoeffer: A Theology of Sociality*. Rev. ed. Grand Rapids: Eerdmans, 1999.

———. "Human Sociality and Christian Community." In *The Cambridge Companion to Dietrich Bonhoeffer*, edited by John W. de Gruchy, 113–33. Cambridge: Cambridge University Press, 1999.

———. "Pacifism and Tyrannicide: Bonhoeffer's Christian Peace Ethic." *Studies in Christian Ethics* 18/3 (2005) 31–47.

———. Review of *Dietrich Bonhoeffer: Reality and Resistance*, by Larry L. Rasmussen. *Conversations in Religion and Theology* 6/2 (2008) 155–65.

———. Review of *Performing the Faith: Bonhoeffer and the Practice of Nonviolence*, by Stanley Hauerwas. *Modern Theology* 21/4 (2005) 674–77.

———. "Sociality, Discipleship, and Worldly Theology in Bonhoeffer's Christian Humanism." In *Being Human, Becoming Human: Dietrich Bonhoeffer and Social Thought*, edited by Jens Zimmerman and Brian Gregor, 71–90. Cambridge: James Clarke, 2012.

Green, Clifford J., and Guy C. Carter, eds. *Interpreting Bonhoeffer: Historical Perspectives, Emerging Issues*. Minneapolis: Fortress, 2013.

Gregory, Brad S. *The Unintended Reformation: How a Religious Revolution Secularized a Society*. Cambridge, MA: Belknap, 2012.

Grenz, Stanley J., et al. *Pocket Dictionary of Theological Terms*. Downers Grove, IL: InterVarsity, 1999.

Griffiths, Paul J. "Witness and Conviction in *With the Grain of the Universe*." *Modern Theology* 19/1 (2003) 67–75.

Grobien, Gifford. "A Lutheran Understanding of Natural Law in the Three Estates." *Concordia Theological Quarterly* 73/3 (2009) 211–29.

Guder, Darrell L., ed. *Missional Church: A Vision for the Sending of the Church in North America*. Grand Rapids: Eerdmans, 1998.

Gunton, Colin, ed. *The Cambridge Companion to Christian Doctrine*. Cambridge: Cambridge University Press, 1997.

———. "The Church as a School of Virtue? Human Formation in Trinitarian Framework." In *Faithfulness and Fortitude: In Conversation with the Theological Ethics of Stanley Hauerwas*, edited by Mark Thiessen Nation and Samuel Wells, 211–31. Edinburgh: T. & T. Clark, 2000.

Gushee, David P. "Dietrich Bonhoeffer and the Evangelical Moment in American Public Life." *Studies in Christian-Jewish Relations* 2/1 (2007) 8–12.

Gustafson, James. "The Sectarian Temptation: Reflections on Theology, the Church and the University." *Proceedings of the Catholic Theological Society of America* 40 (1985) 83–94.

Gustavsson, Roger. "Hauerwas's *With the Grain of the Universe* and the Barthian Outlook." *Journal of Religious Ethics* 35/1 (2007) 25–86.

Hall, Christopher A. *Worshipping with the Church Fathers*. Downers Grove, IL: IVP Academic, 2009.

Hallie, Philip. *Lest Innocent Blood Be Shed: The Story of the Village of Le Chambon and How Goodness Happened There*. New York: HarperPerennial, 1994.

Hamill, Bruce. "Beyond Ecclesiocentricity: Navigating Between the Abstract and the Domesticated in Contemporary Ecclesiology." *International Journal of Systematic Theology* 14/3 (2012) 277–94.

Harink, Douglas. *1 and 2 Peter*. Brazos Theological Commentary on the Bible. Grand Rapids: Brazos, 2009.

———. "For or Against the Nations: Yoder and Hauerwas, What's the Difference?" *Toronto Journal of Theology* 17/1 (2001) 167–85.

———. *Paul among the Postliberals: Pauline Theology beyond Christendom and Modernity*. Grand Rapids: Brazos, 2003.

Harnack, Adolf von. *What is Christianity?* Translated by Thomas Bailey Saunders. 1957. Reprint, Philadelphia: Fortress, 1986.

Harper, Brad, and Paul Louis Metzger. *Exploring Ecclesiology: An Evangelical and Ecumenical Introduction*. Grand Rapids: Brazos, 2009.

Hart, David Bentley. *In the Aftermath: Provocations and Lament*. Grand Rapids: Eerdmans, 2009.

Harvey, Barry. "Augustine and Thomas Aquinas in the Theology of Dietrich Bonhoeffer." In *Bonhoeffer's Intellectual Formation: Theology and Philosophy in His Thought*, edited by Peter Frick, 11–29. Tübingen: Mohr Siebeck, 2008.

———. "The Body Politic of Christ: Theology, Social Analysis, and Bonhoeffer's Arcane Discipline." *Modern Theology* 13/3 (1997) 319–46.

———. "The Narrow Path: Sociality, Ecclesiology, and the Polyphony of Life in the Thought of Dietrich Bonhoeffer." In *Being Human, Becoming Human: Dietrich Bonhoeffer and Social Thought*, edited by Jens Zimmerman and Brian Gregor, 102–23. Cambridge: James Clarke, 2012.

Hauerwas, Stanley. *After Christendom: How the Church Is to Behave if Freedom, Justice, and a Christian Nation Are Bad Ideas*. 1991. Reprint, Nashville: Abingdon, 1999.

———. *Against the Nations: War and Survival in a Liberal Society*. Notre Dame: University of Notre Dame Press, 1992.

———. *Approaching the End: Eschatological Reflections on Church, Politics, and Life*. Grand Rapids: Eerdmans, 2013.

———. *A Better Hope: Resources for a Church Confronting Capitalism, Democracy, and Postmodernity*. Grand Rapids: Brazos, 2000.

———. *Character and the Christian Life: A Study in Theological Ethics*. 1975. Reprint, Notre Dame: University of Notre Dame Press, 2001.

———. "Christian Ethics in Jewish Terms: A Response to David Novak." *Modern Theology* 16/3 (2000) 293–99.

———. *Christian Existence Today: Essays on Church, World, and Living in Between*. 1988. Reprint, Grand Rapids: Brazos, 2001.

———. *A Community of Character: Toward a Constructive Christian Social Ethic*. Notre Dame: University of Notre Dame Press, 1981.

———. *Cross-Shattered Christ: Meditations on the Seven Last Words*. Grand Rapids: Brazos, 2004.

———. *A Cross-Shattered Church: Reclaiming the Theological Heart of Preaching*. Grand Rapids: Brazos, 2009.

———. "The Democratic Policing of Christianity." *Pro Ecclesia* 3/2 (1994) 215–31.

———. "Dietrich Bonhoeffer and John Howard Yoder." In *The Sermon on the Mount through the Centuries: From the Early Church to John Paul II*, edited by Jeffrey P. Greenman et al., 207–22. Grand Rapids: Brazos, 2007.

———. *Dispatches from the Front: Theological Engagements with the Secular*. Durham: Duke University Press, 1994.

———. *Disrupting Time: Sermons, Prayers, and Sundries*. Eugene, OR: Cascade, 2004.

———. "The Ethicist as Theologian." *Christian Century*, April 23, 1975, 408–12.

———. "Faculty Forum with Stanley Hauerwas: Conrad Grebel University (15 March 2002)." *Conrad Grebel Review* 20/3 (2002) 69–80.

———. "Faith Fires Back: A Pre-eminent Theological Ethicist Grapples with the Church, the State, the State of the Church, and the Responsibility of the Religious Community." *Duke Magazine* (January–February 2002). http://dukemagazine.duke.edu/article/faith-fires-back.

———. *God, Medicine, and Suffering*. Grand Rapids: Eerdmans, 1990.

———. *Hannah's Child: A Theologian's Memoir*. 2010. Reprint, Grand Rapids: Eerdmans, 2012.

———. *The Hauerwas Reader*. Edited by John Berkman and Michael Cartwright. Durham: Duke University Press, 2001.

———. "How to Be Caught By the Holy Spirit." ABC Religion and Ethics. November 14, 2013. http://www.abc.net.au/religion/articles/2013/11/14/3891054.htm.

———. "The Humanity of the Divine." *Cresset* 35/8 (1972) 16–17. http://www.valpo.edu/cresset/Hauerwas/June_1972.html.

———. "In a Time of War: An Exchange." *First Things* 120 (2002) 11–14.

———. *In Good Company: The Church as Polis*. Notre Dame: University of Notre Dame Press, 1995.

———. "Jews and the Eucharist." *Perspectives* 9/3 (1994) 14–15.

———. *Matthew*. Brazos Theological Commentary on the Bible. Grand Rapids: Brazos, 2006.

———. "No, This War Would not be Moral." *Time*, March 3, 2003, 45.

———. "On Doctrine and Ethics." In *The Cambridge Companion to Christian Doctrine*, edited by Colin E. Gunton, 21–40. Cambridge: Cambridge University Press, 1997.

———. "On Learning Simplicity in an Ambiguous Age." In *Barth, Barmen and the Confessing Church Today: Katallegete*, edited by James Y. Holloway, 131–38. Lewiston, NY: Edwin Mellen, 1995.

———. *The Peaceable Kingdom: A Primer in Christian Ethics*. Notre Dame: University of Notre Dame Press, 1983.

———. *Performing the Faith: Bonhoeffer and the Practice of Nonviolence*. Grand Rapids: Brazos, 2004.

———. *Prayers Plainly Spoken*. Downers Grove, IL: InterVarsity, 1999.

———. "Remembering How and What I Think: A Response to the *JRE* Articles on Hauerwas." *Journal of Religious Ethics* 40/2 (2012) 296–306.

———, ed. *Responsibility for Devalued Persons: Ethical Interactions between Society, the Family and the Retarded*. Springfield, IL: Charles C. Thomas, 1982.

———. *Sanctify Them in the Truth: Holiness Exemplified*. Nashville: Abingdon, 1998.

———. "September 11: A Pacifist Response: From Remarks Given at the University of Virginia, October 1, 2001." The Ekklesia Project. http://web.archive.org/

web/20050216040529/http://www.ekklesiaproject.org/resources/resource57/index.php?article=57.

———. *The State of the University: Academic Knowledges and the Knowledge of God*. Oxford: Blackwell, 2007.

———. *Suffering Presence: Theological Reflections on Medicine, the Mentally Handicapped, and the Church*. Notre Dame: University of Notre Dame Press, 1986.

———. "The Testament of Friends: How My Mind Has Changed." *Christian Century*, February 28, 1990, 212–16.

———. *Truthfulness and Tragedy: Further Investigations into Christian Ethics*. Notre Dame: University of Notre Dame Press, 1977.

———. *Unleashing the Scripture: Freeing the Bible from Captivity to America*. Nashville: Abingdon, 1993.

———. *Vision and Virtue: Essays in Christian Ethical Reflection*. 1974. Reprint, Notre Dame: University of Notre Dame Press, 1981.

———. *War and the American Difference: Theological Reflections on Violence and National Identity*. Grand Rapids: Baker Academic, 2011.

———. "What is Radical about the Ordinary?" *Scottish Journal of Theology* 64/1 (2011) 96–99.

———. "Where Would I Be Without Friends?" In *Faithfulness and Fortitude: In Conversation with the Theological Ethics of Stanley Hauerwas*, edited by Mark Thiessen Nation and Samuel Wells, 313–32. Edinburgh: T. & T. Clark, 2000.

———. *Wilderness Wanderings: Probing Twentieth-Century Theology and Philosophy*. Boulder, CO: Westview, 1997.

———. *With the Grain of the Universe: The Church's Witness and Natural Theology*. Grand Rapids: Brazos, 2001.

———. *Without Apology: Sermons for Christ's Church*. New York: Seabury, 2013.

———. *Working with Words: On Learning to Speak Christian*. Eugene, OR: Cascade, 2011.

Hauerwas, Stanley, et al., eds. *Growing Old in Christ*. Grand Rapids: Eerdmans, 2003.

Hauerwas, Stanley, et al., eds. *Theology without Foundations: Religious Practice and the Future of Theology*. Nashville: Abingdon, 1994.

Hauerwas, Stanley, et al., eds. *The Wisdom of the Cross: Essays in Honor of John Howard Yoder*. Grand Rapids: Eerdmans, 1999.

Hauerwas, Stanley, with Jason Barnhart. *Sunday Asylum: Being the Church in Occupied Territory*. N.p.: House Studio, 2011.

Hauerwas, Stanley, and Romand Coles. *Christianity, Democracy, and the Radical Ordinary: Conversations between a Radical Democrat and a Christian*. Eugene, OR: Cascade, 2008.

———. "'Long Live the Weeds and Wilderness Yet': Reflections on *A Secular Age*." *Modern Theology* 26/3 (2010) 349–62.

Hauerwas, Stanley, and Stanley Fish. "Miltonian Rebukes in an Age of Reason: A Conversation between Stanley Fish and Stanley Hauerwas." In *"God is Dead" and I Don't Feel So Good Myself*, edited by Andrew David et al., 108–19. Eugene, OR: Cascade, 2010.

Hauerwas, Stanley, and L. Gregory Jones, eds. *Why Narrative? Readings in Narrative Theology*. 1989. Reprint, Eugene, OR: Wipf & Stock, 1997.

Hauerwas, Stanley, and Frank Lentricchia, eds. *Dissent from the Homeland: Essays after September 11*. Durham: Duke University Press, 2003.

Hauerwas, Stanley, and Alasdair C. MacIntyre, eds. *Revisions: Changing Perspectives in Moral Philosophy.* Notre Dame: University of Notre Dame Press, 1983.

Hauerwas, Stanley, and Charles Pinches. *Christians among the Virtues: Theological Conversations with Ancient and Modern Ethics.* Notre Dame: University of Notre Dame Press, 1997.

Hauerwas, Stanley, and Samuel Wells, eds. *The Blackwell Companion to Christian Ethics.* Oxford: Blackwell, 2006.

Hauerwas, Stanley, and John H. Westerhoff, eds. *Schooling Christians: "Holy Experiments" in American Education.* Grand Rapids: Eerdmans, 1992.

Hauerwas, Stanley, and William H. Willimon. *Resident Aliens: Life in the Christian Colony.* Nashville: Abingdon, 1989.

———. *The Truth about God: The Ten Commandments in Christian Life.* Nashville: Abingdon, 1999.

———. *Where Resident Aliens Live: Exercises for Christian Practice.* Nashville: Abingdon, 1996.

Hauerwas, Stanley, and Jean Vanier. *Living Gently in a Violent World: The Prophetic Witness of Weakness.* Downers Grove, IL: InterVarsity, 2008.

Hawksley, Theodora. "The Freedom of the Spirit: The Pneumatological Point of Barth's Ecclesiological Minimalism." *Scottish Journal of Theology* 64/2 (2011) 180–94.

Haynes, Stephen R. *The Bonhoeffer Legacy: Post-Holocaust Perspectives.* Minneapolis: Fortress, 2006.

———. *The Bonhoeffer Phenomenon: Portraits of a Protestant Saint.* Minneapolis: Fortress, 2004.

Hays, Richard B. *The Faith of Jesus Christ: The Narrative Substructure of Galatians 3:14—4:11.* Grand Rapids: Eerdmans, 2002.

———. *The Moral Vision of the New Testament: Community, Cross, Creation; A Contemporary Introduction to New Testament Ethics.* San Francisco: Harper, 1996.

Healy, Nicholas M. *Church, World and the Christian Life: Practical-Prophetic Ecclesiology.* Cambridge: Cambridge University Press, 2000.

———. *Hauerwas: A (Very) Critical Introduction.* Grand Rapids: Eerdmans, 2014.

———. "Karl Barth's Ecclesiology Reconsidered" *Scottish Journal of Theology* 57/3 (2004) 287–99.

———."The Logic of Karl Barth's Ecclesiology: Analysis, Assessment and Proposed Modifications." *Modern Theology* 10/3 (1994) 253–70.

———. "Practices and the New Ecclesiology: Misplaced Concreteness?" *International Journal of Systematic Theology* 5/3 (2003) 287–308.

Herdt, Jennifer A. "Hauerwas among the Virtues." *Journal of Religious Ethics* 40/2 (2012) 202–27.

Heuser, Stefan. "The Cost of Citizenship: Disciple and Citizen in Bonhoeffer's Political Ethics." *Studies in Christian Ethics* 18/3 (2005) 49–69.

Higton, Mike. *Christ, Providence and History: Hans W. Frei's Public Theology.* London: T. & T. Clark, 2004.

Hill, Wesley. "'The Full This-Worldliness of Life': On Dietrich Bonhoeffer." *Books and Culture* (2014). http://www.booksandculture.com/articles/2014/sepoct/full-this-worldliness-of-life.html?paging=off.

Hindmarsh, Bruce. "Is Evangelical Ecclesiology an Oxymoron? A Historical Perspective." In *Evangelical Ecclesiology: Reality or Illusion?*, edited by John G. Stackhouse Jr., 15–38. Grand Rapids: Baker Academic, 2003.

Hobson, Theo. "Ecclesiological Fundamentalism." *Modern Believing* 45/4 (2004) 48–59.
Holland, Scott. "The Problems and Prospects of a 'Sectarian Ethic': A Critique of the Hauerwas Reading of the Jesus Story." *Conrad Grebel Review* 10/2 (1992) 157–68.
Holloway, James Y., ed. *Barth, Barmen and the Confessing Church Today*. Lewiston, NY: Edwin Mellen, 1992.
Holmes, Christopher. "'The Indivisible Whole of God's Reality': On the Agency of Jesus in Bonhoeffer's *Ethics*." *International Journal of Systematic Theology* 12/3 (2010) 283–301.
———. "Wholly Human and Wholly Divine, Humiliated and Exalted: Some Reformed Explorations in Bonhoeffer's Christology Lectures." *Scottish Bulletin of Evangelical Theology* 25/2 (2007) 210–25.
Hughes, Richard T. *Christian America and the Kingdom of God*. Urbana: University of Illinois Press, 2009.
Hunsberger, George H. "Evangelical Conversion toward a Missional Ecclesiology." In *Evangelical Ecclesiology: Reality or Illusion?*, edited by John G. Stackhouse Jr., 105–34. Grand Rapids: Baker Academic, 2003.
Hunsinger, George. *The Eucharist and Ecumenism: Let Us Keep the Feast*. Cambridge: Cambridge University Press, 2008.
———. "To Hauerwas: On Learning Faithfulness in a Fallen World." In *Barth, Barmen, and the Confessing Church Today: Katallegete*, edited by James Y. Holloway, 252–56. Lewiston, NY: Edwin Mellen, 1995.
Huntemann, George. *Dietrich Bonhoeffer: An Evangelical Reassessment*. Translated by Todd Huizinga. Grand Rapids: Baker, 1996.
Hurtado, Larry W. *Lord Jesus Christ: Devotion to Jesus in Earliest Christianity*. Grand Rapids: Eerdmans, 2003.
Hütter, Reinhard L. *Bound to Be Free: Evangelical Catholic Engagements in Ecclesiology, Ethics, and Ecumenism*. Grand Rapids: Eerdmans, 2004.
———. "The Church: Midwife of History or Witness of the Eschaton?" *Journal of Religious Ethics*. 18/1 (1990) 27–54.
———. "Ecclesial Ethics, the Church's Vocation, and Paraclesis." *Pro Ecclesia* 2/4 (1993) 433–50.
———. *Suffering Divine Things: Theology as Church Practice*. Translated by Doug Stott. Grand Rapids: Eerdmans, 2000.
Irenaeus. *Against Heresies*. In *The Apostolic Fathers, Justin Martyr, Irenaeus*, edited by Alexander Roberts and James Donaldson, 833–1391. Ante-Nicene Fathers 1. Grand Rapids: Christian Classic Ethereal Library, 2001. Adobe PDF ebook.
Jenson, Matt. "Real Presence: Contemporaneity in Bonhoeffer's *Christology*." *Scottish Journal of Theology* 58/2 (2005) 143–60.
Jenson, Robert W. "How the World Lost its Story." *First Things* 36 (1993) 19–24.
———. "Luther's Contemporary Theological Significance." In *The Cambridge Companion to Martin Luther*, edited by Donald K. McKim, 272–88. Cambridge: Cambridge University Press, 2003.
———. Review of *After Christendom*, by Stanley Hauerwas. *First Things* 25 (1992) 49–51.
———. Review of *Christ, History and Apocalyptic: The Politics of Christian Mission*, by Nathan R. Kerr. *Pro Ecclesia* 20/3 (2011) 310–12.
———. *Systematic Theology*. Vol. 1, *The Triune God*. New York: Oxford Varsity, 1997.
———. "You Wonder Where the Spirit Went." *Pro Ecclesia* 2/3 (1993) 296–304.

John Paul II. *Evangelium Vitae*. In *The Encyclicals of John Paul II*, edited by J. Michael Miller, 791–894. Huntington, IN: Our Sunday Visitor, 1996.

———. *Veritatis Splendor*. In *The Encyclicals of John Paul II*, edited by J. Michael Miller, 673–771. Huntington, IN: Our Sunday Visitor, 1996.

Johnson, Keith L., and Timothy Larsen, eds. *Bonhoeffer, Christ and Culture*. Downers Grove, IL: InterVarsity, 2013.

Johnson, Kelly S. "Worshipping in Spirit and Truth." In *Unsettling Arguments: A Festschrift on the Occasion of Stanley Hauerwas's 70th Birthday*, edited by Charles S. Pinches et al., 300–314. Eugene, OR: Cascade, 2010.

Johnson, Luke Timothy. "Matthew or Stanley? Pick One." *Pro Ecclesia* 17/1 (2008) 29–34.

Jones, L. Gregory. *Embodying Forgiveness: A Theological Analysis*. Grand Rapids: Eerdmans, 1995.

———. *Transformed Judgment: Toward a Trinitarian Account of the Moral Life*. Notre Dame: University of Notre Dame Press, 1990.

Jones, L. Gregory, et al., eds. *God, Truth, and Witness: Engaging Stanley Hauerwas*. Grand Rapids: Brazos, 2005.

Kallenberg, Brad J. "The Strange New World in the Church: A Review Essay of *With the Grain of the Universe* by Stanley Hauerwas." *Journal of Religious Ethics* 32/1 (2004) 197–218.

Kasper, Walter. *Jesus the Christ*. New York: Paulinist, 1977.

Kaye, Bruce N. *Conflict and the Practice of the Christian Faith: The Anglican Experiment*. Eugene, OR: Cascade, 2009.

Kelly, Geffrey B. "Kierkegaard as 'Antidote' and as Impact on Dietrich Bonhoeffer's Concept of Christian Discipleship." In *Bonhoeffer's Intellectual Formation: Theology and Philosophy in His Thought*, edited by Peter Frick, 145–65. Tübingen: Mohr Siebeck, 2008.

Kelly, Geffrey B., and F. Burton Nelson. *The Cost of Moral Leadership: The Spirituality of Dietrich Bonhoeffer*. Grand Rapids: Eerdmans, 2003.

Kelly, Geffrey B., and C. John Weborg, eds. *Reflections on Bonhoeffer: Essays in Honor of F. Burton Nelson*. Chicago: Covenant, 1999.

Kemp, Walter H. "The 'Polyphony of Life': References to Music in Bonhoeffer's *Letters and Papers from Prison*." In *Vita Laudanda: Essays in Memory of Ulrich S. Leupold*, edited by Erich R.W. Schultz, 137–53. Waterloo, ON: Wilfrid Laurier University Press, 1976.

Kenneson, Philip D. *Beyond Sectarianism: Re-Imagining Church and World*. Harrisburg, PA: Trinity, 1999.

Kenneson, Phillip D., and James L. Street. *Selling Out the Church: The Dangers of Church Marketing*. Eugene, OR: Cascade, 2003.

Kerr, Nathan. *Christ, History and Apocalyptic: The Politics of Christian Mission*. Eugene, OR: Cascade, 2009.

Kirkpatrick, Matthew D. *Attacks on Christendom in a World Come of Age: Kierkegaard, Bonhoeffer, and the Question of "Religionless Christianity."* Eugene, OR: Pickwick, 2011.

Klassen, A. J., ed. *A Bonhoeffer Legacy: Essays in Understanding*. Grand Rapids: Eerdmans, 1981.

Kotsko, Adam. "Objective Spirit and Continuity in the Theology of Dietrich Bonhoeffer." *Philosophy and Theology* 17/1–2 (2005) 17–31.

Krötke, Wolf. "Dietrich Bonhoeffer and Martin Luther." In *Bonhoeffer's Intellectual Formation: Theology and Philosophy in His Thought*, edited by Peter Frick, 53–82. Tübingen: Mohr Siebeck, 2008.

Lapide, Pinchas. "Bonhoeffer und das Judentum." In *Verspieltes Erbe: Dietrich Bonhoeffer und der deutsch Nachkriegsprotestantismus*, edited by Ernst Feil, 116–30. Munich: Kaiser, 1979.

L'Arche Canada. "What is L'Arche?" http://www.larche.ca/en/larche/what_is_larche.

Larsen, Timothy. "The Evangelical Reception of Dietrich Bonhoeffer." In *Bonhoeffer, Christ and Culture*, edited by Keith L. Johnson and Timothy Larsen, 39–57. Downers Grove, IL: InterVarsity, 2013.

Lawson, James Barry. "Theological Formation in the Church of the 'Last Men and Women.'" *Ecclesiology* 9/3 (2013) 335–46.

Lee, Nathaniel Jung-Chul. Review of *Christ, History and Apocalyptic: The Politics of Christian Mission*, by Nathan R. Kerr. *Political Theology* 13/2 (2012) 249–51.

Lee, Phillip J. *Against the Protestant Gnostics*. New York: Oxford University Press, 1987.

Lehenbauer, Joel D. "The Theology of Stanley Hauerwas." *Concordia Theological Quarterly* 76/1–2 (2012) 157–74.

Lehmann, Paul L. "Faith and Worldliness in Bonhoeffer's Thought." *Union Seminary Quarterly Review* 23/1 (1967) 31–44.

Leithart, Peter J. *Between Babel and Beast: America and Empires in Biblical Perspective*. Eugene, OR: Cascade, 2012.

———. *Defending Constantine: The Twilight of an Empire and the Dawn of Christendom*. Downers Grove, IL: IVP Academic, 2010.

Lienhard, Marc. *Luther: Witness to Jesus Christ: Stages and Themes of the Reformer's Christology*. Translated by Edwin H. Robertson. Minneapolis: Augsburg, 1982.

Lindbeck, George A. *The Church in a Postliberal Age*. Grand Rapids: Eerdmans, 2002.

———. *The Nature of Doctrine: Religion and Theology in a Postliberal Age*. Louisville: Westminster John Knox, 1984.

Lockley, Harold. *Dietrich Bonhoeffer: His Ethics and Its Value for Today*. London: Phoenix, 1993.

Lockwood, Lewis. "Cantus firmus." In *The New Grove Dictionary of Music and Musicians*, edited by Stanley Sadie, 3:738–41. London: MacMillan, 1980.

Lohse, Bernhard. *Martin Luther's Theology: Its Historical and Systematic Development*. Translated by Ray A. Harrisville. Minneapolis: Fortress, 1999.

Lovin, Robin W. "The Christian and the Authority of the State: Bonhoeffer's Reluctant Revisions." *Journal of Theology for Southern Africa* 34 (1981) 32–48.

———. *Christian Faith and Public Choices: The Social Ethics of Barth, Brunner, and Bonhoeffer*. Philadelphia: Fortress, 1984.

Luther, Martin. *Luther's Works*. Vol. 1, *Lectures on Genesis: Chapters 1–5*. Edited by Jaroslav Pelikan. Saint Louis: Concordia, 1958.

———. *Martin Luther's Basic Theological Writings*. Edited by Timothy F. Lull. Minneapolis: Fortress, 1989.

———. "On the Bondage of the Will." In *Luther and Erasmus: Free Will and Salvation*, edited and translated by E. Gordon Rupp and Philip S. Watson, 99–334. Philadelphia: Westminster, 1969.

MacIntyre, Alasdair C. *After Virtue: A Study in Moral Theology*. 3rd ed. Notre Dame: University of Notre Dame Press, 2007.

Malesic, Jonathan. *Secret Faith in the Public Square: An Argument for the Concealment of Christian Identity*. Grand Rapids: Brazos, 2009.

Mallard, William. "*Totus Chrisus*, the Whole Christ." In *Augustine through the Ages: An Encyclopedia*, edited by Allan Fitzgerald and John C. Cavadini, 468–70. Grand Rapids: Eerdmans, 1999.

Mangina, Joseph L. "After Dogma: Reinhard Hütter's Challenge to Contemporary Theology: A Review Essay" *International Journal of Systematic Theology* 2/3 (2000) 330–46.

———. "Bearing the Marks of Jesus: The Church in the Economy of Salvation in Barth and Hauerwas." *Scottish Journal of Theology* 52/3 (1999) 269–305.

———. "Church, Cross, and *Caritas*, Or, Why Congregationalism Is Not Enough: A Reply to Stanley Hauerwas." *Pro Ecclesia* 22/4 (2013) 437–54.

———. "Hidden from the Wise, Revealed to Infants: Stanley Hauerwas's Commentary on Matthew." *Pro Ecclesia* 17/1 (Winter 2008) 13–19.

———. *Karl Barth: Theologian of Christian Witness*. Louisville: Westminster John Knox, 2004.

Mannermaa, Tuomo. "Justification and Theosis in Lutheran-Orthodox Perspective." In *Union with Christ: The New Finnish Interpretation of Luther*, edited by Carl E. Braaten and Robert W. Jenson, 25–41. Grand Rapids: Eerdmans, 1998.

Marsh, Charles. "In Defense of a Self: The Theological Search for a Postmodern Identity." *Scottish Journal of Theology* 55/3 (2002) 253–82.

———. *Reclaiming Dietrich Bonhoeffer: The Promise of His Theology*. Oxford: Oxford University Press, 1994.

———. *Strange Glory: A Life of Dietrich Bonhoeffer*. New York: Knopf, 2014.

Marshall, Bruce D. "The Church in the Gospel." *Pro Ecclesia* 1/1 (1992) 27–41.

———. *Trinity and Truth*. Cambridge: Cambridge University Press, 2000.

Marty, Martin E. *Dietrich Bonhoeffer's Letters and Papers from Prison: A Biography*. Princeton: Princeton University Press, 2011.

———, ed. *The Place of Bonhoeffer: Problems and Possibilities in His Thought*. New York: Association, 1962.

Martyn, J. Louis. "The Apocalyptic Gospel in Galatians." *Interpretation* 54/3 (2000) 246–66.

———. *Galatians*. Anchor Bible 33A. New York: Doubleday, 1997.

———. *Theological Issues in the Letters of Paul*. Nashville: Abingdon, 1997.

Matheson, Peter. *The Church and the Third Reich: A Documentary Account of Christian Resistance and Complicity during the Nazi Era*. Edinburgh: T. & T. Clark, 1981.

Matthewes, Charles T. "Appreciating Hauerwas: One Hand Clapping." *Anglican Theological Review* 82/2 (2000) 343–64.

Matthews, John. W. *Anxious Souls Will Ask . . . : The Christ-Centered Spirituality of Dietrich Bonhoeffer*. Grand Rapids: Eerdmans, 2005.

———. "Responsible Sharing of the Mystery of Christian Faith: *Disciplina Arcani* in the Life and Theology of Dietrich Bonhoeffer." *Dialog* 25/1 (1986) 19–25.

McBride, Jennifer M. "Christ Existing as Concrete Community Today." *Theology Today* 71/1 (2014) 92–105.

———. *The Church for the World: A Theology of Public Witness*. Oxford: Oxford University Press, 2012.

———. "Thinking within the Movement of Bonhoeffer's Theology: Towards a Christological Reinterpretation of Repentance." In *Religion, Religionlessness and*

Contemporary Western Culture, edited by Stephen Plant and Ralf K Wüstenberg, 91–109. Frankfurt: Peter Lang, 2008.
McClendon, James Wm., Jr. *Biography as Theology: How Life Stories Can Remake Today's Theology*. 1974. Reprint, Eugene, OR: Wipf & Stock, 2002.
———. *Systematic Theology*. Vol. 1, *Ethics*. 2nd ed. Nashville: Abingdon, 2002.
McFague, Sallie. *Models of God: Theology for an Ecological, Nuclear Age*. Philadelphia: Fortress, 1987.
McGrath, Alister E. *Christian Theology: An Introduction*. 5th ed. Malden, MA: Wiley-Blackwell, 2011.
McIntosh, Mark A. *Divine Teaching: An Introduction to Christian Theology*. Malden, MA: Blackwell, 2008.
McKim, Donald K., ed. *The Cambridge Companion to Martin Luther*. Cambridge: Cambridge University Press, 2003.
Meilaender, Gilbert. "Time for Love: The Place of Marriage and Children in the Thought of Stanley Hauerwas." *Journal of Religious Ethics* 40/2 (2012) 250–61.
Metaxas, Eric. *Bonhoeffer: Pastor, Martyr, Prophet, Spy*. Nashville: Thomas Nelson, 2010.
Metzger, Paul Louis. "Christ, Culture, and the Sermon on the Mount Community." *Ex Auditu* 23 (2007) 22–46.
Migliore, Daniel L. *Faith Seeking Understanding: An Introduction to Christian Theology*. Grand Rapids: Eerdmans, 1991.
Moberly, Jennifer. *The Virtue of Bonhoeffer's Ethics: A Study of Dietrich Bonhoeffer's Ethics in Relation to Virtue Ethics*. Eugene, OR: Pickwick, 2013. Kindle.
Moltmann, Jürgen, and Jürgen Weissbach. *Two Studies in the Theology of Bonhoeffer*. Translated by Reginald H. Fuller and Ilse Fuller. New York: Scribner, 1967.
Moses, John A. *The Reluctant Revolutionary: Dietrich Bonhoeffer's Collision with Prusso-German History*. New York: Berghahn, 2009.
Müller, Hanfried. *Von der Kirche zur Welt: Ein Beitrag zu der Beziehung des Wort Gottes auf die Societas in Dietrich Bonhoeffers theologische Entwicklung*. Leipzing and Hamburg-Bergstedt: Reich, 1966.
Nation, Mark K. "'Pacifist and Enemy of the State': Bonhoeffer's 'Straight and Unbroken Course' from Costly Discipleship to Conspiracy." *Journal of Theology for Southern Africa* 77 (1991) 61–77.
Nation, Mark Thiessen. "'A Blanket License to Commit Evil Acts?' A Fresh Examination of Bonhoeffer's Christological Framing of *Ethics*." *Perspectives in Religious Studies* 40/2 (2013) 143–53.
———. "The First Word Christians Have to Say about Violence is 'Church': On Bonhoeffer, Baptists, and Becoming a Peace Church." In *Faithfulness and Fortitude: In Conversation with the Theological Ethics of Stanley Hauerwas*, edited by Mark Thiessen Nation and Samuel Wells, 83–115. Edinburgh: T. & T. Clark, 2000.
———. "Stanley Hauerwas: Where Would We Be without Him?" In *Faithfulness and Fortitude: In Conversation with the Theological Ethics of Stanley Hauerwas*, edited by Mark Thiessen Nation and Samuel Wells, 19–36. Edinburgh: T. & T. Clark, 2000.
Nation, Mark Thiessen, et al., *Bonhoeffer the Assassin? Challenging the Myth, Recovering His Call to Peacemaking*. Grand Rapids: Baker Academic, 2013.

Nation, Mark Thiessen, and Samuel Wells, eds. *Faithfulness and Fortitude: In Conversation with the Theological Ethics of Stanley Hauerwas*. Edinburgh: T & T Clark, 2000.

Nelson, F. Burton. "The Relationship of Jean Lasserre to Dietrich Bonhoeffer's Peace Concerns in the Struggle of Church and Culture." *Union Seminary Quarterly Review* 40/1-2 (1985) 71-84.

Nessan, Craig L. "What if the Church Really is the Body of Christ?" *Dialog* 51/1 (2012) 43-52.

Neuhaus, John Richard. *Death on a Friday Afternoon: Meditations on the Last Words of Jesus from the Cross*. New York: Basic Books, 2000.

Neuhaus, John Richard, and James A. Nuechterlein. "In a Time of War." *First Things* 118 (2011) 11-17.

Nicolaisen, Carsten. "Concerning the History of the Bethel Confession." In *Berlin: 1932-1933*, edited by Larry L. Rasmussen, 509-13. Translated by Isabel Best and David Higgins. Vol. 12 of *Dietrich Bonhoeffer Works*. Minneapolis: Fortress, 2009.

Niebuhr, H. Richard. *Christ and Culture*. 50th ann. ed. New York: Harper, 2001.

Niebuhr, Reinhold. *Moral Man and Immoral Society: A Study in Ethics and Politics*. New York: Scribner, 1960.

Nissen, Ulrik Becker. "Letting Reality Become Real: On Mystery and Reality in Dietrich Bonhoeffer's Ethics." *Journal of Religious Ethics* 39/2 (2011) 321-43.

Noll, Mark. *A History of Christianity in the United States and Canada*. Grand Rapids: Eerdmans, 1992.

Northcott, Michael. *An Angel Directs the Storm: Apocalyptic Religion and American Empire*. New York: Tauris, 2004.

———. "'An Angel Directs the Storm': The Religious Politics of American Neoconservatism." *Political Theology* 5/2 (2004) 137-58.

———. "Reading Hauerwas in the Cornbelt: The Demise of the American Dream and the Return of Liturgical Politics." *Journal of Religious Ethics* 40/2 (2012) 262-80.

———. "Who Am I? Human Identity and the Spiritual Disciplines in the Witness of Dietrich Bonhoeffer." In *Who Am I? Bonhoeffer's Theology Through His Poetry*, edited by Bernd Wannenwetsch, 11-29. London: T. & T. Clark, 2009.

Nullens, Patrick. "Dietrich Bonhoeffer: A Third Way of Christian Social Engagement." *European Journal of Theology* 20/1 (2011) 60-69.

Ochs, Peter. *Another Reformation: Postliberal Christianity and the Jews*. Grand Rapids: Baker Academic, 2011.

O'Donovan, Oliver. *Ethics as Theology*. Vol. 1, *Self, World, and Time*. Grand Rapids: Eerdmans, 2013.

———. *The Ways of Judgment: The Bampton Lectures, 2003*. Grand Rapids: Eerdmans, 2005.

O'Regan, Cyril. *Gnostic Return in Modernity*. Albany: State University of New York Press, 2001.

Ott, Heinrich. *Reality and Faith: The Theological Legacy of Dietrich Bonhoeffer*. Translated by Alex A. Morrison. London: Lutterworth, 1971.

Pangritz, Andreas. "Dietrich Bonhoeffer: 'Within, not Outside, the Barthian Movement." In *Bonhoeffer's Intellectual Formation: Theology and Philosophy in His Thought*, edited by Peter Frick, 245-82. Tübingen: Mohr Siebeck, 2008.

———. *Karl Barth in the Theology of Dietrich Bonhoeffer*. Translated by Barbara and Martin Rumscheidt. Grand Rapids: Eerdmans, 2000.

———. "'Who is Jesus Christ, for us, today?'" In *The Cambridge Companion to Dietrich Bonhoeffer*, edited by John W. de Gruchy, 134–53. Cambridge: Cambridge University Press, 1999.
Pannenberg, Wolfhart. *Jesus—God and Man*. Translated by Lewis L. Wilkins and Duane E. Preibe. 2nd ed. Philadelphia: Westminster, 1977.
Pfeiffer, Hans. "An Aesthetic Voyage: Dietrich Bonhoeffer's Gradual Approach towards Full Reality and Eberhard Bethge's Contribution to It." *Journal of Theology for Southern Africa* 127 (2007) 63–81.
———. "Cultural Elements in Theology and Language: Translation as Interpretation." In *Interpreting Bonhoeffer: Historical Perspectives, Emerging Issues*, edited by Clifford J. Green and Guy C. Carter, 61–69. Minneapolis: Fortress, 2013.
Phillips, John A. *Christ for Us in the Theology of Dietrich Bonhoeffer*. New York: Harper & Row, 1967.
Pinches, Charles. "Considering Stanley Hauerwas." *Journal of Religious Ethics* 40/2 (2012) 193–201.
———. "Stout, Hauerwas, and the Body of America." *Political Theology* 8/1 (2007) 9–31.
Pinches, Charles R., et al., eds. *Unsettling Arguments: A Festschrift on the Occasion of Stanley Hauerwas's 70th Birthday*. Eugene, OR: Cascade, 2010.
Placher, William C. *A History of Christian Theology: An Introduction*. Louisville: Westminster John Knox, 1983.
Plant, Stephen. *Bonhoeffer*. London: Continuum, 2004.
———. "The Sacrament of Ethical Reality: Dietrich Bonhoeffer on Ethics for Christian Citizens." *Studies in Christian Ethics* 18/3 (2005) 71–87.
Pugh, Jeffrey C. *Religionless Christianity: Dietrich Bonhoeffer in Troubled Times*. London: T. & T. Clark, 2008.
Quirk, Michael J. "Beyond Sectarianism?" *Theology Today* 44/1 (1987) 78–86.
Quispel, Gilles. *Gnostic Studies*. Istanbul: Nederlands Historisch-Archaeological Instituut in het Nabije Oosten, 1974.
Radner, Ephraim. *A Brutal Unity: The Spiritual Politics of the Christian Church*. Waco: Baylor University Press, 2012.
———. *The End of the Church: A Pneumatology of Christian Division in the West*. Grand Rapids: Eerdmans, 1998.
Rasmussen, Larry L. *Dietrich Bonhoeffer: Reality and Resistance*. Louisville: Westminster John Knox, 2005.
———. *Earth Community, Earth Ethics*. Maryknoll, NY: Orbis, 1996.
———. *Earth-Honoring Faith: Religious Ethics in a New Key*. New York: Oxford University Press, 2013.
———. "The Ethics of Responsible Action." In *The Cambridge Companion to Dietrich Bonhoeffer*, edited by John W. de Gruchy, 206–25. Cambridge: Cambridge University Press, 1999.
———. "Response to Clifford Green." *Conversations in Religion and Theology* 6/2 (2008) 165–73.
Rasmusson, Arne. *The Church as Polis: From Political Theology to Theological Politics as Exemplified by Jürgen Moltmann and Stanley Hauerwas*. Notre Dame: University of Notre Dame Press, 1995.
Reimer, A. James. "Hauerwas: Why I'm a Reluctant Convert to His Theology." *Conrad Grebel Review* 20/3 (2002) 5–16.

Reno, R. R. *In the Ruins of the Church: Sustaining Faith in an Age of Diminished Christianity.* Grand Rapids: Brazos, 2002.

———. "Stanley Hauerwas." In *The Blackwell Companion to Political Theology*, edited by Peter Scott and William T. Cavanaugh, 302–16. Malden, MA: Blackwell, 2007.

———. "Stanley Hauerwas and the Liberal Protestant Project." *Modern Theology* 28/2 (2012) 320–26.

Richardson, Neville. "*Sanctorum Communio* in a Time of Reconstruction? Theological Pointers for the Church in South Africa." *Journal of Theology for Southern Africa* 127 (2007) 96–115.

Robertson, Edwin. *Christians against Hitler.* London: SCM, 1962.

———. *The Persistent Voice of Dietrich Bonhoeffer.* Atworth, UK: Eagle, 2005.

Robertson, Pat. "Pat Robertson Clarifies His Comments." Christian Broadcasting Network, August 24, 2005. http://www.cbn.com/about/pressrelease_hugochavez.aspx.

Robinson, John A. T. *Honest to God.* Philadelphia: Fortress, 1963.

Robinson, Marilynne. "Dietrich Bonhoeffer." In *The Death of Adam: Essays on Modern Thought*, 108–25. Boston: Houghton Mifflin, 1998.

Rogers, Eugene F., Jr. *After the Spirit: A Constructive Pneumatology from Resources Outside the Modern West.* Grand Rapids: Eerdmans, 2005.

Rumscheidt, Martin. "The Formation of Bonhoeffer's Theology." In *The Cambridge Companion to Dietrich Bonhoeffer*, edited by John W. de Gruchy, 50–70. Cambridge: Cambridge University Press, 1999.

Schlabach, Gerald W. "Continuity and Sacrament, or Not: Hauerwas, Yoder, and Their Deep Difference." *Journal of the Society of Christian Ethics* 27/2 (2007) 171–207.

Schliesser, Christine. *Everyone Who Acts Responsibly Becomes Guilty: Bonhoeffer's Concept of Accepting Guilt.* Louisville: Westminster John Knox, 2008.

Schlingensiepen, Ferdinand. *Dietrich Bonhoeffer: Martyr, Thinker, Man of Resistance.* Translated by Isabel Best. London: T. & T. Clark, 2010.

Schmid, Heinrich. *The Doctrinal Theology of the Evangelical Lutheran Church.* Translated by Charles A. Hay and Henry E. Jacobs. 4th ed. Philadelphia: Lutheran Publication Society, 1899.

Schmitz, Florian. "Reading *Discipleship* and *Ethics* Together: Implications for Ethics and Public Life." In *Interpreting Bonhoeffer: Historical Perspectives, Emerging Issues*, edited by Clifford J. Green and Guy C. Carter, 147–53. Minneapolis: Fortress, 2013.

Schwöbel, Christoph. "'Religion' and 'Religionlessness' in *Letters and Papers from Prison*." In *Mysteries in the Theology of Dietrich Bonhoeffer: A Copenhagen Bonhoeffer Symposium*, edited by Kirsten Busch Nielsen et al., 159–84. Göttingen: Vandenhoeck & Ruprecht, 2007.

Scott, Jamie S. "'From the Spirit's Choice and Free Desire': Friendship as Atheology in Dietrich Bonhoeffer's Letters and Papers from Prison." *Studies in Religion* 22/1 (1993) 49–62.

Second Vatican Council. *Gaudium et Spes* (Pastoral Constitution on the Church in the Modern World). December 7, 1965. Vatican Archive. http://www.vatican.va/archive/hist_councils/ii_vatican_council/documents/vatii_cons_19651207_gaudium-et-spes_en.html.

Seitz, Christopher R., ed. *Nicene Christianity: The Future for a New Ecumenism.* Grand Rapids: Brazos, 2001.

Sheahen, Laura. "'Why Have You Forsaken Me?' Stanley Hauerwas on Atonement Theology, Mel Gibson's 'Passion' and the 'Chilling' Meaning of Christ's Last Words." Beliefnet. 2005. http://www.beliefnet.com/Faiths/Christianity/2005/03/Why-Have-You-Forsaken-Me.aspx.

Shults, F. LeRon. "A Dubious Christological Formula: From Leontius of Byzantium to Karl Barth." *Theological Studies* 57/3 (1996) 431–46.

Sider, J. Alexander "Friendship, Alienation, Love: Stanley Hauerwas and John Howard Yoder." In *Unsettling Arguments: A Festschrift on the Occasion of Stanley Hauerwas's 70th Birthday*, edited by Charles S. Pinches et al., 61–86. Eugene, OR: Cascade, 2010.

Slenczka, Notger. "Christus." In *Luther Handbuch*, edited by Albrecht Beutel, 381–92. Tübingen: Mohr Siebeck, 2005.

Smith, James K. A. *Desiring the Kingdom: Worship, Worldview, and Cultural Formation*. Grand Rapids: Baker Academic, 2009.

Smith, Robert. "Bonhoeffer and Musical Metaphor." *Word and World* 26/2 (2006) 195–206.

Sonderegger, Katherine. "Epistemological Monophysitism in Karl Barth and Hans Frei." *Pro Ecclesia* 22/3 (2013) 255–62.

Sopko, Andrew J. "Bonhoeffer: An Orthodox Ecclesiology?" *Greek Orthodox Theological Review* 28/1 (1983) 81–88.

Soulen, R. Kendall. *The God of Israel and Christian Theology*. Minneapolis: Augsburg Fortress, 1996.

———. "YHWH the Triune God." *Modern Theology* 15/1 (1999) 25–54.

Stackhouse, John G., Jr., ed. *Evangelical Ecclesiology: Reality or Illusion?* Grand Rapids: Baker Academic, 2003.

Stone, Lance. "Word and Sacrament as Paradigmatic for Pastoral Theology: In Search of a Definition via Brueggemann, Hauerwas and Ricoeur." *Scottish Journal of Theology* 56/4 (2003) 444–63.

Stout, Jeffrey. *Democracy and Tradition*. Princeton: Princeton University Press, 2004.

———. "The Spirit of Democracy and the Rhetoric of Excess." *Journal of Religious Ethics* 35/1 (2007) 3–21.

Stringfellow, William. *Conscience and Obedience: The Politics of Romans 13 and Revelation 13 in Light of the Second Coming*. Eugene, OR: Wipf & Stock, 2004.

———. *An Ethic for Christians and Other Aliens in a Strange Land*. Eugene, OR: Wipf & Stock, 2004.

Stumme, Wayne C., ed. *The Gospel of Justification in Christ: Where Does the Church Stand Today?* Grand Rapids: Eerdmans, 2006.

Tanner, Kathryn. *Christ the Key*. Cambridge: Cambridge University Press, 2010.

———. "Jesus Christ." In *The Cambridge Companion to Christian Doctrine*, edited by Colin E. Gunton, 245–72. Cambridge: Cambridge University Press, 1997.

———. "Trinity, Christology, and Community." In *Christology and Ethics*, edited by F. LeRon Shults and Brent Waters, 56–74. Grand Rapids: Eerdmans, 2010.

Tappert, Theodore G., et al., eds. and trans. *The Book of Concord: The Confessions of the Evangelical Lutheran Church*. Philadelphia: Fortress, 1959.

Taylor, Charles. "Challenging Issues about the Secular Age." *Modern Theology* 26/3 (2010) 404–16.

———. *A Secular Age*. Cambridge, MA: Belknap, 2007.

———. *Sources of the Self: The Making of the Modern Identity*. Cambridge, MA: Harvard University Press, 1989.

Thomson, John B. *The Ecclesiology of Stanley Hauerwas: A Christian Theology of Liberation*. Aldershot: Ashgate, 2003.

———. *Living Holiness: Stanley Hauerwas and the Church*. London: Epworth, 2010.

Tietz, Christiane. "Bonhoeffer's Strong Christology in the Context of Religious Pluralism." In *Interpreting Bonhoeffer: Historical Perspectives, Emerging Issues*, edited by Clifford J. Green and Guy C. Carter, 181–96. Minneapolis: Fortress, 2013.

———. "'The Church is the Limit of Politics': Bonhoeffer on the Political Task of the Church." *Union Seminary Quarterly Review* 60/1–2 (2006) 23–36.

Tinsley, E. J. *The Imitation of God in Christ*. London: SCM, 1960.

Tödt, Heinz Eduard. *Authentic Faith: Bonhoeffer's Theological Ethics in Context*. Edited by Glen Harold Stassen. Translated by David Stassen and Ilse Tödt. Grand Rapids: Eerdmans, 2007.

Tolkien, J. R. R. *The Fellowship of the Ring*. 1954. Reprint, London: HarperCollins, 2001.

———. *The Return of the King*. 1955. Reprint, London: HarperCollins, 2001.

———. *The Two Towers*. 1954. Reprint, London: HarperCollins, 2001.

Torrance, Thomas F. *Incarnation: The Person and Life of Christ*. Edited by Robert T. Walker. Downers Grove, IL: IVP Academic, 2008.

Treier, Daniel J., and Mark Husbands, ed. *The Community of the Word: Toward an Evangelical Ecclesiology*. Downers Grove, IL: InterVarsity, 2005.

Van Harn, Roger E., ed. *Exploring and Proclaiming the Apostles' Creed*. Grand Rapids: Eerdmans, 2004.

Vanier, Jean. *Becoming Human*. The Massey Lectures. Toronto: Anansi, 1998.

———. *Community and Growth*. London: Darton, Longman and Todd, 1979.

———. *Drawn into the Mystery of Jesus through the Gospel of John*. Ottawa: Novalis, 2004.

Visser't Hooft, W. A. "Dietrich Bonhoeffer and the Self Understanding of the Ecumenical Movement." *Ecumenical Review* 28/2 (1976) 198–203.

———. *Memoirs of W. A. Visser't Hooft*. Geneva: WCC, 1976.

Volf, Mirsolav. "'The Trinity is Our Social Program': The Doctrine of the Trinity and the Shape of Social Engagement." *Modern Theology* 14/3 (1998) 403–23.

Waddell, Paul J. "Friendship." In *Unsettling Arguments: A Festschrift on the Occasion of Stanley Hauerwas's 70th Birthday*, edited by Charles S. Pinches et al., 265–83. Eugene, OR: Cascade, 2010.

Wainwright, Geoffrey. *For Our Salvation: Two Approaches to the Work of Christ*. Grand Rapids: Eerdmans, 1997.

Wannenwetsch, Bernd. *Political Worship: Ethics for Christian Citizens*. Oxford: Oxford University Press, 2004.

——— "The Political Worship of the Church: A Critical and Empowering Practice." *Modern Theology* 12/3 (1996) 269–99.

———. "Reading Backwards: Introducing the Hauerwas Reader." *Modern Theology* 20/3 (2004) 457–66.

———, ed. *Who Am I? Bonhoeffer's Theology through His Poetry*. London: T. & T. Clark, 2009.

———. "The Whole Christ and the Whole Human Being: Dietrich Bonhoeffer's Inspiration for the 'Christology and Ethics' Discourse" In *Christology and Ethics*,

edited by F. LeRon Shults and Brent Waters, 75–98. Grand Rapids: Eerdmans, 2010.
Webb, Stephen H. "The Very American Stanley Hauerwas." *First Things* 124 (2002) 14–17.
Webster, John. *Barth's Ethics of Reconciliation*. Cambridge: Cambridge University Press, 1995.
———. *Holiness*. Grand Rapids: Eerdmans, 2003.
———. *Word and Church: Essays in Christian Dogmatics*. Edinburgh: T. & T. Clark, 2001.
Wedemeyer-Weller, Maria von. "The Other Letters from Prison." In *Letters and Papers from Prison*, edited by Eberhard Bethge, 412–19. Enl. ed. New York: Touchstone, 1997.
Weizsäcker, Carl Friedrich von. "Thoughts of a Non-Theologian on Dietrich Bonhoeffer's Theological Development." *Ecumenical Review* 28/2 (1976) 156–73.
Wells, Samuel. "The Difference Christ Makes." In *The Difference Christ Makes: Celebrating the Life, Work, and Friendship of Stanley Hauerwas*, edited by Charles M. Collier, 11–29. Eugene, OR: Cascade, 2015.
———. *Improvisation: The Drama of Christian Ethics*. Grand Rapids: Brazos, 2004.
———. "Stanley Hauerwas (1940–)." In *The Blackwell Companion to the Theologians*, edited by Ian S. Markham, 2:277–93. Malden, MA: Wiley-Blackwell, 2009.
———. "Stanley Hauerwas' Theological Ethics in Eschatological Perspective." *Scottish Journal of Theology* 53/4 (2000) 431–48.
———. *Transforming Fate into Destiny: The Theological Ethics of Stanley Hauerwas*. Eugene, OR: Cascade, 1998.
Werpehowski, William. "Command and History in the Ethics of Karl Barth." *Journal of Religious Ethics* 9/2 (1981) 298–320.
———. "Talking the Walk and Walking the Talk: Stanley Hauerwas's Contribution to Theological Ethics." *Journal of Religious Ethics* 40/2 (2012) 228–49.
Williams, Reggie L. *Bonhoeffer's Black Jesus: Harlem Renaissance Theology and an Ethic of Resistance*. Waco: Baylor University Press, 2014.
Williams, Rowan. *Christ on Trial: How the Gospel Unsettles our Judgement*. Grand Rapids: Eerdmans, 2003.
———. "Presidential Address (Lambeth Conference, 2008)." Dr. Rowan Williams, 104th Archbishop of Canterbury. http://rowanwilliams.archbishopofcanterbury.org/articles.php/1353/archbishops-first-presidential-address-at-lambeth-conference.
———. "The Richard Dimbleby Lecture 2002." Dr. Rowan Williams, 104th Archbishop of Canterbury. http://rowanwilliams.archbishopofcanterbury.org/articles.php/1808/the-richard-dimbleby-lecture-2002.
———. *Tokens of Trust: An Introduction to Christian Belief*. Louisville: Westminster John Knox, 2007.
Willimon, William H. *The Service of God: How Worship and Ethics Are Related*. Nashville: Abingdon, 1983.
———. "Too Much Practice: Second Thoughts on a Theological Movement." *Christian Century*, March 9, 2010, 22–25.
Willimon, William H., et al. *Lord Teach Us: The Lord's Prayer and the Christian Life*. Nashville: Abingdon, 1996.

Willimon, William H., and Stanley Hauerwas. *Preaching to Strangers: Evangelism in Today's World*. Louisville: Westminster John Knox, 1992.

Wilson, Jonathan R. "From Theology of Culture to Theological Ethics: The Hartt-Hauerwas Connection." *Journal of Religious Ethics* 23/1 (1995) 149–64.

———. *Gospel Virtues: Practicing Faith, Hope and Love in Uncertain Times*. Downers Grove, IL: InterVarsity, 1998.

Wind, Renate. *Dietrich Bonhoeffer: A Spoke in the Wheel*. Translated by John Bowden. Grand Rapids: Eerdmans, 1992.

Wolin, Sheldon S. *Politics and Vision: Continuity and Innovation in Western Political Thought*. Exp. ed. Princeton: Princeton University Press, 2004.

———. *The Presence of the Past: Essays on the State of the Constitution*. The Johns Hopkins Series in Constitutional Thought. Baltimore: Johns Hopkins University Press, 1989.

Wright, H. Elliott. "Aftermath of Flossenburg: Bonhoeffer, 1945–1970: An Interview with Eberhard Bethge." *Christian Century*, May 27, 1970, 656–59.

Wright, John. ed. *Postliberal Theology and the Church Catholic: Conversations with George Lindbeck, David Burrell and Stanley Hauerwas*. Grand Rapids: Baker Academic, 2012.

Wood, Susan K. "The Holy Catholic Church, the Communion of Saints." In *Exploring and Proclaiming the Apostles' Creed*, edited by Roger E. Van Harn, 219–32. Grand Rapids: Eerdmans, 2004.

Wüstenberg, Ralf K. *Bonhoeffer and Beyond: Promoting a Dialogue between Religion and Politics*. Frankfurt: Peter Lang, 2008.

Yeago, David S. "The Apostolic Faith: A Catholic and Evangelical Introduction to Christian Theology." Vol. 1, "The Gift of the Life of the Triune God in Jesus Christ." Unpublished manuscript, 2005.

———. "Gnosticism, Antinomianism, and Reformation Theology: Reflections on the Costs of a Construal." *Pro Ecclesia* 2/1 (1993) 37–49.

———. "Messiah's People: The Culture of the Church in the Midst of the Nations." *Pro Ecclesia* 6/1 (1997) 146–71.

Yoder, John Howard. "Armaments and Eschatology." *Studies in Christian Ethics* 1/1 (1988) 43–61.

———. *Body Politics: Five Practices of the Christian Community Before the Watching World*. Scottdale, PA: Herald, 2001.

———. *The Christian Witness to the State*. Institute of Mennonite Studies 3. Newton, KS: Faith and Life, 1964.

———. *The Jewish Christian Schism Revisited*. Edited by Michael G. Cartwright and Peter Ochs. Grand Rapids: Eerdmans, 2003.

———. *Karl Barth and the Problem of War and Other Essays on Barth*. Edited by Mark Thiessen Nation. Eugene, OR: Cascade, 2003.

———. *Nevertheless: Varieties of Religious Pacifism*. Scottdale, PA: Herald, 1992.

———. *The Politics of Jesus: Vicit Agnus Noster*. 2nd ed. Grand Rapids: Eerdmans, 1994.

———. *Preface to Theology: Christology and Theological Method*. Grand Rapids: Brazos, 2002.

———. *The Priestly Kingdom: Social Ethics as Gospel*. Notre Dame: University of Notre Dame Press, 1984.

———. *The Royal Priesthood: Essays Ecclesiastical and Ecumenical*. Edited by Michael G. Cartwright. Scottdale, PA: Herald, 1998.

Zerner, Ruth. "Dietrich Bonhoeffer's Views on the State and History." In *A Bonhoeffer Legacy: Essays in Understanding*, edited by A. J. Klassen, 131–57. Grand Rapids: Eerdmans, 1981.

Ziegler, Philip G. "Christ for Us Today—Promeity in the Christologies of Bonhoeffer and Kierkegaard." *International Journal of Systematic Theology* 15/1 (2013) 25–41.

———. "Dietrich Bonhoeffer—An Ethics of God's Apocalypse?" *Modern Theology* 23/4 (2007) 579–94.

———. "'Not to Abolish, but to Fulfil': The Person of the Preacher and the Claim of the Sermon on the Mount." *Studies in Christian Ethics* 22/3 (2009) 275–89.

Zimmerman, Jens. "Being Human, Becoming Human: Dietrich Bonhoeffer's Christological Humanism." In *Being Human, Becoming Human: Dietrich Bonhoeffer and Social Thought*, edited by Jens Zimmerman and Brian Gregor, 25–48. Cambridge: James Clarke, 2012.

———. "Suffering with the World: The Continuing Relevance of Dietrich Bonhoeffer's Theology." *Crux* 42/3 (2006) 22–36.

Zimmerman, Jens, and Brian Gregor, eds. *Being Human, Becoming Human: Dietrich Bonhoeffer and Social Thought*. Cambridge: James Clarke, 2012.

Zimmermann, Wolf-Dieter, and Ronald Gregor Smith, eds. *I Knew Dietrich Bonhoeffer*. Translated by Käthe Gregor Smith. London: Collins, 1966.

Index

Act and Being (Bonhoeffer), 78, 96
    church as revelation in, 73, 86n79
    God's freedom in, 27, 92, 250–51
    sinful humanity in, 9, 21, 22
Airhart, Phyllis, 106n198
America, 102–3
    Bonhoeffer in, 7–9, 19n13, 188
    Hauerwas and, 114, 154, 188–91
    Hauerwas's criticisms of church in, 2–3, 105–8, 198, 201, 225
anthropology. *See* Christian humanism; incarnation: and anthropology; new humanity; sin
apocalyptic: Christology, 69, 118, 150–51, 205
    and daily life, 200–201
    ecclesiology, 85, 114–17, 217–18
    struggle, 80–81, 104
    theology, 236–37
Aquinas, Thomas, 45, 140, 207
"arcane discipline," 93–95, 186–87, 227
Aristotle, 138n388, 147n433, 207
Augustine, 33, 110, 120n289

Baillie, John, 7–8
baptism, 75, 87, 111, 129
    apocalyptic character of, 85, 89, 141
Barmen, synod and declaration of, 6, 75n16, 133, 158n23
Barth, Karl, 68, 217n30, 223n351, 236, 249–50
    Bonhoeffer, influence on, 5–9, 136n375, 167, 219n336, 230, 233, 235
    Bonhoeffer, personal relationship with, 137n380
    Bonhoeffer's criticisms of, 26–27, 92–96, 232, 235
    on Bonhoeffer's work, 73n1, 82
    christological concentration of, 5–7, 12–13, 151n450, 230
    ecclesiology of, 13, 72
    Hauerwas, influence on, 5–6, 9–12, 42, 44, 47n190, 57n229, 62, 193, 219n336, 230, 233, 235
    Hauerwas's criticisms of, 123–27, 150, 232, 235
    on the state, 161, 193, 219n336
Bender, Kimlyn, 92n120, 126n322
Berlin, University of, 7, 17, 19–20, 73n1
Bethge, Eberhard, 18, 24, 187, 234n5
    and his friendship with Bonhoeffer, 176–77, 179–83, 186n168, 212
    and *Letters and Papers from Prison*, 17, 82–83, 156, 171, 172
Better Hope, A (Hauerwas), 115–16, 190, 211–12
Bischoff, Paul, 29–30
Bonhoeffer, Dietrich: biographical material, 2–3, 17–20, 73–74, 154–57
    conspiracy involvement, 154–56, 159, 182–83, 241–43, 248, 251
    theology, practice of, 2, 8, 21, 143–44, 150, 239
bricklaying, 127–30
Bush, George, 188–89n179, 249

Calvin, John, 23, 120n288
capitalism, 107, 195–97
Carter, Guy, 2n3
Cartwright, Michael, 54n219, 203
casuistry. *See* ethics: casuistry
Cavanaugh, William, 2n2, 153n1, 200n244, 206
Chalcedon, 37–38, 42, 70, 231
 and ecclesiology, 46, 148, 178
character. *See* conformation; virtue: and character formation
"cheap grace," 65, 74–77, 78, 81, 83, 91
 and "arcane discipline," 94, 186–87, 227
Christendom, 3–5, 81, 103–8, 156, 173, 220–23
 See also cultural Protestantism; post-Christendom
Christian humanism, 14, 171–72, 182, 200, 214–18
Christianity, Democracy, and the Radical Ordinary (Hauerwas and Coles), 196–211
Christology. *See* Jesus Christ
Christology lectures (Bonhoeffer), 17–41
church: apostolicity of, 148–52
 catholicity of, 133, 141–48, 205, 219
 discipline, 91–92, 100, 127–30, 135–36, 146, 232
 holiness of, 90–92, 120, 134–40, 232
 invisibility of, 104–5, 108–9, 131, 145–48
 as means and end, 88, 118–19, 150, 152, 232
 mission of, 97, 112–15, 122–23, 148–52, 223–29, 232–33
 as *polis*, 48, 91–92, 108–17, 119, 147
 revelation, as form of, 33, 86–87, 131, 144–46, 149, 237
 and state, 104–5, 110–11, 157–71, 185, 191–98, 218–23, 233
 unity of, 130–34
 visibility of, 40–41, 79–80, 88–92, 108–12, 131, 144–48, 231–32

 and world, 48, 90–92, 109–10, 113–17, 121–23, 153–229, 231–33
Church Growth Movement, 97, 102
Church Struggle. *See* Confessing Church
Coles, Romand, 194, 196–206, 213, 215, 219, 226
communion ecclesiology, 237
Confessing Church, 3n9, 6, 183
 Bonhoeffer's criticisms of, 94–95, 154–55, 182, 184, 224–25
 Bonhoeffer's involvement in, 1n1, 73–74, 92–94, 133, 155, 160n34
conformation: to Christ, 122, 135–36, 152, 218, 232–33, 239
 and epistemology, 95–96, 108
 of God to the human image, 40, 87–88
 and pneumatology, 135, 235
Constantinianism, 103–8, 109, 156, 185, 191, 193
 See also Christendom
cor curvum in se, 21, 28, 87
Cranfield, C.E.B., 220–21
creation, 123, 155, 158, 216, 225
 and Christ, 34, 36, 44, 63, 89, 223
 and fall, 32, 36, 153, 217, 223
 telos of, 110–11, 121, 141, 208
 See also natural theology; orders of creation
cross, 60–64, 134, 189, 209–10, 217
 and discipleship, 75, 78–80, 85, 91, 233, 245
 and non-violence, 43, 51, 120
 and shape of reality, 67, 173, 204
 and suffering, 175, 204
 and vulnerability, 40, 208
 See also, principalities and powers: and the cross; *theologia crucis*
Cross-shattered Christ (Hauerwas), 58–64
cultural Protestantism, 80, 160, 170, 183, 217, 231
 and "cheap grace," 74–77, 83, 94
 See also Christendom
Cyprian of Carthage, 92, 151
Cyril of Alexandria, 21
Cyril of Jerusalem, 63

Dahl, Nils, 49
Dahlem, synod of, 73, 133
De Gruchy, John, 183–84n155, 186–87, 216n327
DeJonge, Michael, 27
democracy, 106, 164–65, 193–99, 204, 209
discipleship: Bonhoeffer and, 75–85, 101, 137–38, 231
 call to, 75, 77–81, 85, 98n158, 112, 135
 Christology and, 43, 45, 75–77, 231
 discipline and, 129–30
 Hauerwas and, 43, 45–48, 56, 108–12, 129–30, 231
 works righteousness and, 81–84, 137–38
 See also cross: and discipleship; epistemology: and discipleship
Discipleship (Bonhoeffer), 18, 25, 40, 101, 145
 "cheap grace" in, 65, 74–77, 94
 Christ and church in, 33–34, 43, 77–81, 84–92, 109, 226
 critique of virtue in, 137–138
 objections to, 81–84
docetism, 46, 49, 87, 139, 178
 modern forms of, 38–39, 53, 64–65, 93, 148
Dudzus, Otto, 20
Duke Divinity School, 5n15, 16n1, 102–3, 213n314
Dula, Peter, 202
Dumas, André, 33, 66n289

Ebionism, 42, 71, 148
ecclesiology. *See* church
ecumenism, 131–33, 155, 158n23, 237–38
epistemology: and church, 86–87, 96, 121–22, 125–26, 149–50
 and discipleship, 46–48, 56, 67, 78, 108–109
 and non-foundationalism, 67
 and revelation, 9, 11, 21–23
eschatology, 48, 53 111–12, 113, 231
 and timefulness, 208, 214–15, 248

See also apocalyptic; Kingdom of God; new humanity
ethics: and casuistry, 10, 142–44
 of Christendom, 104–7
 and church, 91, 110
 and divine commandment, 132, 143, 167, 170, 172, 221, 245
 normativity of Jesus for, 42–43, 46, 49, 55–57, 70, 231
 responsibility, 107, 155–56, 168–69, 182, 242–51
 and theology, 9–12, 105–6, 142–144, 250
 See also tyrannicide; virtue
Ethics (Bonhoeffer), 136n375, 155–56, 242–46
 church in, 88, 134, 150, 182–84, 222, 225–27
 Jesus Christ in, 35–36, 88, 171–73, 174
 mandates in, 165–-71, 222
Eucharist. *See* Lord's Supper
Evangelicalism, 29–30, 238
extra ecclesiam nulla salus, 13, 92, 123, 151, 232

faith, 104, 207
 and revelation, 23, 87, 149
 and works, 10, 54, 78, 81–84
 worldliness of, 174–76
Feil, Ernst, 84
Fergusson, David, 55–57
Finkenwalde: communal life at, 73–74, 81–82, 96, 101, 182, 186
 lectures, 74, 89, 94
 writings, 73–74, 96, 155n11, 159, 219, 226n364
First Things, 189
Ford, David, 77n25, 95, 179
Fowl, Stephen, 113n246
Frei, Hans, 42, 47, 65, 118
friendship, 45, 171
 within church, 171, 179–82, 206–14
 and discipline, 100, 129
 with world, 182–87, 210–11, 213, 228–29, 233
Fuller, Reginald, 78

Gibson, Mel, 61
Gifford Lectures, 7, 68n299, 123–26
gnosticism, 31, 42, 87, 118
    and modernity, 13, 231, 246
God: freedom of, 26–28, 92–93, 95,
    143–44, 249–50
    mission of, 71, 149–52
    participation in life of, 63–64,
        94–96, 125, 140, 176, 184, 218,
        232, 237
    Word of, 20–23, 97–101, 146, 167,
        170, 228
    See also Trinity
Godsey, John, 96
Green, Clifford, 2n3, 156, 244
    on Christ and sociality, 29, 34
    on worldliness, 173n100, 175n110
Grobien, Gifford, 163n46
Gunton, Colin, 55–57
Gustafson, James, 2n3, 113

Harink, Douglas, 69n302, 220,
    236n12
Harvey, Barry, 33, 173n104, 185n163
Hauerwas, Stanley: biographical material, 2–3, 41–43, 101–3, 188–91
    Bonhoeffer, engagement with, 3–4,
        43, 144–45, 150, 190–91, 212,
        219–20, 227, 241–43
    theology, practice of, 2, 12, 41–42,
        50n204, 56–58, 115–116, 150,
        239
Hays, Richard, 41n152, 113n242,
    117n264
Healy, Nicholas, 124
    criticisms of Hauerwas by, 5n17,
        110n227, 117n264, 138n388,
        146–48, 235n6
Hegel, George, 22, 32–33n101, 158
Hill, Wesley, 179n133
Hitler, Adolf, 3n8, 18–19, 66, 75, 170
    oath of allegiance to, 155
    plot to kill, 159–60n30, 241–42,
        247n31
holiness. *See* church: holiness of;
    sanctification
Holl, Karl, 21

Holy Spirit: Bonhoeffer and, 69–70,
    88–89, 91, 95, 142, 235–36
    Hauerwas and, 69–70, 124–25, 142,
        146–47, 235–36
humanism. *See* Christian humanism
"Humanity of the Divine, the" (Hauerwas), 44–45
Hunsinger, George, 193
Huntemann, George, 238n17
Hurtado, Larry, 66
Hütter, Reinhard, 124, 146
hypostatic union. *See* incarnation: and hypostatic union

idolatry, 43, 66, 77, 188–90, 247
Ignatius of Antioch, 236
incarnation, 41–46, 77, 231
    and anthropology, 65, 88, 172, 208,
        247
    and empirical church, 131, 142, 145
    and hypostatic union, 25, 32n96,
        37–39, 62, 150
    misunderstandings of, 65, 82, 93
    and ordinary life, 215–17, 233
    and reality, 70, 141
Israel: and church, 60n261, 110,
    113n242, 185n163, 221
    and knowledge of God, 96
    and the Messiah, 35, 68, 108, 231
    story of, 53–55, 62, 110, 118, 144

Jenson, Robert, 62
Jeremias, Joachim, 135
Jesus Christ: and Jesus of history—
    Christ of faith, 37, 64
    Jewishness of, 35, 49, 53, 59–62,
        68, 108
    lordship of, 64–71, 112, 159, 183,
        186, 203–4, 219, 233
    particularity of, 25, 39, 47–49,
        61–62, 64–66, 116, 231
    person and work, 23–28, 46–49,
        61–64, 71, 122, 150, 151, 230
    presence of, 24–37, 49–50, 52, 85,
        132, 232
    See also cross; incarnation;
    resurrection

"Jesus: The Presence of the Peaceable Kingdom" (Hauerwas), 50–58
"Jesus: The Story of the Kingdom" (Hauerwas), 45–50
Jews, 35, 53, 224, 238
Johansen, Paul, 213n312
John Paul II, 56n225, 126, 196n221, 228
Johnson, Kelly, 238n18
Jones, L. Gregory, 251
justification, 54, 65, 75–77, 82–84, 85, 90–91

Kallenberg, Brad, 56n225, 126n323
Kant, Immanuel, 8, 11, 96
Käsemann, Ernst, 236
Kasper, Walter, 46
Kelly, Geffrey, 3n8, 23n37, 69n303
Kenneson, Philip, 122n299
Kerr, Nathan, 114–17
Kierkegaard, Søren: and Bonhoeffer, 8, 20, 23n37, 181
and Hauerwas, 44–45, 59, 65
Kingdom of God: church and, 81, 109–10, 232, 237
Jesus as presence of, 47–48, 51–52, 54, 135, 151
and the kingdom of the world, 157
Krause, Gerhard, 82n55
Krötke, Wolf, 28n75, 40n45, 167n68

L'Arche, 191, 206–12
Lapide, Pinchas, 35n121, 238n20
Lasserre, Jean, 79, 82
Letters and Papers from Prison (Bonhoeffer), 156
ethical reflection in, 136–37, 142n409, 242–44, 245–46
friendship in, 171, 179–82
Jesus Christ in, 17, 29, 40, 36, 172–73
on the life of faith, 82–83, 98n153, 99n163, 172–79
"Outline for a Book" in, 184–187
"religionless Christianity" in, 35, 172–79, 185n163
liberal theology. *See* theological liberalism

liberalism, 193–97
and church, 65, 107–8, 131, 183, 197–98
depersonalizing character of, 200, 204–5, 210–11
Hauerwas's over-determination by, 114–16, 190, 205
Life Together (Bonhoeffer), 73–74, 84, 96–101, 152
Living Gently in a Violent World (Hauerwas and Vanier), 206–11, 218n335
living out of control, 69, 120, 122, 199, 248
Lord's Supper: and confession of sin, 75, 101
and politics, 111, 120
and presence of Christ, 32, 87, 120, 132, 216, 237
Luther, Martin, 8, 60, 62, 101n173, 137n380
and Christology, 21, 23–24, 25, 40, 145
and the commandments, 222n346
and the Gospel, 49n199, 138
and the Reformation, 76, 160
and sin, 21, 40
and soteriology, 23–24
and the state, 157–58, 160–61, 220n339
Lutheran tradition, 21, 79, 192, 220, 222
Bonhoeffer within, 27, 28n75, 170, 222
Christology of, 23–24, 32, 38
discipleship in, 85, 137, 140
orders of creation in, 158–59, 181
soteriology of, 23–24, 98, 137
the state within, 157–59, 161, 192, 220

MacIntyre, Alasdair, 110
"man for others," 29, 66, 182, 184–87, 216, 243
mandates, doctrine of, 157, 160–71, 178–81, 219–23
Mangina, Joseph, 58n232, 59n233, 95, 110n227, 124–25

marines, 127–30
marriage, 163, 165–66, 167, 180, 215n321, 222
Marsh, Charles, 27n64, 78, 83n61, 179n133, 244n18
Marshall, Bruce, 125
Martyn, J. Louis, 236
martyrdom, 2n5, 125–26, 164, 241n3, 248–49
Matthew (Hauerwas), 58–64, 67n296, 67n298, 69n301, 147n433
Matthews, John, 18
McBride, Jennifer, 33n101
McClendon, James, 3n10, 251
McFague, Sallie, 182n143
Melanchthon, Philip, 23–24
Metaxas, Eric, 238n17, 245n19
Methodist church, 102, 119, 214
missio Dei. See God: mission of
mission. *See* church: mission of; God: mission of
Moberly, Jennifer, 83n61, 136n375, 137n382, 139n391
Moses, John, 165
Müller, Hanfried, 84

narrative, 49, 111, 114–16, 118, 121, 200
Nation, Mark Thiessen, 2n1, 83n61, 241–242n4
nation-state, 11, 35, 114, 199, 205
allegiance to, 63, 66, 77, 105–8
See also church: and state
natural theology, 68, 123, 217
Nazis, 7, 18–20, 97, 165, 183, 184n155
and America, 3, 190
and Bonhoeffer, 2–3, 35, 89n105, 136, 158–159, 170
and church in Germany, 3, 73–74, 75, 164, 224, 251n58
Nelson, F. Burton, 3n8, 69n303
new humanity: church as presence of, 118, 135, 181, 222
and Jesus Christ, 28–29, 68–69, 86–88, 151, 217, 231
Niebuhr, Reinhold, 65, 106n200, 111n236, 244
9/11, 188–91

non-violence. *See* peace
Northcott, Michael, 190
Notre Dame, University of, 101–2, 238n18

Old Testament, 35, 175–6, 185n163
"On Doctrine and Ethics" (Hauerwas), 9–12
orders of creation, 77, 158–59
orders of preservation, 159–60, 162–63, 222
ordinary life, 198–206, 208, 215–16
Origen, 47, 94

pacifism. *See* peace
Pangritz, Andreas, 93n125
Paul, apostle, 6, 33, 66, 191–92, 205n271, 223
and Bonhoeffer, 8, 34, 85–86, 185, 223
on the state, 191–92, 220–21
peace: Christ and, 48n193, 59, 80, 234n5, 244–45, 246
commandment for, 132
community of, 134, 190, 211, 227
the cross and, 43, 51, 63–64, 69, 80, 120
and eschatology, 118, 200–201
Kingdom of, 51, 54, 69, 109–10, 121
as principle, 66, 246
resurrection and, 52, 48n193, 120
See also tyrannicide; war
Pelagianism, 55–56, 130n345, 137n382
Pentecost, 86, 118, 141, 148n439, 189
Performing the Faith (Hauerwas), 190, 219–20, 227, 241–42
Phillips, John, 30, 88n92
pietism, 70, 83, 90, 170, 235
Plant, Stephen, 173–74n104
pneumatology. *See* Holy Spirit
politics, 110–11, 193–213, 218–19, 226–27
Jesus Christ and, 34, 42–43, 47
See also church: as *polis*; democracy; liberalism; nation-state
"polyphony of life," 171, 176–79

"positivism of revelation," 93–96
post-Christendom, 97, 185, 209–10, 223–29, 232–33
  See also Christendom
powers. *See* principalities and powers
prayer, 21, 144, 182
  Bonhoeffer on, 84, 98–99, 186–87, 227n368
  Hauerwas on, 129–30, 207n278
preaching: Bonhoeffer and, 25, 30–31, 85, 143–44, 162, 233–35
  Hauerwas and, 44, 120, 124–25, 193, 233–35
  presence of Christ in, 25, 30–31, 85, 132, 135, 216, 232
principalities and powers, 192, 196, 220–21, 223
  and the church, 48, 104, 151, 153, 201, 204
  and the cross, 48, 51, 69
  naming the, 48, 119, 122, 130
private-public divide, 174, 222
  as characteristic of modernity, 105, 107, 110, 114, 137, 157
pro me, 26–30, 34, 40, 181, 243
Protestant Reformation, 105, 107, 117, 157, 160–61, 220
  and discipleship and ethics, 10, 76, 79, 215
Pugh, Jeffrey, 94n130

radical democracy, 198–206, 219
Rasmussen, Larry, 18, 241n3, 247n31
  on Bonhoeffer's ethics, 139n393, 144n419, 250–251n57
Rasmusson, Arne, 117n267, 120n285, 195
Rauschenbusch, Walter, 47n189, 105–6
reality: and church, 98–99, 131
  and Jesus Christ, 36, 67–68, 70, 141, 161, 166
  and "realism," 111–12, 244
Reformation. *See* Protestant Reformation
"religionless Christianity," 35, 172–79, 185n163

Reno, R.R., 13n54, 103n185
Resident Aliens (Hauerwas and Willimon), 102–17
responsibility. *See* ethics: responsibility
resurrection, 69, 113, 149
  and presence of Christ, 24–25, 52, 56, 71, 85–86, 120
  as vindication of Christ, 40, 48n193, 52, 208, 217, 248
  and worldliness, 175–76, 200–201, 217–18
revelation, 8–9, 26–27, 31, 68, 95–96, 167
  See also church: revelation, as form of
Richardson, Neville, 145n423
Robertson, Pat, 249
Roman Catholicism, 131, 145, 147n432, 157, 158n23, 238

sacraments, 36, 124, 235
  and arcane discipline, 94, 187
  and body of Christ, 87, 148n438
  and ethics, 111, 120, 232
  and the presence of Christ, 25, 30–34, 85, 132, 135–36
  See also baptism; Lord's Supper
sacrifice, 62–63, 108, 110, 228
saints, 82–83, 90–91, 120, 122, 185, 228–29
salvation, 9, 207, 208
  and church, 13, 84–92, 117–126, 147, 226
  and Jesus Christ, 23–24, 28–30, 40, 45–47, 69–71, 150–51
sanctification, 54, 66, 76, 82, 90–92, 119–22
Sanctorum Communio (Bonhoeffer), 73
  bearing one another in, 29, 99–100n166, 245
  collective person in, 28–29, 86
  pneumatology of, 88–89, 222
  relation between Christ and church in, 32–33, 86–87, 149–51
Schleiermacher, Friedrich, 11, 25, 107

Schliesser, Christine, 245n24, 250n56
sectarianism, 183
    and Hauerwas, 2, 113–14, 136–38, 203, 206, 226
Seeberg, Reinhold, 28, 33n101
Sermon on the Mount, 74, 79–80, 111–12, 135, 244
sermons. *See* preaching
Sider, Alex, 202
sin: condition of, 8–9, 21–23, 28–29, 69, 87–88
    confession of sin, 91, 100–101, 119, 129, 134, 135, 227, 235
    doctrine of, 153, 217
    forgiveness of, 52, 69, 100–101, 119, 135, 227
    and Jesus Christ, 39–40, 86
Smith, Robert, 178
Social Gospel, 47n189, 105–6
soteriology. *See* salvation
Soulen, R. Kendall, 60
state. *See* nation-state; church: and state
"State and Church" (Bonhoeffer), 160–65
Stellvertreter, Stellvertretung. See vicarious representative action
Stout, Jeffrey, 1–2n1, 51n206, 195
suffering: of Christ, 8, 29n80, 80, 90
    of Christians, 78, 90, 176, 204, 248
    of God, 45, 176, 204
    of humanity, 63, 96, 175
    and the mentally disabled, 210–211

Tanner, Kathryn, 95, 237n16
Taylor, Charles, 215–16
theocracy, 203–6
theologia crucis, 40, 45, 62–63, 66, 155
theological liberalism: and Barth, 5–6, 82, 94, 124, 235
    Bonhoeffer's criticisms of, 23–25, 26, 29–30
    Hauerwas's criticisms of, 11, 47, 61
    idealism of, 38, 47, 64–65
    and lives of Jesus, 38, 42
"Theology of Crisis and its Attitude toward Philosophy and Science" (Bonhoeffer), 7–9

Time magazine, 2, 188, 189
Tolkien, J.R.R., 113, 197
tradition, 110, 116–17, 119, 127–30, 142, 146
transcendence, 21–22, 27, 34, 175–76, 215–16, 233
Trinity, 57–63, 71, 125, 172n96, 235, 237
Tyrannicide, 156n13, 241–51

Union Seminary, 7–8, 79
United States. *See* America

Vanier, Jean, 191, 206–11
vicarious representative action, 29, 161, 166, 168–170
    of Jesus Christ, 29, 34, 69, 168, 181, 243
virtue, 49, 127–30, 185, 194, 200, 203
    and character formation, 65–66, 109, 120, 135, 146–47, 202
    concerns about, 55–56, 136–40
Visser't Hooft, W.A., 165

Wannenwetsch, Bernd, 138, 144n418
war, 108, 132, 156, 189–90, 228, 246
Webster, John, 12, 24, 73n3
Wedemeyer, Maria von, 97
Wells, Samuel, 58n231, 106n202, 118n269
    on Hauerwas's Christology, 16n1, 46n176, 48n193, 68n299
Wesley, John, 119
Where Resident Aliens Live (Hauerwas and Willimon), 127–30
Williams, Rowan, 132n358, 179n133, 195–96, 205, 226
Willimon, William, 102–12, 114, 120n286, 121, 127–30
With the Grain of the Universe (Hauerwas), 123–26, 217n330
witness: as church's calling, 12, 63, 118, 152, 164, 169, 223–26
    as God's activity, 37, 62, 64, 125–126, 152
    necessity of, 47, 108–9, 123, 126, 149–150, 152
    See also martyrdom

Wolin, Sheldon, 194–97, 199,
    202–3n257, 204
work, 163, 165–66, 167, 222
world. *See* church: and world
worldliness, 14, 35, 141, 171–79,
    214–18, 233
worship, 98, 111, 186–87, 207, 227

Yale Divinity School, 7, 42
Yoder, John Howard, 121n290, 126,
    249–50
    and Constantinianism, 103–5
    and peace, 42–43, 49, 201, 204, 250
    and the state, 191–93, 220–21
Yordy, Laura, 211–12

Ziegler, Philip, 23n37, 27n64, 75n16,
    79n41, 234–235n6
    on Bonhoeffer and apocalyptic,
    69n302, 236n12
Zimmerman, Jens, 27, 28n69, 172n96,
    176n118

www.ingramcontent.com/pod-product-compliance
Lightning Source LLC
Chambersburg PA
CBHW071236230426
43668CB00011B/1466